Social History of the Matthean Community

CROSS-DISCIPLINARY APPROACHES

David L. Balch
editor

FORTRESS PRESS   MINNEAPOLIS

SOCIAL HISTORY OF THE MATTHEAN COMMUNITY
Cross-Disciplinary Approaches

Scripture quotations, unless otherwise noted, are from the New Revised Standard Version of the Bible, copyright © 1989 by the Division of Christian Education of the National Council of the Churches of Christ in the United States of America.

Cover photograph and photograph on page 256 copyright © Frederick W. Norris. Used by permission.

Cover design: Publishers' WorkGroup
Interior design: Publishers' WorkGroup

Library of Congress Cataloging-in-Publication Data

Social history of the Matthean community: cross-disciplinary approaches / David L. Balch, editor.
    p.   cm.
    Includes bibliographic references.
    ISBN 0-8006-2445-9 (alk. paper)
    1. Bible. N.T. Matthew—Criticism, interpretation, etc.
    2. Sociology, Biblical.   I. Balch, David L.
BS2575.2.S665   1991   91-23935
226.2'067—dc20   CIP

The paper used in this publication meets the minimum requirements of American National Standard for Information Sciences—Permanence of Paper for Printed Library Materials, ANSI Z329.48–1984. ∞™

Manufactured in the U.S.A.   AF 1-2445
95   94   93   92   91   1   2   3   4   5   6   7   8   9   10

Contents

PART I
MATTHEW: JEWISH AND HELLENISTIC ASPECTS

PART II
MATTHEW: WOMEN IN AN AGRARIAN SOCIETY

PART III
MATTHEW AND IGNATIUS OF ANTIOCH

PART IV
MATTHEW: SOCIAL SITUATION AND LOCATION

Contributors

David L. Balch
> Professor, Brite Divinity School
> Texas Christian University, Fort Worth, Texas

Robert H. Gundry
> Professor of New Testament and Greek
> Westmont College, Santa Barbara, California

Jack Dean Kingsbury
> Aubrey Lee Brooks Professor of Biblical Theology
> Union Theological Seminary in Virginia, Richmond, Virginia

John P. Meier
> Professor
> Catholic University, Washington, D.C.

Frederick W. Norris
> Professor of Christian Doctrine
> Emmanuel School of Religion, Johnson City, Tennessee

Pheme Perkins
> Professor of Theology (New Testament)
> Boston College, Chestnut Hill, Massachusetts

Anthony J. Saldarini
        Professor of Theology
        Boston College, Chestnut Hill, Massachusetts

William R. Schoedel
        Professor
        University of Illinois, Urbana, Illinois

Alan F. Segal
        Professor and Chairperson, Department of Religion
        Barnard College, New York, New York

Rodney Stark
        Professor of Sociology and Comparative Religion
        University of Washington, Seattle, Washington

L. Michael White
        Associate Professor of Religion and Christian Origins
        Oberlin College, Oberlin, Ohio

Antoinette Clark Wire
        Professor of New Testament
        San Francisco Theological Seminary and
        The Graduate Theological Union, San Anselmo, California

Abbreviations

AB	Anchor Bible
AmerJourSoc	*American Journal of Sociology*
AnBib	Analecta biblica
ANRW	*Aufstieg und Niedergang der römischen Welt*
Arist.	Aristotle
Eth. Nic.	*Ethica Nicomachea*
Pol.	*Politica*
ASOR Monographs	American Schools of Oriental Research Monographs
ATANT	Abhandlungen zur Theologie des Alten und Neuen Testaments
BA	*Biblical Archaeologist*
BAR	*Biblical Archaeologist Reader*
BASOR	*Bulletin of the American Schools of Oriental Research*
BCNH	Bibliothèque copte de Nag Hammadi
Bib	*Biblica*
BJRL	*Bulletin of the John Rylands University Library of Manchester*
BJS	Brown Judaic Studies
BZNW	Beihefte zur ZNW
Cass. Dio	Cassius Dio
Hist.	*Roman History*
CBQ	*Catholic Biblical Quarterly*

CBQMS	Catholic Biblical Quarterly Monograph Series
Clem. Al.	Clemens Alexandrinus
Eclog. proph.	*Eclogae Propheticae*
Strom.	*Stromateis*
1–2 Clem.	*1–2 Clement*
CRINT	Compendia rerum iudaicarum ad novum testamentum
Did.	Didache
Dio Chrys.	Dio Chrysostomus
Or.	*Orationes*
Dion. Hal.	Dionysius Halicarnassensis
Ant. Rom.	*Antiquitates Romanae*
Epictetus	Epictetus
Diss.	*Dissertationes*
Epiph.	Epiphanius
Pan.	*Panarion*
Eus.	Eusebius
Chron.	*Chronica*
Hist. Eccl.	*Historia Ecclesiastica*
FRLANT	Forschungen zur Religion und Literatur des Alten und Neuen Testaments
Herm. Man.	*Hermas, Mandate(s)*
Herm. Sim.	*Hermas, Similitude(s)*
HTR	*Harvard Theological Review*
HUCA	*Hebrew Union College Annual*
IEJ	*Israel Exploration Journal*
Irenaeus	Irenaeus
Adv. Haer.	*Adversus haereses*
Dem.	*Demonstratio Evangelica*
Isaeus	Isaeus
De Philoctem. hered.	*De Philoctemonis Hereditate*
JAAR	*Journal of the American Academy of Religion*
JAC	Jahrbuch für Antike und Christentum
JBL	*Journal of Biblical Literature*
JEH	*Journal of Ecclesiastical History*
JJS	*Journal of Jewish Studies*
Joseph.	Josephus
AJ	*Antiquitates Judaicae*
Ap.	*Contra Apionem*
BJ	*Bellum Judaicum*
Vit.	*Vita*
JQR	*Jewish Quarterly Review*

JRS	*Journal of Roman Studies*
JSHRZ	Jüdische Schriften aus hellenistisch-römischer Zeit
JSNT	*Journal for the Study of the New Testament*
JSNTSup	Journal for the Study of the New Testament— Supplement
JSPSS	*Journal for the Study of the Pseudepigrapha, Supplement Series*
JSSR	*Journal for the Scientific Study of Religion*
JTS	*Journal of Theological Studies*
Justin	Justin Martyr
Apol.	*First Apology*
Dial.	*Dialogue with Trypho*
LCL	Loeb Classical Library
Libanius	Libanius
Ep.	*Epistulae*
Or.	*Orationes*
Mart. Pol.	*Martyrdom of Polycarp*
NovT	*Novum Testamentum*
NovTSup	Novum Testamentum, Supplements
NTD	Das Neue Testament Deutsch
NTS	*New Testament Studies*
PG	Migne, *Patrologia graeca*
Philo	Philo
Quaest. in Gen.	*Quaestiones in Genesim*
Som.	*De somniis*
Spec. leg.	*De specialibus legibus*
Vit. cont.	*De vita contemplativa*
Phlegon	Phlegon
De mirab.	*De Mirables*
Pl.	Plato
Laws	*Laws*
Protag.	*Protagoras*
Pol.	Polycarp
Phil.	*Letter to the Philippians*
Qumran Documents	
CD	Cairo (Genizah text of the) *Damascus (Document)*
1QpHab	*Pesher on Habakkuk* from Qumran Cave 1
1QS	*Serek hayyaḥad (Rule of the Community, Manual of Discipline)*
1QSa	Appendix A (*Rule of the Congregation*) to 1QS

RSR	*Recherches de science religieuse*
RTL	*Revue théologique de Louvain*
SANT	Studien zum Alten und Neuen Testament
SBLDS	Society of Biblical Literature Dissertation Series
SBLMS	Society of Biblical Literature Monograph Series
SBLSBS	Society of Biblical Literature Sources for Biblical Study
SBLSP	Society of Biblical Literature Seminar Papers
SecCent	*Second Century*
SJLA	Studies in Judaism in Late Antiquity
SNTSMS	Society for New Testament Studies Monograph Series
Tac.	Tacitus
Ann.	*Annales*
Hist.	*Historiae*
Theodoret	Theodoret
H.E.	*Historia Ecclesiastica*
TRu	*Theologische Rundschau*
TS	*Theological Studies*
TU	Texte und Untersuchungen
VC	*Vigiliae christianae*
WUNT	Wissenschaftliche Untersuchungen zum Neuen Testament
ZNW	*Zeitschrift für die neutestamentliche Wissenschaft*
ZPE	Zeitschrift für Papyrologie und Epigraphik
ZTK	*Zeitschrift für Theologie und Kirche*

Preface

      "The Social History of the Matthean Community in Roman Syria" was the name of an international, interdisciplinary conference held on the campus of Southern Methodist University in October 1989. The excitement generated in those discussions may be felt in this volume. Alan Segal, a well-known Jewish scholar from Barnard College, discussed "Matthew's Jewish Voice." The chair of that session was Susannah Heschel of SMU, who is herself preparing to publish a dissertation on Rabbi Abraham Geiger's nineteenth-century studies of the Pharisees and Jesus; and Segal's respondent was Anthony Saldarini, a Catholic scholar from Boston College. The Jewish-Christian discussions that occurred in Dallas were memorable, and some of them are recorded in the following pages. The conference was both interconfessional and international: more than eighty scholars from Canada, Austria, and Australia, as well as the United States, participated in these open exchanges.

      Interdisciplinary approaches were employed in attempting to understand this aspect of first- and second-century social history. Antoinette Wire utilized macro-sociological analysis in order to reconstruct gender roles characteristic of scribal communities within advanced agricultural societies, and she thereby shed new light on the literary dynamic of Matthew as well as on the social situation of women in Matthew's community. Frederick Norris discussed mosaics uncovered by archaeologists in and near Antioch in Syria, arguing that the mosaics may serve as evidence of religious attitudes in the region. Sociologist Rodney Stark was prevented from attending, but his paper on the sewers, plagues, and other miseries of ancient Greco-Roman cities and the Christian ethical response to sickness in that world communicates a realistic perception of daily life as experienced by those congregations. Michael White creatively analyzed recent archaeological evidence from Upper and Lower Galilee as well as the shifting geopolitical boundaries of the region in the late first century, and his paper proposes a hypothesis about the origin of the Gospel related to the political and economic crises of those Jewish communities around 92–93 C.E.

William Schoedel, a Patristics scholar, discussed the use of Matthean traditions by the Antiochian bishop Ignatius, including a sketch of what a gospel written by him might have looked like. John Meier responded with a very different view of the literary and theological relationships between the Gospel and the epistles of Ignatius. Finally, Jack Kingsbury, as a literary critic, surveyed the strikingly diverse methods employed and conclusions reached by the presenters and was still able to point out nearly a dozen common assumptions and make challenging suggestions for future research.

The conference was sponsored by the Center for the Study of Religion in the Greco-Roman World, directed at that time by Joseph B. Tyson, Victor Paul Furnish, and William S. Babcock. For years, under Tyson's direction, this center has sponsored many such scholarly events in the Dallas/Fort Worth metroplex and beyond. Such conferences have often involved conversations between New Testament and Patristics scholars, of which the discussion between Schoedel and Meier was one example. In fact, this conference followed an earlier one supported by the National Endowment for the Humanities and directed by Furnish; those papers were edited by William S. Babcock (*Paul and the Legacies of Paul* [Dallas: Southern Methodist University Press, 1990]). The center has been supported principally by SMU and by its provost, Ruth Morgan, and also by the University of Dallas and its provost and dean, John E. Paynter, to whom those attending the conference and those who have benefited from the center over the years expressed a deep sense of gratitude. I received skilled assistance from a colleague at Texas Christian University, Daryl D. Schmidt, who voluntarily assumed many tasks while I was on sabbatical. As several letters after the conference attest, we were also indebted to my student assistant, Julie Pierce of Brite Divinity School, TCU, who made innumerable arrangements for participants: well done!°

The codirectors and participants express gratitude to Marshall D. Johnson, now editorial director of Fortress Press, both for attending the conference and for active editorial encouragement and support in the production of this volume. I wish to thank Mrs. Sharlie Tomlinson, my secretary at Brite Divinity School, for preparing the index of Judeo-Christian Scriptures.

° Julie Pierce was involved in an automobile accident in June 1991 and died July 2, 1991, at Parkland Hospital in Dallas, Texas. Friends and colleagues grieve the loss of her companionship.

Finally, the other codirector of the conference was William R. Farmer, who was pleased to see a conference on his favorite Gospel at SMU in the year before his final one at Perkins School of Theology. During the proceedings we saluted his extraordinary ability to generate interest in and scholarly study of Matthew both in our region and internationally. The conference itself and these essays do not focus on his primary passion, the question of the literary relationships among the Synoptic Gospels, but on an earlier interest in social history as manifested both in his book, *Maccabees, Zealots, and Josephus: An Inquiry into Jewish Nationalism in the Greco-Roman Period* (Westport, Conn.: Greenwood, rev. ed. 1973), and especially in his essay, "The Post-Sectarian Character of Matthew and Its Post-War Setting in Antioch of Syria," in *Perspectives in Religious Studies* 3 (1976) 235–47. Farmer's activities since the conference remind us that he will continue to generate new perspectives and promote lively discussion!

Introduction

_____ DAVID L. BALCH

Matthean Jewish Christianity and early rabbinic Judaism were "twin alternatives"[1] in the last decades of the first century of our era. The authors in this volume discuss the provenance of these two and point to the arc of Jewish settlement in Syria that extended from Galilee and Pella north through Antioch and Edessa. Recent research concludes that within this social world there were numerous Jewish sectarian communities that were hostile toward the emerging leadership, all of whom employed the Torah as a common battleground to legitimate their identity and to challenge other groups. Andrew Overman strikingly concludes that "Matthew and his community claim the same tradition, the same authority, even, at points, the same roles as formative Judaism,"[2] which results in the hostility and antagonism of direct confrontation.

In this volume, Alan Segal proposes "that the hostility to Pharisees one sees in the First Gospel provides one piece of evidence that Christians were both still concerned with what was happening in Jewish communities and synagogues, _still found there,_ and greatly vexed by some of the positions they heard from Christian Pharisees inside and outside of synagogues" (p. 35, my emphasis). He suggests a reversal of the usual scholarly methodology employed to understand these conflicts: typically we use Jewish texts, many dated to the third century or later, to understand earliest Christianity. But

1. Alan F. Segal, _Rebecca's Children: Judaism and Christianity in the Roman World_ (Cambridge: Harvard University Press, 1986) 2.
2. J. Andrew Overman, _Matthew's Gospel and Formative Judaism_ (Minneapolis: Fortress, 1990) 153.

since we know the dates of New Testament books within a narrow range, Segal's method is to reverse this and employ Christian texts to understand developments in Judaism. The concluding sentence of this original essay observes that "given the nature of our Jewish texts, the New Testament may be the most valuable evidence we have about ordinary Jewish life in the first century, even though it has a special perspective and a number of hostile opinions about it" (p. 37). The conflict among Peter, Paul, and James reflected in Christian sources shows a Jewish spectrum of opinion in the first century about how strictly the law is to be observed. The really interesting question is not whether Matthew represents Jewish Christianity, but, "How does the Gospel of Matthew fit into this spectrum of Jewish opinion on the law?" (p. 15). Matthew's cut into Jewish history is biased, but it gives us a unique window we cannot get any other way, since the Mishnah is both later and prescriptive, not a description of common practice.

Anthony Saldarini even more insistently looks at the Matthean community and its spokesperson, the author of Matthew, as deviant Jews (p. 38). "Deviance" is employed as a sociological term that does not imply that the group has been driven out of a society; rather, such deviance and nonconformity are part of every society and function to keep a group related to the whole. "Matthew is deviant not because of disagreement with a 'normative' Judaism but because he is a minority against the majority and because he recommends a more fundamental reorientation of the tradition than many other Jewish movements" (pp. 49–50). Saldarini organizes Matthew's innovations under five headings: core symbols, cosmology, boundaries, laws, and social structure. Jesus, the core symbol, is the Son of God for this apocalyptic group, the boundaries are more open, laws are reinterpreted opening the way for change, and the social structure moves away from priestly and aristocratic leadership toward egalitarian fellowship. These innovations suggest that the movement changed from a reformist, to a conversionist, and finally to an isolationist community, Saldarini argues.

Robert Gundry questions all this, asking how the church in Syria traveled so far and fast from Jewish sectarianism to the Ignatian, urban, cosmopolitan, gentile community described in Schoedel's essay. Rather, Matthew represents a distinctly new people whose church differs from the synagogues of Jews. The differences focus on Matthew's confession of Jesus who is "God with us" (1:23) and who enjoins obedience to all his commandments, not to the Torah, which his new interpretation replaces (28:20). It is not the relation of Matthean Christians to formative Judaism that is sociologically problematic, Gundry argues, but internal conflicts within the Christian community.

Antoinette Clark Wire approaches understanding this Gospel's community with a different question. Inquiring about what gender roles were expected in that society and whether the Matthean community deviated from them, she employs macro-sociological analysis to reconstruct roles characteristic of scribal communities within advanced agricultural societies. She identifies five characteristics of the scribal agricultural Qing (Ch'ing) Dynasty in China (seventeenth to early twentieth centuries), compares these with the Qumran Covenanters and the Pharisees in the Roman East, and applies the results to the community addressed by Matthew's Gospel. The five characteristics are "(1) They reinterpret in writing a revered literary tradition (2) in such a way as to teach concrete ritual and ethical behavior (3) which can assure the proper fulfillment of set roles within a community of identification (4) sanctioned by adequate rewards and punishments (5) in order to reassert right order in a situation where it is perceived to be under some threat" (p. 91).

The third characteristic leads Wire to investigate roles women play in the Gospel. They are not among the "disciples," but do demonstrate faith, perhaps "because exemplary faith is considered most wonderful where least expected" (p. 104). Matthew's narrative and teaching converge on two roles, one played by disciples and the other by people *in extremis,* including women, whose "role of deficiency or dependence is not overcome but is used to challenge others to meet their needs and at the same time to learn humility and faith from them" (p. 106). Their roles are typical of those in scribal communities, but Matthew is distinctive in the central emphasis on these figures without social power as models of faith in God and as challenges to service. The second part of Wire's article seeks an explanation for this distinctive emphasis in the recent origin of these traditions among the nonliterate and economically dependent, although Matthew seems to write for a classically educated and self-sufficient scribal community. Women, who were not taught to read in such a society, are marginalized.

In response, Pheme Perkins raises basic questions. Is the community of Matthew one that determines all facets of life for its members? Does Matthew really envision a "scribal" ethos? Since Matthew is not really scribal *halacha,* a community rule, or a commentary on a prophetic text, is not its narrative genre rather *haggadah*? Another series of questions concerns gender analysis. Perkins notes that rhetorical analysis attends to the literary dynamic internal to the text. The mother of the sons of Zebedee, for example, relieves pressure placed on male characters (Matt 20:20–28; cf. 27:19), which departs from Wire's Chinese parallel. Second, culturally cued literary analysis may answer questions about gender roles, but is there really enough cultural overlap between China and the world of Matthew to produce reliable clues? Third, text and archaeology may be sources of information about the social situation of women.

William R. Schoedel observes that Matthew is the only one of the Gospels to have been exploited shortly after its composition by another early

Christian writer as a major source about Jesus, that is, by Ignatius of Antioch. This observation helps clarify the role played by the Gospel in shaping early Christianity. "Ignatius has the popular culture of the Greek city in his bones" (p. 137). In fact there is only one passage in Ignatius (Smyrnaeans [Sm] 1.2) that could pass for a reference to Jewish Christianity, but it is quite general and "suggests no awareness of Jewish Christianity as a distinctive alternative to the type of Christianity taken for granted by Ignatius" (p. 145)! Ignatius has relatively little interest in the Old Testament, and rabbinic Judaism left no real mark on him (p. 153). How can Ignatius be so deeply indebted to Matthew and so unaffected by its form of Christianity? Quite unlike the Matthew presented by Segal and Saldarini, for Ignatius there is a decisive distinction between Christianity and Judaism (cf. Magnesians [Mg] 8–10), a gap that suggests paying more attention to the Hellenistic in Matthew (p. 145). Heuristically he asks, finally, what a gospel written by Ignatius would have looked like (cf. Trallians [Tr] 9; Sm 1; Ephesians [Eph] 18.2; 19.1, 2–3; pp. 154–75), and includes comments on the possible quotations of Matt 3:15 in Sm 1.1 and of Matt 8:17 in Polycarp (Pol) 1.3 (pp. 157, 166), possibilities he argues against. Surprisingly and unlike Matthew, Ignatius would not have written a Petrine gospel; he models himself rather on Paul (p. 164).

John Meier, in response, raises two questions involving both method and content: Do Ignatius's epistles inform us about the Antiochian or Asian churches; and the larger question, Did Ignatius know the Gospel Matthew itself or simply some special M traditions? To the first question Meier responds with a careful "both/and," and to the second he argues, with Massaux and Köhler and against Schoedel and Koester, that Ignatius knew the written text of Matthew, as evidenced by Sm 1.1, Philadelphians (Ph) 3.1, Pol 2.2, and Eph 19.2–3. Meier adds a strong argument based on the cumulative force of these heterogeneous Matthean traditions in Ignatius's epistles; the simplest solution is that Ignatius knew the written Gospel.

Rodney Stark in a shockingly realistic study suggests that "if we want to understand the immense popular appeal of the early church we must understand how the message of the New Testament and the social relations it sustained solved acute problems afflicting Greco-Roman cities" (p. 189). Based on the few studies of the physical environment of Greco-Roman cities that have been written, he emphasizes the "extraordinary levels of urban disorder, social dislocation, misery, and cultural chaos" (p. 190). With other social scientists, he assumes that "a cultural shift so extreme as the rise of Christianity is possible only during periods of acute social disruption" (p. 190, citing Anthony F. C. Wallace), an assumption related to the fifth characteristic of scribal societies described by Wire. Antioch offers an excellent case study of "the severe physical and social stress on most residents most of the time" in Greco-Roman cities, "an everyday misery . . . punctuated frequently by appalling natural and social disasters" (p. 191). Stark attempts "to show how Christianity [exemplified by Matt 25:35–40] served as an effective revitalization movement that greatly mitigated the chronic misery, disorder, and periodic disasters that afflicted Greco-Roman cities" (pp. 198–99). "In my judgment, a major way in which Christianity served as a revitalization movement within the empire was in offering a coherent culture that was *entirely stripped of ethnicity*" (p. 200, his emphasis). But his major point relates to the periodic epidemics: "Because they were asked to nurse the sick and dying, many of them received such nursing. . . . [t]o cities faced with epidemics, fires, and earthquakes, Christianity offered effective nursing services" (p. 205).

Michael White cautions that "Matthew's polemic against 'their synagogues' (4:23; 9:35; 10:17; 12:9; 13:54; cf. 23:34) cannot be understood as having broken away from the established order of Judaism in Jesus' day" (p. 217). Matthew still has a "sectarian" Jewish identity, assuming circumcision for all males of the community (p. 241 n. 100), although Ignatius is better characterized as a "cultic" revitalization movement, one within a basically foreign symbolic worldview (pp. 224–25). Stimulated by Stark but noting that the Antiochene disasters listed by him date later than Matthew's time (p. 219 n. 30), White inquires how one may locate the crisis situation in Matthew's context. He rules out both Antioch and Galilee proper as the Gospel's place of origin (p. 228). His insightful, original suggestion is that the crisis setting of the Gospel is to be fixed not only in relation to the emergence of the Pharisees, but also by the *shifting geopolitical or administrative boundaries* of Galilee, which would disrupt the market exchange system by establishing new tax zones, in the period ca. 75–125 (p. 233). The death of the Jewish king Agrippa II (ca. 92–93) was a time of massive administrative changes and the occasion for the expansion of rabbinic religious authority in the Yavnean period (ca. 90–120; p. 236). White highlights the Q woe-saying against Chorazin, Bethsaida, and Capernaum, towns that mark the boundary of Lower Galilee; Jesus says it will be better for the Greek cities of Tyre and Sidon, the village culture of Upper Galilee and of gentile contact, in the final judgment (Matt 11:20–24). This distinction symbolizes the Matthean community's situation although it does not explicitly locate it (p. 240).

Frederick Norris, an "armchair archaeologist," remarks that although Antioch was the fourth-largest city of the Mediterranean world, inscriptions and information generally about its history are sorely lacking. Streeter was not correct in saying that influential writings must come from large urban centers, but Norris does outline how the artifacts that remain in and near Antioch may serve as evidence for religious attitudes in the region. Against Festugière, one may cautiously use the mosaics to indicate some religious values of a home's occupants, for example, the personifications of *Soteria* and *ktisis,* the Yakto floor featuring the Constantinian church, the Daphne-Yakto mosaic featuring Isis, another depicting either Isis or Demeter, and three apotropaic mosaics from Jekmejeh, a village west of Daphne.

As codirector of the conference and editor of these essays, I have perceived a difficulty, exaggerated by the fact that the scholar who addressed the conference on the social location of Matthean values in *Greek* culture subsequently became the pro-vice-chancellor of his university and was unable to produce a paper. The conference sought to describe the *social history* of these communities, and yet we are left with an imposing, unexplained social gap between Segal, Saldarini, and White's Matthew embedded in formative Galilean Judaism and Schoedel's Hellenistic Antiochian Ignatius on whom rabbinic Judaism left no real mark. To state the problem from another angle, when one compares allusions to and citations from the four Gospels by second-century Greek Christian writers, a "clear preponderance" of them belong to Matthew, and after Irenaeus, Matthew is *the* Gospel of the church.[3] How and why did a Gospel that concentrates on such "ordinary Jewish issues"[4] become the most popular one in the later Greek church? Hellenistic values are also crucial, of course, to understanding Matthew;[5] Jewish and Greek values are not mutually exclusive. Given this problematic I have written chapter 4 on the Greek political topos "concerning law(s) (περὶ νόμου/νόμων)," arguing that these ideas and practices influence Matthew in 5:17, 19, and 16:19. In the Greco-Roman world, a people or nation could consider themselves legitimate only if they had not "abolished" the laws of their founder: As Romans claimed in the first century to be following Romulus's laws, so Jews claimed still to be practicing Moses' laws. But this idealistic claim is problematic over time: crises bring change and development, so some of the same writers, for example, Dionysius for Rome, Josephus and Matthew for Israel, must legitimate present practices that differ from ancient ones. These ideas from Greek political discussions "concerning laws," that is, claiming that change has not occurred, but then narrating development and rationalizing it, mean that the Jewish-Christian author of Matthew participates in the "selective acculturation" of Greek political ideas and practices seen two centuries earlier in 2 Maccabees.

In the final paper in this volume, Jack Dean Kingsbury surveys these highly diverse essays, commenting on their methodology, on the *eleven* points describing the social location of Matthew's community on which the

---

3. Wolf-Dietrich Köhler, *Die Rezeption des Matthäusevangeliums in der Zeit vor Irenäus* (WUNT 2.24; Tübingen: J.C.B. Mohr [Paul Siebeck], 1987) 522 and 2.

4. Segal, *Rebecca's Children,* 146–47.

5. Most importantly, see Hans Dieter Betz, *Essays on the Sermon on the Mount* (Philadelphia: Fortress, 1985).

authors seem to agree (pp. 262–63), and on the use of source theories. Finally, from his intimate knowledge of the text as a literary critic, he makes significant suggestions for future research.

I

MATTHEW:
JEWISH AND
HELLENISTIC ASPECTS

1

Matthew's Jewish Voice

ALAN F. SEGAL

PAUL AND STRACK-BILLERBECK

The use of Jewish texts wholesale to understand earliest Christianity is too often misleading. Strack and Billerbeck wrote a massive German commentary of the New Testament, patiently going chapter by chapter through the New Testament, and bringing in important passages from Talmud and Midrash. The volumes are often wrongly criticized for their shallow evaluation and lack of comprehensiveness in rabbinic Judaism, but the shallowness problem is not so much their own. It is, instead, the problem of the many scholars whose only contact with rabbinic Judaism was through Strack-Billerbeck. When used together with other sources, it is a very helpful reference work.

The real problem with Strack-Billerbeck is its methodology. It is sometimes possible to learn a great deal about the New Testament from a rabbinic tradition. But methodologically it is impossible to assume that one can study New Testament Christianity, a book whose date is firmly set by the end of the first quarter of the second century, by means of the Mishnah and Talmud, works which can be dated surely to the third century and later. To be sure, there was a period of oral tradition behind every rabbinic work. But we cannot generalize on the duration of the oral stage of the traditioning process. Each tradition must be evaluated according to its own development. Therefore, the Christian evidence is more crucial for understanding and dating the development of rabbinic Judaism than the reverse, which exactly reverses the methodology most often used today.

What we should be doing is compiling a commentary of the Mishnah with the New Testament in its margins. After all, we know the dates of the New Testament documents within a very close range. We should be using the witness of the New Testament (and the church fathers) in the margins of the Mishnah to help understand the world of the first century.[1]

In this paper, I will show that Matthew's Gospel tells us more about Judaism than we have so far exploited.[2] The incident at Antioch, briefly described by Paul in Gal 2:11–18—somehow related to the Jerusalem council recounted by Luke in Acts 15 and so important to understand Paul—was also my starting point for understanding the Gospel of Matthew as well. So we must come back to it later. I wish to show that the earliest Christian community is not yet distinct from the Jewish community; it was a fractious and interesting new sect. By understanding what is happening at Antioch, we also learn something about Judaism.

MATTHEW'S POSITIVE PERSPECTIVE ON TORAH

Matthew has a positive view of Torah in general.[3] Jesus is an accurate and knowledgeable interpreter of the law. This, in general, strikingly distinguishes Matthew from Mark.[4] Matthew takes pains to demonstrate the truth of Jesus' interpretations of the law, over against the accusations of his opponents. This seems to reflect the actual practice of the community that valued Matthew, though not necessarily the practice of Jesus. That is to say, it is more likely to be an accurate view of the Matthean community's views on law rather than Jesus' own. This attempt to presage and understand the community's social view in its records of its founder is nowhere clearer than in Matthew 10. Here the community is told what to expect. They must preach that the kingdom of God is at hand (10:7). They must heal the sick, raise the dead, cleanse lepers, and cast out demons (10:8). They should not take any remuneration for their services, nor carry any wealth. Instead they must go without any baggage

---

1. See some provisional uses of the new method within the Pauline corpus in Alan F. Segal, *Paul the Convert* (New Haven: Yale University Press, 1990).

2. By "Matthew" I mean, of course, the Gospel passed on in his name.

3. Arland Hultgren, *Jesus and His Adversaries: The Form and Function of the Conflict Stories in the Synoptic Tradition* (Minneapolis: Augsburg, 1979). See also W. G. Kümmel, *Introduction to the New Testament* (Nashville: Abingdon, 1966) 80–83. He cites the literature and the consensus that Matthew reflects a Jewish-Christian background. He notes however that it is a Jewish Christianity very open to the admission of Gentiles. For me this automatically raises the suspicion that some varieties of ordinary Judaism were open to proselytizing Gentiles as well. Of course, to establish such a point, one needs to look for direct evidence of it as well. See Segal, *Paul the Convert*, chap. 3.

4. I try not to assume either Markan or Matthean priority, only wishing to distinguish between the ways in which the evangelists interpret their stories. Thus, for present purposes, "Q" essentially means those parts of Matthew that are shared with Luke but not present in Mark.

and accept the charity of those with whom they stay (10:10). This is not merely prophecy or gospel. This is a social handbook for what a proper Matthean disciple should look like. According to Matthew, this role of itinerant preacher was created by Jesus himself.

Numerous features in the Gospel suggest an intimate acquaintance with rabbinic exegesis. Jesus' use of antithesis (5:22–48) and *qal vahomer* (12:9–14) show that the editor wished to portray Jesus as knowledgeable in exegesis.[5] Matthew's use of rabbinic exegetical methods does not of itself prove the redactor's Jewish-Christian origins, for those rules were often adapted from Greek hermeneutical devices, as both Henry Fischel and David Daube have demonstrated.[6] Yet Jesus' derivation of life after death by means of *hekesh* in Matthew 23 is not just a Greek rhetorical technique, since it depends intimately on biblical interpretation. It is supposed to show Jesus' mastery of Jewish exegetical technique to resolve important existential questions. It shows that Matthew knew these techniques intimately.

The costs of this discipleship in Matthew are also clear:

> Beware of them, for they will hand you over to councils and flog you in their synagogues, and you will be dragged before governors and kings because of me, as a testimony to them and the Gentiles. When they hand you over, do not worry about how you are to speak or what you are to say; for what you are to say will be given to you at that time; for it is not you who speak but the Spirit of your Father speaking through you. Brother will betray brother to death, and a father his child, and children will rise against parents and have them put to death; and you will be hated by all because of my name. But the one who endures to the end will be saved. When they persecute you in one town, flee to the next; for truly, I tell you, you will not have gone through all the towns of Israel before the Son of Man comes. (Matt 10:17–23)

Here is a forecasting of the tribulation that Matthew expects from his Jewish neighbors. We see a group of people who are presumed to be part of the synagogue, under its aegis and subject to its punishments, not outside of it like Paul's congregations. The congregation that lies behind the words of Matthew must be Jewish in history and tradition, though there are some

---

5. Admittedly this can be contested. G. Strecker restricts all such evidence of Jewish-Christian background to the level of the primitive tradition; cf. *Der Weg der Gerechtigkeit. Untersuchung zur Theologie des Matthäus* (FRLANT 82; Göttingen: Vandenhoeck & Ruprecht, 1962) 15–39. Of course, if Matthew is prior, then it is still a primitive tradition within Matthew. Contra E. Schweizer, *Matthäus und seine Gemeinde* (Stuttgart: KBW, 1974) 10–12. See Celia Deutsch, *Hidden Wisdom and the Easy Yoke: Wisdom, Torah, and Discipleship in Matthew 11:25–30* (Sheffield: JSOT, 1987) 14–16.

6. David Daube, "Rabbinic Methods of Interpretation and Hellenistic Rhetoric," *HUCA* 22 (1949) 239–64. Matthew's use of the devices is, however, significant in view of the other range of indications in the Gospel. Henry Fischel, *Rabbinic Literature and Greco-Roman Philosophy: A Study of Epicurea and Rhetorica in Early Midrashic Writings* (Leiden: E. J. Brill, 1973).

indications that toward the end of the redaction process this Jewish identity was under siege. What is more important, whatever they think of themselves, some Jews apparently think of them as dangerous *heretics*. The community is cognizant that some of their members (1) are subject to synagogue punishments, and (2) have been reported to authorities. The community in which the Gospel of Matthew exists is for most of its history a kind of Judaism that is wary of non-Jews, as Jesus tells his disciples: "Go nowhere among the Gentiles, and enter no town of the Samaritans, but go rather to the lost sheep of the house of Israel" (Matt 10:5–6).[7] Even if the Matthean community no longer believes in this limitation, it preserves it as an important foundational belief.

Indeed, the Gospel defines a group that accepts instability and asserts mobility as a necessary part of discipleship. Accepting discipleship, the technical terms for which are evidenced more in Matthew than in any other Gospel, includes a commitment to itinerancy. It is not necessarily true, however, that these people did not want to convert Gentiles. Rather, the First Gospel says that the centers of Matthean activity should be in cities that have Jews in them and that one should avoid cities where there are only Gentiles or Samaritans. The targeted group is "the lost sheep of the house of Israel." This term may support a number of different interpretations, but it might easily be ordinary Jews living outside of Pharisaic domination. It is, of course, conditioned by the time frame that the Gospel stories impose upon history. Whatever Jesus' words originally meant, Matthew interprets them as applying to a limited period, as we shall see.

But to discover where Matthew falls in the Jewish legal spectrum, we have to look at Jesus' conflicts in Matthew's eyes. First I will take a few examples of what Matthew appears to say about Torah positively. Then I will attempt to understand the evangelist's negative views about the opposition, particularly the Pharisees. Finally, I will say a few words about the corresponding situation in the Jewish community and try to summarize the social meaning of Matthew's opinions.

Matthew 12:1–8:
Picking Grain on the Sabbath

Matthew, as well as Mark and Luke, reproduces this story. But, in contrast to the other evangelists, Matthew explains that the disciples were hungry on the Sabbath, making clearer the precedent between the disciples' actions and that of David in 1 Sam 21:1–6. For Mark, the issue is only that David is just as guilty as Jesus, not that both were upholding the law. But Matthew has a

---

7. See Amy-Jill Levine, *The Social and Ethnic Dimensions of Matthean Salvation History: "Go nowhere among the Gentiles . . ." (Matt 10:5b)* (Studies in the Bible and Early Christianity 14; Lewiston, N.Y.: Edwin Mellen, 1988).

further conclusion. He mentions priests who profane the Sabbath yet are guilt-less. Citing Hos 6:6, Matthew records Jesus as saying that the disciples are guiltless (12:7); indeed, they actually fulfill the law, though their interpretation differs from those who condemn them, presumably the Pharisees, who are singled out here. Thus, the Pharisees have no authentic claim to their exegesis, but Jesus' claim comes directly from God (12:6–8).

So Jesus and his disciples do not break the law. They only break with the Pharisaic interpretation of the law. This is quite different from Paul's posi-tion that all observances are equally irrelevant. Here the primacy of the law is affirmed, but the Pharisaic authority to interpret is disputed.

Matthew 15:1–20

Even when the issue is explicitly purity laws, Matthew upholds the law. The Markan story about hand washing (Mark 7) contains the summary state-ment that "all foods are clean" (Mark 7:19). Matthew avoids any such extreme statement and argues rather about what the law means: "Do you not see that whatever goes into the mouth enters the stomach, and goes out into the sewer? But what comes out of the mouth proceeds from the heart, and this is what defiles. For out of the heart come evil intentions, murder, adultery, fornica-tion, theft, false witness, slander. These are what defile a person, but to eat with unwashed hands does not defile" (15:17–20). Matthew completely omits the offensive phrase "all foods are clean," the Markan conclusion that invali-dates the Jewish food laws. He also softens the force of Jesus' criticism of the defilement issue in several ways. But note that he does not completely ignore Jesus' criticism of the law. Rather he tries to show that Jesus' criticism of law is actually its true fulfillment.

Although we should not uniquely equate attention to purity laws with Pharisaism, Matthew explicitly takes issue with the Pharisaic interpretation of Torah. He also takes issue with a large part of the Jewish community beyond Pharisaism which equally valued the biblical purity injunctions. But it is not clear that Matthew's understanding of Torah would have cast his community outside of Judaism. Rather it seems likely that the sentiments he articulates could have had a place within Hellenistic Judaism, widely conceived. Socio-logically then, we should think of Matthew's community as a rather left-wing one in terms of obedience to Torah. But it is not one that claims to be beyond Jewish law entirely, as is Paul's.

Matthew 22:34–40

In Mark and Luke this short encounter is stimulated by a scribe (γραμ-ματεύς, Mark 12) or a lawyer (νομικός, Luke 10). In Matthew the Pharisees are behind the test. They send a lawyer to stimulate a controversy. The lawyer asks: "Teacher (διδάσκαλος), which commandment in the law is the greatest?" (Matt 22:36). Jesus responds that the greatest commandment is love, combining Deut 6:5 and Lev 19:18. Like Hillel, Jesus responds that all the law depends on this commandment (Matt 22:39). But the point of the controversy is to show the Pharisees up as hypocrites. This is central for Matthew's understanding of the law. For him Torah is all fulfilled in the command to love (Matt 5:43f., 7:12, 19:19, 24:12, 27:34ff.), and the Pharisees have missed it.

Regardless of Matthew's polemical stance against the Pharisees, basing the law on love is rather close to a rabbinic story about Hillel. Matthew is certainly concerned with the law, though he interprets it more radically than the rabbis did. The rabbinic story ends with the command to the proselyte to go out and study. At the same time, it is not hard to see that these statements harbor a sensitivity to the charge that the Christian community is antinomian. Matthew's community is claiming that its opponents, not itself, are misinterpreting the law, even while defending its own interpretation and practice of the law. As Jesus himself says in Matthew: "Do not think that I have come to abolish the law or the prophets; I have come not to abolish but to fulfill. For truly I tell you, until heaven and earth pass away, not one letter, not one stroke of a letter, will pass from the law until all is accomplished. Therefore, whoever breaks one of the least of these commandments, and teaches others to do the same, will be called least in the kingdom of heaven; but whoever does them and teaches them will be called great in the kingdom of heaven" (Matt 5:17–20).

These teachings are linked to the passion narrative by means of Matt 26:1. "And it happened when Jesus had finished these sayings," so it is viewed as having a direct connection with the events leading up to Jesus' death and resurrection. In 28:20 Jesus' teachings are linked to the resurrection: "Teaching them to observe all that I have commanded you." It is certainly not accidental that both passages sound peculiarly Deuteronomic. Indeed, the love commandment of Matthew is highly reminiscent of Deuteronomic paraenesis. But it is also clear that Jesus' crucifixion and resurrection are new teachings that must inform the whole.[8]

PETER IN MATTHEW

The very favorable view of Peter in Matthew is related to the positive view of law in the Gospel, a perspective that again must predispose us to assume a Jewish-Christian background for the community which produced the

8. Nils A. Dahl, "The Passion Narrative in Matthew," in *Jesus in the Memory of the Early Church: Essays by Nils Alstrop Dahl* (Minneapolis: Augsburg, 1976) 50.

Gospel.[9] I will show that the figure of Peter serves as a kind of eponymous ancestor for the Matthean community. In three passages Matthew portrays Peter as making a significant contribution which is not paralleled by other Gospels. The passages are (1) the incident of Peter's walking on the water (paralleled in Mark 6:45–52), but sinking and being rescued (Matt 14:28–31); (2) Peter's confession of Jesus not only as the Messiah (paralleled in Mark 8:27–33) but as the Son of the living God, followed by Jesus' blessing and promise (Matt 16:16b–19); (3) the question about paying the temple tax in which Jesus tells Peter to catch a fish in which there would be a shekel (17:24–27). All three cases involve a dialogue between Jesus and Peter, while two also involve a miracle done on Peter's behalf. All three passages appear in the so-called fourth book of Matthew (13:53–18:35), in which the evangelist turns his attention to ecclesiastical concerns. It is only in this section that the term ἐκκλησία ["church"] occurs. Chapter 18 is devoted mostly to social relationships within the community. Thus, it appears that the portrayal of Peter is closely associated with the Gospel's understanding of community. Peter may serve as role model and hero of that community.

In Matt 14:28–31, at the scene of Jesus' walking on water, Peter is invited to walk with him. Peter gets out of the boat, walks on water, and comes to Jesus. But when he becomes afraid, he begins to sink. He prays to Jesus, "Lord, save me," whereupon Jesus reaches out his hand and catches him. Jesus reprimands Peter for having little faith (ὀλιγόπιστε). Although there is a partial parallel in John 21:7–8, this basic story seems unique to Matthew. But the setting in John, with the risen Lord, may in fact be more original, because recognition of the "Lord" is appropriate to resurrection scenes.

Since the story specifically criticizes Peter as having too little faith, the import for a Petrine community is not entirely clear. Yet, the basic pattern of discipleship is strongly evident in the story (see also Matt 4:19; 10:1). Jesus bids Peter to come to him, giving him the power to do what Jesus himself can do, even though the story makes the point that Peter's faith is inferior to the Savior himself. It may be especially important that Peter, the rock on whom the church is founded, is saved from sinking. The story emphasizes Peter's preeminence among the disciples. On account of Peter's confession and recognition of Jesus as Lord, the other disciples worship Jesus. It is this worship that most distinguishes Jewish Christians from ordinary Jews.[10]

The theme of confessing Jesus as Lord is again taken up in Matt 16:16b–19. This famous crux cannot be discussed in detail. But it is safe to assume that Matthew reproduces most of the Markan story, expanding it by

9. See esp. R. E. Brown, K. P. Donfried, and J. Reumann, *Peter in the New Testament* (Minneapolis: Augsburg, 1973) esp. 107.

10. Larry Hurtado, *One God, One Lord: Early Christian Devotion and Ancient Jewish Monotheism* (Philadelphia: Fortress, 1988).

insertions.[11] In Matthew, as opposed to Mark, Peter's confession of Jesus as Messiah and "Son of the living God" is considered true and perceptive, since Jesus himself praises it. This confession is further lauded with the evaluation that "flesh and blood" did not reveal it, effectively turning Peter's confession into a revelation. The revelation is the unique part of the story, for all the disciples have similarly confessed Jesus as Son of God (14:33). This passage has the effect of confirming from Jesus' own mouth the special distinction accorded to Peter. Jesus' subsequent acknowledgment that Peter is the rock on which the church is built, itself a statement that works better in Aramaic than Greek, is adumbrated by a series of statements of temporal power that appear to have a Jewish provenance. No one is quite sure of the meaning of the terms "keys of the kingdom" and "binding" and "loosing." Given the importance of these verses for establishing the powers of the church of Rome that rest on these statements, it is unlikely that any agreement will ever be reached throughout Christian scholarship. But the Semitic background to the verses seems clear enough.

In between these statements lies a puzzling rebuke: "Get behind me, Satan! You are a stumbling block to me; for you are setting your mind not on divine things but on human things" (Matt 16:23).[12] Although many different interpretations have been proposed for this verse, to me the most significant association appears to be with Jewish Christianity, which did not especially interpret the suffering of Jesus as meaningful.

It may even be that the statements of binding and loosing are the basis of the *takkanot* which appear to have entered Jewish Christianity concerning various observances of the law.

The final specifically Petrine addition to Matthew is the story of the temple tax (Matt 17:24–27). Tax collectors for the half-shekel tax approach Peter, suspicious of tax evasion. Upon returning to his house, Jesus asserts that they are free from such tolls. However, in order not to give offense, Peter is to go fishing. The first fish that he catches will have a coin which will pay for the tax of both Peter and Jesus.

The miracle story functions to answer a difficulty in the community, that of paying taxes to the temple, which was shortly to become theoretical. But the story in Matthew shows a unique interest in fulfilling Jewish customs. The story points out the special importance of Peter because he is included in the miracle with Jesus. No other disciple is afforded the tax relief Peter attains.

11. See Oscar Cullmann, *Peter—Disciple, Apostle, Martyr* (2d ed.; Philadelphia: Westminster, 1962) 184. Cullmann relates the scene to Luke 22:31–32. But it is quite possible that this scene represents, as does Matt 14:28–31, a postresurrection appearance, set into the life of Jesus.

12. The remark, which appears in Mark as well, seems to be based on his misunderstanding of the necessity of suffering of the Son of man, becoming a stumbling block for Jesus.

From these observations in Matthew, it seems clear that Peter plays a crucial role for the Matthean community. He is one of the first two disciples (Matt 4:18–20), and he is the first (πρῶτος) of the Twelve (10:2). Indeed, his name is a kind of title, since Peter displaces his given name, Simon Bar-Jonah. In the organization of the church, Peter, not Jesus, is the foundation figure. Peter brings up the legal issues about Jewish food regulations (15:15), the payment of the temple tax (17:24–27), and the obligation to forgive (18:21). It was Jesus himself who gave Peter his name and title, as well as the keys to the kingdom. Jesus himself saves him when he is sinking. As in Mark, Peter is the spokesperson for the disciples; but he is not simply that. He is also the recipient of a special divine revelation for which Jesus gives him a unique blessing (16:17).

But he is not an entirely strong character. He is called a man of little faith (14:31), even though he is also praised for having faith (16:17–18). He is cursed as "satan" and a stumbling block because he thinks the thoughts of humans and not the thoughts of God (16:23), and after Jesus' arrest, he denies Jesus. These statements almost sound like a Pauline criticism, and they may, in fact, reflect the point of view of tradents within the gentile Christian community. Because of his compromising position, he may be praised for his judgment but criticized for his lack of faith. By the time of Matthew's Gospel, this term hardly can be innocent of Pauline implications. Let us look at how the Petrine position, especially as discussed in Acts, helped bridge this gap.

Paul's Position

Within the Christian community, the spectrum of opinion about the Jewish law is most easily divided into three. The position of James is that Jewish law remains in effect. Peter has a moderate opinion while Paul has the most radical position. All three positions can be described as growing out of Pharisaism. Paul's position cannot be called a Pharisaic one but, ironically, it comes from Pharisaism since Paul developed it by overthrowing Pharisaism. He converted from being a Pharisee to a member of a new apocalyptic and mystical form of Judaism, which we now call Christianity. And, although it is not in itself a Pharisaic position, Paul is cognizant of and agrees with many Pharisaic beliefs. Paul began from the Pharisaic position that to become Jewish, the entire Jewish law must be performed, as the rabbis maintain afterward, and as he himself must have taught when he was a Pharisee. What he questioned was whether the new converts to Christianity had to become Jewish, if they led ethical, Christian lives without strict conversion to Judaism. Paul did not overturn his Pharisaic past completely when he maintained that the Gentiles need not convert to have a place in the world to come, for this was one of the positions the Pharisees debated and accepted as well. Within rabbinic

Judaism there was also a position accepting that righteous Gentiles are the equivalent of Jews when the issue is salvation (e.g., *t.Sanhedrin* 13:2, *b.Sanhedrin* 105a; *Sifra* 86b; *b.Baba Kamma* 38a).[13] It eventually became the accepted position in Judaism, but it is hard to date exactly. However, the Noahide laws are traceable to the pre-Christian book of *Jubilees* 7:20 (see below). Can it be that these perspectives reflect in some degree ordinary Jewish opinions about the law? In the case of Matthew and James, the answer is yes with some special Christian pleadings. The case of Paul is not as special as first seems, but it is outside the purview of this paper.

Paul overstepped his Pharisaic bounds in insisting that the boundaries between Jewish and gentile communities be dissolved. While it was not strictly against Pharisaic law for Jews and Gentiles to eat together, it was extremely difficult to do so. Not only did the Jewish community observe special rules which were not understood by Gentiles, they were enjoined against gentile foods that were involved in pagan worship. Among other things, Jews were adjured from drinking wine with Gentiles, since there was a presumption that Gentiles poured out libations to idols whenever they drank. There was also a strong prohibition against eating the meat of animals that had been sacrificed to idols before it was made available to secular use. The fact that Jewish Christians understood these rules and naturally followed them, while gentile Christians neither knew them nor understood them, made for great difficulties to Christian unity. Paul's letters show us that his gentile communities were offended, puzzled, and hurt by Jewish Christian sensibilities, their reticence to interact with gentile Christians, and their condemnation of gentile Christian lack of attention to Jewish law. Paul maintained strongly that the Jewish laws that separated Jewish Christians from gentile Christians were no longer necessary. Just as circumcision was no longer necessary to become one community with the Jewish Christians, so restrictions in dietary law were no longer necessary. Paul maintained, therefore, that the works of the law, the special laws of Judaism, were no longer necessary, though the law was good and from God. The Jewish Christian reaction to Paul's preaching is in some ways representative of the Jewish reaction to it.

James

Although Paul perhaps thought he was broadening the borders of Judaism by adding his gentile converts to it, most Christians were not ready for Paul's extreme interpretation of the law. As Paul did not garner most support, the Pharisees and the Pharisaic Christians probably saw in Paul's congregations little or no threat, as even Acts 5:33–39 makes clear. Of course, Acts is not

13. See Segal, *Paul the Convert*, chaps. 3 and 5–8.

automatically trustworthy, but the positions Acts describes appear historical, though Acts has important theological reasons for presenting them in a particular context. According to Acts 15:5 and 21:20, some Pharisees became followers of Jesus while maintaining their standard ritual requirements. For them, the earliest Christian community was in no sense a new religion, distinct from Judaism. Jewish Christians felt that nothing that Jesus had said prevented them from observing Jewish law. This is close to the perspective of James, though James would have been on the liberal side of Pharisaic opinion because he compromised on crucial issues.

James is the brother of Jesus, hereditarily first among the leadership of the Jerusalem church (Gal 1:19; 2:9, 12; Acts 12:17; 15:13). According to Paul, James was an opponent because James's position was that the entire law continued in effect. James must represent the community that remained in Jerusalem, particularly those who before the outbreak of the war against Rome fled Jerusalem to Perea across the Jordan (Eus. *Hist. Eccl.* 3.5.3).

This position, dominant in very earliest Christianity, is now only found in a few places in canonical New Testament literature. The most obvious place is the Epistle of James, which contains the most Jewish theology of the New Testament. In James, there is a strong polemic against the doctrine of faith without works. This seems to be directed against Paulinism, which believed in justification by faith alone. In Rom 4:3–22 and Gal 3:2–7 Paul argues that Gen 15:6, "Abraham believed the Lord: and the Lord reckoned it to him as righteousness," means that Abraham's faith *alone,* not his actions, brought about God's favor. This position has the social utility of reassuring gentile converts to Christianity that they do not have to adopt the whole (or indeed any) of the special laws of Judaism. James 2:14–26 directly contradicts the Pauline opinion, arguing that Abraham's work, not his faith, is what endeared him to God. Thus, the earliest controversy in the church appears to have centered around the fulfillment of the law and, particularly, Paul's rather striking position that faith rather than deeds was the center of Jesus' message. But the import of the controversy had nothing to do with theology in our sense of the term. Rather, it was a live dispute between Christians about the kinds of actions that would define the new Christian community or make one a Christian. Thus, behind the theological issues rests a social rupture between Jewish Christians and gentile converts. The Jewish legal opinion was that gentile converts ideally should convert, performing the entire Jewish law and entering the Jewish community. There were moderate Jews, perhaps interested in assuaging gentile fears that Jews were a threat to the gentile family, who championed the idea that Gentiles need not convert entirely. They could become worshipers of God, or God-fearers, without actually taking up all the Jewish law. They could observe the Noahide commandments, which applied to all

humanity (*b.Sanhedrin* 56b. Cf. *m.Avodah Zarah* 8(9):4–6; *Jubilees* 7:20ff).[14]
But anyone who intended to interact with Jews must be careful not to impinge
on their ritual purity.

This spectrum of opinion, with all of its accumulated knowledge about
the importance of various symbolic actions, moved over into the Christian
community where it received a series of new meanings. Along with official
Pharisaism, Paul said that Christians should be either observant Jews or God-
fearers, interested fellow-travelers, as well. But Paul changed the meaning of
the choice. For the Pharisees, the goal was complete conversion, including circumcision. For Paul that was an unwanted possibility, perhaps an impossibil-
ity, since his gentile converts did not know the law well enough to observe it.
Paul says, "Once again I testify to every man who lets himself be circumcised
that he is obliged to obey the entire law" (Gal 5:3). Furthermore, the effects of
faith in Christ are lost on those who converted totally (Gal 5:4). Christ's
sacrifice would thereafter be irrelevant because they were no longer Gentiles.
Rather, he felt that none of the special laws of Judaism were incumbent upon
the new converts from the Gentiles. There can be no doubt that Paul's position
was the minority one at first, while the majority position was represented by
both Peter and James, whose center of influence was Jerusalem and the original
community, as opposed to the Hellenized cities of the Diaspora, where Paul's
gentile congregations were to be found.[15]

MATTHEW AND THE INCIDENT
AT ANTIOCH

Matthew is often supposed to come from the neighborhood of Antioch.
Concerning Antioch in church history we know of a single and most puzzling
incident. The Antioch incident is datable to the late 40s of the first century,
depending on the outcome of such questions as the date of the Jerusalem council. Since the crisis at Antioch was provoked by the arrival of "certain people
from James" (Gal 2:12), that is, from Jerusalem, it would be important to clarify
the relationship between the church in Jerusalem and the church at Antioch,
were we able to do so. But we cannot, and the reason may be that they themselves were probably not sure about the relationship either. Or else what was
the dispute about? At any rate, the dispute is apparently stimulated by the fact
that Peter originally eats with Gentiles but withdraws under the pressure of
these men from James.

Peter is caught in the middle of this dispute and, as we will see, Peter's

14. See ibid., chap. 5.
15. See ibid., chap. 4.

position becomes the basis of Matthew's understanding of law. We thus see a spectrum of opinion about how strictly Jewish law is to be observed. Furthest on the right wing is James, in the middle is Peter, and on the left wing is Paul. Even James is not nearly so strict as some of the Pharisaic Jews described by the New Testament. It also seems clear from the ensuing story in Acts that Paul is very much on the other extreme from James. The more centrist positions dominate the Jerusalem conference, suggesting that some Jewish law ought to be permitted. Paul is an extremist for the first generation of Christians, though later his position becomes normative.

My first question then is not whether Matthew represents Jewish Christianity. That term is not very helpful because even Paul is a Jewish Christian. Nor is it whether Matthew represents a "Pharisaic" Christianity, because there are many kinds of Pharisees. The really interesting question is: How does the Gospel of Matthew fit into this spectrum of Jewish opinion on the issue of the law? To me the evidence of Christianity is better for understanding first-century Judaism than the other way around. The Christian record merely gives us a cut into Jewish history, from one, biased point of view. But it does give us a unique window into Judaism that we cannot easily get any other way, since the Mishnah is codified at the end of the second century and it is itself a prescriptive code, not a description of common practice. Looking at the Christian evidence from a new point of view we see that it may in fact describe part of the actual range of opinion about Jewish law that existed at the end of the first and beginning of the second century. Paul is on the far extreme, so Matthew must be the descendant of a more compromising position within the Jewish community, one more at ease within the Jewish ritual practices and more susceptible to pressure from it. The issue of table fellowship with Gentiles must have come up even before Christianity. Note that nowhere in rabbinic literature is table fellowship with Gentiles forbidden. What is forbidden is eating nonkosher food or food that has been dedicated to idols. But that does not exhaust the possibilities even for a Pharisaic Jew. And there is no telling what ordinary Jews and diaspora Jews might have done. But there must have been conflicts within the community on how to behave, just as there are conflicts within the Jewish community today on the exact same issues.

What makes Christianity different from ordinary Judaism is that Paul's mission to the Gentiles made such questions crucial to unity within the community, rather than an interesting sidelight. That is to say that the presence of Gentiles who asked for equal communal status precipitated the question in a way that was not necessary in Judaism. And since the Gospel of Matthew is widely felt to represent the Christianity of Antioch a generation or two after Paul, it is particularly interesting to ask the question of Matthew's view toward the law. In so doing, we are really asking what was the outcome of the conflict

in Antioch in the next generation. However, it is not out of the question that
Matthew represents a Christian community living elsewhere. I am very
positively impressed by the arguments of J. Andrew Overman that Matthew
reflects the social conflicts of the Galilee more than Syria.[16] But we shall have
an opportunity to return to these issues.

Paul's Encounter with Peter
at Antioch

The first major crisis between these differing interpretations of Jesus'
teaching about the Jewish law appears to have been at Antioch. The basic texts
for understanding the events are Galatians 2, 2 Corinthians 10–13, and Acts 15
and 21. The events include a church council in Jerusalem and an argument
between Paul and Peter over dietary laws. No one knows for sure which event
came first. We know from Paul's writings and Acts that there was a party that
insisted on circumcision for all converts. Paul calls them false brothers, sham
Christians, interlopers, and even dogs. But it is clear from Galatians 2 and Acts
15 that they are Jews and a force in the Jerusalem community. Furthermore,
most Gentiles who had been converted to Christianity by circumcision and
adoption of Jewish law would have naturally been strong proponents of the
practice. Anything less would have cheapened the meaning of their conversion.[17]

At first the encounter seemed genial. But soon the underlying social
difficulties surfaced, as the church council in Acts 15 makes clear. The positions all seem to correspond to positions within the Jewish community before
Christianity. Within Christianity the issue was sharper than for the rest of the
Jewish community because of Paul's desire to make a single, common community. Some Jewish Christians would only allow Gentiles into community by
means of circumcision, although it is arguable that some Jewish Christians who
insisted on circumcision might have believed, as the rabbis believed, that Gentiles could be saved without circumcision, that is, without becoming Jews. That
is to say, it is not entirely clear that the reason that some Jewish Christians
insisted on circumcision was the belief that only the circumcised would be
saved. Perhaps they believed that only the law-observant could marry and eat
together.

The strict Jewish-Christian point of view did not prevail at the council,
however, for James and Peter apparently admitted that Paul's converts need

16. See J. Andrew Overman, *Matthew's Gospel and Formative Judaism: A Study of the
Social World of the Matthean Community* (Philadelphia: Fortress, 1990).

17. I especially like the solution proposed by John Coolidge Hurd, Jr., *The Origin of
1 Corinthians* (2d ed.; Macon, Ga.: Mercer University Press, 1983). This is the most logical
reconstruction of the evidence. But for my current purposes there is no necessity to accept either
order of events. See Segal, *Paul the Convert*, esp. the appendix.

not submit to circumcision or take upon themselves the full performance of the commandments. I take this as grounds for suspecting that other Jews have believed that Gentiles could be righteous without conversion as early as the first century, given that rabbinic literature manifests the same opinion in the third century. In other words, the notion that this kind of universalism was a Christian innovation needs to be carefully examined.

The council's decision was a compromise. It did not fully accept Paul's position that Gentiles need observe no special laws of Judaism. Rather, James himself, according to Acts, promulgates a series of rules that Gentiles have to follow. These rules are quite similar to the rabbinic formulation of the Noahide Commandments, the minimum rules Gentiles need to observe to be called righteous. Besides their ostensible purpose of actualizing the theology of universalism inherent in Judaism, they have a practical social purpose. They essentially are concessions Gentiles must make if they are to be allowed into commensality and intimate contact with Jews. They safeguard Jews and the purity laws they observe from accidental infraction by well-meaning but ignorant Gentiles. And these rules in their Christian form appear to have been a *desideratum* for at least a century, if the Didache is a good witness: "Now about food: *undertake what you can. But keep strictly away from what is offered to idols, for that implies worship of dead gods*" (Did 6:3). The Didache exhorts Christians to observe as many of the dietary laws as possible. It even mirrors the mishnaic warning against worshiping the dead, interpreting the phrase as pagan gods now known to be "dead." Throughout early church history, the dominant position is almost surely to have been more like the Didache or the Apostolic Decree than Paul's ideological position.[18]

No one knows precisely which event came first, the agreement in Jerusalem or the argument at Antioch. But even if the conflict at Antioch is subsequent to the agreement in Jerusalem it merely underlines the fact that Jerusalem's agreements did not automatically guarantee complete Christian uniformity. The Jewish laws were a higher authority than the successors to Jesus in the minds of many Jewish Christians; the compromise between James and Paul could easily have been ignored or discounted by other Jewish Christians.

In Antioch, diaspora Jewish Christians were less rigorous about adopting the special laws of Judaism for their converts than the most conservative members of the Christian community wanted. It is even possible that Paul was a major leader in this community, provoking the conservative members of the

18. See the extremely helpful article by C. K. Barrett, "Things Sacrificed to Idols," in his *Essays on Paul* (Philadelphia: Westminster, 1982) 40–59. See also Justin *Dial.* 34; Irenaeus *Adv. Haer.* 1.6.3; Clem. Al. *Strom.* 4.15; Novatian *On Jewish Meats* 7. See also Segal, *Paul the Convert*, chap. 7.

church even more, because Paul recommended that his converts accept none of the rules, even though he concedes that one might observe them to keep the peace of the Christian community. Since Peter is also actively missionizing in the area, Peter and Paul come directly into conflict, which surfaces in Galatians 2. Apparently Peter has been fairly tolerant of Paul's converts until the arrival of some Jerusalem delegates who warn Peter to be more circumspect. He ceases to eat with Gentiles and, possibly, to be so charitable about the performance of Jewish law in other respects, though Acts represents the issue of circumcision as having been settled already. In any event, Paul's position, no matter how strongly worded in his own letters, was a minority one within the church at large. Though Paul says that Peter stands condemned and that Barnabas acted hypocritically, the one thing he does not say is that the Antioch Christian community agreed with the Pauline position on law. So it seems likely that Peter's position represented the more common approach in Antioch as well as in Jerusalem during this time.

The entire nature of the conflict seems impossible to establish, given the fragmentary and biased reports that Paul gives us. But it seems clear that there was a deep divide between Paul's communities and the original disciples of Jesus. Paul identifies his opponents as "false brothers secretly brought in," though from 2 Cor 11:15 we know that they can refer to themselves as "ministers of righteousness." They appear to be the same persons whom Acts describes more charitably than Paul as "zealous for the law."

The Pharisaic position in Judaism can comprehend both James's compromise agreement and also the more stringent interpretation of Paul's opponents. This is because some Pharisees and rabbis accepted the intermediate position of God-fearers and respected the ethical purity of righteous Gentiles, while others were suspicious. And every Pharisee would have naturally thought that being Jewish was better than not being Jewish, because Judaism was the religion of God's elected priesthood. But being Jewish was not the only route to salvation. Thus, while some tolerated Gentiles, all would have preferred that the converts become fully Jewish.

The compromise worked out at the first conference—allowing Gentiles into community without circumcision but enjoining certain laws on all—appears to have been held together by the person of James, the brother of Jesus, who served as a symbolic personal guarantor of the mediation. Peter however was the person most representing what the legal position actually was. He allowed that the law was still in effect but that it needs fulfillment in love. James's death by martyrdom apparently helped undo the compromise, or at least brought the underlying tensions to the fore again. Josephus dates the event in the year 62/63 (AJ 20.9.1). Josephus reports that James was indicted as a transgressor of the law by Ananus the Younger, the Sadducean High Priest.

Thereafter he was condemned and executed by stoning. But the incident was widely seen as an injustice, since it provoked a reaction within the wider Jewish community, not just among Christians. The Pharisees appealed to the procurator Albinus, seeking relief from Sadducean "justice." The Christian community was sufficiently upset by the event to emigrate from Jerusalem to Pella in Perea, thus ending the mission of Christianity to the Jewish population of Judea. After the end of the first revolt, some of the Christian exiles returned, according to Epiphanius, but in 135 C.E. when Jerusalem was transformed into a Roman city from which Jews were excluded, the Jewish Christians departed permanently as well. Thereafter the center of the Jewish Christian movement falls between Judea and Antioch, including parts of what are today Galilee, Jordan, and Syria. This area, particularly the arc between Galilee and Antioch, seems to be the setting of the community that produced the final editing of the Gospel of Matthew, though the date for the final editing seems to precede the Second Revolt—that is to say, while Jewish Christians and Jews still had some access to Jerusalem as well. There is no irrefutable evidence that the majority of the writing did not precede the First Revolt as well. But it certainly was a useful document to the Christians living in Galilee and Syria thereafter. In departing Jerusalem, the Jewish Christian community sees Jerusalem's immediate destruction at the hands of the Romans in 70 C.E. as divine retribution for the crime of martyring Jesus and James, among others.[19]

Peter is not the foundation figure of all Jewish Christianity; rather he represents the most heroic apostle of both the Gospel of Matthew and the kind of Christianity that dominated at Rome. But it is fair to say that the relationship between Jewish Christians and gentile Christians must have changed over the important part of a century in which Roman Christianity was forming. In the end, the Gospel of Matthew probably provided a kind of model necessary for the mutual respect of Jewish and gentile Christians. The most recent scholarship on Paul's audience at Rome assumes both a Jewish Christian group and a group of Gentiles loyal to him.[20] The origin and development of the Christian community in Rome recently has been chronicled amply by Peter Lampe.[21] He shows that there are both archaeological and literary grounds for saying that the early Roman Christian community was at first indistinguishable from the Jewish one. This can be seen in "the Edict of Claudius," banishing Jews from

19. S.G.F. Brandon and Georg Strecker's attempt to treat the flight to Pella as unhistorical has been amply discredited by Martin Hengel in *Die Zeloten* (Leiden: E. J. Brill, 1961) 307, Eng. trans.: *The Zealots* (Philadelphia: Fortress, 1989).

20. See, e.g., Francis Watson, *Paul, Judaism, and the Gentiles: A Sociological Approach* (Cambridge: Cambridge University Press, 1987).

21. Peter Lampe, *Die stadtrömischen Christen in den ersten beiden Jahrhunderten: Untersuchungen zur Sozialgeschichte* (WUNT 2.18; 2d ed.; Tübingen: J.C.B. Mohr [Paul Siebeck], 1987, 1989); Eng. trans. forthcoming from Fortress Press.

Rome around 41 C.E., mirrored in Acts 18:2, and the testimony of Suetonius ("*Iudaeos impulsore Chresto*"). Indeed, it may be that Paul's Letter to the Romans has the purpose of trying to recommend to the gentile Christians left in Rome the refugee Jewish Christians who are beginning to return there. Lampe's conclusion is that, Paul's ecclesiology to the contrary, Christianity grew out of the Jewish community in Rome, becoming a separate group only when the number of gentile Christians overwhelmed the Jewish Christians. The reasons for the rapid spread of gentile Christianity in Rome were manifold. Among them was certainly the worsening condition of Jews throughout the empire as a result of the revolts. Then, too, Rome was a magnet for indentured slaves from all over the empire and these people were easily evangelized. Gentile Christians at first lived together with the synagogue as God-fearers, or semiproselytes (Rom 16:7 together with Acts 18).[22]

However, by the time of the Neronian persecution, certain changes can already be seen. As their public and cruel martyrdoms witness, the numerous victims of Neronian persecution lacked any civil rights. Regardless of whether Jews were also so cruelly accused (Tac. *Hist.* 5.5.1), we know that by the time of Nero, Christians now existed in sufficient numbers to be publicly known and scapegoated. Thus, while Jewish Christians may have been equal partners with the Gentiles in the Roman community, by the end of the second century, they appear to be a minority position. This may be typical of many other Christian communities as well. Note, however, that this implies that Jewish Christianity was a living and important force within Christianity for much longer than is usually assumed.

As a variation of Peter's position played out over time, the Gospel of Matthew was in some ways a compromise program to bridge the widening gap between Jewish and gentile Christianity, though Paul would have had nothing but scorn for the attempt. In some respects, Matthew's position appears to be Peter's position, in a more mature, evolved form. Matthew's attitude toward the law comes to clearest expression in 5:17–19: "Do not think that I have come to abolish the law and the prophets; I have come not to abolish but to fulfill. For truly I tell you, until heaven and earth pass away, not one letter, not one stroke of a letter, will pass from the law until all is accomplished. Therefore, whoever breaks one of the least of these commandments, and teaches others to do the same, will be called least in the kingdom of heaven; but whoever does them and teaches them will be called great in the kingdom of heaven." Even more striking is the emphasis of Matthew 23, suggesting that whatever the scribes and Pharisees say should be observed, without even neglecting the lesser matters, such as tithing mint, dill, and cumin (Matt 23:23).

22. Ibid., 55.

Matthew does not exclude those who relax the law from the kingdom. (Neither would the later rabbis, with certain exceptions; see *Sanhedrin* 10.) But fulfillment of the law is contrasted with destroying it, so Matthew's interpretation of Jesus' words promotes its retention. For Matthew, these sayings strongly support loyalty to the law, which is realized or completed by Jesus' interpretation.

Matthew uses the word ἀνομία, lawlessness, to mean rejection of the law. The word occurs in Matthew more often than in any other New Testament document, and Matthew is the only evangelist to use it at all (Matt 7:23; 13:41; 23:28; 24:12). The same point can be made from another distinctively Matthean word, δικαιοσύνη, or righteousness, used seven times in Matthew but elsewhere only in Luke 1:75 and John 16:8, 10. Furthermore, the use of "righteousness" in Matt 5:20 indicates that Matthew understands it as entailing the performance of the commandments of Judaism. As he says, "Unless your righteousness exceeds that of the scribes and Pharisees, you will never enter the kingdom of heaven" (cf. 6:1, and contrast Luke 18:9–14).

Matthew's Jewish Christian attitude can be found in his legal interpretation, by comparison with Mark. In Mark 10:2 the question put to Jesus is: Can a man divorce his wife? but Matthew formulates it as: Can a man divorce his wife *for cause*? (Matt 19:3). For Mark, the issue is one of the applicability of law in general. But for Matthew, the issue is one of the interpretation of law, since Matthew squarely sets Jesus' saying within the rabbinic debate between the schools of Hillel and Shammai about the grounds for divorce. The school of Shammai assumed that the grounds for divorce included only cases of adultery. The Hillelites, who eventually predominated in rabbinic Judaism, deliberately set the grounds to include anything, including burning porridge (*m.Gittin* 10.10; see also Joseph. *AJ* 4.8.23). Matthew's position then is not a pretext for denying the validity of the law. It is an actual position within Jewish legal discourse.

Thus, we see Matthew take an intermediate position, trying to defend against two extreme positions on the law. On the one hand, his polemic is against ἀνομία, lawlessness—in particular against what he considers to be charismatic antinomianism (7:15–23; 24:10f.). This seems to me to be an oblique reference to Paulinism, or extreme Paulinism. Even though Paul objected to extreme forms of charismatic Christianity, his emphasis on the spirit and transformation in place of formal conversion to Judaism made him subject to the charge of overemphasizing charisma over against the law. His disciples and followers in the following generations were even more subject to the charge. To set a middle course, Matthew contrasts reliance on prophetic inspiration and spiritual powers on the one hand and doing God's will on the other. Those who rely on charisma are called "workers of lawlessness." In seeing Matthew's reaction against Paulinism, are we not also seeing a kind of Jewish reaction against Paul's preaching?

Matthew also fights against too literal an understanding of the law, a caricature of Jamesian Christianity and Christian Pharisaism. Although (under different historical circumstances) Petrine Christianity might have been subsumed under the umbrella term Christian Pharisaism, by the time of Matthew the two positions have become irreconcilable. Against Pharisaism, Matthew is a fierce antagonist. He attacks the Pharisees for their overinterpretation of the law (3:7–10; 5:20; 15:12–14; 16:12; 21:28–32, 33–46; and particularly 23:1–36). This can be explained most easily by assuming that the Matthean community has come into active antagonism with the Pharisees in the interim between the earliest Christian generation and the redaction of the First Gospel. Comparing Matthew with the other evangelists only emphasizes this perspective, since Matthew dwells on the crimes of the Pharisees and their hypocrisy far more than any other Gospel. The point of these encounters is to portray Jesus as a legal thinker with a new and deeper understanding of the law, which contrasts with the Pharisees who multiply ordinances by means of the oral tradition. Jesus' interpretation of Torah is continuous with the prophetic protest against mere law-observance.

Finally, Matthew's position can be summarized by Jesus' command that the fulfillment of the commandments is *love* (5:43–48; 7:12; 12:1–8, 9–14; 18:12–35; 22:34–40). This means for Matthew that the entire body of the law is still in effect, but that it must be evaluated through the principles of love that Jesus preached. Matthew steers his readers between the two extremes of Pharisaism and antinomianism. Note, however, that this position is also reconcilable with the Lukan description of the apostolic decree. Gentiles are to be allowed into Christian company without circumcision. They should refrain from doing anything that would antagonize or interfere with Jewish purity laws. This is neither the complete rejection of Gentiles by the right wing, nor the complete antinomianism of the left: "For it has seemed good to the Holy Spirit and to us to impose on you no further burden than these essentials: that you abstain from what has been sacrificed to idols and from blood and from what is strangled and from fornication" (Acts 15:28–29). Thus, Petrine and possibly some of Jamesian Christianity, because of his acceptance of converts, form a middle ground between what Matthew and Luke call Pharisaic Christianity, on the one hand, and the more radical Paulinist position on the other. Theoretically, James and Peter might have been called Pharisaic as well, when thinking about the wide spectrum of belief that existed in non-Christian Pharisaism. But the terms are not applied in this way during the latest phase of Matthew's Gospel. Evidently the terms themselves can be used differently by various participants in the argument. Acts prefers to call only the right wing in Christianity Pharisaism, and Matthew also dislikes Pharisaism intensely.[23]

MATTHEW'S NEGATIVE PERSPECTIVE
ON PHARISAISM AND JEWS

As we have seen, Matthew's theme of Pharisaic persecution is combined with his interest in Jewish law. This distrust goes beyond anything in Luke and Mark. As I have already said, I see this emphasis as necessarily explainable in the social setting of Matthew's community, not in the circumstances surrounding Jesus. Matthew has greatly augmented the conflict stories and emphasized that Jesus' opponents are Pharisees, in places where the other Gospels are less sure of the opponents. In the past, the most knowledgeable scholars on the issue have been able to show that the reasons for this opposition are theological and figure strongly in Matthew's understanding of salvation history. Douglas R. A. Hare shows in *The Theme of Jewish Persecution of Christians in the Gospel according to St. Matthew* that the theme of opposition has theological meaning, and that does not cohere with the actual facts of opposition as we know them.[24] But we must at least outline in what ways Matthew vilifies Jews.

Matthew's anti-Jewish tone is evident in much of his social history. Matthew 21:33–46 is a vineyard parable ending with the moral of 21:43: "Therefore I tell you, the kingdom of God will be taken away from you and given to a nation (ἔθνει) producing the fruits of it" (RSV). This may be taken as a simple statement of Jewish guilt, which reverberates with Matt 27:25: "His blood be on us and on our children!" Matthew holds Judaism or some part of it responsible for the death of Jesus, removing the promises of the prophets as a punishment and transferring them to the church. In the parable of the vineyard, Matthew rewrites Mark to emphasize that the heir dies outside the vineyard, suggesting to me that he may have a social conflict outside of the immediate Jerusalem area in mind. I do not feel that there is an innocent explanation for these statements. Rather they appear to me to reflect an exacerbated social conflict between the Matthean community and a group of Jews whom he refers to as Pharisees (or symbolizes by them), and this causes him, sadly for all subsequent Jewish-Christian relations, to generalize on the entire enterprise of Israel's destiny. I also see it as a triumphalism that attempts to capitalize on the destruction of Jerusalem and the worsening fate of much of the Jewish community in its struggle against the Christian community.

---

23. For a new perspective in the study of Acts, see Donald Juel, *Luke Acts: The Promise of History* (Atlanta: John Knox, 1983) 103–5. See also Robert Brawley, *Luke-Acts and the Jews: Conflict, Apology, and Conciliation* (SBLMS; Atlanta: Scholars, 1988).

24. (Cambridge: Cambridge University Press, 1967).

M's man

⌐Yet, some of the main lines of Matthew's theology precede these events. There is no simple replacement theology; rather Matthew offers a description of a new group that respects the law but excludes faithless Jews. Post-Easter disciples are to learn not just the good news about Jesus but to do the law, understood through Jesus' teachings.⌐

The peculiar use of the term ἔθνος, which has often been taken as a cipher for *Gentile,* has to be investigated in more detail. The key passages are Matt 24:9, 14; and 28:19, as A.-J. Levine has shown. In 24:9 Matthew uses πάντα τῶν ἐθνῶν where Mark would simply say πάντα. But the difference in wording does not necessarily have to mean all the *Gentiles,* as it is frequently interpreted. It could mean all the *nations,* including Israel. Thus the phrase πάντα τῶν ἐθνῶν anticipates Matthew's use of πάντα τὰ ἔθνη ("all the nations") in 24:14 and in Matt 28:16–20. In both cases, the context could imply Jews as well as Gentiles. Indeed, Matthew's prediction that the "good news of the kingdom will be proclaimed throughout the world" (ἐν ὅλῃ τῇ οἰκουμένῃ) may as easily indicate that the preaching will continue throughout the whole world, including the Jews.[25] In rabbinic literature as well, Jews are often distinguished from the other nations, but they may also be included as one among the nations. Thus the issue of keeping the law does not necessarily conflict with the universal mission to the world.⌐

The problems besetting a consistent exegesis of Matthew have been described well by Amy-Jill Levine in her new book, *The Social and Ethnic Dimensions of Matthean Salvation History.* Although many might take issue with a number of her conclusions, her methodological caution seems always well founded. For instance, she cautions against thinking that an interest in the law necessarily conflicts with the universalism of the Gospel. Adding to her argument, I would point out that rabbinic law did not exclude Gentiles from the law, rather included them in a lesser version of it. The most famous formulation of the issue at the beginning of *Midrash Rabba* clearly says that Torah is the tool by which the universe was created and the way in which it is governed. The rabbinic question was not whether Gentiles were subject to Torah, but how much of the Sinaitic revelation they were to perform. The mature answer was that they need do none of it because the Noahide laws explicitly tell Gentiles about their obligations. But this answer reflects a time when Jews were actually a minority among the Gentiles. The earlier formulations of the question reflect social situations when Gentiles were guests in the Jewish state, and thus could be expected to respect Jewish customs to a greater extent. There is no guarantee that the Matthean community subscribed to

---

25. See Levine, *Social and Ethnic Dimensions of Matthean Salvation,* 225–26, contra Douglas R. A. Hare and Daniel J. Harrington, "Make Disciples of all the Gentiles (Mt. 28:19)," *CBQ* 37 (1975) 359–69.

the same idea, but such a concept of universalism within a particular setting seems possible.

The clearest statement of Matthew's complex relationship with Judaism may come from returning to the mission command in chapter 10, where Matthew also mentions the nature of Jewish opposition—whippings in synagogues and appeals to gentile authorities. The sayings there are obviously instructions for Matthew's contemporary church; however, the command to go only to the lost sheep of the house of Israel has been retained from Matthew's earliest sources. For Matthew this specific command must be, first of all, applicable explicitly to the pre-Easter situation. With the crucifixion, Israel the nation has lost its opportunity to be part of the new creation because of the perverse antagonism of its leaders, in particular the Pharisees. But the hope of the resurrection excludes no one. Individual Jews, the lost sheep of Israel, may come into Matthean community if they understand Jesus' special exegesis of law. So too, Jesus' disciples in all nations must learn to keep all that he commanded them on the occasion of the sending out of his apostles to Israel. Hence Jesus is Χριστός διδάσκαλος, crucified Son of God and teacher of law.[26] His community is a community of law, populated by some Jews and by Gentiles. They should not keep the laws as the Pharisees do, but should keep them according to the teachings Jesus gave.

Now the command to stick only to the cities of Judah is replaced by a new apostolic commissioning:

> Now the eleven disciples went to Galilee, to the mountain to which Jesus had directed them. When they saw him, they worshiped him; but some doubted. And Jesus came and said to them, "All authority in heaven and on earth has been given to me. Go therefore and make disciples of all nations, baptizing them in the name of the Father and of the Son and of the Holy Spirit, and teaching them to obey everything that I have commanded you. And remember, I am with you always, to the end of the age." (Matt 28:16–20)[27]

THE PROVENANCE OF
MATTHEW'S GOSPEL

If one were to ask which kind of Christian in the Antioch controversy most closely approximates the Matthean community, the answer is clearly Peter. Matthew's stance on law is surely not Pauline, which I have maintained is a Pharisaic notion overthrown by conversion: "Christ is the end of the Law."[28] Nor does Matthew represent the strict Pharisaic Christian notion

26. Dahl, "Passion Narrative in Matthew," 50–51.
27. Benjamin J. Hubbard, *The Matthean Redaction of a Primitive Apostolic Commissioning: An Exegesis of Matthew 28:16–20* (SBLDS 19; Missoula, Mont.: Scholars, 1974).
28. See Segal, *Paul the Convert.*

described by Acts, for Matthew argues vociferously with the Pharisaic notion. Rather the Jewish voice of Matthew must be closest to the position of Peter, or, less likely, James, the two most centrist positions on law, which appear to dominate in the early church's first generations. And, of course, of the two, Matthew favors most strongly the Petrine claims. As we have seen, Matthew expands on the Petrine claims for primacy in ways the other Gospels do not.[29]

Many scholars have suggested that the geographical setting for the Matthean community must be Antioch, because it was here that Paul most squarely opposed Peter. It is no surprise that Antioch housed a very active and impressive Jewish community. Although Antioch's Jewish population did not reach the size or importance of Mesopotamia or Egypt, it still had a remarkably large and influential community. During the two revolts against Rome, the community was disadvantaged; and it received a great many refugees from each war. But the anxieties of these world events did not permanently inhibit the growth of the community. In fact, they benefited from the hostilities. On the other hand, not much is known about the Judaism practiced there. Kraeling suggests that it was not predominantly rabbinic. Meeks and Wilken see little evidence of rabbinic activity in Antioch.[30]

However, it is arguable that Galilee and Syria should be considered as a single geographical area, if not from every perspective, then at least from the point of view of the development of Jewish and Christian hostility. In the history of earliest Jewish Christianity, the relationship between Galilee and Syria is quite obvious. The Jewish Christian heartland, settled by Jewish Christian refugees from Jerusalem, was an arc of settlement that included both the Galilee, Jesus' home, and Pella, the destination of the Jerusalem refugees, and then arched into Syria through Antioch and Edessa.[31] This is clear from the development and communications in the church. But the same geographical unity is evident in Jewish sources. The Jewish community of Syria was in relatively good communication with that of the Galilee, due to geographical contiguity, except during the rebellions (see Kraeling). After all, it was to this area that Trypho emigrated before he had his supposed dialogue with Justin. This has important ramifications for the social location of Matthew because the Galilee was the center of the rabbinic movement throughout the second century. The cities of the Galilee are the background for the discussions of the Mishnah. The Christian evidence about the dispute between Paul and James

29. It is possible that in a different way and from a different perspective Luke may be doing the same thing, that is, providing a common ground for Jew and Gentile.

30. See Carl H. Kraeling, "The Jewish Community at Antioch," *JBL* (1932) 130–60, esp. 130; and Wayne A. Meeks and Robert L. Wilken, *Jews and Christians in Antioch in the First Four Centuries of the Common Era* (Missoula, Mont.: Scholars, 1978) 1–12, esp. 6–7.

31. See Hans-Joachim Schoeps, *Jewish Christianity: Factional Disputes in the Early Church* (Philadelphia: Fortress, 1964) 21–23, 33.

suggests that *at the very least* there was Christian Pharisaic activity in this area.

In his recent book, J. Andrew Overman suggests that the location of the Matthean community must be Galilee.[32] I will not review all his arguments, except to note that Galilee has an extraordinary importance in Matthew. It can even be seen in the apostolic commissioning cited above. Furthermore, the enemies of the Matthean community are surely the Pharisees or their heirs. Overman argues that the most logical place for Pharisees to have run into the burgeoning Matthean community would be Galilee, since we know that their center of power, Jerusalem, was removed to Galilee after the war against Rome that ended in 70 and again after the Bar Kokhba War of 132–135. So Galilee was a prime location for Pharisees of the late first and early second century. We must also not forget that the Pharisees are rising in power. As the Romans look over the destroyed country, they find the Pharisees, previously a member of the client class, relatively untouched by the revolt. They make ideal candidates for the successors to the old nation state, since they have already been part of a coalition government in the past. The patriarch, living in Galilee, eventually becomes the highest Roman client, nominal head of the Jewish community and, at the same time, the patron of the Pharisaic movement.

Overman's claims are therefore extremely cogent. But we cannot exclude the idea that Pharisees wandered further than Galilee proper. Paul claims to have been a Pharisee and the church tradition makes him a citizen of Tarsus. Josephus records that Queen Helena and Prince Izates were convinced by a stricter Jew (from the Galilee) to undergo circumcision in far-flung Adiabene. The position of this stricter Jew is consistent with Pharisaism, though to be sure it could hardly be called uniquely Pharisaic. So the religious spectrum of lands outside of Judea can be more mixed than scholars usually admit.[33]

The itinerant nature of the disciples that Jesus commissioned in Matthew 10 and 28 makes unnecessary a strict choice between Galilee or Syria. These disciples were constantly traveling and were used to being refugees. Thus, it may be that both Overman and the other scholars are correct in a sense—Galilee and Antioch were merely two fixed points in a rather loosely confederated group of congregations, united by missionaries who were more or less constantly on the move at first. The result was a constantly changing sense of the proper compromise between Jewish Christians and gentile Christians, depending on which apostle was visiting that month. And any discussion of

32. J. Andrew Overman, *Matthew's Gospel and Formative Judaism: The Social World of the Matthean Community.*

33. Furthermore, we may be sure that whatever the term "Pharisee" meant to the earliest church, its meaning changed significantly by the time the Gospel had been written. We must surely understand that the group Matthew called Pharisees (partly anachronistically?) were further along the road to becoming rabbis than the group the earliest church witnessed.

Pharisees in Galilee might just as easily be communicated to the Antioch area, where actual Pharisees were less frequent.

> As you go, proclaim the good news, "The kingdom of heaven has come near." Cure the sick, raise the dead, cleanse lepers, cast out demons. You received without payment, give without payment. Take no gold, or silver, or copper in your belts, no bag for your journey, or two tunics, or sandals, or a staff; for laborers deserve their food. Whatever town or village you enter, find out who in it is worthy, and stay there until you leave. As you enter the house, greet it. If the house is worthy, let your peace come upon it; but if it is not worthy, let your peace return to you. If anyone will not welcome you or listen to your words, shake off the dust from your feet as you leave that house or town. (Matt 10:7–14)

As Ernst Lohmeyer showed in his study *Galilaea und Jerusalem,* the primitive church had its real roots in Galilee, the country native to Jesus, though it is strange that Acts does not mention the Christian communities there.[34] It is possible that Acts itself was written from a more Jewish position than is normally considered possible and that part of its purpose is to convince the Jewish church of the validity of the gentile church. Paul gives us some evidence for Christian activities in Galilee as well. The brothers of Jesus appear to work out of Galilee in their mission, as 1 Cor 9:5 suggests. The church in Damascus may have been founded by them even before the martyrdom of Stephen. Julius Africanus reports (Eus. *Hist. Eccl.* 1.7.14) that Jesus' relatives had spread the gospel, starting from the villages of Nazareth and Cochaba, both Galilean cities.[35]

The area continues to be an important location for Jewish Christianity after the gospel period. Jerome says that the Nazoreans of Beroea and the Jewish Christians believed that those which formerly lived in the darkness of error would be the first to see the light of the gospel (Migne, *series Latina,* 24.125), an obvious reference to Isaiah 9, interpreted in a geographical sense. Thus Galilee becomes the place of prophecy.

Mark 14:28 and 16:7 locate the resurrection of Jesus and the coming messianic kingdom as starting in Galilee. According to Matthew, too, Galilee is the biblical fulfillment of Jesus' mission. In Matt 4:15, Jesus directs his attention to Galilee in order to fulfill the prophecy of Isa 9:1 that a great light would dawn upon the territory of the tribes of Zebulun and Naphtali and upon the way to the sea, upon Perea and Galilee of the Gentiles. Matthew apparently understood this arc of territory to be the land of promise, situated πέραν τοῦ Ἰορδάνου, although Isaiah himself probably had the area encompassed by the

---

34. (Göttingen: Vandenhoeck & Ruprecht, 1936).
35. Schoeps, *Jewish Christianity,* 22–27.

modern areas of Upper and Lower Galilee in mind. Thus, the Matthean community lived in precisely the area that Jesus, while preaching in Capernaum, had called the land of promise. Clearly this enlarged Galilee, from which Syrian cities like Antioch and Edessa can be considered proselytized satellites, was the center of Matthew's attention.

Because of the way in which Christian apostles traveled, the Matthean community could have considered Galilee to have included virtually everything from the present-day Galilee through Antioch. Over time, who would have blamed them for seeking shelter closer to Antioch, for that is precisely what the Jews of the area did in response to hostilities. And the community that produced Matthew must have lived for some time in close association with rabbinic Judaism, which was centered in Galilee. It must also have lived in a place where Greek was spoken and where there was a significant number of Gentiles as well as Jews. These factors virtually uniquely imply northern Palestine and Syria, but it is not clear where. Furthermore, the Q statements implying a peripatetic existence for the earliest Christian apostles imply that the cities in which Christian communities took place were many and that they encompassed the entire area.

The stories of the healing of the Canaanite woman's daughter (15:5–13), as well as the mission command (28:18–20), do not indicate that the Matthean community was gentile. Rather these passages indicate that they were a Jewish Christian community that, like some other Jews, had a positive view of gentile converts.

GALILEE AND SYRIAN
CHRISTIANITY

We have only hints and sideways glimpses of the most interesting period in the later development of Jewish Christianity. It appears, for instance, that many of the Jesus traditions in the Gospel of Thomas come from a Jewish-Christian environment.[36] Logia 2, 6, 12, 16, 23, 27, 31, 39, 44, 62, 64, 65, 68, 69, 71, 81, 84, 88, 90, 93, 95, 99, 104, 107, 109, and 113 contain significant Jewish-Christian influence. Some of the material is quite strikingly Jewish Christian. For instance, Logion 39 states approvingly that the Pharisees and scribes have received the keys of knowledge (see *Homilies* 3.18.3 and *Recognitions* 1.54.7 and also Justin *Dial.* 17.4), implying no criticism of the law, which contrasts even with Matthew, who polemicizes that the Pharisees are hypocrites in spite

36. See Gilles Quispel, "The Gospel of Thomas Revisited," *Colloque international sur les textes de Nag Hammadi* (ed. B. Barc; Quebec, Aug 22–25, 1978; BCNH, section Etudes, 1; Quebec and Louvain, 1981) 218–66. The list of *logia* containing Jewish-Christian influence is to be found on pp. 242–44.

of their being in positions of authority in the community. Thus one of the sources of the Gospel of Thomas was Jewish Christian, quite independent from the canonical Gospels and Q, though it has some affinities with both Q and special Matthew. Since Justin also evidences the tradition, it is possible that the material is just as ancient as the other Gospel traditions and in some cases even more primitive. For instance, the Gospel of Thomas does not allegorize the parables to the extent of the Synoptic Gospels, and may hence be a more primitive tradition. In any event, one of the sources of the Gospel of Thomas must be closely associated with Syrian Christianity, because it is closely related to the Odes of Solomon and the work of Tatian, which culminated in the Syriac Diatessaron. Both of these works are already known to have incorporated Jewish-Christian materials and they, in turn, have distinct parallels with the Gospel of Thomas.[37] Indeed, the foundation story of the church of Edessa, found in Eus. *Hist. Eccl.* 1.13,[38] says that Christianity was brought there by Addai, a missionary sent from Jerusalem. Furthermore, the Cologne Mani Papyrus attests the existence of a Jewish-Christian, baptist, Elkesaite commune in Southern Babylonia.[39] On this basis, Quispel and other scholars date the Gospel of Thomas to the middle of the second century in Edessa.

This impression is confirmed by the Didascalia, written in the first half of the third century, and claiming to set forth a "catholic" doctrine. The author is fully aware of the practice of Jewish law. Furthermore, he is compelled to say, in defending against gnostic heresy, that some heretics also abstain from the flesh of swine and eat only what the law declares pure, preaching circumcision according to the law (202.17–20 = 6.10.4).[40] This suggests that the author knows of a Jewish Christianity or Judaizing Christianity, considered Christian heresy in the third century, which is probably related to the kind we have already seen deeply associated with Syria.

JEWISH REACTIONS TO
JEWISH CHRISTIANITY

The theme of Jewish persecution of Christians in the New Testament has been covered extremely well by Hare.[41] I will summarize some of it here, suggesting in one or two places where I disagree, when relevant. Hare goes

37. L. W. Barnard, "The Origins and Emergence of the Church in Edessa during the First Two Centuries A.D.," *VC* 22 (1968) 161–75.

38. Edited by E. Schwartz, *Griechischen Christlichen Schriftsteller* 9, 1.32–37.

39. A. Henrichs and L. Koenen, "Ein griechischer Mani-Codex," *ZPE* 5 (1970) 97–216.

40. Georg Strecker, "On the Problem of Jewish Christianity," in W. Bauer, *Orthodoxy and Heresy in Earliest Christianity* (Philadelphia: Fortress, 1971) 244–57, trans. from the 1934 second German ed.

41. See Hare, *Theme of Jewish Persecution of Christians.*

into some detail to show that Jewish opposition to Christianity is not systematic, or violent, or sustained. Some early Christians were martyred but these were not systematic Jewish reactions. Rather they were mob actions. And they were not long lasting. Though Justin believes the reports of persecution he encounters in the Gospels, he absolves the Jews of persecuting Christians in his own day after indicting them for previous ages (*Dial.* 16). Furthermore, although he credits Jews with calumnies against Christians, he does not say that these rumors are being spread by Jews in his own day. Consequently, the best conclusion from Justin's witness is that second-century Christians thought Jews responsible for a certain amount of persecution of Christians, but that they had not witnessed it personally.

To be sure, a century earlier the Pharisee Paul claimed to have been a persecutor of Christianity before his conversion, but the Greek word διώκω covers a very wide variety of opposition and Paul's persecution of Christianity appears to have entailed argumentation and warning, rather than physical punishment.[42] I cannot improve on Hare's discussion, though I think that he probably discounts the later Jewish opposition to Paul too quickly. I take seriously Paul's claim that he was subjected to lashes by the Jewish community. This experience and the experience of antinomians like Paul may be responsible for the prophecy in Matthew that some followers will be punished in this way, especially since we can assume that Petrine Christianity attempted to stay in communion with the Jewish community in some ways. But any possible Jewish discipline against Pauline Christianity only underlines the continued acceptance of Matthean Christians within Judaism. As opposed to Paul, who preached either the invalidation or the elective observance of Jewish law, depending on how one chooses to interpret him, the Gospel of Matthew preaches its validity. From a social and legal point of view (insofar as these are distinguishable for second-century Judaism), Matthean Christianity might have remained within Judaism. For that reason the Gospel (and the Christian debate on how much law to observe generally) illustrates the range of Jewish practice in the first century unavailable to us from the Mishnah, which only represents a range of prescribed opinions from the vantage point of the beginning of the third century. That is to say, in spite of their Christian confession, Matthean Christians are within the spectrum of Jewish law observance. What they oppose is the Pharisaic interpretation of the law and their claim of authority to interpret the laws. These issues might in themselves have explained the enmity between Pharisaic Judaism and Matthean Christianity. During the time of Matthew's editorial activity, most Jews were not yet Pharisaic, so Petrine Christians could have been virtually invisible except for their faith commitment

42. Ibid., 60.

to Christ. Rather the Matthean rejection of Pharisaic Judaism must reflect a growing social rift between them and the waxing rabbinic leadership. Perhaps they were angry because the Pharisees championed an opposing legal position, and the Pharisees were successful at galvanizing Jewish opinion to their perspective.

But there were theological reasons for objecting to Christianity as well, some having to do with the growing rabbinic opposition to the central theological tenet of Christianity—that Jesus is Lord and God. As I have shown in my book *Two Powers in Heaven,* the rabbis often have Christianity in mind (and usually Jewish Christianity) when they oppose those who say there are "two powers in heaven." This group, which is called both a heresy (*minuth*) as well as a gentile belief in different places, believes that there are two different gods because God can look like a young man or an old man in Dan 7:9–13 as well as Exod 15:3 and 20:2.[43] Although dualism is not a characteristic of most Christianity, the rabbis describe it in a way that clarifies Christian complicity. Daniel 7:9–13 is characteristic of Christian descriptions of the Christ in his role as the Son of man. Apparently, then, a number of different heresies are debated by the rabbis with these arguments. The majority of the reports, however, describe Christianity, even though Christians consider themselves Trinitarians. The rabbis do not feel behooved to represent their opponents' beliefs exactly.

Furthermore, the issue had been vexing Judaism since the beginning of the first century or before, since Philo uses the very term δεύτερος θεός to describe God (*Som.* 1.227–29; *Quaest. in Gen.* 2.62). That is to say, we can date the intellectual issue generally to the first century and before. But Gospel texts and Matthew itself offer the most convincing evidence of Christian involvement in the issue, because the rabbinic writings themselves cannot be dated with precision. The text of Matthew tells us that during the period of its final redaction, opposition from Pharisaism, rather than Judaism generally, was intensifying.

Hare makes a credible case that any principled Jewish opposition to Christianity was not violent. With the exception of antinomians like Paul and occasional mob actions, I can agree. Rather it would have most often entailed ostracism and excision from the community. The only way to do this was by means of the process of *nidui,* as Luke 6:22 seems to describe anachronistically, or the much-studied *birkat ha-minim,* the curse against sectarians. If Luke is correct in his description of Jewish opposition in Acts, when Christian preachers interrupted services with Christian prayers or sermons, they were simply thrown out. Sometimes a complaint to the authorities followed, for disturbing

---

43. Alan F. Segal, *Two Powers in Heaven: Rabbinic Reports about Christianity and Gnosticism* (Leiden: E. J. Brill, 1977). See also idem, *Rebecca's Children* (Cambridge: Harvard University Press, 1977) 151–62.

the peace. These reports, though possibly exaggerated for polemical effect, retain a certain credibility.

The issue of the dating and meaning of the *birkat ha-minim* must occupy us for a moment. The twelfth paragraph of the central eighteen prayers of the Jewish daily service, known as the *Shemone Esre,* is referred to several times in talmudic literature as *birkat ha-minim.* This paragraph is not really a blessing at all, but a curse against apostates and informers. Most versions of the liturgy today do not mention *minim,* but there was a time when the *minim* appear to have been explicitly mentioned.[44] Furthermore, in 1925, Geniza fragments containing the explicit reference were found.[45]

According to rabbinic literature, the text of the curse is to be traced back to the academy at Yavneh, between the two revolts: "Simeon Hapakuli arranged the Eighteen Benedictions in their proper order in the presence of Rabban Gamaliel at Yavneh. Said Rabban Gamaliel to the sages: 'Is there anyone that can formulate the *birkat ha-minim*?' Up rose Samuel the Lesser and recited it" (*b.Berakot* 28b, j; ibid. 4b, 8a).[46]

Furthermore, Justin Martyr says, around the year 150, in his *Dialogue* 16 (cf. 96), "You Jews pronounce maledictions on the Christians in your synagogues." Epiphanius, who specifies the charge, says that the Jews denounce the *Nazarenes* in their prayers three times a day (*Panarion* 29.9). The latter report seems a bit more sensible than Justin's, which does not distinguish between Jews and gentile Christians, and does not give the context. Furthermore, the old versions of the curse in the Geniza mention both *minim* and *notzrim.*

Reuven Kimelman has questioned whether the church fathers' reports can be identified with the *birkat ha-minim.*[47] He certainly is successful in pointing out some of the difficulties with this passage. There is something illogical about the church fathers accepting the designation *min,* which implies heretic. But I do not think that the issue in the church fathers' reports is the logic or rightness of the charge, only the intent of it. The church fathers only wish to indict the Jews for intolerance; they do not even tell us that the curse was not

44. L. Finkelstein, "The Development of the Amidah," *JQR* n.s. 16 (1925) 156.

45. For an updated bibliography and complete discussion of the textual problems, see P. Schaefer, *Studien zur Geschichte und Theologie des rabbinischen Judentums* (Berlin: Walter de Gruyter, 1978) 53 n. 3.

46. See Gedaliah Alon, *The Jews in Their Land in the Talmudic Age 70–640 C.E.* (trans. Gershon Levi; Cambridge: Harvard University Press, 1989). The Hebrew edition was published in 1967.

47. See Reuven Kimelman, "*Birkat ha-minim* and the Lack of Evidence for an Anti-Christian Jewish Prayer in Late Antiquity," *Jewish and Christian Self-Definition,* vol. 2: *Aspects of Judaism in the Greco-Roman World* (ed. E. P. Sanders with A. I. Baumgarten and Alan Mendelson; Philadelphia: Fortress, 1981) 226–44. See my remarks in the same volume in "Ruler of This World: Attitudes about Mediator Figures and the Importance of Sociology for Self-Definition," 257 and 409 n. 57.

aimed at Christians alone. In other words, contra Kimelman, it does seem to me that the church fathers are referring to the *birkat ha-minim*.

Furthermore, the curse was not written de novo at Yavneh. Apparently Samuel the Lesser merely added the name *minim* to a previously existent curse against apostates and informers.[48] I see no reason to discount the Gospel stories about exclusion from the synagogue service (e.g., John 9:22; 12:42; 16:2) though the phenomenon itself cannot date from the time of Jesus but from the end of the first century and beginning of the second. This is not the same action as the curse, in spite of most scholarly opinion trying to equate them. It appears rather to be a popular reaction to Christian preaching, which was later systematized by rabbinic discussion. Thus, the Jewish opposition to Christianity mirrored in the ἀποσυνάγωγος passages in John are probably popular expressions of dislike rather than a specific rabbinic program. It was a practical way of dealing with a bunch of disruptive Christians wishing to missionize Jews when they were praying in synagogue.

In other words, with care, the Jewish reaction to Jewish Christianity can be understood, but the rabbinic evidence cannot give us a chronology. What Matthew offers us is a window on the developing trouble. It is now commonly assumed that Christians were later included in the term *min*, "sectarian," if they were not its whole or original referent, as Herford thought.[49] In essence we shall never know all we would like to know about the separation between the two communities. But it is not illogical to me to assume that the *birkat ha-minim* was one of the rabbinic weapons against Jewish Christians, and that more formal ostracism is represented in Matthew's Gospel. At the same time, a growing Pharisaic presence in Galilee at the beginning of the second century tells us that the rabbinic movement was beginning to gain the respect of the people. That is something we could not know from the rabbinic texts themselves; but Matthew ironically tells us exactly that.

I would not assume, however, that the curse was the sole reason for the separation between the two communities or even that the curse was successful at it. The Matthean community is not a total stranger to synagogues, though they may be estranged from it. So the Matthean anti-Pharisaism probably represents the first clear evidence that Jewish opposition and the rabbinic approach was having an effect on the Christian community too. The sharpness

48. This context of informers and apostates suggests to me that some Jewish Christians may have informed to the Romans during the period of the revolts against Rome, and certainly that they were perceived as a real problem within the midst of the synagogue. This is speculation, of course, but there is no particular reason why the rabbis would have used such a tool against Jewish Christians if the synagogue were not imperiled by Jewish Christians in the same way that they were imperiled by informers and apostates.

49. R. Travers Herford, *Christianity in Talmud and Midrash* (London: Williams & Norgate, 1903).

of the polemic implies still unsettled boundaries; they must have been competing over some territories. From Matthew's point of view, the competition may
easily have been with the right wing of the church in his day, those people the
church called Christian Pharisees. They must have been somewhat successful
in an atmosphere of rising rabbinic influence. That influence is mainly, as the
core of the rabbinic corpus shows us, one of ritual and purity laws.[50] The battle
in Matthew appears confined to the synagogue because that is the battlefield in
second-century Galilee. The rabbinic movement does not have much direct
influence in the ruling sphere, though their codification of civil law shows that
they felt competent to claim it. Indeed, for centuries thereafter one hears of
Jewish Christians in synagogues, as Meeks and Wilken have shown us so
eloquently.[51] The stakes in battle in the second century then were not the
government of the country but the religious authority to interpret the law in
synagogues and houses. And it appears that the rabbinic approach to purity
and observance was more attractive, in the end, than the Matthean approach.
In this battle must also figure the hearts and minds of converts to Christianity
who were tempted to become completely law observant. That converts could
have been tempted to Pharisaism seems hard to believe today, knowing the
outcome. But it is not hard to understand in context. Paul complains of the
temptation to law observance in Galatia. If one by becoming Christian had
come part of the way to Judaism, why not go all the way, as the Pharisees (and
most others) preferred? Matthew would certainly object to this Pharisaic
approach to conversion.

What I wish to propose is merely that the hostility to Pharisees one sees
in the First Gospel provides one piece of evidence that Christians were still
concerned with what was happening in Jewish communities and synagogues,
still found there, and greatly vexed by some of the positions they heard from
Christian Pharisees inside and outside of synagogues. It goes without saying
that we know considerably less about the Pharisees and their transition to the
rabbinic movement than we would like. In a recent monograph, Anthony Saldarini has maintained that the Pharisees were a client group of the Romans, an
approach that has some real advantages in understanding first-century Pharisaism. This means that in the first century some of the Pharisees entered the
retainer class while others did not. He also uses the Christian evidence to
reveal the meaning of Jewish history, which is methodologically correct.[52] The

50. See Segal, *Rebecca's Children*, 117–41.
51. See *Jews and Christians in Antioch*, 13–52. Also see R. Wilken, *Judaism and the Early
Christian Mind* (New Haven: Yale University Press, 1971), on Cyril of Alexandria, and his subsequent book on Chrysostom.
52. Anthony J. Saldarini, *Pharisees, Scribes, and Sadducees in Palestinian Society* (Wilmington, Del.: Michael Glazier, 1988). For a review of the previous literature, see 7–10. See also
Lee Levine, *The Rabbinic Class in Palestine in the Talmudic Period* (Jerusalem: Yad Yattsrhark

same is true in the second century, but when the rabbinic movement takes hold, the Exilarch's house, a retainer institution, functions as the major native rulers, in the absence of the previous ruling class.[53]

Matthew's hostility to the Pharisees appears to correspond to the period in which the Pharisees were becoming rabbis—that is, extending their ascribed authority in synagogues more widely through Galilee and Syria. That is a rather important perception, which we cannot get from rabbinic evidence at all. Nor do we know exactly how their respect among the people grew. But it is crucial for understanding Jewish history. The synagogues adopted rabbinic authority out of respect for the rabbis' piety and power; they appear to have spurned the Matthean version of Torah interpretation, based on Jesus' principles. Even more importantly, the Christian issues about keeping the law appear to be ordinary Jewish discussions about the law, precipitated by the innovative power of the Pauline bid to break down the ritual distinctions between Jews and Gentiles. Just as is evident in Christian documents, considerable parts of the Jewish community would have agreed with Paul that Gentiles could be saved. Fewer would have agreed that the law provided for a single community composed of Jews and Gentiles. The issue, discussed so thoroughly in Christian sources, is just as much a Jewish issue as a Christian one. But there is a wider issue here. The entire Christian discussion of the law took place within a Jewish context. It is thus a kind of searchlight into the world of first-century ordinary Judaism, though it may be colored specially by a Christian agenda. And Matthew appears to be admitting that the rabbis were more successful at persuading the ordinary Jews of the synagogues of their interpretation of law than were the Christians. He reflects that the same problem was still important within the churches. That is to say, the Pharisees were not just an external enemy for Christians. Their position was to be found within Christianity as well. Matthew attempts to argue against it, both within and without his movement.

The synagogue curse was hardly the only issue separating Jewish Christians and rabbis. But the rabbinic polemic against "Two Powers" allows us to assume that the Matthean dislike of Pharisees was reciprocated by our earliest rabbis. This policy, in turn, formed the basis of the later rabbinic polemics against the Jewish Christians, which is most easily seen in the midrash of the third century and thereafter but is already present in some Tannaitic sources.

It is difficult to ascertain whether the Matthean community, in its latest form represented by the Gospel itself, was entirely sure of its Jewish identity.

Ben Tevi, 1985); and idem, "The Jewish Patriarch (Nasi) in Third-Century Palestine," *Studies in the History of the Jewish People* (Haifa: University of Haifa, 1978) 89–102.

53. This has been supposed in many places. See, e.g., Alon, *Jews in Their Land,* 308–25; Shaye J. D. Cohen, *From the Maccabees to the Mishnah* (Philadelphia: Westminster, 1987) 221–24.

Though some passages, like 21:33–45 and 27:15–26, suggest a replacement theology, they do not necessarily demand a complete separation from Judaism.[54] Thus, the latest phase may represent a period after which the purely Jewish identity of the group had been diluted by conversions of Gentiles.

Nor can the opposition to the community be considered uniform. It is pretty clear that many Jews would not have accepted Matthean Jewish Christians readily within their religious life and that most would have insisted on some purity distinctions between Jews and Matthean gentile converts. But there was no uniformity in Judaism, as the Gospel of Matthew helps show us so well. Thus, we cannot say that Judaism uniformly dismissed Matthean Christians from their midst.

As a corollary to this, scholarship can no longer facilely assume that the Christian movement was unique, and therefore that everything good in Christianity—for instance, its universalism—was unknown in Judaism before it. Each of the sects of Judaism in the first century, including Christianity, was unique in several respects. The Christian evidence appears to demonstrate that ideas we see fully documented in later rabbinic literature were already being discussed in the first-century Jewish community. It is not proper to assume that, even at the end of its canonical development, Matthean Christianity had totally separated from Judaism, becoming a heresy that has nothing further to contribute to our understanding of Judaism. Indeed, given the nature of our Jewish texts, the New Testament may be the most valuable evidence we have about ordinary Jewish life in the first century, even though it has a special perspective and a number of hostile opinions about it.

54. See Deutsch, *Hidden Wisdom and the Easy Yoke*, 16.

2

The Gospel of Matthew and Jewish-Christian Conflict

Most studies of Matthew and Judaism concentrate on four problems: (1) whether Matthew's community is made up of Jewish Christians or Gentiles, (2) whether Israel can still be saved, (3) whether his community is still a Jewish community or has broken away entirely from Judaism, and (4) whether his polemics against Judaism can be somehow separated from anti-Semitism. These studies, mostly by Christians, are Matthew-centric and Christian-centric. That is, they focus on the viewpoint and thought of Matthew in historical context and on Matthew as a Christian who is independent of and equal in stature to his Jewish opponents, in a way similar to church and synagogue today.

This study will look at the Matthean community and its spokesperson, the author of the Gospel of Matthew, as deviant Jews. They have been labeled deviant by the authorities and by many members of the Jewish community in their city or area. Sociologically the Matthean community is a fragile minority still identified with the Jewish community by others and still thinking of itself as Jews. Despite sharp conflicts with the leaders of the Jewish community and subjection to standard disciplinary measures or, better, because of this, the Matthean community is still Jewish. Many of the stigmatizing procedures used by communities against deviants and the countermeasures they provoke can be seen in Matthew's polemics and apologetics.[1] Deviance processes, far from

---

1. The charge that Jesus' marvelous birth was really illegitimate is answered in 1:18–25, and the charge that his disciples stole his body in 27:62–66 and 28:11–15. Charges that followers of Jesus reject the law are probably being refuted in chap. 5, and attacks on the legitimacy of the community leadership in chap. 23.

driving a group out of society, often keep it in. Paradoxically, social theory has established that nonconformity, resistance to social structures, and deviance are always part of any functioning society.[2]

Looked at in this way the Gospel of Matthew (dating from the 80–90s C.E.) fits not only into the development of Christian theological thought but also into the post-70 Jewish debate over how Judaism was to be lived and how that way of life was to be articulated in order to insure the survival of the Jewish community without the temple and its related political institutions. Thus, the Gospel of Matthew should be read along with other Jewish postdestruction literature, such as the apocalyptic works *2 Baruch, 4 Ezra,* and *Apocalypse of Abraham,* early strata of the Mishnah, and Josephus. All this Jewish literature tries to envision Judaism in new circumstances, reorganize its central symbols, determine concretely the will of God in new circumstances, and propose a course of action for the faithful community.

This study of the Gospel of Matthew presupposes the widely held position that the final author exercised strong compositional and creative control over the documents and traditions at his disposal. He ordered and edited them to fit the needs of his community, to convey his understanding of the Jesus movement, and to promote his solutions to community problems.[3] Thus the story of Jesus in Matthew reflects the experience of Matthew's community and its social situation.[4] For example, Matthew's identification of the Twelve with the disciples makes Jesus' followers into a transparency for the community and Jesus' instructions to his disciples into the author's instructions for the community members.[5] Similarly, Matthew's description of conflicts between

---

2. The tension between deviance as destructive and as formative for society is brought out well by Nahman Ben-Yehuda, *Deviance and Moral Boundaries: Witchcraft, the Occult, Deviant Sciences and Scientists* (Chicago: University of Chicago Press, 1985) 3–7. On the positive effects of deviance, see Kai T. Ericson, *Wayward Puritans: A Study in the Sociology of Deviance* (New York: Wiley, 1966) 3–5. For the necessity of deviance, see Emile Durkheim, esp. *The Rules of Sociological Method* (Glencoe, Ill.: Free Press, 1958) 67; and idem, *The Division of Labor in Society* (Glencoe, Ill.: Free Press, 1960) 102. See also George H. Mead, "The Psychology of Punitive Justice," *AmerJourSoc* 23 (1918) 577–602, esp. 591.

3. What is referred to is redaction criticism, which followed form criticism after World War II. The pioneering essays in Matthean studies are found in G. Bornkamm et al., *Tradition and Interpretation in Matthew* (Philadelphia: Westminster, 1963). More recent literary critical and social scientific approaches to the Gospels presume redaction criticism. See also the focus on the narrative as a whole found in "composition criticism" as practiced by William Thompson in "An Historical Perspective on the Gospel of Matthew," *JBL* 93 (1974) 243–62; and idem, *Matthew's Advice to a Divided Community (Matt 17:22–18:35)* (AnBib 44; Rome: Biblical Institute, 1970).

4. G. Barth, "Matthew's Understanding of the Law," in Bornkamm et al., *Tradition and Interpretation,* 111; R. Hummel, *Die Auseindersetzung zwischen Kirche und Judentum im Matthäusevangelium* (Munich: Kaiser, 1963) 154; Douglas R. A. Hare, *The Theme of Jewish Persecution of Christians in the Gospel according to St. Matthew* (SNTSMS 6; Cambridge: Cambridge University Press, 1967) 81ff.; E. Schweizer, *Matthäus und seine Gemeinde* (Stuttgarter Bibelstudien 71; Stuttgart: KBW, 1974).

5. Schuyler Brown, "The Mission to Israel in Matthew's Central Section (Mt 9:35–11:1)," *ZNW* 69 (1978) 73–90, esp. 74–77. For the disciples in the narrative as a transparency for the

leaders of the Jewish community and Jesus indirectly reflect the relationship between his late first-century community and the local Jewish community with which he was in contact. However, such social analysis must avoid turning the text into an allegory by taking into account the influence of earlier traditions, the dynamics of the narrative,[6] and the purposes of the Gospel.

The use of the sociology of deviance in this study implies that the argument over whether Matthew's community is still Jewish, that is, whether it is still in contact with the Jewish community or has irrevocably broken away, is misstated.[7] Categories that place Matthew's community either in or out of Judaism are too absolute and sociologically rigid to be useful analytical tools. Mediating positions, such as G. Stanton's hypothesis that Matthew is separated from Judaism but defining his community's stance over against Judaism,[8] are vague concerning the nature of the relationship and require clarification. A community that has "broken away" from a parent community retains multiple relationships and cannot be understood in isolation. (Even after nineteen hundred years, Christianity must still be defined partly with reference to Judaism.) A tradition and community is always a complex symbolic and social reality including many subcommunities, systems, and groups with shifting boundaries. Most analyses of Judaism and Christianity give too much credence to the majority groups who define boundaries, orthodoxy, orthopraxy, morality, and belief with artificial clarity. What groups say about themselves and each other often reflects what they wish were true rather than what is. Accepting the consensus of scholars that Matthew's Jewish community of believers-in-Jesus had

---

members of the Matthean community, see Ulrich Luz, "The Disciples in the Gospel according to Matthew," *The Interpretation of Matthew* (ed. Graham Stanton; Philadelphia: Fortress, 1983) 98–128, and the previous literature cited there. The apostles in Matthew are neither people called specifically by Jesus (Paul's view) nor a historically past group of founders (Luke), but the disciples (Matt 9:37; 10:1, 2, 42; 11:1). Matthew portrays the disciples much more positively than does Mark by deemphasizing their lack of understanding and fidelity (e.g., the mother of James and John, rather than the disciples themselves, requests thrones on either side of Jesus [Matt 20:20–28; cf. Mark 10:35–45]). For the roles of the disciples in the narrative in relation to Matthew's view of his community, see Luz, "Disciples," 109–11; Jack D. Kingsbury, "The Verb *Akolouthein* ('to follow') as an Index of Matthew's View of His Community," *JBL* 97 (1978) 56–73; in another form, idem, chap. 9 of *Matthew as Story* (2d ed.; Philadelphia: Fortress, 1988); Richard A. Edwards, "Uncertain Faith: Matthew's Portrait of the Disciples," *Discipleship in the New Testament* (ed. F. Segovia; Philadelphia: Fortress, 1985) 47–61; Michael J. Wilkins, *The Concept of Disciple in Matthew's Gospel* (SuppNovTest 59; Leiden: E. J. Brill, 1988).

6. E.g., Edwards, "Uncertain Faith," shows how the disciples, as literary characters in the narrative, carry Matthew's comments on his community.

7. For a review of modern positions that see Matthew's community as closely related to Judaism or separated from Judaism but defining itself against Judaism or separate and no longer arguing with Judaism, see Graham Stanton, "The Origin and Purpose of Matthew's Gospel: Matthean Scholarship from 1945–1980," *Aufstieg und Niedergang der römischen Welt* II.25.3 (ed. H. Temporini and W. Hasse; Berlin: de Gruyter, 1985) 1911–21. This paper will accept Markan priority, the usual solution to the synoptic problem, but suggest that the second-generation author is a Greek-speaking Christian Jew still closely related to Judaism.

8. Stanton, "Origin and Purpose of Matthew's Gospel," 1914–16, 1921.

been engaged in a lengthy conflict with Jewish community authorities and had recently withdrawn from or been expelled from the Jewish assembly, I will argue that it still had numerous negative and positive relations with the Jewish community and many common symbolic elements. In fact, Matthew still had a fading hope that he would prevail and make his program normative for the whole Jewish community.

In order to elucidate the conflictual relationship between Matthew's community and the parent Jewish community, some guidance from the sociological theories of deviance is necessary. First, a hypothesis concerning the identity and location of the Matthean community will be sketched. Then deviance processes and relationships will be elucidated and correlated with data from Matthew's Gospel. Finally, Matthew's community will be defined against known types of deviant associations, including sects.

THE IDENTITY OF MATTHEW'S COMMUNITY

Many descriptions of the Matthean community have assumed its Christian, as opposed to Jewish, identity and in an a priori or subjective fashion relegated the strongly Jewish exhortations and tone of the Gospel to the history of its tradition. On the basis of the text, as will be shown, Matthew's community is a Christian-Jewish group that keeps the whole law, interpreted through the Jesus tradition. Matthew considers himself to be a Jew who has the true interpretation of Torah and is faithful to God's will as revealed by Jesus whom he declares to be Messiah and Son of God. Matthew promotes "a perfected or fulfilled Judaism brought to its goal by the long-awaited Christ."[9] He seeks to promote his interpretation of Judaism over that of other Jewish leaders, especially those of emerging rabbinic Judaism.[10] In his own view, Matthew is simply Jewish. He seeks to legitimate his particular form of Judaism by utilizing the sources of authority in the Jewish community (see chaps. 5–6 and his use of Scripture generally) and by delegitimating the Jewish leaders (see esp. chap. 23).[11] His motivational accounting system is still Jewish. Significantly, he has

9. Donald A. Hagner, "The *Sitz im Leben* of the Gospel of Matthew," SBLSP 1985 (ed. Kent Richards; Chico, Calif.: Scholars Press, 1985) 256.

10. For the specific nature of Matthew's opponents as early proponents of rabbinic Judaism, see J. Andrew Overman, *The Gospel of Matthew and Formative Judaism: A Study of the Social World of the Matthean Community* (Minneapolis: Fortress, 1990).

11. Peter Richardson, *Israel in the Apostolic Church* (SNTSMS 10; Cambridge: Cambridge University Press, 1969) 194, correctly characterizes Matthew thus: "In so far as he works toward a theory of the Church as 'true Israel,' he does it as a Jewish Christian for a Jewish Christian community, as a part of a dispute with a pharisaic Synagogue which is also claiming to be 'true Israel.' In the post-Jamnian situation where a Jewish Christian church might stand alongside a synagogue, each has a deep need to clarify its thinking about its relationship to the cultus and the law. Each is forced to move beyond the attitude before the fall of Jerusalem towards these matters, and in doing so each is tempted to claim that it fully represents 'Israel.' The pharisaic

no name for his group. He does not call it Israel or the people (ὁ λαός); he uses these terms either in their biblical setting or to designate the Jewish people whom Jesus and the Matthean community have tried to instruct and influence. These terms designate all Jews and provide no identifying distinctions among groups within Israel. Matthew does not even use the terms new or true Israel. Rather, members of the Jewish community who reject Jesus, especially the leaders, are excoriated, in the prophetic mode, as unfaithful members of Israel, but still as members. Israel is the concrete community of Jews from which Matthew has been banned, but to which he still thinks that he belongs.[12] Many also understand Matthew to claim that Christianity has replaced Judaism (21:43)[13] as the true or new Israel and that all hope of preaching Jesus to his fellow Jews has been relinquished (28:19).[14] But this is a mid-second-century

community rested its claim basically on continuous tradition; the Christian on the fulfillment of the old and better obedience through the Messiah." It should be noted that the claims to both continuous tradition and fulfillment are equally artificial and are creative initiatives at adapting Jewish tradition to new circumstances.

12. This thesis is contrary to the thesis that Matthew's community is mostly or completely Gentile (and that the Jewish mission is in the past). For the gentile thesis, see Georg Strecker, *Der Weg der Gerechtigkeit: Untersuchung zur Theologie des Matthäus* (3d ed.; Göttingen: Vandenhoeck & Ruprecht, 1971; orig. ed. 1962) 34–35; Hare, *Theme of Jewish Persecution of Christians*, 153; John P. Meier, *Law and History in Matthew's Gospel* (AnBib 71; Rome: Biblical Institute, 1976); R. Walker, *Die Heilsgeschichte im ersten Evangelium* (Göttingen: Vandenhoeck & Ruprecht, 1967). Wolfgang Trilling, *Das Wahre Israel: Studien zur Theologie des Matthäus-Evangelium* (3d ed.; SANT 10; Munich: Kosel, 1964), sees the Gospel community a midpoint, separated from Israel, but claiming to be the true Israel (hence all the Jewish traditions). For vigorous rejections of Strecker's position on the gentile nature of Matthew's community, see M. Hengel, "Zur matthäischen Bergpredigt und ihrem jüdischen Hintergrund," *TRu* 52 (1987) 327–400, esp. 341–48; and Benno Przybylski, "The Setting of Matthean Anti-Judaism," *Anti-Judaism in Early Christianity* (vol. 1; Waterloo: Laurier, 1986) 181–200.

The conflicts Matthew has with the Jewish community leaders and even his alienation from their assembly do not affect his Jewishness sociologically or psychologically. He considers himself a Jew and fights for his interpretation of Jewish life. He is seen as a Jew by the surrounding communities, by the Jewish authorities who discipline him, and by other believers-in-Jesus. He affirms the validity of Jewish law understood in the correct way (5:17–20) and the authority of the Jewish community leaders, though not their practice nor their legal interpretations (23:1–36, esp. vv. 2–3). He mitigates Christian rejection of purity and dietary laws (15;1–20; cf. Mark 7:1–23, esp. 19) and gives reasons for letting his disciples pick grain on the Sabbath (12:1–8; cf. Mark 2:23–28). Thus he seems to be one of a diminishing number of Christian Jews who accept the whole Jewish law and way of life, understood according to the teaching of Jesus, as normative.

Contrary to the position defended in this study, many commentators assign Jewish-Christian laws and interests in Matthew to earlier stages in the community history. This sorting of materials by how Jewish they are tends to be arbitrary, circular, and based on Christian, theological salvation history schemes that purport to account for an evolutionary Christian development away from Judaism. More importantly, many assign the anti-Jewish polemics (e.g., 6:1–18; 10:17–23; 21:28—22:14; 23:1–36; 27:43) to earlier stages in the community history and hold that the break with Judaism is so final that there is no current conflict or that serious conflict is in the past.

13. Hare, *Theme of Jewish Persecution of Christians*; David E. Garland, *The Intention of Matthew 23* (Leiden: E. J. Brill, 1979). Especially chap. 23 is a Matthean redactional unit expressing in a most fervent way the author's engagement with the Jewish authorities.

14. See Douglas R. A. Hare and Daniel J. Harrington, "Make Disciples of All the

position which assumes that the two communities are separate and Christianity is established.[15] Matthew does not use this salvation history scheme, but reflects real history, that is, real people in a struggle for the future of Judaism. Imposition of eras of salvation has obscured the Jewishness of Matthew's community and his engagement in Jewish community struggles in the name of Jesus.

Contrary to the claims of the usual salvation history schemes, the Jewish mission is still open in Matthew.[16] This can be seen in his portrayal of the Jewish crowds. His treatment of the Galilean crowds is fundamentally friendly with some ambiguity. Usually they are Jesus' audience and marvel at his teaching or miraculous deeds (e.g., 7:28; 22:33; 12:23). For the most part, they are not directly attacked as the leaders are, but rather seen as misled (9:36); they are excoriated and rejected only when linked to their leaders in such a way that Jesus' and Matthew's appeal to them is rejected by a whole city (11:20–24; 23:27–39; 27:25). Matthew still hopes to win part of Israel away from their false leaders. For this reason the crowds, who represent the people of the Jewish community with which Matthew was in contact, are often portrayed as searching, as needing leadership and instruction, and as neutral or goodwilled.[17] At other times they are condemned for rejecting Jesus and for ill will, that is, for following the traditional Jewish leaders instead of Matthew (26:47, 55; 27:15,

---

Gentiles (Matthew 28:19)" *CBQ* 37 (1975) 359–69. Contrary to this position, which understands ἔθνη (foreigners) in the limited sense of Gentiles, the Greek term ἔθνος (nation, people) can be used to refer to the Gentiles (nations), as opposed to the Jews, but it is not a technical theological term in Matthew. ἔθνος can be a nation, a people (ethnic group), but also any kind of band of people or association. In 21:43 the ἔθνος to which the kingdom of God will be given is the Matthean community. However, this Matthean ἔθνος is not thereby characterized as gentile. Rather, it is a Christian-Jewish group which replaces the Jerusalem-based group of Jews as the faithful interpreters and observers of God's will.

15. This view comes out most clearly in Justin *Dial.*, where Christians are said to be Israel and the true Israelite race [*genos*] (123; 135). For a thematic development of these themes, see Marcel Simon, *Verus Israel: Etude sur les relations entre Chrétiens et Juifs dans l'Empire Romain* (Paris: de Boccard, 1948); Eng. trans. *Verus Israel: A Study of the Relations between Christians and Jews in the Roman Empire, 135–425* (New York: Oxford University Press, 1986).

16. The view that the mission to Israel is in the past and is now closed was commonly held (see the authors cited in n. 12). It is based on understanding *ethnē* in 28:19 as referring exclusively to non-Jews, on a periodization of chaps. 24–25 that associates the destruction of Jerusalem with the end of the Jewish mission (see Thompson, "Historical Perspective"), on a reading of chap. 10 that places the Jewish mission in the Palestinian past, and similar exegetical arguments. Many recent interpreters hold that the Jewish mission is still open, or at least not closed in principle. See J. Meier, "Nations or Gentiles in Matthew 28:19?" *CBQ* 39 (1977) 94–102; Kingsbury, *Matthew as Story*, 154; K. Tagawa, "People and Community in the Gospel of Matthew," *NTS* 16 (1969–70) 160; and Amy-Jill Levine, *The Social and Ethnic Dimensions of Matthean Salvation History: "Go nowhere among the Gentiles ..." (Matt. 10:5b)* (Studies in the Bible and Early Christianity 14; Lewiston, N.Y.: Edwin Mellen, 1988). Levine argues that Matt 28:19 does mean "Gentiles," but that the Gospel as a whole leaves the Jewish mission open. Hummel, *Auseinandersetzung*, 156 n. 72, 157–61, correctly stresses the integral connection and close relationship between Matthew's community and other Jewish communities.

17. Richardson, *Israel in the Apostolic Church,* 193.

20–25).[18] But the Jewish people are still recruitable, still not beyond salvation, not irrevocably condemned (as they are in later Christian literature). For this reason the Jewish mission is still open for Matthew.[19]

Matthew attacks the Jewish leaders unceasingly in an attempt to delegitimize their authority and teaching and to win the people over to his interpretation of Judaism. Matthew's polemics, even his famous attack on the scribes and Pharisees as hypocrites (chap. 23), and his underlying view of Judaism are nuanced. Matthew attacks the Jewish leadership (scribes, Pharisees, and Jerusalem leaders) and their interpretations of how the Jewish community should live in order to replace their understanding of Torah and Jewish life with his community's reformed program. He is dealing with real time, concrete history, and living people.

DEVIANCE AS PART OF A
FUNCTIONING SOCIETY

Calling the Matthean community a deviant Jewish community is in traditional categories a pejorative labeling. Most ancient and many modern societies treat deviant behavior as objectively evil because it is seen as contrary to divine or natural order or as inspired by evil powers (demonic possession, witchcraft, etc.).[20] Within the taken-for-granted, everyday world, moral and cultural norms are right and good, and that which is different is at best strange and at worst wrong and evil. This common-sense judgment of deviance has been severely qualified by cross-cultural comparisons and modern theories of deviance, which show that social consensus and explicit norms for what is considered deviant change with time. Customs, mores, social relationships, and laws develop and adapt to new circumstances and outlooks. Even "hard" deviance, such as murder and theft, are defined differently according to culture and era.

The study of deviance is crucial to the understanding of culture and community. What a society considers deviant is intimately related to its identity, shows where it draws its boundaries, and exposes key structures and values in its social and symbolic system.[21] To study what a society rejects is to study

18. Matt 27:25 refers to the Jerusalem leadership and people and is post-eventum prophecy, that is, a response to the actual destruction of Jerusalem and its leaders and people in 70. The crowds in chaps. 26–27 are the crowds in Jerusalem and seem to be a subset of, or different from, the crowds in Galilee.

19. At the same time, Matthew is urging his community to include fully a gentile mission.

20. In a review of several theories of deviance, Stephen J. Pfohl, *Images of Deviance and Social Control: A Sociological History* (New York: McGraw-Hill, 1985), entitles his chapter on the traditional idea of deviance "The Demonic Perspective: Otherworldly Interpretations of Deviance."

21. Ben-Yehuda, *Deviance and Moral Boundaries,* 19–20.

what it is.[22] Thus consideration of the conflicts between Matthew and the dominant Jewish community will reveal how each conceives of and lives life. What Matthew defends is what is crucial to him, and what he attacks is probably important to his opponents' view of Judaism. Both communities share many values and know each other's weak points.

The study of deviance must be set in a broad context. The struggle to define and sanction some behaviors and their attendant attitudes as deviant is always political in the broad sense and involves a power struggle for control of society.[23] Competing political interest groups promote particular modes of living; they symbolize society in coherent ways and condemn others who are different. Far from being a subjective, foolish debate about preferences, these conflicts concern the basic shape of society, the relationships that will hold the society together, and the symbolic universe that makes sense out of the flux of life. For example, critical reading of biblical history has revealed the constant competition and conflict between the Yahweh-only Israelites and the Yahwist-Baalist Israelites. For much of monarchic Israel, mixed worship of Yahweh and Baal was the norm. Only in the exile did the Yahweh-only group prevail and definitively stigmatize its opposition in the documents collected into the Bible. Likewise, the Matthean community, the early rabbinic community, and other Jewish groups competed for control of Jewish life. Since every society is built upon previous societies or stages in its own history, that history, plus physical, social, and intellectual circumstances, and the power relationships among the members of the society greatly influence what is normative and deviant at any time.

Recent theories of deviance have stressed the processes whereby some people, behaviors, and ideas are declared deviant.[24] While I shall use these studies, I shall give greater attention to the larger questions of social order and structure, of how groups interrelate within a whole system, and of how social

22. Ericson, *Wayward Puritans*, 22–23. What we fear is what is likely to emerge as deviance, probably because our fears are centered around what we value, and so someone who thinks and acts differently does so concerning matters that are important for all in the society.

23. See recently, Edwin M. Schur, *The Politics of Deviance: Stigma Contests and the Uses of Power* (Englewood Cliffs, N.J.: Prentice-Hall, 1980).

24. Surveys of various sociological theories with a critique of each can be found in Pfohl, *Images of Deviance*; and Nanette Davis, *Sociological Constructions of Deviance: Perspectives and Issues in the Field* (Dubuque, Iowa: William C. Brown, 1975). Labeling theory is ably expounded by Edwin H. Pfuhl, *The Deviance Process* (New York: Van Nostrand, 1980). A seminal book is Howard S. Becker, *Outsiders: Studies in the Sociology of Deviance* (New York: Macmillan, 1963). Many aspects of deviance theory are based on the fundamental work of Max Weber and Emile Durkheim.

Recent work stresses the viability of deviant behaviors and the oppressive causes of deviance. It has often neglected to relate deviance to larger social structures and the nature of society, a weakness which will be avoided here. The theory that society is only process (Garfinkel) will be avoided here.

conflict and deviance relate to stability and change in society. I shall work within a broadly functionalist theory of society, but with attention to the symbolic interaction and power struggles analyzed by labeling theory.[25] Every society has norms and patterns of behavior and thought, and every society contains a great variety of behaviors and viewpoints clustered around the center. The boundaries of a society, which are more or less sharp, depending on a variety of factors, define the normative from the deviant.[26] At the same time, the creation of boundaries and norms for discerning that which is acceptable and that which is not, is an intricate process requiring great social effort. Much of our behavior is in itself ambiguous and indifferent. Thus, defining deviance is a struggle to bring order to human activities and the meanings we see in them.[27] Defining deviant behavior also helps a society limit the virtually infinite range of custom and outlook to a finite and coherent whole. It is a sign that a society has voluntarily restricted itself to a constant and stable pattern of activity.[28]

Deviance is a necessary part of a functioning society in several senses.[29] Specifically, it is part of the larger social processes associated with stability and change, continuity and adaptation.[30] It keeps the society from rigidifying and failing to fulfill its necessary functions. In the present case, Jews in Palestine and southern Syria had to adapt, or perhaps better, reconstitute their symbolic worlds, and their social-political worlds as well, in the aftermath of the destruction of the temple and its leadership. Jerusalem, the symbolic and political center of Palestinian Judaism, was eliminated with grave community consequences which had to be met with innovative solutions drawn from the tradition. Jewish literature of the period, including the Gospel of Matthew, testifies to several approaches adopted by different Jewish groups.

In any social system, especially in one in crisis like the Palestinian Jewish social system after the destruction of the temple, what is within the boundaries of the society and what is not, what is deviant and what is accepted is a matter of dispute. The competing rabbinic, apocalyptic, revolutionary, and Christian-Jewish movements are a rich field for analysis. The early rabbinic movement, with its emphases on Torah, purity, Sabbath observance, tithing, and so on, and its vision of a Torah-centered life, probably seemed strange and

25. Davis, *Sociological Constructions of Deviance*, chap. 5, esp. p. 118.
26. For an approach to group definition that depends heavily on social boundaries, see Yehudi A. Cohen, "Social Boundary Systems," *Current Anthropology* 10 (1969) 103–17.
27. Paul Rock, *Deviant Behavior* (London: Hutchinson, 1973) 73.
28. Ericson, *Wayward Puritans*, 10. Ericson quotes Durkheim to the effect that if a society were to be uniformly good by normal criteria, more and more trivial traits of behavior would be marked as deviant (p. 26).
29. See n. 2 above.
30. Ben-Yehuda, *Deviance and Moral Boundaries*, 1–20, esp. 3.

deviant to many loyal Jewish farmers in Palestinian villages. Matthew's community had enough fundamental disputes with the majority of Jews to be classified as deviant in a stronger qualitative and quantitative sense than many other Jewish movements (see the next section). And Matthew's own text testifies to the heightened tension within Jewish society caused by his new teachings.

Even though deviant positions are often spoken of as outside the pale, sociologically and historically they are part of the whole. For example, reformed Judaism is rejected by some Jews today as deviant, as not authentically Jewish, yet even to those rejecting reformed Judaism, the members of that movement are Jews. In addition, the reformed movement is patently Jewish historically and sociologically. Deviant groups remain part of the whole. They modify a social, political, or religious system that they judge does not make sense or work, but they build their new world with materials from the old world they share with those who have declared them deviant.

The deviance that is always part of society has predictable effects on society. Even though those in control often wish to eliminate deviance and see it as an evil, deviance is caused by social relationships and has both beneficent and negative effects on society. If there is a quantitatively and qualitatively small amount of marginal deviance that can be controlled by the majority, then deviance helps to define and strengthen social boundaries and promote cohesion. If there is a large amount of fundamental deviance, this is a sign of and cause of significant social change.[31] The constitutive function of deviance can be seen clearly in the sociology of tradition. As defined by S. N. Eisenstadt in Weberian terms, tradition is:

> the routinized symbolization of the models of social order and of the constellation of the codes, the guidelines, which delineate the limits of the binding cultural order, or membership in it, and of its boundaries, which prescribe the "proper" choices of goals and patterns of behavior; it can also be seen as the modes of evaluation as well as of the sanctioning and legitimation of the "totality" of the cultural and social order, or of any of its parts.[32]

Tradition is often habitual and unreflective and thus tends to be constrictive. But tradition may also be conscious and elaborated and in this way creative. The rabbinic sages are parade examples of creative traditionalists.

Tradition crystallizes the construction of reality, often initiated by a creative leader or group, and contributes to the rationalization of social goals, values, and meaning.[33] Traditions are often founded by deviant leaders and

---

31. Ibid., 14–15; Ericson, *Wayward Puritans*, 13.
32. S. N. Eisenstadt, *Tradition, Change, and Modernity* (New York: Wiley, 1973) 139. See also E. Shils, *Center and Periphery* (Chicago: University of Chicago Press, 1975).
33. Eisenstadt, *Tradition, Change, and Modernity*, 127, 139.

groups who have succeeded in establishing themselves. In fact, any tradition, culture, or society has within it deep tensions between competing symbolic systems, norms, groups, and interests. The very specification of cultural boundaries and norms contained in a tradition is open to and often invites redefinition and change.[34] Linguistic usage, social categories, cultural sensitivities, and shared experiences all undergo constant change, either gradual or sharp. Boundaries are never completely stable and fixed, but rather approximate and under constant modification.[35] Conflict with and affirmation of tradition pervades all aspects of life, society, and thought at all times. Even the most radical revolutionary is set within a cultural tradition which he or she draws from and reacts against.

DEVIANCE IN
THE GOSPEL OF MATTHEW

One cannot be deviant unless one is a member of the community. The Gospel of Matthew and the community behind it are Jewish in that they accept all the fundamental commitments of first-century Judaism, but argue about their interpretation, actualization, and relative importance. In the Gospel, as in other Jewish works, God rules (kingdom of heaven), cares for his people (6:25–34), and communicates to them his will. Israel and its special relationship to God and its history permeate the Gospel. The Bible is the authoritative source for knowing God, God's will, and God's purposes. Thus Matthew quotes the Bible frequently and often solemnly in the formula quotations. Prophets, ancient and contemporary, true and false (Elijah in 11:14 and 17:9–13; true prophets in 23:34; false in 7:15; 24:11) are invoked, as is Moses (17:3).[36] Numerous biblical laws, later Jewish laws, and community norms are affirmed or accepted as part of his world by Matthew: the commandments (19:18), alms, prayer and fasting (6:1–18), care for the poor, powerless, and sick (preaching and miracles of Jesus), biblical virtues (5:1–12; 11:5; 12:17–21), faith (17:14–20; 21:21–22), observance of the Sabbath (24:20; 12:1–14) and purity rules (15:1–20; 23:25–26; 8:1ff.), tithing (23:23), observance of temple ritual (12:3–5; Passover in 26), divorce in case of adultery (1:18–19; 5:32; 19:9),[37] Jewish

---

34. Ibid., 140–41. Ericson, *Wayward Puritans*, 7–8, stresses the intricacy of the processes and relationships involved in deviance and the arbitrariness of much of the behavior labeled normal or deviant.

35. Ericson, *Wayward Puritans*, 12.

36. Josephus reports a number of leaders claiming prophetic or messianic warrants for their leadership in the first century. See Richard Horsley and John S. Hanson, *Bandits, Prophets and Messiahs: Popular Movements at the Time of Jesus* (Minneapolis: Winston, 1985).

37. The Matthean exception allowing divorce because of πορνεία (some kind of immorality) has been interpreted by some, in the light of Qumran legislation, as marriage within forbidden degrees of kinship. See J. A. Fitzmyer, "The Matthean Divorce Texts and Some New Palestinian Evidence," *To Advance the Gospel: New Testament Essays* (New York: Crossroad, 1981) 79–111.

community leaders, and standard community discipline (10:17, 23; 23:2–3) are presumed. Resurrection of the dead, a final judgment, and a typical apocalyptic scenario are woven into the text. Finally, circumcision is not mentioned. Most commentators assume, on the basis of Pauline letters and the influx of Gentiles into most Christian communities by the late first century, that no New Testament community circumcises. However, it is worth considering whether Matthew's silence on the issue implies that his community takes circumcision for granted.[38]

Matthew's Jewish community is, nevertheless, a deviant community. Though the list of practices and symbols Matthew shares with his fellow Jews is long (and more could be added to the list), in most cases Matthew modifies the interpretation or actualization of the law so that it conflicts with other Jewish groups. Matthew's disputes over how Jewish law and life are to be interpreted should not lead commentators to the conclusion that he is no longer Jewish (in his own eyes or sociologically speaking). Nor should a covert notion of a universal normative Judaism be introduced. In the first century, especially after the destruction of the temple, there was no normative Jewish teaching, practice, or authority, but rather a traditional way of living Judaism with many local variations and some striking dissident voices. It was only after a century or two of recruiting followers and gaining community influence that the rabbinic leaders made an impact on Palestinian Judaism and could claim to be normative; it was even longer before talmudic Judaism became normative for all diaspora Jewish communities. Matthew is deviant not because of disagreement with a normative Judaism but because he is a minority against the majority and

---

Traditionally πορνεία had been understood as adultery. Recently this view has been subsumed into an argument that any sexual interference in a marriage (adultery, rape, etc.) would have forbidden the resumption of that marriage according to first-century norms. See Markus Bockmuehl, "Matthew 5.32; 19.9 in the Light of Pre-Rabbinic Halakhah," *NTS* 35 (1989) 291–95.

38. A strongly Jewish-Christian community such as Matthew's, which is not afraid to disagree explicitly and vocally with the majority of Jews in many particulars of law, is unlikely to have kept silent on the status of circumcision. Even in the second century Christian authors raise the issue of circumcision in order to say it is not needed or it is ineffective. It is most probable that if circumcision were not practiced, Matthew would have discussed it as he discusses and justifies many other deviations from common Jewish practice. For the possibility of circumcision, see S. Brown, "The Matthean Community and the Gentile Mission," *NovT* 22 (1980) 193–221, esp. 218. Most interpreters assume that the problem of circumcision had been solved in the negative. See recently Hagner, "*Sitz im Leben* of the Gospel of Matthew," 258, and the more traditional typology of Raymond Brown, "Not Jewish Christianity and Gentile Christianity but Types of Jewish/Gentile Christianity," *CBQ* 45 (1983) 74–79. Most interpreters see Matthew as very much Christian and so cannot conceive of a late first-century community of believers-in-Jesus circumcising. This view is influenced by Paul's rejection of circumcision for Gentiles and the influx of Gentiles who dominated many (most?) communities of believers-in-Jesus by the end of the first century. But in the first century the boundaries of Christianity varied greatly. Paul's position that Gentiles were free of the law was strongly opposed and became the majority view only gradually, long after Paul's death. Many Christian-Jewish communities survived into the second century and some beyond. Matthew fits with these Christian-Jewish communities.

because he recommends a more fundamental reorientation of the tradition than many other Jewish movements. Matthew modifies or rejects many specific Jewish practices and teachings that he attributes mostly to the scribes and Pharisees. He is probably responding to the leaders of an early form of rabbinic Judaism who are competing with him for the loyalties of the local Jewish community.[39]

Matthew's innovations can be roughly classified under five headings: core symbols, cosmology, boundaries, laws, and social structure.

Core Symbols. A key change from the majority view of Judaism found in the text of the Gospel and in the Matthean community is the rising status of Jesus as Son of God, authoritative teacher (9:8 etc.), and crucified savior.[40] Though Matthew's community does not believe that Jesus is divine in the way later Christian theologians and councils defined it, the belief in and focus on Jesus is escalating and will eventually take the Jesus communities away from Judaism. As a consequence of this focus on Jesus as central authority and symbol, Torah becomes subordinate to both Jesus and his interpretation of its provisions, as articulated in a unique way by Matthew.

The law as a core symbol has an altered status and role in Matthew's symbolic world. Though the commandments and the law as a whole are affirmed (5:17–19; 19:16–20), in each instance Matthew, through Jesus, counsels a further effort to reach perfection (5:48 [see also 5:20]; 19:21–22) and gives further instructions (5:21–47; 19:23–30) to guide that effort. The commandments themselves, besides being modified (see "Laws," below), are also subsumed under the two greatest commandments, love of God and neighbor (22:34–40). Though these commandments are biblical, the apologetic and rhetorical use made of them shifts the emphasis from a careful study of Torah to a more flexible use and adaptation that fits the needs of Matthew's changing, alienated community. For example, when Matthew criticizes the scribes and Pharisees' practice of tithing, he affirms tithing itself but puts the emphasis on "the weightier matters of the law: justice and mercy and faith" (23:23). All these central symbols and affirmations are Jewish, but Matthew's community has rearranged and reweighted them.

---

39. See Overman, *Matthew and Formative Judaism.*

40. This usually forms the centerpiece of Christian analyses of Matthew. It has been neglected here in order to get a different purchase on the Gospel and community. As noted above, a small amount of deviance, qualitatively and quantitatively, can be controlled by the majority and can strengthen the community boundaries. A large amount is a threat to the community and a sign of significant social change. The growing focus on Jesus and neglect of the Jewish way of life by Christian Jews and their gentile brethren at first firmed up Jewish community boundaries and identity and then led to a deep rupture. Matthew's community stands in the early stages of this process.

Cosmology. A strong apocalyptic orientation with the promise and threat of divine judgment is a characteristic of a deviant minority group under pressure. Divine mandate and sanction justify change and invalidate the current norms in view of the apocalyptic crisis. Future orientation produces a revised version of what society should be. New revelation and the need for conversion[41] become most comprehensible in this situation. It is no accident that the rabbinic leaders who gradually gained control of Jewish society through a very traditional program of reform masked innovations under the guise of immemorial tradition and eschewed apocalypticism as a fundamental organizing principle for their reform of Judaism.

Boundaries. The boundaries of the Matthean community are more open and the membership requirements have been modified. Sinners and tax collectors, that is, those marginalized in Jewish society, are welcomed (9:10–11; 11:19; 21:31–32) in conscious opposition to the Jewish community which, according to Matthew, declared them deviant. Enemies must be pacified (5:38–48, 9) so that the Matthean community can avail itself of all available social groups. The chosenness of the larger Jewish community has been qualified (chaps. 21–22, esp. 21:43; 3:9–10) and non-Jews are included systematically from the Magi in chapter 2 to the command to preach to all nations at the end (28:16–20). Though the Matthean community is very Jewish in tradition, thought, and practice, it has in principle (though perhaps not very much in fact yet) opened its boundaries to non-Jews. Cautiously and tentatively, Matthew is redefining Israel, even though he reserves the words Israel and people (λαός) for the Jewish community alone. He does not declare himself a new or true Israel, nor does he give his community a new name over against Israel. That will be left to the next generation. Rather, prompted by the inclusion of Gentiles and marginal groups such as the poor, sick, and outcasts, and influenced by biblical passages that are inclusive of these groups, Matthew constantly defends the Gentiles' right to faith in and salvation from Jesus. In Matthew's case this adherence to Jesus seems to involve an acceptance of much of the Jewish way of life as well.

Laws. The reinterpretation of many laws, customs, and outlooks has an aggregate impact on Matthew's community and alienates it from the majority of Jewish communities. A stress on inwardness, rather than adherence to traditional practices, institutions, and leaders (chaps. 5, 6, 23, esp. the charge of hypocrisy), opens the way for change, legitimates the deviants through appeal

---

41. Strictly speaking, neither Matthew nor his fellow Jews were converts to another religion. However, as the deviant way of living Judaism becomes stronger, it becomes sociologically legitimate to speak of conversion, that is, moving from one community to another.

to different norms and higher authorities, and shakes the given norms and their defenders (symbolized by scribes and Pharisees). Specifically, Matthew rejects the washing of hands (15:20) and qualifies the importance of purity regulations without rejecting them totally (15:11; cf. Mark 7:19). He opposes the use of oaths emphatically (5:33–37; 23:16–22) and rejects divorce except for πορνεία [some kind of sexual immorality] (5:31–32; 19:1–12). He modifies the interpretation of Sabbath (12:1–13) and subordinates it to other values. As noted above, he affirms tithing but puts the emphasis on "the weightier matters of the law: justice and mercy and faith" (23:23).

Social Structure. Matthew has moved decisively away from the prevailing modes of leadership and social organization. The temple and its priestly and aristocratic leadership had already been destroyed, and Matthew sheds no tears for them. In the narrative the temple and its supporting institutions function as part of Judaism, but their legitimacy is severely qualified. The temple will be destroyed (24:2, 15), must be cleansed (21:12–13), is less important than mercy (Hos 6:6 quoted in 9:13; 12:7) and is subordinate to something greater [Jesus] (12:6). The leaders "sit in the chair of Moses" (23:2) but are hypocrites who give a bad example. The Matthean community has its own inner order (18) and its own mode of leadership (23:4–12, 34) which conflict with those of the larger Jewish community. Matthew's community, like most new groups, stresses egalitarian relationships with little differentiation and specialization. Fellowship rather than hierarchy keeps the community together.

Matthew's disagreements with the dominant forces in the Jewish community are more thorough than this list would indicate. The choice and arrangement of materials in Matthew's Gospel suggest that the author envisions a thoroughly reformed Jewish society as the correct response to God's will and that he contrasts it negatively with the mode of living Judaism found in the Jewish community at large. He expounds his own program and seeks to delegitimize his opponents' program—an exercise typical for the leader of a deviant group. A few examples must suffice. The first of Matthew's five sermons begins with the eight (or nine) beatitudes proposing fundamental attitudes and patterns of behavior for Matthew's community. The final sermon on the end of the world (chaps. 24–25) is preceded by seven woes against the scribes and Pharisees who are called hypocrites and blind guides (23:13–36). These blessings and curses define the broad outline of how Matthew conceives of society and what he opposes in the Jewish society surrounding him.[42]

42. The relationship between the Sermon on the Mount and the denunciation of the scribes and Pharisees has been noted by Davies, *The Setting of the Sermon on the Mount* (Cambridge: Cambridge University Press, 1964) 291–92, and J. Schniewind, *Das Evangelium nach Matthäus* (NTD; Göttingen: Vandenhoeck & Ruprecht, 1962) 225. The significance of this relationship is discounted by Davies-Allison, 440–41.

The seven woe oracles (23:13–36) are not a random selection of complaints, but a structured series of charges aimed at key aspects of the outlook, practices, and leadership roles in the Jewish community. The first two woes concern membership in the community. The Jewish leaders prevent their members from joining Matthew's community, and they attract Gentiles to the Jewish community, thus frustrating the recruitment goals of Matthew's community. The next three woes, concerned with oaths, tithes, and purity, attack the legal system (oaths), economy (tithes = taxes), and customs (purity rules) that hold the Jewish community together and give it identity. Finally, the last two woe oracles bring to a climax the attack against the personal ethics and intentions of the leaders with charges of lawlessness and murder. These woes are preceded by a rejection of leadership titles, such as rabbi, teacher, and father, and are knit together by continual charges against the motives and perceptions of the leaders, that is, their inner selves. They end with a charge of homicide against the prophets in the past and the leaders of the Matthean community (prophets, wisemen, and scribes—23:34) in the present. Matthew seeks to present the current form of Jewish society as misguided and corrupt in its practices and leadership.

The Beatitudes that begin the Sermon on the Mount (chaps. 5–7), like the woes in chapter 23, stress the inner attitudes of the community and the patterns of its behavior. Its members should be merciful, meek, pure of heart, and peacemakers; they mourn and seek justice; they know suffering for they are poor in spirit and persecuted (the beginning and end of the series). The sense one has of this community is that it is neither powerful nor established. It seeks to make the best of its minority, deviant status. The reward offered at both the beginning and end of the Beatitudes (5:3, 10) to those who adhere to this code is the kingdom of heaven, that is, life under the rule of God rather than the Jewish community excoriated in chapters 6 and 23 and elsewhere in the Gospel. They will see God, possess the land, and enjoy justice, mercy, peace, and comfort. This is in direct contradiction to the society promoted by the scribes and Pharisees which, according to Matthew's tendentious view, neglects justice and mercy (23:23), places burdens on people (23:4), keeps cups and dishes pure, but not their hearts (23:25), appears just, but is hypocritical (23:28), and kills God's messengers (23:31–32) rather than creating peace and harmony. Thus Matthew brackets his account of Jesus' deeds and teaching with a vision of a new society and an attack on an alternate program (one which has succeeded quite well for almost two thousand years, it must be noted).

Many other sections of Matthew's Gospel support this interpretation of Matthew's program and purpose. Chapters 11 and 12 are paralleled by chapters 14 and 15 in treating the identity and status of Jesus and John the Baptist, in defending them against attack, and in showing the people's need for

their care and leadership. These chapters also show the opposition of the Pharisees and the conflicts over food and purity, that is, over the boundaries of the
community. The sermons of Jesus, woven out of traditional and new material
by the author, mirror the struggles of this deviant Jewish community, which
seeks to recruit new members with mixed success (chap. 10), is losing members
due to the embattled situation of the community (chap. 13), and is divided by
disputes and defections (chap. 18). Against this depressing scenario Matthew
arrays his interpretation of the words and works of Jesus—not a spiritual hope
only, but a concrete vision of a different society, Jewish but different.

THE MATTHEAN COMMUNITY AS A
DEVIANCE ASSOCIATION

The changes Matthew has introduced into his interpretation of Judaism
are typical of those found in deviant communities and religious sects. Social
movements that deviate from the majority usually originate because there are
steering problems within a society. They respond to a lack of focus and direction in a society, a decentering and loss of self and meaning. Movements such
as these attempt to resolve contradictions among the social, political, religious,
and economic orders and revitalize the society through reinvigorated central
symbols and patterns of behavior.[43] When large numbers of people have been
labeled deviant by the dominant forces in society and have been rejected in
some effective way, they may organize into voluntary associations aimed at
defending and restoring respectability to their so-called deviant behavior.
Typically, they challenge the conventional standards by which community
members are measured, seek to delegitimate the societal leaders who control
the definitions of deviance, and ultimately seek to change the social order. In
other words, they use the very techniques used to render them deviant in the
first place in order to justify their deviance and turn the tables.[44] Matthew uses
all the sources of Jewish teaching and authority to achieve legitimacy, and he
constructs an alternate community myth, centered on Jesus, to make a foundation for his community. The realities of Jewish history and life are rewoven into
a new tapestry.

The disputes with the Jewish community leadership and the changed
customs in the Matthean community have led Matthew's community to form
its own assembly and to compete with other Jewish assemblies for members.[45]

43. Davis, *Sociological Constructions of Deviance,* 239–40.
44. Pfuhl, *Deviance Process,* 130–47.
45. Matthew has Jesus refer to "your" or "their synagogue" a number of times in a way that
indicates opposition between him and the teachers in the synagogues or at least distance from the
synagogue (4:23; 9:35; 12:9; 13:54; 10:17; 23:34). See also "their scribes" in 7:29. The first two
curses against the scribes and Pharisees (23:13, 15) accuse them of preventing Jews from joining

Commentators argue whether Matthew is part of a Jewish federation of syna-gogues[46] or has turned its back on Judaism for good.[47] This dichotomy is false. Matthew is too enmeshed in Judaism to be cut off, and there is no official league for him to belong to. It is most probable that Matthew's community thought of itself as authentically and faithfully Jewish but was viewed by its parent community as a deviant form of Judaism. Both these Jewish communi-ties, along with many other Jewish communities, sought to survive and adapt in a changing world. There is some evidence that the Matthean community was not successfully recruiting new members and was losing adherents to the other Jewish community (13:1–30, 36–43; 11:16–24; 18:6–14). If so, this would explain the harsh tone of Matthew's polemics and the elaborate defense he makes of faith in Jesus as the correct way of being faithful to God's will.

At any rate, Matthew's community engages in many of the functions of a deviant association. It recruits members, is developing a coherent worldview and belief system, articulating an ideology and rhetoric to sustain its behavior, and devaluing outside contacts and norms. The formation of such a voluntary association requires adjustment to a new situation, the need to assign new com-munity functions and status rankings, and the creation of new community goals.[48] All of these activities are carried out in the narrative through the ser-mons and other teachings of Jesus. In the words of G. Stanton, "The evangelist is, as it were, coming to terms with the trauma of separation from Judaism and with the continuing threat of hostility and persecution. Matthew's anti-Jewish polemic should be seen as part of the self-definition of the Christian minor-ity."[49]

A bewildering array of categories and terms has been developed by anthropologists and sociologists, especially those studying new religious move-ments in Third World countries and religious movements that are reacting against the incursions of Western culture.[50] Some suffer from such a general

---

Matthew's community and of converting Gentiles to their community and thus "stealing" them from Matthew's.

46. Stanton, "Origin and Purpose of Matthew's Gospel," 1911–14, for summaries of posi-tions. See esp. E. Lohmeyer-W. Schmauch, *Das Evangelium des Matthäus* (2d ed.; Göttingen: Van-denhoeck & Ruprecht, 1958) 335–41; P. Bonnard, *L'Evangile selon Saint Matthieu* (Neuchâtel: Delachaux, 1970) 333; Bornkamm, *Tradition and Interpretation in Matthew*, 43; Hummel, *Ausein-andersetzung*, 31.

47. See Stanton, "Origin and Purpose of Matthew's Gospel," 1916–21, for positions which see the Matthean community as gentile; see esp. Hare, *Theme of Jewish Persecution of Christians*, 104–5; Trilling, *Das Wahre Israel*, 94–95; 13–14; 70ff.; Strecker, *Gerechtigkeit*, 34–35. Others, including Stanton, hold that the Matthean community is clearly separate but still identifying itself in opposition to Judaism ("Origin and Purpose of Matthew's Gospel," 1914–16).

48. Davis, *Sociological Constructions of Deviance*, 216.

49. G. Stanton, "The Gospel of Matthew and Judaism," *BJRL* 66 (1984) 264–84, esp. 274.

50. For an analysis and critique of some categories, see Bryan Wilson, *Magic and the Millennium: A Sociological Study of Religious Movements of Protest among Tribal and*

formulation that they can fit an enormous number of movements without distinction.[51] Others are particular to a given cultural area, such as cargo cults in the Pacific. The evidence found in Matthew's text will be analyzed briefly using two typologies in order to develop a general, cross-cultural characterization of this particular community. The first typology consists of four categories conventionally used to classify deviance associations. The second is Bryan Wilson's typology of seven types of sect which seeks to describe exhaustively corporate forms of deviance[52] because it stresses the positive approach of deviant communities and thus more accurately reflects their own goals rather than the majority groups' evaluation of them. It must be borne in mind, however, that these categories are ideal types. Few movements fit neatly into one category. Rather, at any one time a group may be characterized more or less strongly by more than one category and over time may move from one to another.[53]

Deviance associations have been conventionally classified into four types, using two criteria. Those who seek acceptance by society are *conformative,* and those who seek societal change are *alienative.* Those who focus on the needs of their own members are *expressive,* and those who seek to have an

---

Third-World Peoples (London: Heinemann, 1973) 484–92; Anthony F. C. Wallace, "Revitalization Movements," *American Anthropologist* 58 (1956) 264–81, esp. 264–65, 267.

51. See Wilson, *Magic and the Millennium,* 487–89, for a critique of Wallace on this score. Wallace defines a revitalization movement as "a deliberate, organized, conscious effort by members of a society to construct a more satisfying culture." Certainly the Matthean and emerging rabbinic communities fit this definition, but it leaves too many important characteristics of the movement unanalyzed.

52. Wilson uses the modern Christian category "sect." However, he modifies this formerly parochial category to fit new religious movements. In Troeltsch's classic typology, especially as popularly used, "sect" is contrasted with "church" on theological and behavioral grounds and within Christian context. For difficulties and imprecisions endemic to the church/sect distinction, along with that of denomination or free church, see B. Johnson, "On Church and Sect," *American Sociological Review* 28 (1963) 539–49; Alan W. Eister, "Toward a Radical Critique of Church-Sect Typologizing: Comment on 'Some Critical Observations on the Church-Sect Dimension,'" *JSSR* 6 (1967) 85–90. For the argument that Troeltsch uses these terms as proper to Christianity and as a historical explanation of the development of Christianity, see Theodore M. Steeman, "Church Sect, Mysticism, Denomination: Periodological Aspects of Troeltsch's Typology," *Sociological Analysis* 36 (1975) 181–204. However, the term has come to have a wider meaning and to embrace groups reacting against any society on a variety of grounds. In modern sociology the word "sect" is increasingly applied to religiously based groups that are politically active in their society. If "sect" is understood in this sense, then Matthew's community and the rabbinic group that formed after the destruction of the Temple, as well as many other groups, may be validly understood as sects. Sect formation must be understood as a form of deviance. Sects are groups of people who have accepted their deviant status and formed voluntary organizations to promote their way of life either within or apart from society. Bryan Wilson relates his seven types of sect to deviance in this way: "Concern with transcendence over evil and the search for salvation and consequent rejection of prevailing cultural values, goals, and norms, and whatever facilities are culturally provided for man's salvation, defines religious deviance." The seven types of sect respond to the world differently, partly because they have different ideas of salvation based on different definitions of evil and how it is to be overthrown (Wilson, *Magic and the Millennium,* 21).

53. Wilson, *Magic and the Millennium,* 49, 38, 35.

impact on society are *instrumental*.[54] Thus, Matthew's community seems, at the time the Gospel was written, to be an *alienative-expressive* group offering its adherents a new Christian-Jewish world as an alternative to the conventional Jewish world (i.e., various types of traditional Jewish society with a range of norms and viewpoints). It defends and justifies its way of life against opposition and seeks to establish a firm and reliable identity. Though the Matthean community has its own assembly, it is not withdrawn from Jewish society as a whole, for it still seeks to recruit members from society at large.[55] It still operates within a Jewish world, following the interpretation of Judaism attributed to its prophetic teacher, Jesus.

Whether Matthew still hopes to replace the Jewish leaders and their interpretation of Judaism is questionable. Probably at an earlier stage in the community's history, before opposition had solidified, the community of Christian Jews was an *alienative-instrumental* group seeking to change significantly the social order and worldview of the dominant types of Jewish society.[56] But the Gospel of Matthew reads like the literature of a group with a stabilized deviant identity.[57] Because of the conflict and resultant differentiation, the members of Matthew's community find their core identity and their "master status" in being believers-in-Jesus.[58] All other aspects of their Jewish life and worldview are filtered through this central commitment which has alienated them from many fellow Jews and colored all their activities and relationships. In the next generation this "master status" would crystallize in a Christian identity and lead them to drop their Jewish identity. Thus Matthew's Gospel entered the mainstream of the non-Jewish, second-century Christian church.

Bryan Wilson's typology of seven types of sect is built upon the group's relationship with and reaction to its host society.[59] He has created this typology

---

54. Two standard expositions of this typology can be found in Pfohl, *Images of Deviance and Social Control*, 315–17; and Pfuhl, *Deviance Process*, 269–73.

55. On recruitment, see Pfuhl, *Deviance Process*, 131.

56. It is likely that at an even earlier stage the Palestinian Jesus movement was more like a subculture, in which the members functioned both as members of their group of believers-in-Jesus and as respectable Jews.

57. Pfuhl, *Deviance Process*, chaps. 5–6.

58. The concept "master status" denotes a primary trait of a person to which all others are subordinate. Though we all occupy multiple social positions, statuses, and roles, one may predominate. In a racially stratified society such as the USA being black is a master status. Pfohl, *Images of Deviance and Social Control*, 291; Pfuhl, *Deviance Process*, 163–65; Everett C. Hughes, "Dilemmas and Contradictions of Status," *AmerJourSoc* 50 (1975) 353–59.

59. Wilson, *Magic and the Millennium*, 16–26. His earlier typology had only four types and was based on different principles. See Bryan Wilson, ed., *Patterns of Sectarianism: Organization and Ideology in Social and Religious Movements* (London: Heinemann, 1967), esp. the introduction, 1–21, and "An Analysis of Sect Development," 22–45. This latter work contains a list of characteristics of sects which is often used as a shopping list of things to look for in groups. The presence of a number of characteristics does not make a group a sect unless these characteristics can be related to one another in some systematic way in a theoretical context.

in an attempt to categorize exhaustively all corporate forms of deviance at a level abstract enough to be usable cross-culturally, but concrete enough to distinguish important defining characteristics.[60] The types focus on the goals of the groups and so they allow us to understand their choices and activities. Thus sects are not simply groups with certain doctrinal views, but active units of society that cause reactions among other groups and sometimes directly effect changes in society.[61] A quick review of his typology will aid in understanding the nature of Matthew's community and other Jewish groups. The seven types of sects can be sorted according to three larger categories: objectivist, subjectivist, and relationalist. The objectivist sects, the revolutionist, introversionist, reformist, and utopian, seek change in the world. The revolutionist awaits the destruction of the social order by divine forces. Apocalyptic groups fit this type. The introversionist withdraws from the world into a purified community. The Essenes fit this type. The reformist seeks gradual, divinely revealed alterations in society. The Pharisees and Jesus with his disciples probably fit this type. The utopian seeks to reconstruct the world according to divine principles without revolution. The subjectivist sect, namely, the conversionist, seeks change in the person through emotional transformation now, with salvation presumed to follow in the future after evil has been endured. Because of alienation from society, a new community is formed. Early Christians fit this type. The relationist sects, the manipulationist and thaumaturgical, seek to adjust relations with the world. The manipulationist seeks happiness by a transformed subjective orientation which will control evil. The gnostics fit this type. The thaumaturgical response seeks relief from specific ills by special, not general, dispensation. Magicians and healers, including Jesus, fit this type.[62] The seven types are not totally separate from one another, nor are they rigid. A group can have more than one response to the world at one time, though usually one is dominant and the others subordinate.[63]

The first-generation Jesus movement in Palestine was most probably a reformist movement within Judaism that was also characterized by thaumaturgical and millennial hopes. Jesus is pictured as preaching a more satisfying

60. Wilson, *Magic and the Millennium*, 16–17, 19. Wilson is generally sympathetic in his analysis of sects, but like most modern Western social scientists, he assumes a "higher absolute value for Western political organization and rationality." Cf. Hillel Schwartz, "The End of the Beginning: Millenarian Studies, 1969–1975," *RSR* 2 (1976) 7.

61. For the connection of over six thousand African Christian sects with independency movements, nativizing movements, and a myriad of other culture factors, see David B. Barrett, *Schism and Renewal in Africa: An Analysis of Six Thousand Contemporary Religious Movements* (Nairobi: OUP, 1968). Barrett's typology is concretely related to the African system, while Wilson's is more abstract and universal.

62. Wilson, *Magic and the Millennium*, 23–26, 38–49.

63. Wilson has found that in the modern period the two most common forms of response to social change are the thaumaturgical and revolutionist (thus the title of his book, *Magic and the Millennium*).

way of living Judaism, that is, a reformed Judaism. He addresses people's needs by miraculous cures and also by offering comfort and solace to those in distress.[64] In addition, though not an active revolutionary leader, he promises and threatens an apoc⸱⸱ptic, revolutionary society with a new economic, political, and religious order ruled by God (the kingdom of God). This kingdom will sweep away the evils of this world. As the Jesus movement moved out of Palestine, it took on more aspects of a conversionist movement, with the millennial/revolutionist emphasis left in the background (with the notable exception of the book of Revelation). The late-first-century Matthean community had such close relations with the Jewish community that it had probably been a reformist movement that became a sect (deviance association) in response to the rejection of its program for the reform of Judaism.[65] The community Matthew addressed seems to be giving up its reformist goals and deemphasizing its immediate apocalyptic hopes. It retained the millennarian orientation of the Jesus movement as a cosmic grounding and ultimate goal. Typical of religious movements and sects, the Matthean community and the Jesus movement generally did not achieve relief through palpable divine intervention, but the intellectual and emotional engagement with such hopes gave the community a sense of the future.[66] The Matthean community developed a restorative ethic and self-consciously constructed new social arrangements. Yet, the author of this social vision was still closely connected to Judaism and did not yet involve the development of a new and independent identity.

Thus, the Matthean community is moving toward a new community organization. First, it is still residually reformist and millennarian/revolutionist. Second, it has deemphasized the thaumaturgical. The final commission to the disciples is to preach, teach, and baptize (28:19–20), not exorcise and heal (contrast 10:7–8). Even prophets, though part of the community (10:41; 23:34), are treated with suspicion (7:15; 24:11, 24). Third, Matthew's emphasis on bringing non-Jews into the community (28:19) and on the integrity of his own community (in contrast to the alleged hypocrisy of the leaders of the majority Jewish community) suggests that the community is moving toward a conversionist orientation that seeks to bring a mixed group of people into the community (21:43). For the author, that new community is still Jewish and

---

64. Though most modern Christian groups do not stress miracles, the comforting aspect of thaumaturgy is preserved in various aspects of pastoral practice and care and in the affirmation of personal worth in the face of the modern, impersonal, technological world. See Wilson, *Magic and the Millennium*, 502–3.

65. Though sects can function as political interest groups seeking to change society, they demand such commitment from members that they usually operate as self-selected and intermittently operative communities (ibid., 32). This is because "sects are usually value-oriented movements, seeking total change at cosmic, social or individual level" (ibid., 491).

66. When this happens "they obtain a new dimension of social consciousness and create new forms of social organization" (ibid., 494).

will still adhere to the bulk of Jewish law and custom. The author still has a waning hope that other Jews will join him. However, the orientation of the Matthean community is changing from reformist to isolationist (vis-à-vis Jewish society), and it is beginning to create a new community withdrawn from Judaism and the empire as well.[67]

CONCLUSION

Though many contemporary Christians cannot conceive of Matthew retaining a Jewish identity, Matthew in fact accepts the identity of the Jewish community because it is the overwhelming, real presence in his life world. (For Justin Martyr, less than a century later, Judaism is patently other and at some distance.) Matthew insists on his allegiance to Jesus by carving out a deviant Jewish identity for his sectarian Jewish community. This situation is only transitional. Accepting this deviant status will quickly lead Matthew's community and the communities that subsequently used his Gospel to adopt an integral new identity with many secondary deviance characteristics[68] and a "gentile" Christian interpretation of Matthew's text to go along with it.

Matthew lost the battle for Judaism. Within Christianity his way of following Jesus died out for the most part during the following generation. His Gospel was used by later Christians in order to make sense out of Christianity's relationship to Judaism, but fidelity to Torah in Matthew's sense was nonoperative and so "fulfillment" of Torah was understood in a different way.[69] From the viewpoint of deviance theory, Matthew's community or its successors were engulfed by their deviant role and adopted their deviance as a "master status," that is, as the set of values and characteristics that defined and controlled all other aspects of their lives.[70] Within a short time, because of both rejection by the majority of the Jewish community and the dominance of non-Jewish believers-in-Jesus, most communities like Matthew's became sociologically Christian, that is, they lost their identification with Judaism and became a

67. In general the New Testament writings do not envision the reform of the empire at large. The apocalyptic strains of early Christianity, especially the book of Revelation, envision the destruction of the evil empire, not its reform. This attitude expecting the destruction of the kingdom was transferred to Judaism by later generations of Christians who took over the empire.

68. Secondary deviance is a set of deviant attitudes and behaviors acquired by a person after and because of being labeled deviant for some primary behavior or trait. See Pfuhl, *Deviance Process*, 201ff., 234–38; Pfohl, *Images of Deviance and Social Control*, 291.

69. E. Massaux, *Influence de l'evangile de Matthieu sur la litterature chrétienne avant saint Irénée* (Louvain: Publications Universitaires, 1950), traces the literary influence of Matthew in the second century. For the milieu of Matthew and later developments, see G. N. Stanton, "5 Ezra and Matthean Christianity in the Second Century," *JTS* 28 (1977) 67–83; and Luz, "Disciples in the Gospel according to Matthew," 115–19.

70. Schur, *Politics of Deviance*, 13; and Edwin M. Schur, *Labeling Deviant Behavior* (New York: Harper, 1971) 69–81.

separate, competing group. Late first- and early-second-century Christian and Roman literature testifies to the separate identity of Christians. Yet the lines of demarcation should not be drawn too sharply. The Jewish influence remained so strong that Marcion felt compelled to revise radically Christian symbols and boundaries in the mid-second century, various churches fought over changing the commemoration of Jesus' death and resurrection from 14 Nisan to a Sunday in the late second century, and in the late fourth century John Chrysostom excoriated his gentile Christians for worshiping with Jews in the synagogue.[71]

71. *Logoi kata Ioudaion* (*Homilies Against the Jews* or better *Discourses Against Judaizing Christians*), most recently translated into English by Paul W. Harkins in *The Fathers of the Church*; vol. 68, *Discourses Against Judaizing Christians* (Washington, D.C.: Catholic University Press, 1979).

3

A Responsive Evaluation
of the Social History
of the Matthean Community
in Roman Syria

_____ ROBERT H. GUNDRY

Alan Segal and Anthony Saldarini agree that Matthew's community thought of itself as within the pale of Judaism and that other Jews accepted the community as within that pale despite its deviance.[1] Antoinette Wire's description of Matthew's community as scribal, that is, halakic, tends in the same direction.[2] So also does Pheme Perkin's haggadic description.[3] Both descriptions contain some truth, because especially but not only under the Mark-Q hypothesis, Matthew pares down narratives to make room for teaching[4] yet adds haggadah-like narratives about the nativity, Peter's walking on the water, the coin in the fish's mouth, Judas's suicide, the dream of Pilate's wife, the resurrection of the saints, two earthquakes, the guards at the tomb, and the angel of the Lord's descent from heaven and rolling away the stone from the door of the tomb.[5]

But the imperial, cosmopolitan outlook of William Schoedel's Ignatius[6] militates against a Jewish sectarian definition of Matthew's community. Ignatius does not even seem to know an alternative Jewish Christianity in Antioch or

1. In the end, though, Segal nearly pulls the rug out from under his own thesis by saying, "It is difficult to ascertain whether the Matthean community, in its latest form [as] represented by the Gospel itself, was entirely sure of its Jewish identity" (p. 36).

2. See chap. 5, below.

3. See chap. 6, below.

4. Cf. H. J. Held, "Matthew as Interpreter of the Miracle Stories," *Tradition and Interpretation in Matthew* (London: SCM, 1972) 168–92.

5. Matt 1:18–2:23; 14:28–33; 17:24–27; 27:3–10, 19, 51b–53, 62–66; 28:2, 4, 11–15.

6. See chap. 7, below.

within hailing distance. So whether or not Ignatius knew and used Matthew, as John Meier argues,[7] but all the more if Ignatius did know and use Matthew, how did the church in Antioch or thereabouts travel so far and fast from Jewish sectarianism? The difficulty of answering this question casts doubt on the hypothesis that Matthew's community really was a Jewish sect bent on reforming Judaism or was a Jewish sect just now in the process of coming out of Judaism.[8] But if Matthew's community had already made a clean break with Judaism, regarded itself as a separate entity, and was so regarded by others, it was already on its way to becoming the Ignatian community. Matthew's great emphasis on evangelizing all the nations[9] fits such a separation. So also his urban thinking[10] leads toward Ignatius's urban thinking.

But what should we say to the arguments that Matthew's community was still only a Jewish sect? The argument that Matthew's anti-Pharisaism puts his community in an intramural debate with post-70 Judaism overlooks his special use of the Sadducees,[11] who left no heirs in post-70 Judaism and against whom the Matthean community could not carry on any kind of debate, much less an intramural one, especially not up in Syria or Galilee, far from the Sadducean base of power in Jerusalem and the temple, now destroyed. To say that Matthew's use of ἐθνικός, "Gentile," as a term of disapprobation[12] implies his community's membership in Judaism overlooks his use of "Jews" in 28:15 as a party different from his community. The anarthrousness of the noun (not "*the* Jews," but "Jews") stresses qualitative difference. Alone, Matthew's multiplication of "their synagogues"[13] might be taken as an intramural epithet. But combined with the use of "Jews" as a third party, the phrase seems to mean Jewish synagogues over against the church, which includes Jews without being Jewish.

Matthew's use of ἐκκλησία[14] ["church"] can hardly be taken in a Jewish, Septuagintal sense; for Paul had long since used the term in a differentiatingly Christian sense, and he himself, as well as the book of Acts, tells of his ministry in Antioch.[15] So his usage must have been known there and roundabout. Moreover, not only does Matt 21:43 give the kingdom to a nation

7. See chap. 8, below.

8. Saldarini describes as "fading" Matthew's hope that he would prevail and make his program normative for the whole Jewish community. This description gives some ground to a definition of Matthew's community as not Jewish sectarian.

9. See esp. Matt 28:19–20.

10. G. D. Kilpatrick, *The Origins of the Gospel according to St. Matthew* (Oxford: Clarendon, 1946, 1959) 124–25.

11. Matt 3:7; 6:1, 6, 11, 12; 22:23 par., 34.

12. Matt 5:47; 6:7; 18:17.

13. Matt 4:23; 9:35; 10:17; 12:9; 13:54; cf. 23:34. Only 4:23 has a synoptic parallel.

14. Matt 16:18; 18:17 (bis).

15. Gal 2:11–14 (cf. 1:22); Acts 11:19–30; 12:25–13:3; 14:26–15:2, 30–35; 18:22–23.

(ἔθνος) producing its fruits; Matt 1:21 identifies this nation as Jesus' people
(λαός). He will save them from their sins. They are the ones who call his name
Immanuel—"they," as distinguished from all known textual traditions of Isa
7:14, quoted in Matt 1:23. So we have not just a reforming sect within the
people of God, Israel, or a sect barely in the process of losing its reformative
spirit, but a distinctly new people whose church-assembly differs from the
synagogue-gatherings of Jews. Just as this people belong to Jesus, so also does
the church ("*his* people"), which the people are ("I will build *my* church," Matt
16:18).[16]

Not only are this people or church set over against the synagogues of
Jews; this people or church do not enjoy "continued acceptance ... within
Judaism" (as Segal says they do). Compared with Mark and Luke, Matthew has
intensified the element of persecution,[17] including persecution in synagogues
and Jewish courts;[18] and Matthew says in 23:13 not only that the scribes and
Pharisees do not themselves enter the kingdom but also that they keep others
from entering. So Matthew's community and non-Christian Jews reject each
other. They are on the outs. Consequently a continuing mission to the Jews
aims solely at conversion, not at all toward reformation.

Non-Christian Jews and the community of Matthew might well be on
the outs. His Jesus is Immanuel, "God with us" (1:23); and this Jesus says to his
disciples, "I am with you always, to the end of the age" (28:20). He both
sandwiches himself as the Son between the Father and the Holy Spirit in the
great commission (28:19) and replaces the "God" of "Immanuel" with his own
ever-present "I" (28:20). One might think to find an analogy in the Jewish doctrine of the two powers in heaven (so Segal), but here in Matthew is a recent
historical figure quoted as saying while he was on earth that he would stay with
his disciples here, not in heaven, and do so in accordance with the divine title
with which his people call him (see 18:20, too). This high Christology of
Matthew and its fundamental difference from anything known to Judaism,
including the two powers doctrine, is almost bound to have fixed a great gulf
between Matthew's community and Judaism. Segal and Saldarini have soft-
pedaled that difference (though credit goes to Saldarini for describing the
rising status of Jesus as "a key change").

Segal and Saldarini have also soft-pedaled the didactic difference
between Matthew's Jesus and teachers in Judaism. Matthew 28:20 enjoins

16. Against Saldarini's statement that Matthew "has no name for his group."
17. Cf. R. H. Gundry, *Matthew: A Commentary on His Literary and Theological Art*
(Grand Rapids: W. B. Eerdmans, 1982) 649 s.v. "Flight from persecution," against Segal's dependence on Douglas R. A. Hare, *The Theme of Jewish Persecution of Christians in the Gospel
according to St. Matthew* (SNTSMS 6; Cambridge: Cambridge University Press, 1967), who
underplays the element of actual persecution.
18. Matt 10:17, 23.

obedience to all Jesus' commandments, not to the Torah. Granted, Jesus interprets the Torah in giving his own commandments (5:17–48). But the antithetical manner in which his interpretation replaces the Torah—and it is the quoted
and paraphrased Torah itself, not other Jewish teachers' interpretations of it,[19]
which his interpretation replaces—this antithetical manner exceeds even the
first-person style in which the temple scroll of a deviant Jewish sect repromul-
gates the Torah. Thus the antithetical manner puts distance between
Matthew's community and anything recognizably Judaistic, unless one wants to
stretch "Judaistic" well beyond normal usage.

At the same time that the Matthean Torah looks more different from
Judaism than Segal and Saldarini have allowed, it also looks more Pauline than
they have recognized. We have been told that Matthew interprets the Torah
according to the love commandment and fights Paulinism as well as Pharisaism.
But in his most anti-Judaistic letter, Paul too interprets the law as fulfilled in
that commandment (Gal 5:14; cf. Rom 13:8, 10). This same Paul quotes and
paraphrases other parts of the Torah as well—much of the Decalogue, for
example[20]—in giving instructions to largely gentile Christians, and does not
engage in provocatively antithetical interpretation of the Torah after Matthew's
manner, but diplomatically describes the Torah as holy and just and good and
even spiritual (Rom 7:12, 14), and argues Matthew-like that he does not abro-
gate it but establishes it (Rom 3:31). Differences remain, of course; but if we
take all the evidence into account, not just Paul's slogan "not under law but
under grace" (Rom 6:14), he and Matthew stand closer together than sometimes thought.

Segal's association of Matthew with Peter as opposed to Paul also runs
into problems. Not only does Matthew alone mention Peter's sinking and
Jesus' calling him "little faith" (14:30–31). Matthew is the only one to bring in
Judas's suicide and butt it up against Peter's denials (26:69–27:10), a parallel
made the more unhappy for Peter by the adverb "bitterly," which describes his
weeping in 26:75 and which Mark 14:72 does not have (though Luke 22:62
does). Matthew also does not contain the command that the women tell Peter
about the resurrection (as in Mark 16:7) or the reference to an appearance by
the risen Jesus to Peter (as in Luke 24:34 and 1 Cor 15:5). Would a Gospel
growing out of a Petrine sociological compromise allow Peter to start so grandly
and fade out so miserably?

But a compromise between Judaism at large and Christian Judaism is
not what Matthew aims to strike. In the first place, an evangelist who seeks
such a middle course is unlikely to put such huge emphasis as Matthew does on

19. Gundry, *Matthew*, 83–84, 87, 89–90, 91–92, 94, 96–97.
20. Rom 7:7; 13:9.

discipling all the nations.[21] Discipling them would only add to the sociological problem he is supposedly trying to solve. Nor does discipling all the nations look like a program for reforming Judaism. The more troublesome sociological problem of Matthew's community does not have to do with the relation of a Christian Judaism to the rest of Judaism, but with relations inside Matthew's community between tares and wheat, bad fish and good, true disciples and false. With the partial and passing exception of a response by Michael White,[22] we are hearing nothing at this conference about Matthew's community as a large and mixed body (as opposed to "a fragile minority," Saldarini), about the desire to weed out the tares, about the counterdemand for tolerance till the judgment, about the prohibition of making individual judgments against the genuineness of a fellow disciple, about the necessity on occasion of collective discipline, about the growing coldness of love on the part of the many, about intramural betrayal and hatred in addition to betrayal by others and hatred by all the nations, about the expansive treatment of much-needed mutual forgiveness, about the danger of being thrown out from the wedding feast even though you are a "friend" (ἑταῖρε), like Judas, whom Matthew's Jesus ironically calls his friend.[23] Surely here is grist for the sociological mill. But we are missing it. We are too fixated on the relation of Matthew's community to Judaism.

And it is exactly the interior features of Matthew's community that pose problems for Rodney Stark's paper, too.[24] Who would want to join a community not only under persecution but also at war with itself and needing a hard kick in the seat of the pants with the moral rigorism of Matthew's Gospel? Mark 10:30 promises houses, brothers, sisters, mothers, children, and fields along with persecutions right now, in this age, as well as eternal life in the age to come; but the severity of persecution and the intramural problems brought on by it in Matthew's community forestall such a this-worldly promise in the parallel Matt 19:29, which therefore limits itself to the by-and-by. Even the traveling preachers in Matthew's community need stiffer rules than in Mark or Luke. They are not to acquire money, whereas in Mark and Luke they are not to take any along. In Matthew's community, they appear to have been acquiring from

21. The combination of this emphasis and Jewishness fits the description in Acts 11:19–26; 13:1–3; and passim of the church in Syrian Antioch better than it fits a Galilean church whose shape is shrouded in mystery. The emphasis on discipling all the nations also puts a roadblock in the way of Saldarini's suggestion that as a Jewish sect Matthew's community took circumcision for granted. The greater the emphasis on bringing Gentiles into Judaism, the greater the need to emphasize circumcision—or to defend a nonrequirement of circumcision. The absence of circumcision from Matthew therefore combines with the emphasis on discipling all the nations to disfavor Jewish sectarianism.

22. See chap. 11, below.

23. Matt 5:21–26; 6:14–15; 7:1–6; 13:24–30, 36–43, 47–50; 18:15–18, 21–35; 22:11–14; 24:10, 12; 25:1–13; 26:50.

24. See chap. 9, below.

their audiences gold as well as copper and silver, which appear in Mark and Luke, respectively.[25]

Only some of Matthew's community have risked their own safety by feeding, giving drink to, clothing, entertaining, and visiting the sick and imprisoned fugitives from persecution, those who flee from one city of Israel to another, whom Jesus calls the least of his brothers (10:23, 40–42; 25:31–46). These little ones appear not to be marginal Christians, sinning Christians, as Wire suggests,[26] but Christians suffering the results of persecution and liable to be caused to sin, that is, to apostatize under persecution, if their fellow professing Christians do not help them, as some (the goats) are failing to do though some (the sheep) are helping. Matthew's community is a sociological shambles. No wonder he wants them to go disciple all the nations. At least they will stay out of each other's hair.

25. Cf. Matt 10:9 with Mark 6:8; Luke 9:3.
26. See chap. 5, below.

4

The Greek Political Topos
περὶ νόμων and
Matthew 5:17, 19, and 16:19

DAVID L. BALCH

"Do not think that I have come to abolish (καταλῦσαι) the law or the prophets; I have come not to abolish but to fulfill" (Matt 5:17). First, I observe that the verb translated "abolish" is a key term in Greek political discussions of a state's or a people's constitution and laws. The same root occurs in another crucial verse later in the Gospel: "I will give you [Peter] the keys of the kingdom of heaven, and whatever you bind on earth will be bound (δεδεμένον) in heaven, and whatever you loose on earth will be loosed (λελυμένον) in heaven" (Matt 16:19). It is a problem that δέω, the verb paired in this second verse with λύω, is not its usual twin; the typical opposite of "abolishing" is "guarding" (φυλάσσω). So, second, I observe that three verbs belong to the same semantic domain: δέω, δεσμε(ύ)ω, and φυλάσσω.[1] One can see the relationship between these roots in various biblical texts, for example, all three of them in Isa 42:7 (LXX), "I have given you as a covenant to the people, a light to the nations, to open the eyes that are blind, to bring out the prisoners from the dungeon (ἐκ δεσμῶν δεδεμένους), from the prison (ἐξ οἴκου φυλακῆς) those who sit in darkness." The two verbs δέω and δεσμεύω refer to persons or things bound/in chains, φυλάσσω to "guarding" persons or things bound/in chains. And all

---

1. Johannes P. Louw, Eugene A. Nida et al., *Greek-English Lexicon of the New Testament Based on Semantic Domains* (New York: United Bible Societies, 1988) vol. 1, para. 18B, 37C, 37H, 37I, 37J. I am grateful to Ronald F. Hock and Daryl D. Schmidt for helpful conversations while I was puzzling about the relationship between these verbs. The Thesaurus Linguae Graecae has been indispensable for tracing aspects of the history of the topos, and I am thankful to Dean Leo G. Perdue of Brite Divinity School/Texas Christian University for facilitating use of the TLG at TCU.

three belong to Matthean legal vocabulary. Besides 16:19 quoted above, note that when Jesus tells the rich young man to keep the commandments and lists some from the Decalogue, he replies, "I have kept/guarded (ἐφύλαξα) all these . . ." (19:20). Later, Jesus advises his disciples to do whatever the scribes and Pharisees teach, although they do not practice. "They tie up (δεσμεύου- σιν) heavy burdens hard to bear . . . , but they themselves are unwilling to lift a finger to move them" (23:4). The second observation, that these three verbs are closely related, makes it possible to trace the use of the metaphor of "bind- ing, tying up, or enchaining" in Greek legal discussions. These two observa- tions are fundamental to the following argument, which traces the meaning of these verbs in two philosophers, Plato and the Stoic preacher Dio Chrysostom, and in two historians, Dionysius of Halicarnassus and Josephus, before inter- preting the meaning of the verbs for 2 Maccabees and Matthew.

Plato was preceded by Protagoras in the use of this language; he spoke of "bonds of friendship that bring people together" (δεσμοὶ φιλίας συναγωγοί; Pl. *Protag.* 322C).[2] Similarly, while speaking of the nurture and education of children, Plato mentions "unwritten laws," which are called "ancestral cus- toms" (*Laws* 7.793B). These

> act as bonds (δεσμοί) in every constitution, forming a link between all its laws (both those already enacted in writing and those still to be enacted). . . . Bearing this in mind, Clinias, we must clamp [bind] together (ξυνδεῖν) this State of yours, which is a new one, by every possible means, omitting nothing great or small (μέγα μήτε σμικρόν)[3] in the way of laws, customs and institutions; for it is by all such means that a State is clamped [bound] together (ξυνδεῖται), and neither kind of law is permanent without the other." (793CD, trans. Bury in LCL)[4]

With the exception of the prepositional prefix, this is precisely the verb of Matt 16:19, "whatever you bind on earth . . ."

These verbs occur in the context of an extensive philosophical-political discussion concerning a people's constitution and laws.[5] In Plato's *Laws*, the Athenian asks about abolishing a kingdom (βασιλεία καταλύεται), for example, the one formed by Argos, Messene, and Lacedaemon. They swore to one another, according to laws binding (ἔθεντο) on all, that the rulers would not become more severe and that the people would not abolish (καταλύσειν) the monarchy (3.683E–684A). The Athenian declares that

2. Heinrich Ryffel, ΜΕΤΑΒΟΛΗ ΠΟΛΙΤΕΙΩΝ: *Der Wandel der Staatsverfassungen* (Noctes Romanae 2; Bern: Paul Haupt, 1949) 30–31.
    3. Cf. Matt 5:18: ". . . not one letter, not one stroke of a letter, will pass from the law . . ."
    4. Plato wrote the *Laws* not long before his death in 347 B.C.E.
    5. See Ryffel, ΜΕΤΑΒΟΛΗ ΠΟΛΙΤΕΙΩΝ, chap. 3 on Pl. *Laws*, books 3–4 and chap. 4 on Arist. *Pol.* 5.

the part of the soul that feels pain and pleasure corresponds to the mass of the populace in the State. So whenever this part opposes what are by nature the ruling principles—knowledge, opinion, or reason,—this condition I call folly (ἄνοια), whether it be in a State, when the masses disobey the rulers and the laws, or in an individual, when the noble elements of reason existing in the soul produce no good effect. (3.689B)

Still appealing to a specific case, the Athenian compares the Persian Empire with Attic civic polity. Athenians had an ancient constitution with "Reverence ... causing us to live as the willing slaves of the existing laws" (αἰδώς, δι ἥν δου-λεύοντες τοῖς τότε νόμοις ζῆν ἠθέλομεν; 3.698b; cf. 3.700A, D). When the Persians approached Greece,

> this created in them a state of friendliness one towards another—both in fear which then possessed them, and that begotten of the past, which they had acquired by their subjection (δουλεύειν) to the former laws. . . . a man must be subject to this if he is to be good (though the coward is unfettered and un-affrighted by it). (3.699C)

Magistrates are "ministers" of the laws, and

> the salvation or ruin for a state hangs upon nothing so much as this. For wher-ever in a State the law is subservient and impotent, over that State I see ruin impending; but wherever the law is lord over the magistrates, and the magis-trates are servants to the law (δοῦλοι τοῦ νόμου), there I descry salvation and all the blessings that the gods bestow on States. (4.715CD)

Dio Chrysostom, a Stoic preacher in the time of Matthew and Josephus, wrote essays "on law" (*Or.* 75[58] and "on custom" (*Or.* 76[59])[6] which show how Greeks interpreted these ideas *both negatively and positively.* Early Stoics valued natural law, which could be realized only to a limited extent in the laws of any city or people.[7] Chrysippus condemned the laws of all cities, a thought reflected in Dio Chrysostom's seventy-fifth *Oration.* Negatively, civic laws are merely human inventions, while (natural) customs are accepted by all.

> We know of many laws which have been repealed by those who made them, because they judged them to be bad (πονηρούς); but no one could readily point to a custom which had been dissolved (λελυμένον). . . . Besides, while laws are

6. Trans. Crosby in LCL. First I list the discourse number as given in the LCL edition, then in brackets [ ] the discourse number according to the critical edition by J. de [H. von] Arnim, *Dionis Prusaensis,* 2 vols. (Berlin: Weidmann, 1893; reprint, 1962). Hans von Arnim, *Leben und Werke des Dio von Prusa* (Berlin: Weidmann, 1898) 155–58 places *Or.* 75 and 76 in Dio's early, Sophistic period before his exile in 83 (cf. pp. 138–39, 147). For other texts belonging to this topos, see the Stobaean chapter 4.2, περὶ νόμων καὶ ἔθων, in Stobaeus, *Anthologium* (ed. C. Wachsmuth and O. Hense; Berlin: Weidmann, 1958) 4.115–83.

7. Andrew Erskine, *The Hellenistic Stoa: Political Thought and Action* (Ithaca, N.Y.: Cor-nell University Press, 1990) 113, 115, 152.

preserved (φυλάττονται) on tablets of wood or of stone, each custom is
preserved within our own hearts. . . .[8]
And, speaking generally, while one might say that the laws create a polity of
slaves [cf. Plato], our customs, on the contrary, create a polity of free men.
(76.2, 3, 4, trans. Crosby in LCL)

In a discourse "on freedom" (Or. 80[63]),[9] Dio claims that the philosopher is
obedient to the ordinances of Zeus rather than to some imperfect, earthly law-
giver, and half the essay contrasts being free with being "bound" by human laws
(80.7–14). Even Solon made bad laws (πονηροὺς ἔγραφε νόμους; 80.4); but
people abandon the law of nature and "guard" statute books and slabs of stone
(80.5)! However, about the mid-second century B.C.E., Stoics changed and
attempted to tie justice more closely to the laws of the city,[10] a positive
(Roman) evaluation of law reflected in Dio's seventy-sixth Oration :

> Those who strictly observe (φυλάττονες) the law have firm hold on safety; while
> those who transgress it destroy first of all themselves and then their fellows too,
> providing them with an example and pattern of lawlessness (ἀνομίας) and
> violence. . . . A city cannot be saved if the law has been destroyed (λυθέντος).
> (75.1, 10)[11]

In his later Roman Stoic stage, Dio addresses the emperor Trajan in Rome concerning "kingship," concluding his discourse with precisely this contrast: Heracles abolishes (κατέλυε) the power of tyrants, but Trajan has him as a helper
and protector (φύλαξ) of his government (Or. 1.84).[12] I conclude that these
soundings in the philosophers Plato and Dio show that this constitutional
language enjoyed widespread use.[13]

8. Cf. 2 Cor 3:3, 6–7 and Philo Spec. leg. 4.149–50.

9. C. P. Jones, The Roman World of Dio Chrysostom (Cambridge: Harvard University
Press, 1978) 135, suggests a date of ca. 83 C.E. for Or. 80.

10. Erskine, Hellenistic Stoa, 152–53.

11. Cf. Herodotus 3.82 (trans. Godley in LCL): "I hold therefore, that as the rule of one
man gave us freedom, so that rule we should preserve; and, moreover, that we should not repeal
(λύειν) the good laws of our fathers; that were ill done." Cf. Xenophon Hellenica 2.3.32, cited by
Ryffel, ΜΕΤΑΒΟΛΗ ΠΟΛΙΤΕΙΩΝ, 50.

12. Anthony R. R. Sheppard, "Dio Chrysostom: The Bithynian Years," L'Antiquité Clas-
sique 53 (1984) 157–73, at p. 172 assigns Or. 1 to 99/100 C.E.

13. Ronald F. Hock writes (letter dated Dec. 29, 1990): "A few remarks about your issue
and the rhetorical tradition: I looked over the relevant sections of a number of rhetorical treatments of an exercise called 'proposal of a law.' (I will cite Theon [1st c. A.D.], Hermogenes [late
2nd], Nicolaus [5th], Doxapatres [late 11th], and the P-scholia [10th?].) This exercise is the last of
fourteen compositional exercises which were called progymnasmata. As the fourteenth it not only
is the most complex compositionally, but also suggests the goal of education to be the ability to
propose (or oppose) a law for the city. . . . I never found the word καταλύειν or δεσμεῖν or
φυλάσσειν. . . . You are probably right in saying that Matthew is drawing upon philosophical traditions. Still, let me give you some references. . . . Theon uses τίθημι instead of "binding" (1.254,
5, C. Walz, Rhetores Graeci [1932–36]). Other terms for introducing or making a law are γράφειν
(Hermogenes Progymnasma 12 [p. 26, 16, H. Rabe, Rhetores Graeci (1926)]); Doxapatres, 2.553,
25; 558; 12 Walz; and P-scholia, 2.669, 2 Walz) and εἰσφέρειν (Doxapatres, 2.553, 23–24). Words
for "abolishing" include λύειν (Doxapatres, 2.553, 5–6, 23–24, 25; 558, 6 Walz) and ἀναιρεθῆναι

Of particular interest for the interpretation of Matthew, however, is the usage by historians. Dionysius of Halicarnassus,[14] a historian who wrote during Augustus's reign, employs these idealistic ideas in his history, but utopian conceptions do not always correspond to the crises, changes, and developments of a people's or a city's history. The verb "abolish" is used to describe the most fundamental revolution in Roman history, the abolishing of the Roman monarchy in favor of a dual consulship (see Dion. Hal. *Ant. Rom.* 1.8.2; also 2.27.3; 5.1.1). Dionysius tells the story of the ousting of the ancestral king Lucius Tarquinius in *Ant. Rom.* 4.41–85. Among Tarquinius's many corrupt actions were his abolition of the original form of taxation, in order to charge the poor and the rich the same, and his prohibition of assemblies, lest large numbers meet for the abolition (κατάλυσις) of his power (4.43.2). The prime mover in the "abolition" of this tyranny was Lucius Junius Brutus (4.67.4; cf. 5.7.4). One of Brutus's speeches during these events addresses the question concerning the form of government to establish as they "abolish" the kingship (4.72.1). Paradoxically(!), it is asserted that, unlike Tarquinius, Brutus "observes/guards" (φυλάττων) the laws and customs (5.8.5).

The same language was used not only of the state, but also of marriage. Dionysius writes of rituals in the original Roman constitution legislated by Romulus, the sharing of which "forged the compelling bond of an indissoluble union (εἰς σύνδεσμον δ' ἀναγκαῖον οἰκειότητος ἔφερεν ἀδιαλύτου), and there was nothing that could annul these marriages" (*Ant. Rom.* 2.25.3, trans. Cary in LCL; compare Arist. *Eth. Nic.* 8.1162A 27–28). Dionysius (2.25.7) then observes that the first Roman to divorce (ἀπολῦσαι) his wife was ever afterward hated by the Roman people. Again, the idea of a "bond" is used positively and opposed to "loosing."[15]

There are many examples of this usage: an important civic disturbance in Roman life occurred in the consulship of Titus Romilius and Gaius Veturius,

(Doxapatres, 2.553, 29 Walz). I should note that you have pairs τίθημι/λύω (Doxapatres, 2.553, 5–6 Walz) and εἰσφέρω/λύω (Doxapatres, 2.553, 23–24 Walz). Lastly, note that Nicolaus differentiates between ψήφισμα and νόμος in the sense that the former is enacted for a time but the latter forever (p. 77, 8–11, J. Felten, *Rhetores Graeci* [1913]). This distinction would support the notion in your sources that 'law' is not to be changed."

14. On Dionysius, see Clemence Schultze, "Dionysius of Halicarnassus and His Audience," *Past Perspectives: Studies in Greek and Roman Historical Writing* (ed. I. S. Moxon, J. D. Smart, and A. J. Woodman; Cambridge: Cambridge University Press, 1986) 121–41. See also my preliminary article comparing the genre of Dion. Hal. *Ant. Rom.* and Luke-Acts, "The Genre of Luke-Acts: Individual Biography, Adventure Novel, or Political History?" *Southwestern Journal of Theology* 33/1 (1990) 5–19. Dionysius began writing the twenty volumes of his *Ant. Rom.* in Augustan Rome in 7 B.C.E., a work which became the model a century later for Josephus's twenty-volume *AJ*.

15. Cf. the use of terms in Dion. Hal. *Ant. Rom.* 7.44.1: Marcius is accused of trying to dissolve/abolish (καταλύειν) the unalterable compact of unity between plebeians and the senate, which is secured by bonds (δεσμοί) unlawful to dissolve.

resulting in both consuls being condemned and punished (narrated in Dion. Hal. *Ant. Rom.* 10.33 and 49). Later, Titus Romilius gave a speech advising the senate to send ambassadors to Greek cities in Italy and Athens asking for their best laws, ones suited to the Roman way of life, so that the senate might then appoint lawgivers and restructure the government (10.51). As the story goes, during the following year (451 B.C.E.) Rome was afflicted with a pestilence more severe than any in the three hundred years since the state was founded. Most of the slaves and half the citizens died, since their servants and friends did not supply them with necessities (10.53.1). During this period many innovations and unseemly customs were introduced into the worship of the gods; but when the gods had no mercy, even these rites were abandoned (10.53.5–6).[16] Meanwhile, the ambassadors returned from Greece and the Greek cities in Italy, but the consuls were unwilling for the aristocracy to be abolished (κατα-λῦσαι). Appius Claudius, one of the next consuls, however, wanted to establish laws for the fatherland (10.54.7). Despite the advice of some to guard the customs of their ancestors (πατρίους φυλάττειν ἐθισμούς; 10.55.3), Appius advised that ten persons be appointed and rule as the two consuls had done previously, and that all other magistracies be abolished (καταλύσθαι; 10.55.4) as long as the decemvirs held office. The offices of tribunes, aediles, quaestors, and other traditional ones were indeed abolished (κατελύθησαν; 10.56.2), and the lawmakers established a different form of government (10.57.1). When the people saw that these ten no longer preserved/guarded (φυλάττοντας) the same democratic and modest form of government (10.59.4), in the cause of liberty the Romans abolished (καταλύουσι) the decemvirate (11.1.1). In the course of this debate, Valerius Potitus addresses the "tyrant" Appius: "If you maintain (φυλάττῃς) your usual arrogance toward everybody, what tribunes shall I call upon to assist me? For this relief to oppressed citizens has been abolished (καταλέλυται) by you decemvirs . . ." (11.4.6).[17]

In an excursus on the subject,[18] Dionysius asserts that he is recording "time-honoured customs, laws and institutions which they [Romans] preserve [guard] down to my time just as they received them from their ancestors" (*Ant. Rom.* 7.70.2). The established rituals for worship of the gods "both the Greeks and barbarian world have preserved [guarded] for the greatest length of time and have never thought fit to make any innovation (καινοτομεῖν) in them, being restrained from doing so by their fear of the divine anger" (*Ant. Rom.*

---

16. See chap. 9, below, Rodney Stark.

17. Passages in Dionysius and other Greek authors who employ this terminology are quoted by Eusebius *Preparation for the Gospel* 2.8; 4.16.

18. Note that in the conclusion to book 1, in his most apologetic chapter, Dionysius refers (*Ant. Rom.* 1.90.2) to the later excursus (7.70–73) proving that the Romans have guarded their ancient traditions, a cross-reference which indicates how important the argument was to him.

7.70.3). For example, Dionysius discusses the custom of competing naked in athletic contests and concludes: "Thus it is plain that the Romans, who preserve [guard] this ancient Greek custom to this day, did not learn it from us [Greeks] afterwards nor even change it in the course of time, as we have done" (*Ant. Rom.* 7.72.4).

Josephus, the Jewish historian, employs the same language. The Maccabean queen Alexandra, he writes, allowed the Pharisees too much influence. They took advantage of her and "became the real administrators of the state, at liberty to banish and to recall, to loose and to bind (λύειν τε καὶ δεσμεῖν), whom they would. In short, the enjoyments of royal authority were theirs . . ." (*BJ* 1.111, trans. Thackeray in LCL).[19]

In his later work, *Jewish Antiquities,* Josephus narrates that Moses delivers the constitution to Israel (*AJ* 3.83–286) and then he gives a second, ordered summary of it (*AJ* 4.196–319). This is their legal constitution in peacetime: "May there never come a time for amending (καινίσει) aught therein and establishing the contrary (τὸ ἐναντίον μεταβαλεῖ) in its place" (4.292, trans. Thackeray in LCL). In times of crisis and war, "May neither foreigner invade it [this land] . . . whereby ye shall be led to actions contrary to those of your own fathers and destroy the institutions which they established: and may you continue to observe laws which God has approved as good and now delivers to you!" (4.294). Moses calls a final assembly, which the women and children and even the slaves are required to attend, making them swear to the observance/guarding (φυλακή) of the laws; nothing is more important than the observance of these laws (4.309). If any of their blood relations would try to confound and abolish (καταλύειν) the constitution and laws, individuals and the nation should rise in their defense (4.310). Later, as Josephus retells stories in the biblical book of Judges, he writes:

> But the state of the Israelites went from bad to worse through their loss of aptitude for toil and their neglect of the Divinity. For, having once *parted from the ordered course of their constitution,* they drifted into living in accordance with their own pleasure and caprice, and thus became filled with the vices (ἀναπίμ-πλασθαι κακῶν) current among the Canaanites. So God was wroth with them. . . . (*AJ* 5.179–80, adapted; emphasis mine. Cf. 5.113, trans. Thackeray and Marcus in LCL)

The people even demand that the last judge, Samuel, appoint for them a king, an outrage on the "former [aristocratic] constitution" (6.35–36). He warns them against rushing into this "change" (μεταβολή; 6.39). The government

---

19. Cited by J. Andrew Overman, *Matthew's Gospel and Formative Judaism: The Social World of the Matthean Community* (Minneapolis: Fortress, 1990) 13, 105, as a parallel to Matt 16:19. However, it is incorrect that the terms in *War* 1.111 and Matt 16:19 are the "same," and Josephus writes of binding and loosing persons, a better parallel to Matt 18:18 than to 16:19.

then fell from aristocracy to monarchy (6.83). Samuel accuses the people of great impiety, of being traitors to God's worship and religion (6.88, 90); nevertheless, Josephus does not write that Moses' constitution has been "abolished." The frightened people pray that God might forgive and pardon them (6.92–93). The story of King Saul follows immediately, stressing the consequences he experienced for not following the commands of Moses (6.133, 137, 141, 144, 149, 151).

The thought of *AJ* 5.179–80 (quoted above) is the polar opposite of Matt 5:17, 20. Josephus observes that when a people departs from their constitution, they are "filled/contaminated" with vices; Matthew asserts that when the laws are not abolished, the people are "filled" with "righteousness."

In both Dionysius and Josephus, one from Greece and the other from Palestine, both writing in Rome a century apart, there is the utopian idea that the founder's constitution, whether that of Romulus or Moses, was instituted for the entire history of their people, and that it is impious and unjust to change it. Nevertheless, as the narrative unfolds, both writers must deal with the historical experience that fundamental change has indeed occurred. Dionysius explains this by claiming that the rulers became corrupt and that what is perceived as a new government really follows Romulus's original constitution. Lucius Junius Brutus, who proposes the change from monarchy to dual consulship, also suggests the appointment of a "king of sacred rites" (Dion. Hal. *Ant. Rom.* 4.74.4). Although they decide not to establish the kingship again, the two annual magistrates "hold the royal power" and "perform the functions which had belonged to the kings" (4.84.4, 5). Rome develops without a break in continuity.[20]

This claim is made not only of Romulus and Moses, but also of Isis: "On the stele of Isis it runs: 'I am Isis, the Queen of every land, she who was instructed of Hermes, and whatsoever laws I have established (ἐνομοθέτησα), these can no man make void" (λῦσαι; Diodorus of Sicily, *Library of History* 1.27.4; trans. Oldfather in LCL).

Further, as Segal, Saldarini, and White all observe in their essays in this volume, Matthew reflects a conflict over leadership in the Jewish community. Similarly, Dionysius's excursus in *Ant. Rom.* 7, which offers proof that the Romans have not abolished but have guarded their ancient customs and laws, is written in the context of his argument attempting to persuade his fellow Greeks that the Romans justly rule the world. Romans are not barbarians but an ancient people who have guarded Romulus's constitution (Dion. Hal. *Ant. Rom.* 1.4–5, 89–90). The logic is that those who guard their ancient customs

20. On development and change in Roman history, cf. the extraordinary Table of Claudius, discussed by Arnaldo Momigliano, *Claudius: The Emperor and His Achievement* (Westport, Conn.: Greenwood, 1981) 6ff., esp. 11–19, a reference I owe to Edwin Judge.

and laws are the legitimate rulers who avoid divine wrath and are favored by divine fortune/providence. Therefore, Greek political thought concerning law argued positively that citizens should be "slaves" of the constitution, should be "bound/chained" by its laws, and that a people should "guard/preserve" the customs of the fathers "by which they [Romans] attain to so great prosperity" (Dion. Hal. *Ant. Rom.* 7.70.5; cf. 2.3.6).

On the other hand, as documented above, historians found this utopian, idealistic conception difficult. There is discontinuity in history, with the result that crucial aspects of Romulus's or Moses' constitution and laws had indeed been "changed" (Josephus) or "abolished" (Dionysius). This tension is built into Greco-Roman and Hellenistic-Jewish narratives about their past, for example, in the stories of the abolition of the tyranny of King Lucius Tarquinius by Lucius Junius Brutus in Dion. Hal. *Ant. Rom.* 4, and the change of the Mosaic, aristocratic constitution into a monarchical one in Joseph. *AJ* 6.

Matthew 5:17, just as a Hellenistic-Jewish audience would expect, makes the claim that Moses' law has not been "abolished," but in the same chapter, the antitheses do change some of them.[21] Dionysius, Josephus, and Matthew faced a similar dilemma. Dionysius's whole work consistently claims that the Romans have kept the customs of the fathers, but in *Ant. Rom.* 4, he must narrate a revolution that rejected kingship and substituted dual consulship in Rome. Josephus narrates Moses' demand that the laws not be abolished, but then describes how the people established kingship, a non- or even anti-Mosaic institution. Matthew, too, paradoxically both claims that the law has not been abolished, and immediately describes changes.[22]

Matthew 16:19 is even more amazing.[23] Peter, the one who "says and hears in an exemplary way for all disciples what every disciple could say and

21. See John Meier, *Law and History in Matthew's Gospel* (Rome: Biblical Institute, 1976).

22. Similarly, Dio Chrys. *Or.* 12[11] extensively quotes the earlier Stoic Posidonius, who argued that the divine has no "form," and therefore, that images of gods and goddesses should not be made. Dio himself *reverses* this and argues that images reveal the nature of the gods. Arguing against the earlier opinion of Posidonius in his own philosophical school, Dio still claims to be "guarding" the tradition (*Or.* 12.85)! See David L. Balch, "The Areopagus Speech: An Appeal to the Stoic Historian Posidonius against Later Stoics and the Epicureans," *Greeks, Romans, and Christians: Essays in Honor of Abraham J. Malherbe* (ed. David L. Balch, Everett Ferguson, and Wayne A. Meeks; Minneapolis: Fortress, 1990) 52–79, esp. 69–72.

23. On its context within the Gospel see John P. Meier, *The Vision of Matthew: Christ, Church and Morality in the First Gospel* (New York: Paulist, 1979) 106–21. Very briefly, Matt 15:1–20 treats the halachic question of purity, concluding in 15:11 that "nothing which goes into the mouth makes a person unclean," a conclusion which the author clarifies with the following story (15:21–28) of a[n unclean] Canaanite woman whose faith is accepted. The halacha which one loosens or binds is related to the persons one includes or excludes. Then in 16:5–12, which introduces the pericope that includes 16:19, Jesus warns the disciples against the yeast of the Pharisees and Sadducees, that is, their "teaching" (διδαχή; 16:12; cf. 23:3–4 and 8). In this context Matt 16:19 focuses more on the halacha/the teaching which is bound or loosened, 18:19 more on the persons included or excluded, although the two are closely related.

hear,"[24] is given the power "to bind and to loose" by Jesus. This is hardly typical either of Greco-Roman or of Jewish legislators with respect to the "laws of the fathers." It forms a striking contrast to both Dionysius's assertion that Greeks and barbarians have guarded their ancient laws and made no innovations and Josephus's story of Moses promulgating divine law which is not to be abolished. Dionysius stresses the people's "fear of divine anger" if they were to make changes (*Ant. Rom.* 7.70.3). Josephus records Samuel's accusation that the people are traitors to God's worship for wanting a king, and they pray that God forgive and pardon them (*AJ* 6.88–93). Matthew 16:19 does not refer to divine wrath, records no accusation,[25] and mentions no need to pray for forgiveness when a law is "loosed." In giving disciples this power, Matthew's Jesus also differs from Isis. In the antitheses of Matt 5:21–48, Jesus interprets and annuls certain Mosaic commandments; 16:19 similarly empowers Peter and the disciples to bind and loose. Whereas Jesus himself had once commanded them to "go nowhere among the Gentiles" (10:5), the resurrected Christ now sends them to "make disciples of all nations" (28:19). This flexibility is surprising enough for the legislator himself; it is even more surprising that this power to "loose" laws would be given to Peter and all the disciples (16:19).[26]

First, 2, and 4 Maccabees narrate analogous conflicts. Many "seeking righteousness and justice" (1 Macc 2:29) follow Matthias into the wilderness, where the forces of Antiochus Epiphanes "attacked them on the sabbath, and they died, with their wives and children and livestock, to the number of a thousand persons" (2:38). In the subsequent narrative, the kinds of tensions noticed above in Dionysius, Josephus, and Matthew are maintained. On the one hand,

> And all said to their neighbor (καὶ εἶπεν ἀνὴρ τῷ πλησίον αὐτοῦ): "If we all do as our kindred have done and refuse to fight with the Gentiles for our lives and for our ordinances, they will quickly destroy us from the earth." So they made this decision (ἐβουλεύσαντο) that day: "Let us fight against anyone who comes to attack us on the sabbath day; let us not all die as our kindred died in their hiding places." (1 Macc 2:40–41)

In this crisis, we learn little about who decided and how, but the earlier Hasidic

24. Eduard Schweizer, "Matthew's Church," *The Interpretation of Matthew* (ed. Graham Stanton; Philadelphia: Fortress, 1983) 129–55, esp. 136. Cf. Raymond E. Brown, Karl P. Donfried, and John Reumann, *Peter in the New Testament* (Minneapolis: Augsburg; New York: Paulist, 1973) 83–101 and 106–7, esp. 95–101; their assumption that to "bind and loose" is exclusively or in origin Semitic (pp. 91, 96) is incorrect.

25. Matt 16:23 // Mark 8:33 concern a different issue.

26. Cf. 18:18, on which see Günther Bornkamm, "The Authority to 'Bind' and 'Loose' in the Church in Matthew's Gospel: The Problem of Sources in Matthew's Gospel," *Interpretation of Matthew*, 85–97. The interpretation of Richard H. Hiers, "'Binding' and 'Loosing': The Matthean Authorizations," *JBL* 104 (1985) 233–50, that this terminology refers to magic, is not persuasive.

practice of not fighting on the Sabbath was changed. On the other hand, even though they are fighting on the Sabbath, they are still said to be offering themselves "for the law" (2:42); they "show zeal for the law," and accept the exhortation to "give your lives for the covenant of our ancestors" (2:50). Phrased in terms of Greek politics, they have not "abolished" Moses' law by fighting on the Sabbath; but to employ a word used by Josephus, they have "changed" it. The difficulties faced by the writers of 1 Macc 2:29–48 and Matt 12:1–8 do not differ qualitatively.

First Maccabees, however, does not use the language of Greek politics and law which we are considering to clarify the problem; 2 and 4 Maccabees do. Judas Maccabeus "re-established the laws that were about to be abolished" (2 Macc 2:22).[27] But Jason, the corrupt high priest, "abolished (καταλύων) the lawful ways of living and introduced *new* customs (ἐκαίνιζεν) contrary to the law" (2 Macc 4:11, RSV; cf. 8:17; Acts 6:14). The old man Eleazar, in contrast, refuses to "abolish" the law of his country (4 Macc 5:33) by eating pork. Rather, by their martyr deaths the seven brothers "abolish" the tyranny (4 Macc 11:25; cf. 1:11; 17:2).[28]

The Gospel of Matthew consistently maintains this polarity, claiming not to "abolish" the laws, but granting the power to "loose" them. With an emphasis significantly different from 2 Macc 4:11, the Jewish-Christian scribe who interprets Moses' laws in Matt 13:52 is "like the master of a household who brings out of his treasure what is *new* and what is old (καινὰ καὶ παλαιά)." The Matthean Jewish scribe has a new understanding gained through Jesus' parables. The question, "Have you understood all this?" (13:51), forms an inclusio with the cognitive language at the beginning of the chapter (13:11, 13–15, 18, 23). Hans Dieter Betz has demonstrated that what Matthean disciples are to "know" is given in an "epitome," the Sermon on the Mount,[29] including the antitheses interpreting Mosaic commandments. These scribes-disciples are also to bind and loose (16:19), perhaps even "loosing" the "old" and "binding" the "new" (combining 13:52 and 16:19) in a way which is alien to 2 Maccabees, nevertheless insisting that the Mosaic way of life has not been "abolished."[30] Novelty is opposed by 2 Macc 4:11 and by Joseph. *AJ* 4.292, but

27. C. Habicht, *2. Makkabäerbuch: Historische und legendarische Erzählungen* (JSHRZ 1.3; Gütersloh: Gerd Mohn, 1979) 170, 175–76 suggests that the epitomizer wrote this section of the book in 124 B.C.E. The following citation (4:11) apparently comes from Jason ca. 160 B.C.E., an eyewitness of the deeds of Judas the Maccabee (Habicht 177). Jason and his epitomizer are Jews who use this terminology two centuries earlier than 4 Maccabees, Matthew, and Josephus.

28. Cf. Dio Chrys. *Or.* 1.84; 75.2, 4 and 76.2, 4 for references to the abolition of violence and tyranny.

29. Hans Dieter Betz, *Essays on the Sermon on the Mount* (trans. L. L. Welborn; Philadelphia: Fortress, 1985) 1–16.

30. The Table of Claudius (see n. 20 above) is parallel. The emperor assumes Roman law, narrates change and development, but still sees continuity in Roman history.

accepted in Matt 13:52 and 16:19. These different emphases resulted in sectarian alienation within formative Judaism. Further, the Matthean approach to law differs qualitatively from the claims of Isis quoted above from Diodorus.

Matthew 5:19 also uses λύω: "Therefore, whoever breaks [annuls] (λύσῃ) one of the least of these commandments, and teaches others to do the same, will be called least in the kingdom of heaven; but whoever does them and teaches them will be called great in the kingdom of heaven." Luz argues that καταλύω in 5:17 and λύω in 5:19 are synonyms,[31] but Matthew must be distinguishing these verbs. First, in 5:17 Jesus denies that he has come "to abolish (καταλῦσαι) the law or the prophets," that is, the whole of the Mosaic Torah, while in 5:19 the reference is to "whoever annuls (λύσῃ) one of the least of these commandments." Matthew's language itself contrasts abolishing the whole with annulling/loosing a single commandment. Second, this fits the basic assumptions seen above in Dionysius and Josephus, that Romulus's and/or Moses' constitutions and laws as a whole must be guarded/not abolished for the nation or people to be legitimate, but that in a crisis, individual institutions and laws such as kingship, aristocracy, the prohibition of divorce, and not fighting a war on the Sabbath can be changed—with great difficulty, usually involving bloodshed, divine anger, and prayer for forgiveness. Third, in his discussions of Matt 5:17–20, Ulrich Luz nowhere notices or explains the tension between the uses of λύω in 5:19 and 16:19.[32] In the first text there is a negative judgment on annulling any single one—even the least—of the commandments, while in the second, Jesus authorizes Peter "to loose/annul" "whatever" (ὃ ἐάν), without a reference to divine wrath or any need to pray for forgiveness. That such a decision is possible makes Matt 16:19 similar to 1 Macc 2:40–41, although in Matthew we learn more about who is authorized to make such decisions.

Luz sees only one fracture in the narrative of Matthew and in the history of the community.[33] The commission of the risen Lord is antithetically contrasted with the command of the earthly Jesus (28:19f.; 10:5f.).[34] Historically, the community failed with its mission to Israel; then the whole course of the story of Jesus told in the Gospel lays the foundation for this fracture.

31. Ulrich Luz, "Die Erfüllung des Gesetzes bei Matthäus (Mt 5,17–20)," *ZTK* 75 (1978) 398–435, at 409 n. 55 and 415 with nn. 82–83.

32. There is also tension in Overman, *Matthew's Gospel and Formative Judaism,* between 72ff. on Matthew's understanding of law and 113ff. on the authority of Peter and the disciples. Cf. "In the teaching of Jesus that follows [5:17], no part of the law, however small, will be done away with" (88) with "Here [in 18:18 and 16:19] the decisions of the community and its leaders are depicted as possessing the authority and sanction of heaven" (131). This contrast reflects tension within the Gospel itself.

33. Ulrich Luz, *Matthew 1–7: A Commentary* (trans. W. C. Linss; Minneapolis: Augsburg, 1989) 84–85.

34. Cf. Amy-Jill Levine, *The Social and Ethnic Dimensions of Matthean Salvation History: "Go nowhere among the Gentiles . . ." (Matt. 10:5b)* (Lewiston, N.Y.: Edwin Mellen, 1988).

Therefore, Luz suggests, the evangelist calls them to a new undertaking, a deliberate, new venture, the gentile mission.

There is, however, a second fracture in the Gospel between 5:19 and 16:19.[35] Whatever idealistic theory says about not abolishing Romulus's or Moses' laws, historical crises bring imperatives for decision and change. Just as for the Hasidic group whose story is narrated in 1 Maccabees 2, the Matthean community faced some crisis in which some leader(s) had to decide to loose/change one or several of the commandments. And in such a crisis situation, a community needs legitimate authority to make the decision credible. The crisis might have included the decision to leave Jerusalem on the Sabbath when Roman armies surrounded it.

> So when you see the desolating sacrilege standing in the holy place . . . , then those in Judea must flee (φευγέτωσαν) to the mountains. . . . Pray that your flight may not be in winter or on a sabbath. (Matt 24:15–20; cf. Eus. *Hist. Eccl.* 3.5.2–3, a historical tradition according to Alan Segal, p. 26 above)

It might have included a decision about paying some new taxes with Roman coins (Matt 22:15–22) or the community moving north farther into Syria (cf. Michael White's essay, p. 240 below). It certainly included the decision for a mission to the Gentiles. At some later point in the community's history, the evangelist "remembered" Jesus authorizing Peter and/or the disciples to loose/annul individual laws, with no distinction between the "least" and the "greatest" commands and no need to be forgiven for the change. Peter/the disciples may have modified the traditional interpretation of Exod 20:8 ("remember the sabbath . . .") or of Exod 20:4 ("you shall not make for yourself an idol, whether in the form of . . .") or of Lev 15:31 ("Thus you shall keep the people of Israel separate from their uncleanness . . ."). Thus Peter, the person responsible for such an authoritative decision, may be compared to Lucius Junius Brutus, the person eulogized by Romans for "abolishing" the ancestral Roman tyrannical kingship while paradoxically guarding Romulus's constitution (see p. 72 above), or with a different Lucius Junius (Brutus) who was later responsible for instituting the new office of the tribunes to protect the plebians (see Dion. Hal. *Ant. Rom.* 6.22–90, esp. 6.87.3; 89.2).[36]

---

35. Cf. Betz, *Essays on the Sermon on the Mount,* 132–54, who contrasts Matt 7:21–23 (Jesus as just an advocate at the judgment) with 10:32–33 (the higher Christology of Jesus as the judge).

36. "Do not be horrified at the idea of introducing this reform on the ground that it is new. . . . What need now for me to remind you how the power of the dictatorship, greater even than that of the consuls, was invented by our forefathers for use in the more dangerous wars and more serious civil commotions? Or how, in order to give aid to the Plebs, tribunes of the Plebs were created? What need to recall the transfer of power from the consuls to the decemvirs, and later, when that tenfold kingship was abolished, back again to the consuls?" (The Table of Claudius, quoted from Momigliano, *Claudius* 11, 12, cited n. 20 above).

Both Matt 5:17–20 and 16:13–20 have been heavily redacted by the evangelist, and no exegesis of the former (including an interpretation of the two ἕως ἄν clauses of 5:18) can be correct that ignores the latter's break with it, a break that allows more change in Moses' individual commandments than does either 2 Maccabees or Josephus and even legitimates change over against Jesus' own prohibition recorded in 10:5–6, just as Jesus' antitheses had "loosed" some of Moses' individual commandments. To use a modern (so an anachronistic) analogy, the second fracture in the Gospel is a break from an Orthodox (5:19) toward a Conservative Jewish (16:19) practice of law, a change legitimated christologically (5:17, "I have come ...," and 16:19, "I will give ...").

When the Matthean community began to sever its connections with other groups in formative Judaism, move toward the larger church, and accept the four-Gospel canon,[37] Matt 16:19 would give the community a legitimate way to loose/annul even a great commandment, for example, circumcision. This process had already begun, however, by the final editing of Matthew; the whole Gospel moves toward the conclusion in 28:16–20, legitimating making disciples of all nations. Theory does not absolutely precede practice: some converts from the nations had been baptized; there were (uncircumcised[38]) gentile males in the Matthean community by the time the conclusion was written. And as Alan Segal emphasizes in his conclusion (see p. 37),[39] this universalism is one possibility within first-century Judaism, not a uniquely Christian possibility. The proclamation of the resurrected Lord in Matt 28:19 makes this a "binding" legal possibility for Matthean Jewish Christians.

In Jewish Christianity, the two (idealistic and experiential) poles maintained in tension with each other by Dionysius, Josephus, and Matthew are collapsed by the Gospel of the Ebionites: "I came to abolish (καταλῦσαι) sacrifices, and unless you cease sacrificing, wrath will not cease from you" (Epiph. *Pan.* 1.30.16.5).[40] Likewise, Ptolemy's gnostic "Letter to Flora" (in Epiph. *Pan.* 1.33.3–7)[41] goes beyond Matthew in abolishing this polarity.

37. Harry Gamble, "The Pauline Corpus and the Early Christian Book," *Paul and the Legacies of Paul* (ed. William S. Babcock; Dallas: Southern Methodist University Press, 1990) 265–80, at p. 279 notes, however, that the Gospels circulated separately throughout the second century and that only in the early third century is there a codex, p45, that contains the four Gospels with Acts. Michael R. Greenwald, who participated in our discussions at the 1989 conference, makes observations on the second-century process of legitimation in "The New Testament Canon and the Mishnah as Consolidation of Knowledge in the Second Century," SBLSP 1987 (ed. K. H. Richards; Atlanta: Scholars, 1987) 244–54.

38. If they had been circumcised, they would no longer be "Gentiles."

39. Cf. Alan F. Segal, *Paul the Convert: The Apostolate and Apostasy of Saul the Pharisee* (New Haven: Yale University Press, 1990) 194–201.

40. Cited by Wolf-Dietrich Köhler, *Die Rezeption des Matthäusevangeliums in der Zeit vor Irenäus* (WUNT 2.24; Tübingen: J.C.B. Mohr [Paul Siebeck], 1987) 283.

41. Cited by Köhler, *Die Rezeption*, 346–47. Trans. Frank Williams as *The Panarion of Epiphanius of Salamis, Book I (Sects 1–46)* (Nag Hammadi Studies 35; Leiden: E. J. Brill, 1987) 198–204.

But the one portion, the Law of God himself, is again divided into some three parts. One is the pure legislation unmixed with evil, and this is properly termed the "law" which the Savior came not to destroy, but to fulfil (ὃν οὐκ ἦλθε κατα- λῦσαι ὁ σωτὴρ ἀλλὰ πληρῶσαι [Matt 5:17]). (If he fulfilled it, it was not foreign to him, but it needed fulfillment; it was not perfect.) Another part is mixed with inferior matter and injustice, and the Savior abolished this as incongruous with his nature. . . . (5.1)

Ptolemy's language matches the Gospel of the Ebionites with respect to sacrifices:

> Outwardly and in bodily observance they were abrogated; spiritually they were adopted, with the names remaining the same but the actions altered. (5.9)

This frank abolishing of laws recalls the Stoic Dio Chrysostom's negative atti- tude toward human law (e.g., *Or.* 76.2–3; and 80.4 on Solon's "evil" laws), not Matthew's insistent polarity rejecting "abolishing" while accepting "loosing."

On the other hand, just as there were certainly Jewish [-Christian] voices to Matthew's left, so there were other Jewish [-Christian] voices on the right,[42] who were unwilling to "loose" laws, much less to "abolish" them, groups referred to by Justin *Dial.* 47.[43] Segal (p. 17) points to Did. 6:2–3, "For if thou canst bear the whole yoke of the Lord, thou wilt be perfect, but if thou canst not, do what thou canst. And concerning food, bear what thou canst, but keep strictly from that which is offered to idols, for it is the worship of dead gods" (trans. Lake in LCL). I add that when the Didache instructs concerning wandering teachers, it cautions: "But if the teacher himself be perverted and teach another doctrine to destroy (εἰς τὸ καταλῦσαι) these things, do not listen to him, but if his teaching be for the increase of righteousness and knowledge of the Lord, receive him as the Lord" (cf. again Joseph. *AJ* 5.79–80 and Matt 5:20).

In conclusion, I suggest that ideas from the Greek topos "concerning law(s)" (περὶ νόμου/νόμων) are employed in Matt 5:17, 19 and 16:19, a topos whose origins are as early as Greek philosophical debates about law as seen in Protagoras and Plato, and in Dio Chrysostom, as well as in the historians 2 Maccabees, Dionysius, and Josephus. By the process social anthropologists

---

42. Cf. the reference to Matt 5:17 in Shab. 116b, discussed by Luz, "Erfüllung des Gesetzes bei Matthäus," 404; also Luz, *Matthew 1–7*, 262. Compare Boaz Cohen, "The Shulhan Aruk as a Guide for Religious Practice Today," *Law and Tradition in Judaism* (New York: Ktav, 1969) 62–99, at p. 71: "It is my deepest conviction that traditional Jewish law as codified in the Shulhan Aruk can be best brought into harmony with contemporary conditions by interpretation, and not by innovation or abrogation." The article is quite "Matthean," that is, legalistic, but still to the right of Matthew. Cohen has no way to loose/annul a counterproductive biblical or rabbinic law (see, e.g., 90 on Yoreh De'ah 113 and 93–96 on Deut 24:1–4); Matthew does.

43. See the discussion by Georg Strecker, "On the Problem of Jewish Christianity," Walter Bauer, *Orthodoxy and Heresy in Earliest Christianity* (ed. Robert Kraft and Gerhard Krodel; Philadelphia: Fortress, 1971) 241–85, esp. 273–76, 279.

call "selective acculturation," the ideas and terms were taken over by Jewish authors, by 2 and 4 Maccabees, Josephus, Matthew, and the Gospel of the Ebionites.[44] This Greek language concerning law as well as the ideas and values it conveys served as one of the bridges between the Hellenistic-Jewish Gospel of Matthew and the second-century urban Greek church.

As Alan Segal argues, the New Testament reflects a spectrum of ordinary first-century Jewish opinion about how strictly the law is to be observed: Matthew is Petrine, occupying a position between James (cf. Acts 11:19; 15:1), the Galatian Judaizers opposed by Paul,[45] those opposed by Justin *Dial.* 47, and others in formative Judaism on the right hand, and Paul and the Gospel of the Ebionites on the left hand. As Saldarini suggests, Matthew is recommending a fundamental reorientation of the tradition, reinterpreting in a way that opens the way for change, and, I add, for "loosing" some laws. This adaptability, openness for change, and authorization for "loosing" some laws moves the Matthean community further toward incorporating gentile converts and integration into the larger church. Also, as is clear in Dionysius's narration of the abolition of Tarquinius's kingship while still maintaining that the Romans have guarded their ancient constitution, in Josephus's narration of the introduction of kingship in Israel while they prayed for the covenant God's forgiveness, and in Matthew's "loosing" some Mosaic laws without needing such forgiveness, the debate occurs in the context of dispute about legitimate practice, authority, and leadership.

Within the context of the conference represented by the essays in this

44. On "selective acculturation" see B. J. Segal et al., "Acculturation: An Exploratory Formulation," *American Anthropologist* 56 (1954) 973–1002. Field studies are summarized in B. J. Segal, ed., *Acculturation: Critical Abstracts, North America* (Stanford Anthropological Series 2; Stanford: Stanford University Press, 1955). There is "enthusiastic acceptance" of some elements from the donor culture by the receiving culture and "firm rejection" of others (Segal, "Acculturation," 985). I utilize this category in "Hellenization-Acculturation in 1 Peter," in *Perspectives on 1 Peter* (ed. Charles H. Talbert; Macon, Ga.: Mercer University Press, 1986) 79–101. Further work on the comparative meaning of this terminology in Greek and Hebrew sources is needed. See [H. L. Strack and] P. Billerbeck, *Kommentar zum Neuen Testament aus Talmud und Midrasch* (Munich: C. H. Beck, 1926, 1959) 1. 738–42 and 4. 297–333. David E. Aune writes (letter dated Dec. 29, 1990): "The Jewish background is somewhat slighted, particularly with regard to rabbinical terminology. One Jewish formula, found in Deuteronomy, is the add-subtract-change formula found throughout the Greco-Roman world in legal contexts, curse formulas, historians, etc. (Deut 4:2, Ep. Aristeas 221–23; Philo *De vita Mosis* 2.34; Joseph. *AJ* 12.109; *Ap.* 1.42; *BJ* 1.26). This formula is favored by the rabbis also (*b.Megilla* 14a; *b.Sanhedrin* 101a; *b.Sabbat* 116b; Midrash Ruth 2.4; Num. Rabbah 10 etc.).... I also wonder whether the pattern of no change–change–rationalization is not extremely widespread and belongs to the phenomenology of legal institutions." Dean Bruce Corley, at a meeting of the Seminar on the Development of Early Catholic Christianity on Feb. 21, 1991, also suggested comparing Tosepta Ḥullin 2.22–23 and 4QMMT (Miqsat Ma'aseh Torah, Qumran 4) as discussed by L. H. Schiffman, "The Temple Scroll and the Systems of Jewish Law of the Second Temple Period," *Temple Scroll Studies*, ed. G. J. Brooke (*JSPSS* 7; Sheffield: JSOT, 1989) 239–55.

45. Cf. Luz, *Matthew 1–7*, 87, 268.

volume, another conclusion follows from this interpretation of legal terminology in Matt 5:17, 19 and 16:19, that is: as Pheme Perkins suggests (p. 123
below), Matthew is primarily story (*haggadah*), not specified life-style
(*halacha*). The legal terminology discussed above is best understood as it
occurs in the *historians* Dionysius of Halicarnassus and Josephus, who claim
not to be abolishing Romulus's or Moses' laws, but who simultaneously narrate
change and development in the life-styles of Rome and Israel, respectively.
The *social history* of the Matthean community, perhaps its exodus from
Jerusalem or its move from Galilee north into Syria and certainly its leaders'
decision to accept Gentiles, is fundamental to understanding the Gospel. And
in the process of the community's discontinuous historical experience, Mosaic
laws (in the antitheses) and even Jesuanic imperatives (10:5–6) are modified,
"loosened" as authorized by Jesus (16:19). At the conclusion of this study, I
find myself agreeing with the literary critic whose evaluations closed the
conference and now conclude the book:

> Focus attention on these [five great] speeches [in Matthew], however, and it
> soon seems only logical to claim . . . with scholars too numerous to mention, that
> Matthew consists fundamentally of two distinct elements, "story" and "speech."
> Weigh the relative importance of these elements, and the conclusion seems
> compelling: "speech" is primary and "story" is secondary. . . . From a literary-
> critical standpoint, this understanding of Matthew's Gospel will not do.[46]

I add that from the standpoint of the legal terminology employed by Matthew,
this understanding will not do either. To employ a phrase describing the canon
that James Sanders has taught us, Matthew's Jesus declares that in future
crises, Peter and the disciples have the authority to "loose/annul" particular
Mosaic laws and even his own imperatives. These commandments are "adaptable for life."[47]

46. Jack Dean Kingsbury, *Matthew as Story* (2d ed.; Philadelphia: Fortress, 1988) 105–6.
47. James A. Sanders, "Adaptable for Life: The Nature and Function of Canon," *Magnalia
Dei: The Mighty Acts of God. Essays on the Bible and Archaeology in Memory of G. Ernest Wright*
(ed. F. M. Cross et al.; New York: Doubleday & Co., 1976) 531–60. Indeed, Sanders suggests
(p. 535) that the "Torah is best defined as story (*muthos*) with law (*ethos*) embedded in it," also a
good description of Matthew.

II

MATTHEW:
WOMEN IN AN
AGRARIAN SOCIETY

5

Gender Roles in a Scribal Community

ANTOINETTE CLARK WIRE

Recent study of the meaning of gender in Matthew's Gospel has raised questions about the social world within which this text is written.[1] It becomes important to know whether Matthew's Gospel reflects the gender roles conventional for its setting or ones that deviate from the expected. The problem is to determine what is expected. Standard social conventions can be reconstructed in a number of ways to illuminate different aspects of the situation. Gender roles reflected in Matthew's Christian sources could be taken as a baseline for comparison, as might the configurations of gender in first-century Judaism. Some scholars are working with the help of anthropological models and cultural comparison to analyze Hellenistic literary texts at large. They hope to define the social construction of gender in the Roman East and to use this as a base for studying gender roles in early Christianity.[2] I want to test another approach to what was conventional by using macro-sociological analysis to

1. Janice Capel Anderson, "Gender and Reading," *Semeia* 28 (1983) 3–28, considers the symbolic significance of gender in Matthew's Gospel and the role of the implied reader of Matthew in relation to a feminist interpreter. Stuart L. Love's paper, read at the 1989 Society of Biblical Literature annual meeting, "A Macro-sociological Analysis of the Role of Women in the Gospel of Matthew," is significant for the issues raised in my chapter both in problem area and method.

2. Karen Torjesen, *Sex, Sin and Woman: Social Histories of Theological Ideas* (San Francisco: Harper & Row, forthcoming). See also an application of this method to the symbolic use of gender roles in Gnostic texts in Karen L. King, "Ridicule and Rape, Rule and Rebellion: Images of Gender in the *Hypostasis of the Archons*," *Gnosticism and the Early Christian World*, vol. 2 of *Essays on Antiquity and Christianity in Honor of James M. Robinson* (Sonoma, Calif.: Polebridge, 1990).

reconstruct the gender roles characteristic of scribal communities within advanced agricultural societies.[3] If I can identify the community Matthew addresses as scribal and locate certain primary factors that determine gender roles in such communities, another base is provided for evaluating how Matthew's gender construction is congruent and/or deviant within its social world.

Beginning from the role of scribes in agricultural society as delineated by macro-sociological analysis, I identify five characteristics of what I call "scribal communities" from recent work done within a more accessible agricultural society, Qing (Ch'ing) Dynasty China.[4] These characteristics are confirmed to be a viable gauge for scribal communities in the Roman East by showing that they appear in two other groups in Matthew's century, region, and ethnic group.[5] The five characteristics are then applied to the community addressed in Matthew's Gospel. This provides a comparative framework for considering what gender roles in scribal communities are distinctive to the Matthean context.

In the second part of this study I try to account for gender role configurations in Matthew's setting that do not appear to be standard in scribal communities. I adapt, for this purpose, a model developed to compare levels of literacy and social domination in Qing China.[6] This allows me to test whether the community addressed by Matthew's Gospel does or does not share the socioeconomic and literacy levels that characterize most scribal communities.

3. For a general introduction, see Gerhard E. Lenski and Jean Lenski, *Human Societies,* rev. ed. (New York: McGraw-Hill, 1982). This is applied more specifically to questions of social stratification in Gerhard E. Lenski, *Power and Privilege: A Theory of Social Stratification,* rev. ed. (Chapel Hill: University of North Carolina Press, 1984).

4. On clans in China, see Maurice Freedman, *Lineage Organization in Southeastern China* (London: University of London Press, 1958, 1965); idem, *Chinese Lineage and Society: Fukien and Kwangtung* (New York: Humanities, 1966); and Maurice Freedman, ed., *Family and Kinship in Chinese Society* (Stanford, Calif.: Stanford University Press, 1970). A more detailed study of the clan rules is available in Hui-chen Wang Liu, *The Traditional Chinese Clan Rules* (Locust Valley, N.Y.: J. J. Augustin for the Association of Asian Studies, 1959); and in her concise "An Analysis of Chinese Clan Rules: Confucian Theories in Action," *Confucianism in Chinese Civilization* (ed. Arthur F. Wright; Stanford, Calif.: Stanford University Press, 1975) 16–49.

5. These are the Pharisees and the Qumran communities among first-century Palestinian Jews. To me the most convincing work to date on the setting of Matthew's Gospel has been done by B. T. Viviano and H. Dixon Slingerland, who set it in a Greek-speaking city of the Decapolis or Mediterranean coastal Palestine in the last quarter of the first century (Viviano, "Where Was the Gospel According to Matthew Written?" *CBQ* 41 [1979] 533–46; Slingerland, "The Trans-jordanian Origin of St. Matthew's Gospel," *JSNT* [1979] 18–28). For the Decapolis thesis, see the recent review of the Pella flight traditions in C. Koester, "The Origin and Significance of the Flight to Pella Tradition," *CBQ* 51 (1989) 90–106. Much of my study would also be relevant for the traditional thesis of Antiochene provenance since Matthew cannot be located there unless Antioch is taken as another context for the postwar interaction of Jewish scribal communities.

6. David Johnson, "Communication, Class, and Consciousness in Late Imperial China," *Popular Culture in Late Imperial China* (ed. David Johnson, Andrew J. Nathan and Evelyn S. Rawski; Berkeley, Los Angeles, and London: University of California Press, 1985) 56.

Finally, I ask whether the recent migration of the Christian tradition from a social sector low in both social dominance and literacy can account for Matthew's distinct emphases.

Part I: Scribal Communities

SCRIBES IN AN
AGRICULTURAL SOCIETY

Distinct from horticultural society in its wake and industrial society yet to come, agricultural society is based on the technology of the animal-drawn and iron-tipped plow.[7] This broad type of social organization apparently first grew up in the great river valleys of the Near East and has been dominant across the world until recent times. The technology of the plow allowed societies for the first time to produce the surpluses necessary for building major cities. The wealth for this was extracted from food producers by the rulers who conquered sufficient land to support a governing class of about 2 percent, themselves served by a retainer class of less than 5 percent and supplied with luxury goods by a yet smaller merchant class. The great gap between these people and the peasant majority—not to speak of the yet more marginal land-less artisans, the unclean and the expendable—meant that retainers and merchants lived near a steep cliff. They had somehow to parlay their educational, military, social, or commercial skills into services wanted by those who governed and their retainers or find themselves among the peasants whose physical labor at subsistence fueled the society. At every level, social organization was patriarchal, an apparent consequence of intensive plow agriculture dominated by land-owning males, which in turn motivated dowry systems to compete for landed sons-in-law, with accompanying tight controls on women's sexual and social lives.[8] Yet the poor majority often could not afford the accepted sexual division of labor if every able-bodied person in the family was needed to carry out each season's work.

Religious leaders are probably best not seen as a separate class in

7. On agricultural social organization, see Lenski, *Power and Privilege,* 189–296; and Gideon Sjoberg, *The Preindustrial City: Past and Present* (New York: Free Press, 1960).

8. This summarizes the conclusion of an extensive cross-cultural study by Martin King Whyte, *The Status of Women in Preindustrial Societies* (Princeton: Princeton University Press, 1978) 156–66. He refers to earlier work by Jack Goody, "Inheritance, Property and Marriage in Africa and Eurasia," *Sociology* 3 (1969) 55–76; and idem, "Bridewealth and Dowry in Africa and Eurasia," *Bridewealth and Dowry* (ed. J. Goody and S. J. Tambiah; Cambridge: Cambridge University Press, 1973). See also the discussion of women in agricultural society in M. Kay Martin and Barbara Voorhies, *Female of the Species* (New York: Columbia University Press, 1975) 276–322; and the comparison of different theories of sexual stratification in Alice Schlegel, ed., *Sexual Stratification: A Cross Cultural View* (New York: Columbia University Press, 1977) 1–40.

agricultural society.[9] Where a religion was long integral to a culture, religious leaders might even belong to the governing class and function in intimate alliance with the ruler. Far from these were the nonliterate artisans of religion who sold homemade charms, potions, and prayers to the poor and could in the worst times stir them up against their fate. But in large part, religious leaders were retainers parallel to the military officers and tax officials, providing a skilled service to those in power—in their case literacy and knowledge of the sacred cultural tradition by which the people lived. Although in some technologically advanced agricultural societies literacy became dissociated from religion, more commonly learning to read was learning the ancient religious texts, though many retained only enough literacy for practical matters such as record keeping. The scribes taught governing-class males to read the tradition with its procedures and warnings, did such study on their behalf, and were expected to promote orally in the society at large such rituals and values as would assure the stability of the regime.

Though an officer, merchant, or even well-off peasant might occasionally hire a scribe to teach his sons, significant knowledge of the tradition outside the ruling group occurred only in what I will call "scribal communities." Here scribes and their kin, sometimes joined by others who were devoted to the tradition, formed voluntary associations to foster its study and to practice the life it demanded. Such associations could be considered suspicious if the tradition celebrated was not that of those who governed, and they might be driven underground or stamped out. But where they could present themselves as carrying out the retainer's task of fostering peace and order among the people—or where the regime was too weak to control them—they might be tolerated and provide a base for the religious tradition to develop in ways not strictly reduced to the legitimating functions of official religion.

THE CLAN IN QING CHINA AS A
SCRIBAL COMMUNITY

In order to specify the general characteristics of what I am calling a scribal community before considering such Jewish groups in first-century

9. Lenski speaks of a priestly class whose livelihood depends on religious roles, but he finds this the most variable class in agricultural society, ranging from those virtually in the governing class to those serving to legitimate their power by educating the governing class and supporting its authority in terms of the tradition. Therefore it seems more appropriate to classify religious leaders in agricultural society among other retainers with similar serving and legitimating roles except where they share governing authority (Lenski, *Power and Privilege*, 219–96). Sjoberg stresses the divisions between higher and lower clergy, which I think can be better honored when they are recognized to come from more than one class (Sjoberg, *Preindustrial City*, 256–84).

Palestine, I turn to studies of the Chinese clan in the Qing Dynasty (1644–1911). Some data is available concerning clans in the earlier Tang, Song, and Ming Dynasties, but the distinctive genealogical books of each clan, which include their own versions of the Confucian rules, survive in greatest number from the later centuries of this ancient agricultural society.[10]

Although China at this time was technologically more advanced than the Roman East in its widespread use of printing, the laborious carving of whole pages of a book in characters onto blocks of pear wood did not bring a new social order as moveable type and industrialization did later.[11] Literacy in the most educated southeastern cities of China in this period would not have reached 20 percent, and most of it was of the minimal sort needed to keep records.[12] The examination system for government service based on the Confucian classics was one of the incentives for those who traced themselves back to a common ancestor to organize their clan and support any who showed some promise of achieving through examination the scholar/official status with its great benefits to all related parties. But this organizing of the clan, which meant above all the recovery and further amassing of genealogical data and ritual celebration of ancestors in specially designated halls, would not have been possible except on the foundation of an accepted patriarchal social structure and morality. It was apparently the function of the clan rules, which we find in these genealogical books, to interpret the ancient Confucian classics so as to define every clan member's duty and elicit such practice in each generation through knowledge of rewards and punishments.

Five characteristics of a scribal community in agricultural society can be drawn from recent anthropological studies of these clans:[13] (1) They reinterpret in writing a revered literary tradition (2) in such a way as to teach concrete ritual and ethical behavior (3) which can assure the proper fulfillment of set roles within a community of identification (4) sanctioned by adequate rewards and punishments (5) in order to reassert right order in a situation where it is perceived to be under some threat.

The Chinese clans reinterpret in writing a revered written tradition in the variety and at the same time the consistency of their clan rules. They draw on all periods and collections of Confucian teachings, especially on the classics concerning appropriate family ritual, but prefer the more recent and practical

10. See the bibliography of genealogies in Liu, *Traditional Chinese Clan Rules,* 194–203. Her study is based on the 151 clan rules from these genealogies housed at Columbia University.

11. Evelyn Sakakida Rawski, *Education and Popular Literacy in Ch'ing China* (Ann Arbor: University of Michigan Press, 1979) 109–24.

12. Ibid., 1–23, 140. This is an average of Rawski's figures for female and male literacy.

13. In addition to Liu's description and analysis of the sources, see the field work on Chinese lineage organization by Maurice Freedman and others (see n. 4 above). On the clans in popular education, see Rawski, *Education and Popular Literacy,* 28–32, 55, 62–64, 70, 84–88.

writings and can even incorporate Buddhist and Taoist teachings and Ming imperial edicts.[14] One primary tendency in interpretation is to slight the Confucian teachings calling for broad human responsibility. Instead the stress is put on responsibility within the lineage,[15] and there more for supporting the education of promising advanced students than of poor beginners. Books studied in clan schools are likely to be the classics on filial virtue, not the character books for self-teaching that name daily and exotic objects.[16]

This is because learning is intended to improve daily human behavior, as noted in the second characteristic of a scribal community. The rules are so specific as to advocate prompt tax payments and clan investment in land and to oppose witchcraft and expensive weddings.[17] These injunctions, as well as those delineating all the many required acts of filial piety in daily life and ancestral hall ritual, are directed to the men. The silence in this context on such key issues as a mother-in-law's relations to her son's wife[18] probably reflects both the male authors and the intended male readers.

The genealogies themselves, which are the primary texts of the clans, demonstrate the third characteristic, that everything depends on proper fulfillment of set roles.[19] The highest dignity goes to the oldest male of the oldest surviving line. A clan often chooses a public leader in addition to the senior male, recognizes those who donate money for clan buildings or benevolences, and honors the few who pass the examinations and become scholar/officials thus balancing and confirming the priorities given to age, male gender, wealth, and wisdom. Though the eldest is expected to set an example of consulting with others and they may in extreme cases remonstrate with him, his final decision is never to be questioned. In this hierarchically ordered world, ritual is as important as daily conduct and "the essence of ritual is status differentiation."[20] Because something like one hundred coins are due when a son becomes sixteen and first attends the biannual banquet, the poorest relatives may never be active in the clan; and butchers, soldiers, prostitutes, and entertainers are not to be enrolled at all.

The primary sanctions for this ordering of society, the fourth characteristic, are the level of honor or shame that one is given within it, the highest achievement for men being that of the scholar/official who passes the final government examinations and becomes an imperial officer, the highest for

14. Liu, "An Analysis of Chinese Clan Rules," 21–25.
15. Ibid., 42.
16. Rawski, *Education and Popular Literacy,* 109–24.
17. Liu, "An Analysis of Chinese Clan Rules," 25–30.
18. Ibid., 24, 40–41.
19. Relationships within families and clans according to these clan rules are described in Liu, *Traditional Chinese Clan Rules,* 47–107.
20. Ibid., 16, 158–65.

women being the status of chaste widow granted by imperial decree on clan petition after decades of devotion to her husband's memory. The greatest shame for a woman according to clan rules comes from bringing shame on her husband through childlessness or any family disturbance, the most extreme being overt disobedience or adultery. Men are shamed when their impropriety or insubordination brings shame on the clan. Though some clans undertake a summary evaluation of each member once a year,[21] in general, social control is effectively internalized. In the case of overt or repeated offenses, punishment ranges from written censure or financial penalties to corporeal punishment or handing over to the state. A man who marries his widowed sister-in-law could be expurgated from the genealogy. Men traditionally bear public punishment in place of women family members as a lesser shame, but retribution on women can take place within the family, and, as one clan rule reads, "If she takes her own life, it is her own fault."[22]

The only characteristic of scribal communities that might be controversial in its application to the Chinese clan is the final one, that right order is being reasserted in response to some threat. But if "threat" is interpreted broadly to include social problems lasting over decades and centuries as the clans themselves did,[23] then this description is very illuminating. At least two crucial problems in the structure of agricultural societies may have contributed to the widespread organization of clans in rural south China. Because imperial confiscation of land and labor could befall anyone rich enough to make it worthwhile, people doing well on the fertile and accessible rice lands of China's southeast had reason to use what surplus was left from taxation to support their most promising members training for imperial exams in the hope of producing scholar/officials who could support the clan in return.[24] A second besetting threat in agricultural society—that of more mouths than could be fed—encouraged extended families to organize in order to expand landholdings at the expense of other clans and restrain sons from individual ownership claims until the father's death. In times of retrenchment younger sons were forced off the land or had to remain single and serve the older brother to sustain the

21. Ibid., 134.
22. For this quotation and punishments in clan practice, see ibid., 87–89; and idem, "An Analysis of Chinese Clan Rules," 42.
23. Here Liu's descriptions of the clan's cultivation of imperial scholar/officials and its problems with sons struggling over land have been linked with Lenski's analysis of agricultural society to propose some rationale for the long survival of these communities (Liu, "An Analysis of Chinese Clan Rules," 33–34, 38–40; and Lenski, *Power and Privilege*, chap. 9). See also Jack M. Potter, "Land and Lineage in Traditional China," *Family and Kinship in Chinese Society* (ed. Maurice Freedman; Stanford, Calif.: Stanford University Press, 1970) 121–38, a study of the relation of clan organization to prosperity in agriculture.
24. Liu, *Traditional Chinese Clan Rules*, 5, 110–11, 193; idem, "An Analysis of Chinese Clan Rules," 30–37.

family standard of living. The relative success of the clan system in meeting these endemic threats in agricultural society made it nearly impossible for its most marginal members—young women and the poor in particular, and those without resources to organize their own clans—to overcome its consistent exploitation of them.[25]

THE QUMRAN COVENANTERS
AND THE PHARISEES AS
SCRIBAL COMMUNITIES

Applying to the Qumran community and to the Pharisees this five-point typology of a scribal community in agricultural society shows both the use and the limits of such characterization.[26] The limits are obvious in the historical sources, which prove that these communities are not identical. Scribal roles in agricultural societies and the functions of communities that supported these roles seem to have varied considerably. Only much broader research on such communities can determine which characteristics turn out to be more generic and which are more variable. Meanwhile the rough pattern of a scribally oriented community as just described can provide a framework for seeing in new ways the distinctive aspects of each such community through their common elements. The description will be inadequate to the religious faith of each group except as its ideology corresponds to the social reality of its religious practice.

The Qumran community, taken broadly in its monastic and socially integrated forms, is unquestionably a group reinterpreting in writing a revered literary tradition (witness their extensive library found in the Dead Sea caves).[27] Their Teacher of Righteousness revealed to them the meaning of the prophetic books—mysteries thought not to have been understood by the prophets themselves—which point to the community's election in a final evil time and to an ultimate messianic interpretation of the law and vindication of

25. One successful effort lasting over a century is documented by Marjorie Topley in "Marriage Resistance in Rural Kwangtung," *Women in Chinese Society* (ed. Margery Wolf and Roxane Witke; Stanford, Calif.: Stanford University Press, 1975) 67–88.

26. Already the choice of the term "scribal" to characterize such communities is problematic because words we translate "scribe" are commonly used in the Roman East and are not applied in this way to communities. But as A. J. Saldarini has shown in a recent comprehensive study of the social role of scribes in Jewish society in this period, "scribe" was a category applied to a broad range of people at various levels of the society earning their living by their literacy, roughly parallel in our time to the many people titled "secretary" (*Pharisees, Scribes and Sadducees in Palestinian Society: A Sociological Approach* [Wilmington, Del.: Michael Glazier, 1988] 241–76). Therefore it seemed to be a relatively neutral term under which to group a cross-cultural sample of literacy-oriented communities in agricultural societies.

27. For an English translation of the texts free from excessive speculation on the lacunae, see Geza Vermes, *The Dead Sea Scrolls in English* (3d ed.; London: Penguin Books, 1987).

the faithful.[28] Meanwhile, all boys in the towns from ages ten to twenty[29] are to study the law, and those who choose the desert way of perfection are to study all their lives, including one-third of each night. This study is expected, as the second characteristic notes, to engender the humility, patience, and understanding necessary for doing God's will, in both the daily rituals of purification, prayers, and meals, and the Sabbaths and festivals set eternally by the sun and the law, as well as in every aspect of the monastic or familial common life.[30]

The third characteristic of scribal communities—that they seek the proper fulfillment of set roles within their community of identification—seems to be belied by the focus on the individual decisions of all who take the oath of the covenant in this community,[31] and by the annual ranking of all the monastics strictly according to their conduct. The stipulation that fathers or husbands can annul only the oaths of women that are not consonant with the covenant even hints at the possibility of some kind of covenanting among women.[32] But the monks who enter and sit and speak in the order of the perfection of their spirits are ranked by conduct strictly within the four set roles of priests, Levites, Israel, and proselytes, very much in that order.[33] It seems that these same priestly standards of holiness exclude from the council of the community the maimed, blind, retarded, minors, and—assumed so much that it is unspoken—the women.[34]

The final two characteristics of scribal communities are unmistakable at Qumran. Rewards and punishments provide sanctions for community values, by immediately honoring or isolating its members in response to their daily conduct,[35] as well as by the promise of ultimate retribution—great progeny and glory for those with families,[36] and a seat at the messianic meal for the monks when holiness is consummated and God's vengeance taken against every enemy and deserter.[37] The purpose of each one's living according to his rank in holiness is to reassert the right order of humanity in humble service before God in the present time of great threat, when the essential temple service of God has been irremediably violated. This threat is also experienced economically because priests cut off from the temple no longer are fed from the offerings.

28. 1QS 4.2–6; 1QpHab 7.1–5.
29. 1QSa 1.6–9.
30. 1QS 3.6–9; 5.1–6.8.
31. The thesis of an annual covenant renewal ceremony at Qumran has been developed by Vermes in his introduction to *Dead Sea Scrolls in English*, 15–18. On free individual commitment, see 1QS 5.5–10; CD 15.5–6, 14.3–6.
32. 1QSa 1.4–5; CD 5.9–10; 16.10–12.
33. 1QS 5.1–6.23; 9.5–7; 1QSa 1.22–2.3; CD 14.3–6.
34. 1QSa 2.3–11.
35. 1QS 6.24–7.25; 8.20–9.5.
36. CD 2.11–12.
37. 1QSa 2.11–22; 1QM 11–19; CD 7–8.

They and their people must structure a new life together in the discipline and hardship of self-support.

In spite of inadequate source material for a full description, the Pharisees of first-century Palestine can be identified without difficulty as a scribal community according to the characteristics outlined.[38] Their reinterpretation of the revered literary tradition is not carried out in writing, but reference to past interpreters is common by the century's final decades; and the eventual reshaping of their work into a fixed form by the end of the second century as found in the Mishnah shows the extent to which interpretations were being orally retained.[39] This process is later described as a transmission of oral Torah from Sinai, parallel to the transmission of the written Torah. In its early stages it reflects the Pharisees' confidence in the all-sufficient authority of the written Torah and in their ability to teach disciples in each generation how to continue its right interpretation.[40]

Second, the purpose of this interpretation is to foster the concrete ritual and ethical action demanded by the Torah. Josephus, the New Testament, and the earliest traditions of the Mishnah all point to a particular focus of the Pharisees on ritual purity, specifically purity in growing, tithing, and preparing of food, and purity at all times—especially at life's transitions and on holy days— of those who prepare the food and those who eat together.[41] But this is not seen as separable from the doing of good deeds, as reflected in Hillel's call to "love your neighbor as yourself" and Yohanan ben Zakkai's stress on "mercy, not sacrifice."[42]

Third, this conduct alone can assure the proper fulfillment of the roles intended for humanity and the natural world by the Creator who gave the Torah. Everything is pure when related properly to the one designated by

38. Even those who question the continuity between the Pharisees before 70 and the sages at Yavneh concede that any radical discontinuity is belied by reappearance of the same leaders, the same stories, and the same focus on resurrection, tradition, and meticulous observance of tithing and purity laws, as well as by an increased spotlight in the late century on the Pharisees' significance before the war (Shaye J. D. Cohen, "The Significance of Yavneh: Pharisees, Rabbis and the End of Jewish Sectarianism," *HUCA* 40 [1984] 27–53). Cohen further suggests that the rabbis never call themselves Pharisees because the sectarian meaning of that name is no longer appropriate in a time when divisions among Jews must be tolerated or absorbed rather than accentuated. A. J. Saldarini prefers a sociological explanation of the decreased sectarianism from the lack of a powerful system against which to react, in this case the temple just destroyed (*Pharisees, Scribes and Sadducees,* 8 n. 1).

39. Jacob Neusner, *From Politics to Piety: The Emergence of Pharisaic Judaism* (New York: Ktav, 1979) 81–100; idem, *Oral Tradition in Judaism: The Case of the Mishnah* (New York and London: Garland, 1987).

40. The process of teaching is vividly depicted in Jacob Neusner, *A Life of Yohanan Ben Zakkai: c. 1–80 C.E.* (Leiden: E. J. Brill, 1970) 97–120. See also E. Schuerer, G. Vermes, F. Millar, and M. Black, *The History of the Jewish People in the Age of Jesus Christ (175 B.C.–A.D. 135)* (Edinburgh: T. & T. Clark, 1979) 2. 332–34, 417–27.

41. Neusner, *From Politics to Piety,* 78–92.

42. Neusner, *Yohanan ben Zakkai,* 39–40, 188–92.

Torah to sanctify the world through acts of intellect and will. Jacob Neusner identifies this one for the Mishnah not as God alone but as God in heaven and the Israelite male on earth whose "will and deed constitute those actors of creation that work on neutral realms, subject to either sanctification or uncleanness. These are the Temple and table, the field and family, the altar and hearth, woman, time, space, transactions in the material world and in the world above as well."[43] That no act of a woman's will can sanctify any situation for the Pharisee and rabbi may be too extreme a statement, but the Pharisee does see himself as the one responsible for sanctifying all the world as the way of his own sanctification. Every male Jew is considered free to join this study and doing of Torah, and special reverence is given to old and learned men.

Fourth, the rewards and punishments that sanction this order are less spoken then assumed,[44] but summary statements of the Torah often warn or promise recompense in the world to come, and the sanctified life of Torah study is taken as its own reward through the divine presence in it.[45] In this world the impure are to be excluded from the crucial table fellowship. After 70 C.E. the sages are known to have banned some among their own number who rejected the decision of the majority.[46] The identification of the *minim* and the time when the curse against them was inserted in the eighteen benedictions is still too widely contested to be used as evidence that first-century rabbis legislated an expulsion of Christians from Judaism.[47]

Fifth, this life lived according to written tradition is perceived to reassert right order in a situation where it is threatened. The Pharisees' pure table fellowship in homes, as if imitating that required of priests in the temple,

---

43. Jacob Neusner, *The Oral Torah: The Sacred Books of Judaism: An Introduction* (San Francisco: Harper & Row, 1986) 25, see also 5–8.

44. Neusner, *Oral Tradition in Judaism*, 122.

45. For examples of summary statements referring to just retribution, see *Pirqe Aboth* 1.7; 2.1, 7, 19, 20, 21; 3.19, 20; 4.13, 29. On the study of Torah as its own reward, see *Pirqe Aboth* 2.8, 9; 3.3, 7; 4.2, 12.

46. This does not presuppose that the Yavneh sages were yet more exclusive than had been the prewar Pharisees (see Cohen, "Significance of Yavneh," 36–42). Such recognized authority may have brought with it stricter internal and external disciplines.

47. Lewis Martyn concludes after sifting evidence that John 9:22 probably refers to an official institution of the benediction against Christians in first-century Yavneh, but he notes that Wayne Meeks and Morton Smith favor a second-century date (*History and Theology in the Fourth Gospel* [2d ed.; Nashville: Abingdon, 1979] 56–57). Although Jakob Jocz dates the twelfth petition curse in the first century and considers that it was aimed at Hebrew Christianity, he doubts that the reference to the "nozrim" was original (*The Jewish People and Jesus Christ: A Study in the Controversy between Church and Synagogue* [London: SPCK, 1962] 51–57). Similarly, William Horsby accepts a late first-century date for the curse and considers Christian sources sufficient evidence that it was directed primarily against them, though the early wording cannot be reconstructed ("The Benediction of the Minim and Early Jewish-Christian Controversy," *JTS* 33 [1982] 19–61). Geza Vermes, on the other hand, argues for identification of the minim as Jewish Hellenists who held that the Torah was falsified (*Post-Biblical Jewish Studies* [Leiden: E. J. Brill, 1975] 169–77).

suggests that at some point they considered the temple to be defiled or at least to be insufficiently present among the people to sanctify Israel. Once having taken on themselves this task of making the people God's temple, they apparently sought to realize it however the political situation allowed, learning self-discipline when their influence was sparse and being ready after the temple's destruction to begin regulating the religious life of the Jews by Roman consent.[48] If this is the case, they were subject throughout to the threat of lacking or losing the social, economic, and political privileges of a retainer class by which they perceived themselves better able to extend their sanctified table to all Israel.

MATTHEW AS A SCRIBAL COMMUNITY

The five characteristics of scribal communities will now be tested on Matthew's Gospel. Granting that one document is insufficient evidence to reveal all aspects of the community it addresses, no other early Christian text can be determined in advance to represent the same setting.

The ethos of Matthew is not that of a school—of writing, reading, studying, copying, learning. Instead the Gospel deals with authoritative speech—Jesus' speech, his acts that fulfill what was spoken earlier by the prophets, and the speech and acts of subsequent witnesses to Jesus. All this speech and action announces the coming of the kingdom of heaven with its promises and demands. This means that authority is not shown to be essentially written, but in practice it is written, both in the prophets' expectations so much cited[49] and in the writers' interpretation of their fulfillment through Jesus' recent speech and acts. Even the written Christian sources that mediate this news about Jesus are treated with respect without being identified as sources.

Among other clear signs that the Gospel of Matthew is interpreting revered written tradition are its understanding of law and its stance toward the Pharisees and scribes. Jesus comes to fulfill not only the prophets but "the law and the prophets" (5:17–19), a phrase applied by a number of Jews in this period to the authoritative writings as a whole[50] and used in Matthew to identify the golden rule and the double commandment as summary statements of

48. Neusner sees them after Herod's accession intent on piety rather than politics, a piety that schools them to leave external politics to Rome after the 70 C.E. war (*From Politics to Piety*, 54–66, 90–92, 143–54). A. J. Saldarini, on the other hand, stresses that they were never apolitical in the century before the war but competed for power in minor ways where a small sect could, as in the struggle with Jesus' faction (*Pharisees, Scribes and Sadducees*, 132–33, 277–97).

49. Matt 1:22; 2:5, 15, 17, 23; 4:14; 8:17; 12:17; 13:35; 21:4–5; and, following Mark, Matt 3:3; 13:14; 15:7.

50. 2 Macc 15:9; 4 Macc 18:10; Ben Sirach Preface; John 1:45; Rom 3:21 as cited in W. D. Davies and Dale C. Allison, *A Critical and Exegetical Commentary on the Gospel according to Saint Matthew* (Edinburgh: T. & T. Clark, 1988) 1. 484.

what the writings demand (7:12; 22:40). These summaries are not presented as replacements for the full written law but as its establishment down to the jot and tittle. Only after Matthew has first confirmed the law (5:17–20) does he describe Jesus eating with sinners, healing on the Sabbath, and not having to pay the temple tax, explaining in each case from the law and prophets the over-ruling text or judgment: God demands mercy rather than sacrifice (9:13; 12:7); God's kingdom has priority over the temple (12:6; 17:25–26); a man's life is worth more than that of a sheep (12:12).

The same respect for the law and its right interpretation is seen in the treatment of the scribes and Pharisees. Though they are under bitter attack for their conduct and for the hypocrisy of not acting as they speak, what they teach is recognized to be the righteousness that those in the kingdom must exceed (23:2–3, 13–36). Entering the kingdom requires going beyond what was said to the ancients forbidding murder, adultery, and violation of reciprocity to no less than the complete and impartial goodness of a God who sends rain on just and unjust (5:20–48).

It is not surprising, therefore, that the term "scribe," which can apply to anyone learned, is also used positively in Matthew for disciples. The writer warns a scribe among other disciples that there is no retainer for discipleship and challenges the disciples as scribes trained for the kingdom of heaven to apply both the new and the old (8:19–21; 13:52). Such scribes will be numbered in the long line of prophets and the wise whom Jesus in Wisdom's role sends out continually to provoke people with God's righteousness (23:34; 5:12; 11:19).[51] The author of Matthew, who begins with the word "book" and refers twice to "this gospel" (24:14; 26:13; cf. 1:1), may well be wearing the persona of a scribe and intend this text to fulfill Jesus' closing commission to "teach them to obey everything that I have commanded you" (28:20).[52]

This comes close to the second characteristic of scribal communities

51. It is also possible that the question about the great commandment that Mark attributes to a scribe commended by Jesus is attributed by Matthew to a Pharisaic lawyer because he wants to stress at this point the negative characterization (Mark 12:28–34; Matt 22:34–40).

52. That the writer refers to his own texts as "this gospel" is proposed by Joseph A. Grassi, "Matthew as a Second Testament Deuteronomy," *Biblical Theology Bulletin* 19 (1989) 23–29, citing Robert H. Gundry, *Matthew: A Commentary on His Literary and Theological Art* (Grand Rapids: Wm. B. Eerdmans, 1982) 480. In general, interpretation of Matthew stressing its continuity with Jewish tradition is in something of a revival in recent years, either by emphasis on the Gospel's use of Jewish-Christian materials as in Hans Dieter Betz, *Essays on the Sermon on the Mount* (Philadelphia: Fortress, 1985), or by focus on the Gospel's own Jewish orientation as in Donald A. Hagner, "The *Sitz im Leben* of the Gospel of Matthew," SBLSP 1985 (Atlanta: Scholars Press, 1985) 243–69; Ulrich Luz, *Das Evangelium nach Matthäus* (1. Teilband; Mt 1–7; Zürich: Benziger; Neukirchen-Vluyn: Neukirchener, 1985) 60–77; Davies and Allison, *Matthew*; and Amy-Jill Levine, *The Social and Ethnic Dimensions of Matthean Salvation History: "Go nowhere among the Gentiles" (Matt. 10:5b)* (Lewiston, N.Y., and Queenston, Ontario: Edwin Mellen, 1988). Earlier important defenders of the Gospel's Jewish-Christian provenance are G. D. Kilpatrick, *The Origins of the Gospel according to Matthew* (Oxford: Clarendon, 1946) 101–39; Reinhart Hummel, *Die Auseinandersetzung zwischen Kirche und Judentum im Matthäusevangelium* (Munich: Chr. Kaiser,

that they interpret the tradition in order to foster concrete ritual and ethical action. The priority on action in this Gospel might be questioned on the basis that it begins with the record of a birth and the proclamation of God's kingdom at hand (1:18–25; 3:2; 4:17) rather than with demands. Jesus' first speech announces "Blessed are the poor in spirit" and "You are the light of the world" before going on to say what the law requires (5:1–16). Yet the kingdom is proclaimed only following the word "repent!" or in conjunction with acts of healing (3:2; 4:17; 10:7–8), and the Beatitudes in Matthew are not so much announcements of good news to the poor and hungry as challenges to become poor in spirit and seekers for righteousness. Even the statement "You are the light" immediately becomes the challenge "Let your light shine before others, so that they may see your good works and give glory to your Father in heaven" (5:3, 6, 14–16). As in sayings of the rabbis, the demand for humility and purity in heart is never contrasted with doing and teaching the commandments. Ritual acts of almsgiving, prayer, and fasting are no less important than the Decalogue because only the person whose eye is single can seek God's kingdom and righteousness without distraction (6:1–18, 22–34). The Sermon on the Mount ends with the warning not simply to "hear these words" but to "hear these words and act on them" like the wise man who builds his house on rock (7:24–27).

I will return to the third characteristic of set roles in the scribal community after reviewing briefly the fourth and fifth. Rewards and punishments are in high profile in Matthew. A final judgment is expected that includes Sodom and Tyre and the Ninevites as well as the Galilean cities and all the nations, where the sheep will be separated from the goats (10:15; 11:20–24; 25:31–46) and the wicked cast out to weeping and gnashing of teeth (8:12; 13:42, 50; 22:13; 24:51; 25:30). The rewards apparently compensate for injustice and do not come to those already rewarded by human praise (5:3–12; 6:1–6, 16–18). Although it is imperative to live responsibly in anticipation of

---

1963); and Kenzo Tagawa, "People and Community in the Gospel of Matthew," *NTS* 16 (1969–70) 149–60.

Davies and Allison's chart surveying scholars' proposals in the last one hundred years on the author's own ethnic identity (*Matthew*, 10) shows that recent stress on the Jewish context is in reaction against a thesis not proposed before mid-century that the writer is a Gentile. This view is based largely on the call to gentile mission (24:14; 28:19), the rejection of the "sons of the kingdom" in favor of those coming from "east and west" (8:11–13), and the taking of the vineyard away from the tenants to give it to "a nation producing the fruits of it" (21:43). But gentile mission is significant in some other branches of first-century Judaism, and there are multiple precedents in Jewish traditions for rejection of irresponsible leaders such as the scribes and Pharisees Matthew depicts in the tenant parable (21:23, 33–46).

Davies also takes with renewed seriousness the external evidence through Papias concerning the apostle Matthew as a collector of materials in Hebrew, perhaps the material behind the Q source. It may also be significant that the writer of this Gospel, by first naming as "Matthew" the tax collector whom Jesus calls and listing Matthew among the Twelve as "the tax collector," shows a special interest in this outcast but literate figure who, at least by the early second century when the Gospels are titled, has become his apostolic legitimation.

God's judgment, a number of parables stress that it is not possible meanwhile to judge oneself superior to others, since God's justice and mercy remain beyond human grasp (13:24–30, 36–43; 18:23–35; 20:1–16; 25:31–46).

That Matthew is reacting to a threat, a fifth characteristic of a scribal community, is clear in the Gospel's concerted redactional apology. The author insists that Jesus does not lack a messianic lineage and name, nor a messianic place and time of birth (1:1–2:23). Jesus' baptism does not make him a disciple of John (3:14–15), and Jesus does not come to abolish the law or the prophets (5:17–20). The apology reappears strongly in the telling of Jesus' last days: he is not defenseless at his arrest (26:52–54), he is not held guilty by the Romans (27:19–26), and he is not resurrected by grave robbers (27:62–66; 28:11–15). These and other less explicit elements of apology suggest that the author is answering a countergospel, a narrative that if it was ever pieced together made Jesus out to be an imposter, a threat to religious and civil order, and a fraud, very much in the dress used by Josephus for prewar pretenders and prophets, with a touch of Lucian's satire of prophetic frauds thrown in.[53]

In contrast, the author's traditional messianic, legal, and resurrection claims on Jesus' behalf probably reflect the values of those whom the writer wants to persuade concerning Jesus. Jesus' announcement that it is children who enter the kingdom is rephrased: "Unless your righteousness exceeds that of the scribes and Pharisees, you will never enter the kingdom of heaven" (5:20). This is explicated in terms of keeping the law so rigorously as to take God's perfection to be the measure for one's own. Thus the righteousness of God reorders a person's life to overcome all anxieties and meet all needs (5:6; 6:33). In terms of ritual, baptism "fulfills all righteousness" (3:15) and "doing righteousness" means carrying out the traditional Jewish religious practices of almsgiving, prayer, and fasting without receiving human praise (6:1–18). The threat to this author can only be coming from the center of the religious community, from people who would like to write Jesus off as another false prophet. The writer responds by claiming the center for Jesus who teaches the greater righteousness and for his followers who are "persecuted for righteousness sake" (5:20, 10).[54] Jesus becomes the one reasserting right order against those who

53. Joseph. *BJ* 2.258–265; 6.281–309; *AJ* 20.97–99; Lucian of Samosata, *Alexander the False Prophet* and *The Passing of Peregrinus*. This denigration of Jesus is different from earlier charges that Jesus is prince of demons, blasphemer, and threat to the temple, but the Gospel of Matthew takes up that debate as well (9:32–34; 12:22–30). On how Matthew shows Jesus the deviant become Jesus the prominent, see Bruce Malina and Jerome Neyrey, *Calling Jesus Names* (Sonoma, Calif.: Polebridge, 1988).

54. Benno Przybylski's recent careful study, *Righteousness in Matthew and His World of Thought* (Cambridge: Cambridge University Press, 1980), recovers the Jewish context of Matthew's concept of righteousness through a comparative study of "righteousness" in the Dead Sea Scrolls, Tannaitic sayings, and Matthew. This becomes problematic only when his own theological absorption with the dichotomy of righteousness as work and as gift requires him to say that Matthew has developed this view of righteousness strictly as a hermeneutical concept for successful communication with Jews. In contrast, he sees Matthew's view of salvation developed

threaten it with hypocrisy and deceit.[55] Although there is no direct indication in
Matthew that the author hopes his community will gain retainer status in post-
war society, this Gospel's claim to legitimacy at a time when Roman rule co-
exists with the courts at Yavneh does enter it in competition to represent the
true Israel.

I return now to the third characteristic of scribal communities to ask if
the Gospel of Matthew cultivates set roles within a community of identification.
It is not possible here to investigate all the ways in which roles can be fostered
in narrative and in teaching and weigh the relative importance of each for this
writer. It will be assumed that roles developed in either narrative or teaching
may have exemplary significance for readers and that this will be strongest
where they corroborate each other. To limit the scope of this review, emphasis
will be put on exemplary roles implied and developed in the author's redaction
of Mark and Q as existing source documents.[56]

In Matthew's Gospel Jesus is not developed as a figure to imitate
beyond what is already said in the sources (16:24; 20:22–28), and Jesus'
opponents are not presented as exemplary, leaving two major narrative roles for
consideration—that of the disciples and that of the people Jesus heals or helps.
The disciples are explicitly credited with understanding Jesus' teaching or
obeying his instructions at several points where they are not so described in
Mark's narrative (13:51; 16:12; 17:13; 21:6; 26:19; 28:16). Yet at the same time
their inadequate faith is highlighted in Matthew by an extensive use of the
epithet "little faiths" with which Jesus rebukes them (6:30; 8:26; 14:31; 16:8; cf.
17:20). In a similar fashion the disciple Peter is given new prominence in this
Gospel by being named as the church's foundation and promised the power "to
bind and to loose" (10:2; 14:28–29; 15:15; 16:19; 17:24; 18:21). But Matthew
adds the incident of his sinking when walking toward Jesus on the water and in
no way softens Peter's rebuke of Jesus' suffering and Peter's ultimate denial of
Jesus (14:30–31; 16:22–23; 26:33–35, 58, 69–75). If this is intended as a model
for believers in Matthew's community, it is as much warning as instruction.

This raises the question whether the writer intends future believers to

---

independently of this in affirmations of God's will that not one perish and consequent human
discipleship (pp. 116–22). It would be more accurate to recognize that all concepts—including
our own concerning Matthew—are hermeneutical without ceasing to be constructive, shaped as
they are by both the threats and positive challenges facing their users.

55. This need not predetermine a set view of Judaism at Yavneh as an exclusive and persecuting movement. Cohen's proposal that the rabbis sought to absorb rather than exterminate
sectarian differences ("Significance of Yavneh") could have been perceived by Christian Jews as a
particular threat and give rise to further assertions of Jesus' distinctive authority. In this sense
Matthew's argument, in contrast to the accusations of the Fourth Gospel, is a Christian participation in the Yavneh-period debates.

56. Anderson, "Gender and Reading," applies a literary and reader-response analysis to
character roles in Matthew's Gospel with particular attention to women characters and readers.
My results, reached by different methods, in several ways confirm hers.

identify with the disciples. Only the Twelve are called "his disciples."[57] Although the Gospel's closing commission charging them to make further disciples by baptizing and teaching suggests the next generation would also bear this role, in these cases the noun is not used but only the verb, "to make disciples" or "to be made a disciple." This verb, found in this Gospel alone, refers not to the Twelve but to the scribe "discipled for the kingdom," to Joseph of Arimathea, and to those made disciples in the final commission (13:52; 27:57; 28:19). Clearly others to come will be given training and expected to bear responsibility, but it is in some derived sense, as if as disciples of disciples.

Women are not named among Jesus' disciples in Matthew's Gospel. The writer apparently assumes that women are "embedded" in male relatives,[58] adding two female figures to the story line—Pilate's wife and the mother of the Zebedees—to take pressure off their male relatives, and giving secondary roles to the women in Jesus' family after his birth so that Joseph is warned in a dream to "take the child and his mother" to safety, and his brothers are each named but not "all his sisters" (27:19; 20:20; 2:13, 14, 20, 21; 13:55–56). The sentences carried over from Mark that make women the witnesses to Jesus' death, burial, and empty tomb do not make them disciples,[59] and even when this Gospel tells that Jesus appears first to the women, it is to send them to inform the disciples/his brethren (27:55–56, 61; 28:1–8). A writer who does not take these women to be disciples—or even to be made disciples by this event—will hardly have expected women readers to take that role.[60]

A second exemplary narrative role is carried by people who receive Jesus' aid. Whether leper, paralytic, demon-possessed, blind, or hungry, they are presented to the reader as "the lost sheep of the house of Israel" to whom Jesus sends out the Twelve after his own intensive ministry of compassion for the crowds "harassed and helpless, like sheep without a shepherd" (9:35–10:6, following 8:1–9:34). The people's miracle stories are shortened, and their sharp portraits fade into a single background for Jesus who demonstrates

57. Jesus' warning in 8:18–22 to "a scribe" and then to "another disciple" about the rigors of discipleship is ambiguous in its address but could well be intended to refer to some among those later chosen as the Twelve, since they are not named and given authority until 10:1–16.

58. This assumption is characteristic of Mediterranean societies as described by Bruce Malina, *The New Testament World: Insights from Cultural Anthropology* (Atlanta: John Knox, 1981) 100–101, a sociological way of saying what Neusner describes in *Oral Torah*, 5–6, 24–25.

59. The redactional history of the Joseph of Arimathea narrative tells most strongly against reading "who also himself was made a disciple" to refer back and include the women of the previous story in this group of disciples (27:57). The words that refer back appear also in Mark but with less likelihood of pointing to the women in particular because of a longer introduction to the story about Joseph of Arimathea. This suggests that Matthew's apparent reference back to the women is an accident of the shortened intervening clause rather than an intended reshaping of the women's role by the author.

60. This, of course, does not put in question Anderson's observation that women readers can and do hear themselves addressed as disciples in this Gospel ("Gender and Reading," 21–26). But we can also ask whether we want to take a role not offered to our sisters who first told the story.

his power again and again for those with faith. Gentiles who depend on him are only a more extreme evidence of Jesus' authority where faith is in no way expected (8:5–13; 15:21–28). Women are prominent in the stories demonstrating faith, perhaps again because exemplary faith is considered most wonderful where least expected (8:14–15; 9:18–26; 14:21; 15:21–28, 38).[61]

The separate narrative roles of the desperate people and of the disciples are often sharply juxtaposed in the author's redaction. The centurion in this Gospel is taken as a sign of those who will come from east and west to the messianic banquet while "the heirs of the kingdom" are thrown out because Jesus has not found one person in Israel—including, we assume, his disciples—with such faith (8:10–12). In the two chapters of the Gospel where most of the stories of desperation and extraordinary faith are gathered, Matthew includes from Mark sharp warnings to potential disciples as well as the story of a storm in which Jesus rebukes the disciples for their fear and little faith (8:23–27).

The disciples are inserted with some difficulty into the story of the Canaanite woman. This cannot be in order to chaperon the interchange, since the location has already been changed from indoor secrecy to outside a house or town; nor can it be even to relieve Jesus of the role of her opposition, since Jesus and the disciples compete in that. Rather, the disciples' demand to "send her away," as in the preceding and similar following feeding stories (14:15; 15:33), indicates their dismissal of her importance. At first Jesus confirms their judgment—"I was sent only to the lost sheep of the house of Israel" (15:24)—but this is suddenly reversed when she adapts his proverb to win her case on his terms and to win Jesus' praise of her great faith before the disciples.

The story of the anointing woman is particularly striking. Here Matthew changes his source to identify those who object as disciples, with the result that Jesus rebukes the disciples and praises her, even though her role is not to seek help but to give. This means that characterizations typical of those who come to Jesus for help are extended in Matthew's Gospel to women who are supporters of Jesus. So, for example, both Peter's mother-in-law and the women who follow Jesus to Jerusalem are said to serve him or provide for him (27:55; 8:15). In this way the two narrative roles of the suppliant and the disciple are sharpened by being juxtaposed. On one side, both those who seek aid and the women followers are praised in the presence of the disciples for their surprising faith and humble service, while on the other side the disciples are called, understand, obey, and are given authority, but are continually challenged to learn what the first group already demonstrates.

---

61. The same lack of expectation that women have great faith favors them in persecution and martyrdom stories as well: 2 Macc 7:20–42; 4 Maccabees 16–19; *Acts of Paul and Thecla* 21–22, 28, 31–36; *The Martyrdom of Perpetua and Felicitas*; Eus. *Hist. Eccl.* 5.1.17–19, 25–26, 40–42, 53–56.

Turning from the narrative to the speech material of this Gospel, we find again two major roles being projected for the hearers' possible identification. One role is that of the people being addressed by Jesus' teaching. Jesus' repeated references in this Gospel to Gentiles as those with whom the reader does not want to be associated make it probable that Matthew is addressed by a Jew to Jews (5:47; 6:7, 32; 18:17; cf. Luke 6:33). His sayings about adultery, divorce, enemies, and celibacy, as Matthew gives them, all assume that they are spoken by a man to men (5:28, 32, 45; 19:9–12; cf. Mark 10:12). Were the writer thinking of Jesus speaking to women as well, these teachings would not so consistently refer only to the concerns of males about looking at a woman to desire her, marrying a divorced woman, or making oneself a eunuch. This way of speaking is not adequately explained by laws that allow only men to divorce, by customary ways of speaking, by conservative transmission of Jesus' words, or by the writer's lack of sensitivity to a female audience, though all of these may be present. However Jesus once spoke, this writer transmits him in order to address men. One is reminded of the way that the Chinese clan rules written for men ignore the crucial relationship of daughter-in-law and mother-in-law.

The second major role reflected in the teaching in Matthew is that of the "little ones," a characterization developed from the sayings following Mark's first passion prediction. This role of the "child" or "little one" stretches from very near the start of Matthew's first discourse of Jesus to the end of the last (5:19; 25:40, 45), and is especially articulated at the climax of three of these discourses (chaps. 10, 18, 25) and throughout chapter 18 as the answer to the disciples' programmatic question, "Who is the greatest in the kingdom of heaven?" (18:1). Jesus first answers them, "Unless you change and become like children, you will never enter the kingdom of heaven"—making this role the model of humility for the disciples (18:3). But then the focus shifts to the "little ones" as other people whom the disciples must welcome. Who these people are is not immediately clear. In dependence on Mark, Matthew initially identifies the one needing welcome as a disciple in need of "a cup of cold water" (10:42; cf. Mark 9:41), reflecting the apparent origin of the challenge to feed the "little ones" in the dependence of Jesus and his followers on others for food (Mark 9:33–50; Matt 10:1–42). But when the disciples are charged in Matthew to welcome the "little ones who believe in me" whose "angels continually see the face of my father" (18:6, 10; cf. 11:11), they are warned not to cause them to stumble or lead them astray but to forgive them without limit (18:6–14, 21–22). This clearly refers to marginal believers, whom the disciples must forgive in order to "regain your brother" (18:21; cf. 18:15, 35). Yet in the culminating parable of the final discourse the problem again is physical need and "all the nations"—including especially the disciples being instructed in these parables (24:3; 26:1)—are to be judged according to their response toward the sick, hungry, and naked. "The least of these my brethren" whom they are to receive almost surely includes believing women in its genitive plural, whether or not they are understood among those needing forgiveness for going astray in the previous section (18:15–35).

The narrative and teaching in Matthew thus converge on two roles the writer recognizes and apparently cultivates in this community of identification. One is this role of people *in extremis*—in the narrative those who plead for help and exhibit a completely unexpected and exemplary faith, in teaching the "least of these," dependent or prone to cause offense, but whose angels behold the face of God in heaven. The other is the role of disciples who are made responsible by Jesus' teaching for the discipling of others and yet prove to be "little faiths" when put to the test. The modern reader would like to take these as two ways to depict the one ambiguous role of someone yet coming to full faith and responsibility. But the Gospel does not collapse the two. In the narrative the disciples remain a distinct, numbered group, not incorporating all followers of Jesus. And those whom their story in turn seeks to disciple through Jesus' teaching are Jewish and male and can be expected to know and do the law. In the education of these people the other "little people" are held up as a challenge to grow in faith from their example and to take responsibility for their need. This role of the "little one" may be temporary for the sinning disciple until he can be "regained as a brother," but it is not clear that others can make this transition. Women and Gentiles seem to function as believers of another category, as do the proselytes at Qumran who also enter the congregation by rank, but after the Israelites, who in turn come after the priests. So in Matthew the women's role of deficiency or dependence is not overcome but is used to challenge others to meet their needs and at the same time to learn humility and faith from them.

A preliminary assessment of Matthew's context according to the five characteristics of scribal communities shows that it is appropriately so classified. This applies also in the third characteristic of reasserting right order through set roles. Responsibility belongs to a designated group of males in the group to identify the right order which the tradition requires and to regulate communal life to this end. Although greater honor is given in this Gospel to those who do God's will than is given to those who teach but do not do it, and greater status in the kingdom of heaven is given to the "little ones" who see God's face, these do not translate into prestige on earth because they do not involve power in the community. Instead this honor and status work through narrative and sayings as teaching devices to warn those who are given responsibility to increase their faith and to do justice. Because women appear only in these modeling roles and not in roles of responsibility, functioning gender roles in the community do not show signs of diverging significantly from those in other scribal communities.

Yet within this general agreement there are two factors related to gender roles that might be considered distinctive. On the one hand there seems to be a direct critique of patriarchal authority in Jesus' demand, transmitted only in this Gospel, not to call anyone rabbi, father, teacher, or master (23:8–10). This could indicate that such conduct does occur, but it also shows opposition to the elevation of patriarchal and teaching roles. Such opposition may be linked to the writer's critique of "this generation" who hear but do not do Jesus' words, of the Pharisees who do not practice what they preach, and of the disciples who understand Jesus and even obey orders but are faithless in times of crisis. In contrast, those who lack power in the community, including its women, have become positive examples for the powerful of humility and faith, warning them that the righteousness God rewards is not in hearing or even speaking the truth, but in doing God's will (7:24–27; 12:46–50; 21:28–32; 23:2–3). Second, the "little ones" who set this standard of greatness in the kingdom are, because of their physical vulnerability, a challenge to those who are responsible for caring for them—under threat of God's judgment for neglecting Jesus in need (25:31–46).

Neither of these two factors can be considered distinctive in the sense of unique. Early Jewish texts can also depict women as models of faith beyond all expectation and in contrast to men; witness the Book of Judith and a number of stories in the rabbinic haggadah.[62] At Qumran such narratives of contemporary events may not have been considered appropriate for writing, but they cannot thereby be demonstrated not to have existed. In Qing China the widespread popular religions of the Earth Mother, Buddhist worship of Guan Yin, and the veneration of regional female deities probably were also present in clan families, especially among women and unlettered men, providing heroic tales of strong and faithful women. But only in Matthew do we find, of the communities reviewed, the critique of patriarchal hypocrisy in contrast to the faith of marginal people occupying an important place at the center of the tradition. It is also the case that all the scribal communities cited praise the men who lead them for their humility and for dealing justly with those who are dependent.[63] Yet Matthew's warnings are particularly stringent, as can be seen in the parables that climax Jesus' last two speeches, which make treatment of the offending and the least into the single standard of God's judgment. In all, it seems best to say that though Matthew's community is not distinctive among scribal groups in articulating such values, it is distinctive in its central emphasis

62. Jdt 7:19–32; 8:11–36; 14:1–7; *b. Ta'anit* 23ab; *y. Sota* 1.4; *y. Horayot* 3.4.
63. Liu, *Traditional Chinese Clan Rules,* 48–69, 98–106; *Pirqe Aboth* 1.2, 10, 12, 17; 3.1, 12, 16, 22; 4.4, 7, 22, 29; 1QS 5.26–27, 8.1–4, 1QH 3, 4, and passim.

on figures without social power, including women, as models of faith in God and as the challenge to service.

Part II: Gender Role Variations in Scribal Communities

The second part of this chapter will investigate further the nature of scribal communities to find factors that might account for Matthew's greater emphasis on women as examples for faith and as incentives to good works. I turn to another study of Qing China which develops a model distinguishing levels of literacy and social dominance in advanced agricultural society. My proposal is that a deviation of Matthew's community from other scribal groups in either literacy or socioeconomic power might help explain the particular emphases in this community. A less educated or less economically stable community might be more prone to identify with its own disadvantaged members. A further possibility is that the recent arrival of the Christian tradition at a high literary and economic level from a very different origin might help to explain distinctive emphases in this community.

SCRIBAL COMMUNITIES
AND CULTURAL COMMUNICATION

In his introduction to a collection of essays on popular culture in late imperial China, David Johnson shapes a model for distinguishing the major social groups involved in cultural communication in this agricultural society.[64] He is looking for a way to chart the "travels" of an opera as it makes its way from the romance and military combat popular in the market town to become an epic of family and state honor appropriate for performance at the clan hall.[65] Similarly, secret religious texts attract women in one period with stories of the celibate princess Miao Shan, while in a later time they offer escape to the Eternal Mother in ways attractive to peasants, migrants, and monks without temples.[66] The role of language and literacy in such cultural sea changes is crucial, and interested bilingual people are needed to carry an oral tradition

---

64. Johnson, "Communication, Class, and Consciousness." The nine sectors described suggest gradations of difference that extend theoretically to as many units as there are people.

65. Tanaka Issei, "The Social and Historical Context of Ming-Ch'ing Local Drama"; and Barbara Ward, "Regional Operas and Their Audiences: Evidence from Hong Kong," both in *Popular Culture in Late Imperial China* (ed. David Johnson, Andrew J. Nathan, and Evelyn S. Rawski; Berkeley: University of California Press, 1985) 143–60, 161–87.

66. David L. Overmyer, "Values in Chinese and Sectarian Literature: Ming and Ch'ing Pao-chuean"; and Susan Naquin, "The Transmission of White Lotus Sectarianism in Late Imperial China," both in *Popular Culture*, 219–54, 255–91.

across dialect borders, or, since written Chinese characters are universal (as is the Greek language in the urban Roman East), the literate may provide the bridge once a story is in writing.[67] But Johnson finds he cannot chart the "cultures within a culture" based on literacy alone because power relations are also determinative.[68] Once killed, a favorite local bandit is transformed by the gentry's patronage into a quiet saint, and the drowned girl taken as Sea Goddess by the boat people and pirates is turned by imperial edict and fine temples into the protector of sea merchants.[69] In the reverse direction, women and servants introduce the men of a household to oral stories and thereby have a creative impact on men's texts.[70]

This means that the independent significance of social power and literacy cannot be ignored. What is needed on the most simple level is a two-factor grid of four quadrants, because literacy is not always congruent with social dominance nor orality with social dependence, even in imperial China where examinations in the classics were required for all government posts. Nonliterates with some social power, such as the women and servants mentioned, affect the cultural product, and the learned who have become dependent survive by teaching their skills and perhaps their discontent to others.

To provide a more sensitive tool, Johnson breaks down his grid further to include three levels of both literacy and social power.[71] He distinguishes

67. Johnson, "Communication, Class, and Consciousness," 35–40.

68. Ibid., 44–50. Here Johnson notes the parallel work done in European social history by Carlo Ginzburg and Eugen Weber showing the key role of social power in a person's cultural mentality.

69. Robert Hegel, "Distinguishing Levels of Audience for Ming-Ch'ing Vernacular Literature: A Case Study"; and James L. Watson, "Standardizing the Gods: The Promotion of T'ien Hou ('Empress of Heaven') along the South China Coast 960–1960," both in *Popular Culture*, 112–42, 292–324; David Johnson, "The Wu Tzu-hsue Pien-wen and Its Sources," *Harvard Journal of Asiatic Studies* 40 (1980) 93–156, 465–505; and idem, "Epic and History in Early China: The Matter of Wu Tzu-hsue," *Journal of Asian Studies* 40 (1981) 255–71.

70. *Popular Culture*, ed. D. Johnson et al., 61–62.

71.

CHIEF SOCIAL-CULTURAL GROUPS

	greatest	SOCIAL DOMINANCE	least
greatest	classically educated; legally privileged	classically educated; self-sufficient	classically educated; dependent
L I T E R A C Y	literate; legally privileged	literate; self-sufficient	literate; dependent
least	nonliterate; legally privileged	nonliterate; self-sufficient	nonliterate dependent

(Adapted from David Johnson, "Communication, Class, and Consciousness in Late Imperial China," *Popular Culture in Late Imperial China* (ed. David Johnson, Andrew J. Nathan and Evelyn S. Rawski; Berkeley: University of California Press, 1985) 56.)

levels of education. At the top are the classically educated, then come the functionally literate, and at the bottom are the people of nonliterate or oral culture. What he calls social dominance is laid out in columns; at the left are those who are legally privileged, in the center those who manage to be self-sufficient, and at right the dependent. This yields nine sectors, or what he calls "cultural mentalities," which are of course not evenly occupied. The majority in agricultural society inhabit the lower right square with no education or independence. Yet this scheme presses on the reader more subtle distinctions than might otherwise be made for those with some measure of either literacy or economic self-sufficiency. Johnson says that position in the dominance system determines point of view, while position in the communication system determines the manner of expressing it. I find it more accurate to say that both systems as he describes them are gauges of social dominance, one economic and the other cultural, and there are points of view and styles of presentation indigenous to each.

Rather than trying to summarize Johnson's application of this model to social groups reflected in the texts of late imperial China, I will attempt an application to first-century Palestine, focusing on the scribal communities reviewed above as known through their texts, with particular interest in women's social roles.

There are some difficulties in transferring Johnson's categories. In the Western classical world the effort to be self-sufficient on the basis of one's own labor would usually have been considered inferior in comfort and dignity to dependence on a well-disposed benefactor.[72] Therefore Johnson's category of the "self-sufficient" will be used to include everyone not legally privileged who has sufficient resources, usually in land or family connections, to support at least a modest household, or who has sufficient skill and position as an artisan, merchant, teacher, or soldier to attract patrons. The dependent are those vulnerable at any moment to an empty plate—tenants, landless people for hire, beggars, and unpatronized artisans and writers. Another difficulty in cross-cultural adaption of the model is that imperial China was a more stable and culturally integrated society than the Roman East. Therefore I limit my use of the grid to one century, one ethnic group, and one region—the Jews of first-century Palestine—to assure that I have a population sufficiently integrated to allow comparisons between cultural types.

Among first-century Palestine's Jews, the classically educated and

72. The greater dignity of not-working over working in the Roman East is described by Richard Rohrbaugh, "Methodological Considerations in the Debate over the Social Class Status of Early Christians," *JAAR* 52 (1984) 536, 541, who cites M. I. Finley, *The Ancient Economy* (London: Chatto & Windus, 1973) 40–51. On the conventions of friendship and benefaction in the Roman Empire as they impact urban Christians, see Peter Marshall, *Enmity in Corinth: Social Conventions in Paul's Relations with Corinthians* (Tübingen: J.C.B. Mohr [Paul Siebeck], 1987).

legally privileged were few. Roman citizenship, if not always a classical Greek education, probably belonged to the Herodian and some other wealthy families and to Jews from Hellenistic cities once allied with Rome, though citizenship could not protect against imperial disfavor. Men in the high-priestly families had legal and economic privileges from Roman recognition of their religious authority, and they would have been classically educated in Hebrew and literate enough to function politically in Greek. Their cultural impact through the temple while it stood can hardly be overestimated, but their effective power was restricted by direct Roman appointment of the high priest and by Roman domination over the priestly vestments and the holy city throughout most of this period. Roman favor itself compromised the authority of the Herodians and high priests except among other privileged people. Merely literate and legally privileged Jews may have been a slightly broader group of people with Roman connections but less education—merchants from Hellenistic cities, perhaps, or high tax functionaries and other officials. The nonliterate with legal privileges would have been largely freed slaves of Roman citizens (though some slaves were educated) or women in wealthy families. In learned families where the men were classically educated the women's lack of literacy would have been more socially debilitating than in those merely literate circles where men acted out their legal privilege in commerce or politics and wives and daughters might become secondarily involved. In all, legally privileged Palestinian Jews were few.

Writers and readers in the scribal communities described above are closer to the category at the top of Johnson's central column, those who are classically educated and self-supporting. Most Pharisees were classically educated in the Torah and studied it by avocation, supporting themselves as was traditional in their families or taking up some trade close to the home of their teacher in order not to accept money for their teaching. After Yohanan ben Zakkai established the academy at Yavneh, the sages did make court decisions in religious law with growing Roman recognition, yet it is unclear to what extent this can be considered a retainer with economic advantages. At least it allowed them in the following period to raise money among Jews without interference for support of the schools and the poor.

Any group of Pharisees probably also included some from the classically educated and dependent group—witness the stories of the poverty of Rabbi Hanina ben Dosa.[73] He and other rabbis better known for healing than teaching may not have advanced—for lack of skill, time, or interest—to the level of a classical education and would be better grouped with the literate and dependent. The women of the Pharisees' and rabbis' families were not taught to read

---

73. *b. Ta'anit* 24b–25a.

Torah and were therefore nonliterate, though the exceptional case of female literacy probably occurred in learned families. Women lived in a world ruled by Torah and had to learn its interpretation wherever they were affected, which means a woman's oral Torah must have developed. In all, the circle who ate together in ritual purity probably extended down the literacy gauge in the self-supporting part of the population and to a lesser extent in the dependent part as well. But because communal identity was so focused on the classical education in Scripture studies toward which all the males were directed, the nonliterate in the community were probably unable to realize major social influence even in self-supporting families.

The Qumran community will also have been in large part classically educated and self-supporting, at least in its monastic form in good times. Texts from the first century show the monks' education in both copying and interpreting the Scriptures in exegesis, law, and liturgy. Their self-supporting nature is suggested by their practice of absorbing the assets of members after two years in the community, by the substantial nature of the material remains of their monastery and parchments, and by their "work" which could have included grazing or winter farming in the wadis around Qumran.[74] The part of the community living in families throughout Israel could have provided a further base for financial support.

But as Palestine became more impoverished in the first century through famine, high taxes, mal-government, withholding of temple tithes from poor priests, and, finally, war, town dwellers would have had less to give and, at last, no monks to give to. Schools were legislated for sons of town dwellers,[75] but many would not have completed or retained this education and daughters were not taught, with the result that this religious group extended into the merely literate and nonliterate population. Although some of these nonliterate women were from self-supporting families, their participation in a tight covenant community which reserved the "way of perfection" for highly educated celibate males left them with little or no access to social power. The community's culture was built on written Scripture by reworking scriptural genres, and those who did not read and write were not able to help create the culture.

Of course most Jews were not wealthy or part of scribal communities and did not have the opportunity for a classical education. It is difficult to estimate what percentage of the male population had had some synagogue or private education and could be classified as literate. Recent studies in late imperial China have reversed an earlier assumption that only the legally privileged were educated. Failures in examinations to enter the privileged

74. On "work," see 1QS 5.14; 6.2; on economic transactions, 5.17; 7.6–8.
75. 1QSa 1.6–9.

scholar/official status have been estimated at 98 percent of participants in the Qing period, producing a group of about five percent of adult males who were classically educated but had to make their own living by some form of teaching, advising, or writing for those not classically educated. This teaching in turn produced a larger fund of at least literate people who kept accounts for merchants, wrote the family genealogy, or sang ballads and read almanacs to the nonliterate.

First-century Palestine was a very different place, without even Qing China's rudimentary printing and with a growing struggle between foreign political power and local groups. Yet here also tax collectors and farm managers kept accounts and someone wrote the deeds and last testaments. Such people would have been self-sufficient in good times. Some nonliterate people with a little land or a few sheep or boats could support themselves part of the year or were members of families where someone made a living. But the dependent class in Palestine seems to have been growing throughout the first century as the exploitation of the Herods and procurators was passed down in the population to prey on the least. Even some classically educated people were unable to feed themselves in hard times, and the functionally literate needed skills other than literacy to avoid dependence. The nonliterate and dependent remained the largest group of all, including as it did virtually all women in dependent families and most men in a society where land was increasingly concentrated in a few hands. A group of people this large could doubtless be distinguished into nine further subcategories, ranging from the sharp survivor to the non-surviving.

MATTHEW'S GOSPEL AS
CULTURAL COMMUNICATION

Because we see no sign in Matthew that its writer or audience had legal privilege, and because we must assume that the writer and at least the primary intended audience could read, the left column (legally privileged) and lower strip (nonliterate) in Johnson's grid are not the central location of this text. The task remaining is to determine on the rest of the grid whether this author and these intended readers were classically educated or merely literate and whether they were self-sufficient or dependent. Whether or not we consider this Gospel's grasp of the Torah and prophets to be adequate to Scripture's divine-human drama and its vision of God's mercy and justice on earth, we cannot deny that the fulfillment of Torah and prophets by Jesus is constitutive for the Gospel's worldview. When this is set beside other indications of scribal practice—apology in light of tradition, first signs of case law in procedures and exceptions, reference to "scribes trained for the kingdom," and a diction and syntax more elevated than the sources—the evidence for classical education rather than a trade-oriented literacy is more than sufficient. Knowledge is knowledge of the authoritative tradition, and anything new is confirmed by consonance with it.

But this does not tell the extent of such education in the community. Practical factors would seem to militate against educating everyone: one son in a family would be hard enough to spare from pressures to make a living, one text at most in the community would make many readers redundant since others could as well listen, and one language in this Greek-speaking community could be the limit of many people, though the Hebrew Scriptures were apparently known to a few. Yet none of these factors would be an insuperable barrier to wide reading and reciting of Scriptures. Competence in Greek could be taken as acceptable. And other scribal communities did not let the pressures of few texts and many mouths to feed prevent practice of their devotion to the tradition through wide-spread education in it. Particularly if this community originated in a larger scribal context such as that established by Qumran town dwellers, Pharisees, or other apocalyptic or wisdom-oriented groups, the practices of learning would already be in place and new texts could be added to the old. Of course some would not get beyond reading the familiar texts with difficulty, and more than half of the group—women, small children, and the disabled—would not be expected to read, but scribal values can be assumed to have fostered at least basic scribal practices.[76]

What then of the consistent critique of scribal consciousness throughout this Gospel? None is to be called "rabbi" or "teacher"; they must do what the scribes preach but not what they practice; they are not to be like the hypocrites who love to make their religion public; better even to say no and obey than to say yes and do nothing (23:8–10, 2–3; 6:2, 5, 16; 21:28–32). I take this as evidence not of distance from scribal life but of intimate knowledge of its dangers. The polemical narrative context of these teachings may reflect the community's dissociation from others too close for comfort on the scribal path, perhaps those from whom the community emerged and toward whom community members might be most likely to defect.

If this reading of a mixed community dominated by the classically educated is accurate, the significance of female models and "the least of these" in Matthew probably does not reflect special identification with the nonliterate. In fact, gender roles in a classically educated community of this kind tend to be

76. To contest this, one would have to argue, first, that the fulfillment quotations are drawn from a Christian source rather than knowledge of Scripture; second, that scribal values are so dominant in the culture that they are shared by groups lacking a tradition of education and/or means to pursue it; or, third, that the writer is working to foster scribal values in a group yet strange to them.

polarized by the great contrast between the educated and nonliterate sexes. Whatever women's experience of faith, they remain dependent on others to read and interpret the tradition that sets the pattern for their lives. This essentially passive rather than active relation to the key step in tradition making not only leaves them without recourse when others determine their practice but also marginalizes them as examples of virtue or objects of need in texts written primarily with the education of others in mind. The scribal practice of not educating females causes this impact on women in particular. Theoretically the roles establishing right order and determining education in a scribal community could be set in terms of age or wisdom or ethnic group rather than gender, and the experience of the Therapeutrides in Egyptian Judaism of this period is a case in point.[77] But some groups are bound to be marginalized by the education of others in the scribal community. And because there are no signs pointing to the quite different environment of women in Egypt for the provenance of Matthew, we must assume that women in this classically educated group are by definition nonliterate, as has been found in the other scribal communities in its setting and confirmed by the roles given women in Matthew.

A second explanation for unusual depiction of women and marginal people in the Matthean community might be based on economic status. Writers and readers who are not self-sufficient but dependent in society at large might have affinity with other dependent people in the community. This is not to say that living standards would have been shared equally by both sexes in any household, since the impact of poverty on the two sexes in agricultural society could differ considerably. To increase output, or at least to maintain some income and social status in times of dependence, the scarce resources of the family would likely be used for its primary producers to do their work—in our author's case perhaps for parchments and time to write—leaving less for the others. Yet severe economic straits could make a household unable to sustain a traditional division of tasks at all and press everyone into common physical labor, diminishing the power differential within the group, but under very stressful circumstances. The production of this Gospel itself is witness that this latter stage has not been reached, at least in the writer's household.

Scholars have recently proposed that the people for whom this Gospel was written lived in relative prosperity.[78] The urban setting of this Gospel,

77. Philo *Vit. cont.* 28–29, 32–33, 68–69, 75–76, 83–89.

78. Herman Waetjen, *The Origin and Destiny of Humanness* (San Rafael, Calif.: Omega Books, 1976) 29–31; Robert H. Smith, "Were the First Christians Middle-Class? A Sociological Analysis of the New Testament," *Currents in Theology and Mission* 7 (1980) 260–76, reprinted in *The Bible and Liberation* (ed. Norman Gottwald; Maryknoll, N.Y.: Orbis Books, 1983) 441–57; Jack Dean Kingsbury, *Matthew as Story* (Philadelphia: Fortress, 1986) 125–26; Michael Crosby, *House of Disciples: Church, Economics and Justice in Matthew* (Maryknoll, N.Y.: Orbis Books, 1988) 39–43.

suggested by the writer's locating the Galilee ministry among "cities" (9:1; 10:5, 11, 15, 23; 11:1, 20) and giving Jesus his own residence (4:13; 9:1, 10; 13:36), already indicates a living standard different from that in rural areas at this time. The systematic urban exploitation of the rural people surrounding each city in the Hellenistic and Roman periods occurred through high taxes on indigenous landowners forcing them to sell, high rents for land to farm, and low wages for hired farm workers. Further evidence of the urban setting of Matthew's Gospel is found in the fact that, while Mark often states large sums in terms of the denarius usable for workers' wages, Matthew prefers to speak of gold, silver, and talents not in rural circulation.[79]

But in this world of moneyed people it was also possible to become no longer self-sufficient, a particularly painful fate. The Gospel community's texts, genealogies, and stories reflect cultural level but not necessarily present economic condition and cannot assure a strong financial position. This can only be determined, if Johnson is right, from direct or indirect information in the text or from its reflecting points of view typical of the socially dominant. And this process is made more difficult by my correction that social dominance may be either cultural or economic, and the dominance sustained by education may continue when the dominance of wealth falls away—if not too far or too long. So it is necessary to consider whether the Gospel shows signs of specifically financial insecurity or the confidence characteristic of the economically self-sufficient. Because the writer's traditions come from a rural origin where dependence is widespread, such signs must be shown to permeate the writer's interpretation of the tradition and not only the sources.

Three possible signs of economic crisis for the community require evaluation. The first, already addressed, concerns the healing stories and references to the "least of these," especially if they are told by Matthew so as to encourage the reader to identify with the economically marginal and be confident of God's delivery. Jesus' role as healer and as one who identifies himself with the least and demands mercy for the needy is newly emphasized in this Gospel (4:23–24; 8:16–17; 9:13, 35; 12:7; 18:5; 25:31–46). But the narrowing of these stories to focus on faith in Jesus' power dims identification with those in need (8:10; 9:18–22, 28). Instead the reader is drawn into identification with the disciples who are to follow Jesus in the healing and serving ministry (9:35—10:8; 18:1–35), and the punishment meted out to those without mercy is clearly a warning to the complacent rather than comfort for the oppressed (18:35; 25:46). Although some hearers of the Gospel are apparently among the "least of these," where the writer develops this tradition

---

79. Mark 6:37; 14:5; Matt 2:11; 10:9; 18:24; 23:16–17; 25:15–28; 26:15; 27:3–9; 28:12–15. For an analysis of the coinage and its significance, see Kingsbury, *Matthew as Story*, 125–26.

most fully "the little one" is called the sinning brother, indicating that economic need in the community is not a major concern of the author (18:7–35).

The predictions of persecution and defection in this Gospel and its apologetic interest are also possible indirect signs of economic distress. A group not recognized by others as it sees itself may be socially rejected or defamed. Unless its members own land, they must provide services to others for a living and are vulnerable to economic sanctions. When in this Gospel Jesus predicts that wickedness will multiply and many people's love grow cold (24:12), the question is whether this sensitivity of the writer reflects the chill of complacent prosperity after fervent beginnings or the chill of unexpected marginality and loss. Not only here but in many passages where the writer adds detail about hard times to come, the focus is on false prophets leading people astray and causing the least to stumble so that people betray and hate each other (24:10–12; 7:15, 21–23; 10:21–23; 18:6–22). Such apparent conflict within the Jewish or Jewish-Christian community could have an economic side, but this is not stated. Instead the emphasis is on the crucial witness at this time to the Gentiles. Perhaps this church has been moving its economic and even social base toward the broader Greek-speaking world and may therefore not be suffering economically. The difference between the writer's vilifying of Herodian rulers and exoneration of the Gentile Pilate could support this (2:1–23; 14:1–12; 27:11–26). Gentile associations would of course bring on further accusations of impurity from fellow Jews and require yet stronger defense that this Gospel's interpretation of Jewish tradition was the strict one. But this would not be evidence of economic hardship.

A final possible sign that this community was in economic straits is the Gospel's extraordinary stress on faith and dependence on God. The question is whether or not this reflects a situation of economic need. The Lord's Prayer is framed with an opening assurance that God "knows what you need before you ask," but at the end this need is explained not in terms of bread or debt release but in terms of forgiveness of trespasses against God (6:7–14). Giving away your clothes and loaning whatever your borrower wants—even selling what you have and giving it to the poor—is interpreted as the way to be perfect (5:38–48; 19:21). But there is no sign that this is meant to encourage resignation by those who have experienced losses. Rather Matthew calls for a chosen way of giving in imitation of God, dramatized in the narrative by rich people such as the Magi and Joseph of Arimathea, as well as in parabolic figures such as the forgiving master, the vineyard owner with his laborers, and the king letting everyone into his feast (5:48; 2:11; 27:57–60; 18:23–35; 20:1–16; 22:1–10). Recompense on earth for this generosity is best avoided or at least not to be expected (6:1–18; 13:28–30, 47–50; 19:29; cf. Mark 10:29–30). All this assumes a financial base with which to be generous. And this Gospel's focus on spiritual rather than material transformation suggests a community with enough to eat: a great harvest is interpreted in terms of understanding, bread in terms of teaching, and the Beatitudes teach dependence on God rather than assuming dependence for food (13:19, 23; 16:11, 17; 5:3–12). Theologically speaking, this Gospel does not consistently proclaim a profligate God for the dependent but rather a righteous God for the self-sufficient, a God who models and rewards a generosity measured out according to righteousness (7:15–27; 12:33–37, 46–50; 13:41–43, 47–50; 18:28–35; 19:28–30; 22:11–14; 25:9–13, 20–30).

Matthew's writer and primary readers seem to be firmly located at the center top of Johnson's grid among the self-sufficient and classically educated, with the writers of all the scribal communities discussed. This leaves no ready explanation for the significant if secondary role Matthew gives the suppliants and "the least." A further possible explanation is that the wide variety of levels in literacy and economic security within the community have encouraged a writer to allow the marginal a certain passive status as models of faith and intimacy with God. While not themselves challenged to understand and act as disciples, they would then have a function as the standard of greatness and the examples of faith for those that do. Yet some variety of literacy and economic levels has also been found within the other scribal communities without widespread modeling by marginal people. It therefore seems unlikely that the origin of this emphasis can be attributed strictly to a wider scope of social groups in the community, though this might encourage retention of such stories and sayings once they are accepted.

Another possible explanation for the stress in this community on the faith and needs of the marginal is the recent origin of the traditions about Jesus in a nonliterate and economically dependent sector of the culture. David Johnson's use of the nine "cultural mentalities" to chart the travels of folk legends through late imperial China may be adapted to chart the cultural route of the traditions about Jesus. Not only do the stories and sayings change as they move from one cultural group to another, but their implication for gender roles differs in different communities. Any schematization oversimplifies what is in reality not the neat stepping of a tradition from one type of group to another but a spreading of multiple traditions "overland" in many directions at once without necessarily leaving the initial setting. The texts Matthew knows give indications of beginning with stories and prophetic sayings by and to the nonliterate and economically dependent. Some of these sayings later appear among the literate and dependent in a collection (Q), while stories and other sayings appear as a Gospel for the literate and perhaps mixed dependent and self-sufficient (Mark) before Matthew's by no means final writing of the tradition in a largely classically educated and self-sufficient scribal community.

For the first stage we have no primary evidence and can only extrapolate backward from written texts. In the history of Chinese folk traditions Johnson and others have traced back from imperial cults and literary texts to find behind the great Li Mi the legend of a desperate rural bandit, behind the Empress of Heaven a village girl with spiritual powers, and behind the noble Wu Tzu-hsue a wronged provincial official.[80] Analogously, Gospel traditions suggest that Jesus began as a healer and teacher in the charismatic rabbi tradition[81] who proclaimed the arrival on earth of a new divine order based on God's unlimited generosity and true judgment. He led his followers to Jerusalem and was crucified as a threat to the existing religious and political order. Doubly marginal people including sick, possessed, gentile, and outcast women were prominent in this movement, both as witnesses to their own transformation and apparently as the first witnesses that Pilate and the priests had not been able to destroy Jesus (Matt 21:31–32; Mark 5:25–34; 7:24–30; Luke 7:36–50; 8:2; 13:10–17; John 4:7–42; Matt 28:8–10; John 20:11–18).

The writers of the Q source transcribed a collection of Jesus' sayings that had apparently been drawn together and shaped by Christian prophets who continued to make these announcements after Jesus' time. The sayings were thereby sharpened for concrete use against those who rejected them and for better hearing in the towns and finally in the cities of Palestine. Women were apparently active among these prophets in the Aramaic-speaking countryside, during the bilingual transition, and in the Greek-speaking cities as well[82]—except in the writing and reading which may not yet have been formative. The point of view expressed in the sayings shows that dependent people were still largely offering their new resource to others like themselves.

Mark, in its epic chain of scenes with its ironic mode, reflects traditions originating among oral storytellers who show a dependent peoples' searing critique of power, the power of both authorities and disciples. In this circle, women told the stories of their healings; and these stories, if not the individual people, traveled to women storytellers across distances and into the Greek city culture. In this writing, the author apparently plays an increasing role, both stylistically in linking chains of stories with summaries and materially in exalting Jesus' suffering as a model for believers. The women may be distanced in two ways from this work: (1) they are not literate writers or readers and

---

80. See n. 69.

81. The parallel is drawn to Hanina ben Dosa by Geza Vermes in *Jesus the Jew: A Historian's Readings of the Gospels* (Philadelphia: Fortress, 1973) 72–78. See also idem, *Post-Biblical Jewish Studies*, 178–214. For a consonant interpretation of the Gospel miracle stories, see my "The Structure of the Gospel Miracle Stories and Their Tellers," *Semeia* 11 (1978) 83–113.

82. Our knowledge of the oral tradents of this period, including women among them, can only be drawn from the Gospel accounts of the itinerants following Jesus (Mark 10:29; cf. Luke 18:29; Mark 15:40–41; Luke 8:1–3; Matt 27:55–56), from Paul's earlier letters describing those who traveled among the city churches (1 Cor 1:11, 16:19; Rom 16:1–5, 7, 12), and from the language of the Sayings Source itself (Luke 12:51–53; 13:20; Matt 21:31–32; Luke 17:35).

continue to work orally, and (2) they—except for a few among the self-sufficient—probably do not teach Jesus as one who calls the powerful to humble service but continue to herald him as one who gives power to the weak.

A further transition in this sequence occurs when a scribal community takes these traditions and demonstrates that Jesus is the fulfillment of Torah and prophets and therefore the long-awaited climax of Israel's written tradition and the restoration of the right order of humanity before God. Certain men chosen to make disciples in this way of righteousness by teaching observance of all Jesus' commands are the model for one part of the community. "The least" in this Gospel are still called greatest in the kingdom and set the example of great faith, a vestige of the earlier oral gospel that the women and other non-literates transmitted. But here the tradition in its written form has taken from them the active roles of carrying and shaping the gospel.

Conclusion

The group addressed in Matthew can be classified sociologically as a scribal community according to common characteristics found in the late imperial Chinese clan, at Qumran, and among the Pharisees. These groups share a parallel function in advanced agricultural societies of restoring in a certain part of society at a time of threat the practice of set roles demanded by written sacred tradition. I have not investigated in each case to what extent this restoration serves the power structures of the respective agricultural society and to what extent it serves the traditional values and the position in society of the particular community. But it has been shown that the set roles called for in this restoration do in each scribal community serve the interests of those who are permitted the literacy necessary to read and interpret the sacred tradition, to the marginalization of women who are not taught to read.

Matthew differs from the other scribal communities reviewed because it is written not only to train male disciples in knowledge and action but makes prominent use in this task of the stories of marginal people, including women, to exemplify faith and practice. This suggested the possibility that this community has either a lower economic or literary level than is expected in such scribal communities and therefore identifies more closely with the needy and women. But a review has shown that the writer and primary readers of Matthew give every indication of being self-sufficient and classically educated, as is characteristic of the other scribal communities studied. The spread of the membership of this community across the less literate and economically secure quadrants of the culture is not unique.

I have suggested that the distinctive role of marginal people in this scribal community may be a vestige of the migration of the Jesus tradition from nonliterate and economically dependent culture into self-sufficient and classically educated culture. This vestige may be present not only in a literary sense but also in a social sense. Alongside this Gospel using marginal people's stories to instruct those the writer thinks bear responsibility for the tradition, very likely an oral tradition is operating in which peoples' voices still directly challenge others to faith.[83] In Matthew's text, gender roles reflect the assumptions of the writer and those participants in the scribal community for which this instruction is written. The gender roles in the continuing oral gospels will likewise have reflected their tradents and audience—including those in the difficult setting of nonliterates in scribal communities. This will have paralleled the oral Torah taught and practiced among wives and daughters of the Pharisees and any oral covenant vowed by women related to Qumran. But because Matthew's written Gospel is so much dependent for its sources on recent popular traditions, it gives more—though still indirect—evidence of these women's traditions than we have in the other scribal communities considered.

83. The polemic against false prophets in Matthew is probably not only an effort on the author's part to dissociate the community from nonliterate and apocalyptic practices but also a negative judgment against certain Christian oral traditions that compete with the writer's vision (7:15–23; 24:10–12).

6

Gender Analysis:
A Response to
Antoinette Clark Wire

PHEME PERKINS

Before turning to the problems of gender analysis raised by Professor Wire, I would like to suggest that three common assumptions underlying the discussions thus far need further analysis and clarification. In some instances, our willingness to use a common vocabulary may mask very different assumptions about what is meant in each case.

1. *What is meant by community?* Wire's sociological evidence from China speaks of a community that determines all facets of life for its members. Such a community integrates religious symbols and practice into the larger sociocultural forms of existence differently than may have been the case for the Matthean community. Those members of this conference who hold that Matthew's community is still part of a larger Jewish community may hold that this Jewish community is the one defining an individual's social world. A. J. Saldarini has already reminded us that we need to clarify what "church" represents in Matthew's context, since it can be used loosely for an "association." The extent to which such an association structures social interaction remains undefined. We are similarly unclear about the semantic range of the term "ethnos" in Matthew. Does it mean "gentile" as opposed to Jew, "gentile" as opposed to Jew and non-Jewish Christian, "nation," or "people"?

2. *What is meant by scribe?* There seems to be a general acquiescence to claims about Matthew that situate him in the context of scribal interpreters of tradition. This agreement presumes that Matthew's statements in passages

like 13:52 and 23:1–3 imply that Matthew accepts the underlying orientation of scribal or Pharisaic interpretation of the tradition. But is a scribal or Pharisaic ethos really the one Matthew envisages for his community? The "scribes" of Wire's Chinese examples, persons from clans whose literacy in a shared tradition allows them access to new centers of imperial power, hardly fits the Pharisaic situation in Jesus' time in any case. It is much more apposite to the sons of the provincial aristocracy who gained access to Roman circles through education and the administrative bureaucracy of the empire.

3. *What is the significance of the gospel genre?* Much of the descriptive language used about Matthew so far in this conference depends upon redactional elements in those passages where Matthew deals with legal rulings or claims that prophetic texts are fulfilled in Jesus. Yet Matthew's Gospel hardly qualifies as halacha even if he does appear more sensitive to legal nuances than Mark does. Nor does his application of prophetic texts require a written, scribal searching of the text such as we find at Qumran. Suppose we begin instead from the fact that Matthew has not composed either a community rule or an interpretation of a prophetic text. Matthew has presented us with a narrative work. If it is to be compared with Jewish writings of the time, then the category of haggadah would seem to be a more appropriate one. Wire has correctly pointed out that Matthew's Gospel is preoccupied with authoritative speech acts. She takes that preoccupation to confirm the view that Matthew advocates scribal interpretation of the Torah. But there are authoritative speech acts in the world of oral traditions, too. Matthew's narrative speaks to a general audience, not to one accustomed to scribal literacy.

THREE APPROACHES
TO FEMINIST ANALYSIS

Wire has adopted a method of comparative social analysis in order to allow us to draw some conclusions about gender relations in the Matthean community. In order to evaluate her proposals, I would like to adopt a typology of types of feminist interpretation of the Old Testament from Katherine Sackenfeld of Princeton Seminary.[1]

1. *Rhetorical analysis* attends to the literary dynamic internal to the text. For example, one finds in Matthew fewer indications of surprising, anomalous behavior of females than in the stories commonly analyzed by feminists in Old Testament studies. Where we do find it, as in the story of the

---

1. Katherine Sackenfeld, "Feminist Biblical Interpretation," *Theology Today* 46 (1989) 154–68.

Canaanite woman whose daughter is healed, the message of the story is sharply pointed at the male disciples, as Wire has observed. The Canaanite woman has to overcome a double obstacle in Matthew's version. First, the disciples seek to push her aside. Then, Jesus invokes the restriction of his own ministry to the "lost of Israel" (a restriction already placed on the mission of the disciples in Matt 10:5) to refuse her request. The narrative function of such "little ones" is to pose a contrast or challenge to the disciples.

In addition, female characters may appear to relieve pressure that might be placed on male characters for behavior that is not approved as in the case of the mother of the sons of Zebedee and the wife of Pilate. The intervention of the female characters moderates the male quest for power or dominance. Wire has shown that there is a narrative ambiguity in Matthew over the attribution of power and authority to Jesus' followers. Thus, Matthew departs from her Chinese parallel in which power and authority clearly followed upon attaining certified scribal learning.

2. *Culturally cued literary analysis* insists that we cannot ascertain the literary or rhetorical dynamics of the text without developing hypotheses about the likely meanings its words, images, and stories would have conveyed to speakers in a given culture. How do we establish such cultural cues? Is there really enough overlap between China and the world of Matthew to permit cues developed from evidence about that setting to fill in gaps in our knowledge of Matthew's world? In the presentations by E. A. Judge and Abraham Malherbe, we saw some examples of how cultural cues might be developed. The association of gnomic, inscribed wisdom with the gymnasia, places in which males gathered for various forms of verbal and physical interaction, might be said to support Wire's contention that Matthew envisages males as the new disciple-scribes of the tradition. However, we also have been reminded that Matthew presumes an unusual social context of responsibility toward others and inter-action among persons that bring words into the Christian speech patterns that do not fit the relationships of the Greco-Roman city. Words like "mercy" and "brother" have an egalitarian usage unlike the "friendship" vocabulary of the period.

The paper by Frederick W. Norris on the archaeology of Antioch raised questions about the cultural cues Christian speech patterns might have raised for the nonliterate. Σωτηρία presents an image of the health attained through healing. Wire has emphasized the importance of Jesus' healing for the marginal persons in the Gospel and seen concern for them as an obligation transmitted to the disciples. We also learned that δικαιοσύνη could mean fair weights and measures in the marketplace. This context situates it within the realm of fair dealings between individuals, not the realm of scribal debates about the law or even religious status. If such a translation is given the term, then we might argue that Matthew is presenting the point of view of "justice" that emerges from "below," not from a scribal class attaching some privilege to its learning. Wire's paper itself questions the common assumption that Matthew's community was a prosperous one based upon the emphasis on larger amounts of money than we find in Mark and the existence of prosperous individuals in the narrative.

3. *Text and archaeology* may be used as sources for information about the social situation of women at particular points in history. Unlike the previous two methods, this approach is not interested in the dynamics of the biblical narrative. To address the question raised by Wire, whether or not Matthew's community was anomalous, we ought to focus upon the question of the role played by women in cultic change. Unlike Luke-Acts, Matthew does not provide direct evidence of such involvement. Some of the Chinese material Wire discusses points to cases in which the folktale traditions that circulated among women came into the literate traditions of the males. Closer to home, we are familiar with the interest in Judaism among families of the Roman aristocracy, which seems to have been particularly true of women—at least, they are the ones against whom charges are lodged.[2] John Chrysostom castigates Christian women in Antioch for partaking of Jewish festivals and attending the synagogue.[3] In doing so, he presumes that the blame attaches to Christian husbands who do not keep their wives away from the synagogues. Could the invisibility of women in Matthew reflect some ambiguity over their role either in the spread of Christianity or in the adherence to Jewish practices that Matthew rejects? If so, more was at stake than the embeddedness of women in husbands and other related males which Wire notes as typical of scribal cultures.

AN UNRESOLVED QUESTION

Finally, there remains an unresolved question of method that might be put to all of our discussions thus far. What weight ought to be given to the literary composition of Matthew? Could the Gospel have apologetic aims, which in the desire to provide the Christian movement with the appearance of a respectable tradition has cast its Jesus as one who disputes with the Pharisees? The difficulty then becomes one of determining whether or not Matthew's interest in the appearances of scribal debate is really an indication of

2. See the list of examples assembled by J. Gager, *The Origins of Anti-Semitism* (New York: Oxford, 1963) 60–62.
3. See the text cited in Ross Kraemer, *Maenads, Martyrs, Matrons, Monastics* (Philadelphia: Fortress, 1988) 59–60.

social relationships within the community or is a literary fiction. Matthew has created an "implied author" and "implied audience" whose respectable opposition to Pharisaic excesses could deceive no one but the ἔθνη.

III

MATTHEW AND IGNATIUS
OF ANTIOCH

7

Ignatius and the Reception of the Gospel of Matthew in Antioch

_____ WILLIAM R. SCHOEDEL

The Gospel of Matthew is the only one of our Gospels that seems to have been exploited within a few years of its composition by another early Christian writer as a major source of information about the words and deeds of Jesus. That writer was Ignatius of Antioch, and the phenomenon is so unusual that Antioch or some location near Antioch has often been suggested as the place of composition for the Gospel of Matthew. The purpose of this study is to explore the social and religious situation that obtained in Antioch at the time of Ignatius and to assess the role that the Gospel of Matthew played in shaping the Christianity known to us from this source. It is an intriguing fact that although Ignatius had moved decisively beyond the social and religious horizons of the First Gospel, Matthew or material of a Matthean type still looms so large in his world. The phenomenon is made even more intriguing by the possibility just alluded to that it was not the Gospel of Matthew itself on which Ignatius relied, but that he depended in whole or in part on materials of a Matthean type that continued to circulate apart from the Gospel. This may have something to do with the fact that such materials were absorbed with such apparent ease in the rather different theological climate reflected in the letters of Ignatius. At the same time it would also mean that we have in Ignatius a window, however small, on the religious world out of which the Gospel of Matthew arose.

It does not prove easy, however, to use the letters of Ignatius for these purposes. Some would say that it is impossible to use them at all.[1] For it is

1. The following abbreviations are used here for the letters of Ignatius: Eph (Ephesians),

being argued again today that it is not only the long recension of the letters of Ignatius that is inauthentic, but also the short one on which we all rely. This is hardly the place to examine the diverse opinions of Weijenborg, Rius-Camps, and Joly on this matter. Suffice it to say that in my view the letters of the shorter recension are indeed authentic and that the reviews and studies mentioned below in the note show why this is the more probable view.[2] In my opinion, then, it is not uncritical to rely on the shorter recension of the letters of Ignatius for whatever light they may shed on the life of the Christian community in Antioch sometime in the first or second quarter of the second century.

For our purposes it would be helpful to be able to place Ignatius and his letters as early as possible in the second century. The date suggested by Eusebius in his *Chron.*, 107–108 C.E., and still often found in the handbooks today, would serve us well in that respect. Unfortunately, Eusebius seems not to have been relying on anything more definite than his own judgment in this matter.[3] And when he came to write his church history, he was satisfied to place the martyrdom of Ignatius in the days of Trajan, 98–117 C.E. (*Hist. Eccl.* 3.21–22). One recent writer has made an interesting argument for the year 115 C.E. by building on the discussion of Ignatius by John Malalas (*Chronographia* 11; *PG* 97.417b), though it is granted that unfortunately Malalas is not known for his accuracy and that he includes highly questionable comments also in his treatment of Ignatius.[4] Another scholar has recently argued for a date of about 120–135 C.E. on the basis of a reexamination of the problematic list of bishops of Antioch given by Eusebius.[5] I cannot see that there is anything in the letters out of harmony with such suggestions, and I do not find strong reasons to prefer one rather than the other. Probably any date between about 105 C.E. and 135

Tr (Trallians), Mg (Magnesians), Rom (Romans), Ph (Philadelphians), Sm (Smyrnaeans), Pol (Polycarp).

2. William R. Schoedel, "Are the Letters of Ignatius of Antioch Authentic?" *Religious Studies Review* 6 (1980) 196–201; idem, *Ignatius of Antioch* (Hermeneia; Philadelphia: Fortress, 1985) 5–7. For reviews of Reinoud Weijenborg (*Les lettres d'Ignace d'Antioche* [Leiden: E. J. Brill, 1969]), see esp. P.-Th. Camelot, *Bib* 51 (1970) 560–64; Antoine Wenger, *Revue des études Byzantines* 29 (1971) 213–16; Ilona Opelt, *Gnomon* 46 (1974) 251–55. For a discussion of J. Rius-Camps, *The Four Authentic Letters of Ignatius, the Martyr* (Christianismos; Rome: Pontificium institutum orientalium studiorum, 1979), see Robert Joly, *Le dossier d'Ignace d'Antioche* (Université Libre de Bruxelles, Faculté de Philosophie et Lettres 69; Brussels: Éditions de l'Université de Bruxelles, 1979) 121–27. For discussions of Joly's own arguments, see C. P. Hammond Bammel, "Ignatian Problems," *JTS* n.s. 33 (1982) 62–97; R. Gryson, "Les lettres attribuées à Ignace d'Antioche et l'apparition de l'épiscopat monarchique," *RTL* 10 (1979) 446–53; R. Winling, "A propos de la datation des Lettres d'Ignace d'Antioche," *RSR* 54 (1980) 259–65.

3. Cf. Adolf Harnack, *Geschichte der altchristlichen Literatur bis Eusebius*, Teil 2: *Die Chronologie* (2 vols., 2d ed.; repr. Leipzig: Hinrichs, 1958) 1.388–406.

4. Klaus-Gunther Essig, "Mutmassungen über den Anlass des Martyriums von Ignatius von Antiochien," *VC* 40 (1986) 105–17.

5. Charles Munier, "A propos d'Ignace d'Antioche: observations sur la liste épiscopale d'Antioche," *RSR* 55 (1981) 126–31.

C.E. must be allowed as a possibility for the martyrdom of Ignatius and the writing of his letters. Evidence of the use by Ignatius of gospel material in a form independent of our Gospels would probably favor a date at the earlier end of the range of possibilities.

There is a further difficulty that we must face at this point. By our account, Ignatius did indeed lead the Christian community in Antioch at a time not too distant from that of the writing of the Gospel of Matthew. But Ignatius is known to us only from six letters to churches in Asia Minor and another to the church in Rome, all of which he wrote on his way to Rome under the supervision of a Roman guard. He did not write back to his own church, and he tells us very little about it directly. Our first task, then, is to report the little that we can glean from the letters about the church in Antioch.

IGNATIUS AND THE CHURCH
IN ANTIOCH

Ignatius refers to his own church as "the church in Syria" in the conclusions of the four letters written from Smyrna (Eph 21.2; Mg 14; Tr 13.1; Rom 9.1). In the conclusions of the three letters written from Troas he refers to it as "the church in Antioch in Syria" (Ph 10.1; Sm 11.1; Pol 7.1). We do not know why there is this difference, but it may have something to do with the good news that he heard about the church in Antioch after arriving at Troas. We shall return to that point later.

At the conclusions of the letters written from Smyrna, Ignatius regularly introduces the mention of his church by urging that prayers be made for it. And he regularly adds a remark that indicates that he is from that church unworthy though he may be. In the letters written from Troas, Ignatius revises his formulation of these thoughts by indicating that the prayers for the church in Antioch have been answered and by adding a request that ambassadors be sent to Antioch to congratulate the Antiochian Christians. Only in the letter to the Smyrnaeans does he again use his earlier language of self-depreciation (Sm 11.1), and I believe that here it is considerably softened by the context in which it is found.

Mention of "Syria" alone as the place from which Ignatius comes appears elsewhere in the letters, including both those written from Smyrna and those written from Troas (Eph 1.2; Rom 2.2; Sm 11.2; cf. Ph 11.1). This fact warns us against trying to make too much of the difference in terminology noted above.

Associated with several of the concluding passages already discussed are remarks that state or imply that Ignatius comes as a prisoner from Syria, and this point is explicitly made also in one other passage (Eph 1.2).

More significant is a passage in which Ignatius identifies himself as "the bishop of Syria" (Rom 2.2). It is not impossible that he held some vaguely defined ecclesiastical jurisdiction over all of Syria, but little that we know about the early history of the episcopacy prepares us for such an understanding of the bishop's role. It is more likely that Ignatius is again referring to his church in Antioch.

We know about one other person who seems to have belonged to the church in Antioch at this time. For Ignatius refers to two men who caught up with him in Troas and brought him the good news about matters in Antioch (Ph 11.1; Sm 10.1). They are named Philo of Cilicia and Rheus Agathopous of Syria. Presumably Rheus Agathopous was from Ignatius's own church in Antioch. Both men seem to have had the title of "deacons" (Sm 10.1). And since Philo alone sends a greeting to the Smyrnaeans (Sm 13.1), he may have replaced the deacon Burrhus who had served as secretary or messenger for Ignatius until he reached Troas (Ph 11.2). Rheus Agathopous, on the other hand, may well have turned back to Antioch at that point. The name "Rheus" does not occur otherwise and may be a mistake. "Agathopous" means "swift-footed." The name is not often encountered and serves most frequently as that of slaves or freedmen or as a Roman cognomen.[6]

There was evidently a close relation between Antioch and one or more communities in Cilicia since Philo plays such an important role in the unfolding of events. It seems almost useless to speculate why this may be. In particular, it seems unlikely that Ignatius's jurisdiction should be extended still further to include parts of Cilicia. He notes (Ph 10.2) that "the nearest churches" have already sent bishops, "and others elders and deacons," to congratulate the church of Antioch. The statement projects the expected image of separate communities ruled by bishops and their assistants and interrelated by less formal means. It is likely that churches in Cilicia were among the neighboring churches who responded so admirably from Ignatius's point of view. And one or more of them may have been willing to bear the expense of sending the deacon Philo to be with Ignatius just as the Ephesians (with the help of the Smyrnaeans after the arrival of their leaders in Smyrna) sent the deacon Burrhus to accompany their visitor for the remainder of his trip in Asia (Eph 2.1; Ph 11.2; Sm 12.1).

The good news that Philo and Rheus Agathopous brought was that the church in Antioch was now "at peace" (Ph 10.1; Sm 11.2; Pol 7.1). It has traditionally been assumed that this is a reference to the end of the persecution in Antioch that brought with it the arrest of Ignatius. There can be no doubt that some pressure had been put on the Christians of Antioch and that for some

6. Schoedel, *Ignatius*, 214 n. 13.

reason their leader had been singled out to be sent to Rome to be thrown to the beasts in the arena. I have been convinced, however, by the arguments of P. N. Harrison that the "peace" that was restored in Antioch had to do with the restoration of unity among the Christians there.[7] If this is correct, the arrest and journey of Ignatius under guard served to draw them together and prompted them to acknowledge the authority of the man who had been taken from them and who was now waiting to hear of their reactions through messengers like Philo and Rheus Agathopous. The purpose of the request to send ambassadors to Antioch, then, was "to confirm the Christians at Antioch in their present newly attained unity."[8] This is not the place to argue the point in detail. It seems to me to make more sense of a number of things that we shall presently note. I shall try, however, not to make too much depend on what must remain a somewhat speculative interpretation of the data.

Such are the points that I have been able to glean from the letters of Ignatius that tell us something directly about the Christians in Antioch early in the second century. There is, of course, one other fact of great importance to us. The bishop of this community was a man who looked at the world and responded to issues as we in fact see him doing in these seven letters, and that surely also tells us something about the outlook of his followers in Antioch. We turn, then, to examine the shape of the Christian movement and its environment as Ignatius saw it.

THE SOCIAL PERSPECTIVES OF IGNATIUS OF ANTIOCH

It will, I think, prove useful first to gather together what can be said about Ignatius's view of the larger world in which he lives and then go on to show how he understands the interrelation of the geographically separate communities of Christians and the maintenance of unity within the individual communities.

The Mental Map of Ignatius

If Ignatius had never given thought to any city other than Antioch, he was forced to do so by his arrest and deportation to Rome. In this connection he generally names cities and their provinces. He not only knows that Antioch is in Syria, but (as we learn from the inscription of each of the letters) that Ephesus is in Asia, Magnesia on the Maeander, Tralles in Asia, the Roman church "in the place of the district of the Romans," Philadelphia in Asia, and

7. Percy Neale Harrison, *Polycarp's Two Epistles to the Philippians* (Cambridge: Cambridge University Press, 1936) 90–104; Schoedel, *Ignatius*, 212–14, 250–51, 278–80.
8. Harrison, *Polycarp's Two Epistles*, 95.

Smyrna in Asia. The reference to Magnesia as Magnesia on the river Maeander was probably intended to distinguish this city from other cities of the same name and especially its near neighbor Magnesia "under (mount) Sipylus" (cf. Livy 37.44–45). When the travelers were unexpectedly whisked away from Troas, Ignatius thinks to tell Polycarp that it is a matter of a "sudden sailing from Troas to Neapolis" (Pol 8.1). There is enough here to show that Ignatius thought of the world in which he lived in terms of the geographical realities of the Roman Empire. The cities of the empire form the links in the chain of Christian communities that stretches between him and Rome.

One detail emphasizes the alertness of Ignatius to practical considerations in this regard. In writing to the Romans, the date of his writing is given as the 24th of August in the Roman manner (Rom 10.3). Ignatius no doubt wishes to make it possible for the Christians in Rome to calculate the time of his arrival and to prepare themselves to welcome him. For Ignatius does not otherwise indicate the date in his letters, and the lack of any reference to the year shows that ordinary concerns in such dating are not operative. The Roman system of dating was well known in the East,[9] but the location of the date here and its form are totally atypical for the Hellenistic letter.[10] All of these points indicate Ignatius's awareness of time and space as a Roman was likely to view them.

The list of cities in the particular chain of Christian communities found in these letters is determined by the route followed by Ignatius's Roman guard. But Ignatius superimposes upon his travels a meaning derived from the journeys of Christian predecessors. In particular, he speaks of the Ephesians as providing a "passage for those slain for God" and goes on to call them the "fellow initiates of Paul, [a man] sanctified, approved, worthy of blessing, in whose steps may it be mine to be found when I reach God, who in every letter remembers you in Christ Jesus" (Eph 12.2). The Ephesians were among the most enthusiastic of Ignatius's supporters. They sent several people to greet him in Smyrna, and they left Burrhus behind to minister to him. As we shall see, it is possible that Ignatius had expected to be taken to Ephesus rather than Smyrna and that careful preparations had been made for his arrival. From the beginning, then, he saw himself walking in the footsteps of the great apostle Paul.

Ignatius, however, adds new and very personal dimensions to his interpretation of his journey. For him "Syria" and "Rome" form the two eyes of an ellipse that dominate his conception of the Roman world. He understands

9. Ludwig Hahn, *Rom und Romanismus im griechisch-römischen Osten* (Leipzig: Dieterich, 1906) 38, 85, 122, 124, 129, 229, 245.

10. Frances Xavier J. Exler, *The Form of the Ancient Greek Letter: A Study in Greek Epistolography* (Washington, D.C.: Catholic University of America Press, 1923) 78–100; Orsolina Montevecchi, *La papirologia* (Torino: Società Editrice Internazionale, 1973) 67–70.

himself to have been "put in bonds from Syria for the common name and hope, hoping . . . to attain to fighting with beasts in Rome" (Eph 1.2), and he speaks of the messengers who have preceded him "from Syria to Rome" (Rom 10.2). Such geographical references are relatively neutral, but Ignatius also adds a mythological dimension to them that ties Syria and Rome together at a deeper level; for "God judged the bishop of Syria worthy to be found at the sun's setting having sent him from the sun's rising"; and he adds that "it is good to set from the world to God that I may rise to him" (Rom 2.2). The journey from Syria to Rome, then, reflects the path of the sun, which in turn symbolizes a dying and rising to God (cf. Mag 9.1).

There is more. For Ignatius also patterns his progress on that of a con- quering hero. "I am fighting wild beasts from Syria to Rome, through land and sea, by night and day, bound to ten leopards . . ." (Rom 5.1). Robert Grant speaks of the bishop's use of the "regal-imperial style" here.[11] For Ignatius, like Paul before him (2 Cor 11:23–27), draws on a form that is found in inscriptions that detail the exploits of kings and generals.[12] Thus the opening words of the passage are modeled on a line like "I fought from Whitetown to the land of the Sabaeans"; and other details point in the same direction.[13] It is no doubt also as conquering hero that Ignatius thinks of himself when he looks back on part of his journey and says that the churches who received him dealt with him "not as a transient traveller," noting that "even churches that do not lie on my way according to the flesh went before me city by city" (Rom 9.3).[14]

The overwhelming significance of the city of Rome as a political and geographical fact here determines the images with which Ignatius works. But obviously Ignatius's victory is paradoxically achieved by going to his death in the capital. Thus the movement of Ignatius from the rising to the setting sun is a movement that leads to death and, at the same time, life. It is a movement against Rome. The mental geography of the bishop here is strikingly different from that of the defenders of Roman power who sense no such movement but speak more conventionally of Rome ruling from the rising to the setting sun.[15] Possibly Ignatius's mental map was shaped in part by the feeling of other Orientals that the East would rise up against Rome and be delivered. Accord- ing to an anti-Roman oracle preserved by the early second-century historian Phlegon, "There will come [against Rome] a most brave and spirited host from Asia afar whence are the risings of the sun."[16] In any event, it is clear that Rome

11. Robert M. Grant, *Ignatius of Antioch* (Apostolic Fathers 4; Camden, N.J.: Nelson, 1966) 90.
12. Cf. Anton Fridrichsen, "Zum Stil des paulinischen Peristasenkatalogs 2 Cor 11:23ff.," *Symbolae Osloenses* 7 (1928) 25–29; 8 (1929) 78–82.
13. Schoedel, *Ignatius*, 178.
14. Ibid., 190–91.
15. Wilhelm Gernentz, *Laudes Romae* (Rostock: Adler, 1918) 118–24.
16. Phlegon *De Mirab.* frg. 32, in Karl Müller, *Fragmenta historicorum Graecorum* (5

apart from the Christians who live in it has strongly negative significance for Ignatius and that in some sense he pits "Syria" against it.

The Church and the World

Rome, of course, is part and parcel of the "world" that stands opposed to God and God's people, whose lives are marked by suffering and death (Mg 5.2). Ignatius knows that pagans will wrong the Christians of Ephesus through boastfulness, slandering, deceit, and fierceness, and that Christians will endure all this in imitation of their Lord: "Who was wronged more? who was defrauded more? who was rejected more?" (Eph 10.1–3). Behind this hostility stands "the Ruler of this age" (Satan) whose abuse we must endure (Mg 1.2).

But Ignatius was no apocalyptist, and there are countervailing tendencies in his attitude toward the world. In a rare use of the word he refers to the pagan opponents of the Christians as those to whom the Ephesians are to prove themselves "brothers" (Eph 10.3).[17] He counsels unceasing prayer for them since "there is hope of repentance in them" (Eph 10.1). Significantly, hope for the repentance of schismatic teachers among these same Ephesians is almost abandoned by Ignatius (Eph 7.1).[18] In another community Ignatius shows himself concerned for respectability in the eyes of pagans. He fears that disunity will provide a pretext for the Gentiles to slander Christians. And he quotes a version of Isa 52:5 as a warning against such a turn of events: "Woe to him through whom my name is slandered" (Tr 8.2). This passage was to have a long history in the early church for calling Christians to the maintenance of high standards of behavior.[19] Similarly, Ignatius is so pleased with Polybius, bishop of Tralles, that he suggests that even the "atheists" (pagans, apparently) "respect" him (Tr 3.2). Ignatius clearly values such respect highly.

The tension in Ignatius's attitude displayed here is partly resolved by noting that with but two exceptions (both in Mg 5.2) all uses of the term "world" are found in Ignatius's letter to the Romans (2.2; 3.2; 3.3; 4.2; 6.1; 6.2; 7.1). The dark powers of the world are seen as manifesting themselves most tellingly and irreversibly in the larger political structures that impinge on the

---

vols.; Paris: Didot, 1841–70) 3.616. For background to such sentiments, see Harald Fuchs, *Der geistige Widerstand gegen Rom in der antiken Welt* (Berlin: de Gruyter, 1938) 31–36. For some qualifications, see John J. Collins, *The Sibylline Oracles of Egyptian Judaism* (SBLDS 13; Missoula, Mont.: Scholars, 1972) 38–44.

17. A few apologetically sensitive church fathers from a later period evince a brotherly attitude toward pagans (see Justin *Dial.* 96.2; Clem. Al. *Strom.* 5.14, 98.1; 7.14, 86.1).

18. Ignatius is somewhat more hopeful of the repentance of false teachers elsewhere (Sm 4.1; 5.3; Ph 3.2; 8.1).

19. Schoedel, *Ignatius*, 150–51. Cf. W. C. van Unnik, "Die Rücksicht auf die Reaktion der Nicht-Christen als Motiv in der altchristlichen Paränese," *Judentum, Urchristentum, Kirche: Festschrift für Joachim Jeremias* (ed. Walther Eltester; BZNW 26; Berlin: Töpelmann, 1960) 221–34.

lives of Christians. The immediate social environment of the Christian communities is experienced in less threatening terms. Being "hated by the world"
may be the very definition of Christianity for Ignatius (Rom 3.2); but he
chooses to view as his spiritual superiors those who like the Ephesians have
served as "a passage for those slain for God," yet who are obviously in no
immediate danger of persecution themselves (Eph 11.2–12.2). Ignatius's sense
of unworthiness here and elsewhere seems too intense to be merely conventional self-depreciation. As we have suggested, it may even have been called
forth by the loss of unity in the Christian community of Antioch. And it may
well be especially the presumed preservation of unity among the Ephesian
Christians from apostolic times (Eph 11.2) that accounts for Ignatius's self-
designation as their inferior. Such factors complicate any picture that we may
develop of the tension in Ignatius's view of the relation between the church and
the world. But he is apparently prepared to come to terms with the urban
world around him in a certain spirit of openness.

One reason for this is that Ignatius has the popular culture of the Greek
city in his bones. I cannot lay out the evidence in detail here. Let me simply
summarize the results of previous research.[20] Ignatius's writing reflects
the Hellenistic conception of the letter as a matter of "conversing" with the
addressees (Eph 9.2) and displays numerous epistolary formulas and transitional devices not learned from Paul. Ignatius also shows significant indebtedness to the popular rhetorical strategies of "Asianism."[21] Moreover, numerous
theological and ethical themes in Ignatius reflect the influence of Hellenistic
conceptions, which sometimes penetrate deeply into the fabric of his thought.
This is particularly true when he develops theological topics and ethical norms
in terms of the widespread Hellenistic commonplace that sets silent deeds
against empty words. Also interesting for our purposes is an emphasis in Ignatius on "concord" that seems to derive from a civic and intercivic ideal of the
period. It is significant that when his treatment of it is lifted from the civic to
the ecclesiastical level (Eph 4.1–5.1), Ignatius can enrich the notion with
images that reflect the higher cultural life of the Greek tradition rather than
biblical materials. Similarly, when Ignatius says, "I sing the churches," and
calls for unity (Mg 1.2), he probably models himself in part on the Hellenistic
rhetorician whose task it sometimes was to sing the praises of communities and
at other times to urge concord and friendship between them or between the
warring groups within them.[22] If I am on the right track in this regard, Ignatius

---

20. Schoedel, *Ignatius*, 17, directs the reader to the relevant parts of the commentary.
21. Othmar Perler, "Das vierte Makkabäerbuch, Ignatius von Antiochien und die ältesten
Märtyrerberichte," *Revista di archeologia cristiana* 25 (1949) 47–72.
22. Schoedel, *Ignatius*, 104.

felt at home in the Greek city at a profounder level than at first would seem likely.

The tension in Ignatius's attitude toward the world receives what may almost be regarded as formal theological formulation. Ignatius knows that such phenomena as disunity arise from acting "according to the flesh" (Mg 6.2) and that "fleshly people cannot do spiritual things, nor yet spiritual people fleshly things; just as faith cannot do the things of faithfulness, nor yet faithlessness the things of faith" (Eph 8.2). Here is a strong echo of the Pauline (and Johannine) opposition between the flesh and the spirit. Yet Ignatius almost immediately goes on to offer what amounts to a correction of the traditional formula: "But what you do even according to the flesh, that is spiritual; for you do all things in Jesus Christ" (Eph 8.2). The motif in its corrected form coheres with Ignatius's repeated uses of flesh and spirit together to express the totality of a Christian's commitment and with his insistence that flesh and spirit were conjoined in the God-Man (Eph 7.2; cf. Sm 3). Indeed, it is precisely the reality of the flesh of Christ that is appealed to by Ignatius in his debate with docetists to make sense of his own suffering and martyrdom (Tr 10; Sm 4.2). Thus in a curious way, enthusiasm for martyrdom is for Ignatius a way of confirming the significance of what is done in the flesh. At the same time, the day-to-day behavior of Christians in the community is covered by the same formula and is evidently accorded a significance comparable to that of martyrdom. I sense an inner connection between these theological developments and the greater rootedness of Ignatius in the culture of the Greek city.

Even Ignatius's enthusiasm for martyrdom could be interpreted in terms familiar to the pagan world. Thus he echoes a pagan ideal when he declares that Christ taught Christians "to despise death" (Sm 3.2).[23] No wonder that even Epictetus (*Diss.* 4.7.2) and Marcus Aurelius (11.3.2) accorded a grudging admiration to Christian fortitude in the face of death and other misfortunes. At the same time, Marcus Aurelius found something theatrical in Christian martyrdom. And Ignatius's insistence that he chooses death in the arena voluntarily and intends to urge on the animals to attack him (Rom 4–5) would surely have seemed unnatural to the emperor. This very attitude was soon more carefully scrutinized by Christians themselves, and we find the church of Smyrna rejecting voluntary martyrdom (*Mart. Pol.* 4) and commending the caution of Polycarp in this regard (*Mart. Pol.* 5–6). The church, then, was finding ways of linking the traditional values of Greco-Roman society with the perspectives of the new faith. If I am right, Ignatius made significant contributions to such developments.

23. Ibid., 227–28.

The Church "Catholic"

The church that is thus both set apart from the world and subtly linked with it is for Ignatius the whole church. Ignatius is the first to use the term "catholic" to describe its universality (Sm 8.2). He describes it as preexistent in terms that hover somewhere between Gnostic and Jewish categories (Eph inscr).[24] He reflects the imagery of the cosmic "body" to describe the church (Sm 1.2; cf. Eph 4.2; Tr 11.2). And he knows that the geographically separated churches are manifestations of one transcendent reality: "Wherever the bishop appears, there let the congregation be; just as wherever Jesus Christ is, there is the whole church" (Sm 8.2). Such are the theological categories that set the tone for Ignatius. As we have seen, however, Ignatius also depends on the experience of the church in the Roman Empire for his picture of the universal church. We turn, then, to ask what at the practical level served to bind the geographically distinct churches together in the experience of Ignatius of Antioch.

In this connection everything revolves around Ignatius himself as a charismatic figure who, as he himself says, dealt with the churches as "a man set on union" (Ph 8.1). He is speaking in this context of unity within the individual churches that he visits, but clearly the united action of all the churches in such matters as the recognition and support of their visitor from Antioch is also involved. It would be foolish, of course, to think that the visit of a potential martyr was something that the churches could expect all that frequently. Ignatius could say to the Ephesians that they were a "passage for those slain for God" (Eph 12.2), but hagiography has always run to exaggeration. It is more fruitful for us to think of the strategies followed by Ignatius and his friends to call forth support for him and his cause as building on less highly developed practices and outlooks that served to link one church with another.

Ignatius did not claim to direct the minds and hearts of the churches of Asia in terms of some formal authority vested in him. He says, "I do not give commands as being someone" (Eph 3.1), and, "I do not command you as Peter and Paul; they were apostles" (Rom 4.3; cf. Tr 3.3). Instead, Ignatius presents himself simply as one who has been considered worthy of God to suffer and who will learn to be a disciple with the assistance of those to whom he addresses his letters. His authority, then, is charismatic; and it is charismatic to such an extent that he plays the role of the spirit-driven prophet in warning the Philadelphians against divisive activity (Ph 7.1).

But the authority of the charismatic can be fostered, and there is considerable evidence that Ignatius and his friends gave attention to cultivating the Christian communities of Asia and beyond. Consider the following account of

24. Ibid., 37–39.

the movement of people and letters surrounding Ignatius's journey: Messengers had been sent to Rome already from Syria to alert the Romans to Ignatius's future arrival (Rom 10.2). As the group crossed Asia someone had to have gone on to Ephesus, Magnesia, and Tralles to inform them of Ignatius's approach. These communities sent representatives to meet Ignatius in Smyrna. Five came from Ephesus (Eph 1.3–2.1: their bishop Onesimus, the deacon Burrhus, as well as Crocus, Euplus, and Fronto). Four came from Magnesia (Mg 2: their bishop Damas, the elder Bassus, the elder Apollonius, and the deacon Zoticon). One came from Tralles (Tr 1: their bishop Polybius). The deacon Burrhus stayed with Ignatius (at the expense of the Ephesians and later also of the Smyrnaeans) as far as Troas. Crocus probably carried the letter to the Romans from Smyrna to supplement the activity of the previous embassy.[25] The amount of support from Ephesus suggests that Ephesus may have been the point from which the Roman soldiers had expected to go by sea to Rome. Moreover, such a route was common. If that was the original plan, it was changed for some reason, so that the group turned north at the fork in the road near the juncture of the Lycus and Maeander rivers, passed through Philadelphia, and reached Smyrna sometime in August where Ignatius was welcomed warmly by the Christians of the community and their bishop Polycarp. There Ignatius received his visitors from the cities to the south. And there too he wrote letters back to these cities and on to Rome. When Ignatius reached Troas not long afterward, he wrote a letter to Philadelphia and two letters to Smyrna. All required messengers for their delivery. Meanwhile, still other messengers, Philo and Rheus Agathopous, had stayed behind to find out what was going to happen in Antioch; they saw to it apparently that people from nearby churches went to congratulate that church when all went as hoped; and they somehow remained sufficiently in touch with the movements of Ignatius to find their way through Philadelphia and to catch up with him in Troas. Philo, as we have seen, replaced Burrhus in Troas. Finally, Ignatius asked all the churches with whom he had been in contact to send representatives or letters to congratulate the church in Antioch (Ph 10; Sm 11; Pol 8). We learn from Polycarp's letter to the Philippians that Ignatius later made the same request at Philippi and that he met with success in these endeavors (Pol. *Phil.* 13.1).

That adds up to an enormous amount of activity and expense. And it probably makes more sense as a response to a victory for Ignatius's cause among the Christians of Antioch than to the end of the persecution of Christians in Antioch. In any event, it surely represents an exaggeration of the normal forms of interchange that took place between the churches. Nevertheless,

25. Ibid., 191.

the reception of Ignatius gives us some understanding of the function of displays of hospitality to traveling Christians as a factor in creating and maintaining the sense of belonging to a widespread brotherhood. In this connection note also the importance of the letter as a literary form in supporting such networks. Thus Ignatius builds on Hellenistic conceptions of the letter as a substitute for personal presence to foster a deeper sense of the united action of the churches of Asia in recognizing their visitor.[26] Moreover, after the immediate occasion of Ignatius's letters had passed, they were collected and sent to at least one church at its request, Philippi, presumably to keep alive the spirit that had been released by the passage of Ignatius through its midst (Pol. *Phil.* 13.2). It should also be noted that at the conclusion of all of Ignatius's letters greetings and requests for prayers are found that serve to link one community with another in their common hope. These themes are intensified by Ignatius who chooses to regard the restoration of peace in Antioch as the result of the united prayers of the churches with whom he has been in contact (cf. Sm 11.1; Pol 7.1) and who believes that such prayer will also lead to the successful conclusion of his own martyrdom (cf. Ph 5.1).

We naturally ask ourselves whether Ignatius ever encountered opposition. Occasionally there is the suggestion that all were not as enthusiastic as he thought they ought to be. Thus he compliments Burrhus with the wish that all would imitate him in his service to God (Sm 12.1), which is surely being measured here by his service to Ignatius. But something closer to outright opposition to Ignatius seems to have taken place in Philadelphia. He became involved in a theological discussion with some of the Christians there, felt as though they had tried to deceive him, and cried out under the impetus of the spirit that all strife should be avoided (Ph 7.1). Some of them in turn suspected that he had been informed in advance of the division in the community (Ph 7.2). In retrospect Ignatius defends himself in such a way that we are led to suspect that even his supporters thought that he had gone too far (cf. Ph 6.3–8.1). He now talks as though what he had found in Philadelphia was that all evil elements were in the process of being removed from the congregation (Ph 3.1), but he inadvertently reveals that the opposition is still very active in the church. For later in the same letter he speaks of those who had dishonored Philo and Rheus Agathopous as they followed Ignatius through Philadelphia and on to Troas (Ph 11.1). There can be little doubt that these were the same people who had resisted Ignatius himself. Evidently, then, it took an intense person like Ignatius to polarize such situations and to introduce sharper definitions of Christian truth and Christian behavior in the churches. Something very similar happened in Smyrna. Here Ignatius argues heatedly that the denial of the reality

26. Ibid., 43, 245.

of the Lord's flesh and the Lord's suffering involves the denigration of his own martyrdom. At the same time, he reveals that he was apparently admired by the very docetists whom he criticized (Sm 5.2: "For what does anyone profit me *if he praise me* but blaspheme my Lord?"). Thus it is likely that the theological lines were not drawn as sharply in Smyrna as Ignatius would like to have seen.

Ignatius also experienced some competition from other visitors. Thus there had come to Ephesus people whom he identifies as wild beasts and rabid dogs who have brought with them "evil teaching" of an unspecified variety (Eph 6.2–9.2). Against these the Ephesians are to stop their ears (Eph 9.2; cf. Tr 9.1; Sm 4.1; 7.2). The virtues of hospitality, then, can be abused. But this leads us into the problem of the control of the life and thought of the local Christian community, to which we now turn.

"Attuned to the Bishop like Strings to a Cithara"

Traditional investigations at this point take up the matter of Ignatius's conception of the ministry, for his letters are the first to describe Christian communities ruled by a single bishop in conjunction with groups of elders and deacons. It is a complicated issue, and it is not always clear what the discussion is all about. Let me simply indicate my conviction here that Ignatius's concern for a union of minds and hearts in the Christian community outweighs any interest in the formal definition of the authority of the ministry. Some corollaries of this are that the notion of episcopal or presbyterial succession is absent from Ignatius (as most commentators agree), that there is a genuine collegiality between the three orders of the ministry, and that the elaborate comparisons between the three orders of the ministry on the one hand and God (or Christ), the apostles, and a Christlike service on the other hand do not amount to a legitimation of episcopal authority in terms that are essentially different from those found in the literature of the New Testament. In short, Ignatius does not work with a conception of highly differentiated roles in the life of the Christian community. In contemporary theological terms we might say that the bishop in Ignatius is the sacrament of the unity of the local church. Thus the elders are said to be "attuned to the bishop like strings to a cithara," and it is assumed that in the "concord and harmonious love" of the congregation "Jesus Christ is sung" (Eph 4.1). Such concord is most surely realized in eucharistic worship (Eph 5.2–3), and calls to come together more frequently in worship are simply one of the more obvious signs of the depth of Ignatius's concern in this connection (Eph 13.1; 20.2; Pol 4.2). There can be no doubt that Ignatius would have spoken in the same terms about the Christian community in Antioch as he does about those in Asia.

Of course conflict was not absent from these same communities.

Indeed, as we shall see, dissent was suppressed. And it is probably precisely this that prompted the need to treat not only visible troubles in a congregation but those "unseen" as well (Pol 2.2). The remark is closely associated with medical language, and the impression is left that Ignatius is speaking of things that fester under the surface of the life of the community.[27] We have already seen that pressure from the pagan environment played its part in fostering a show of unity among the Christians and that internal tensions were viewed by Ignatius as more threatening to the community than external threats. One knows where pagans stand, whereas those who claim to be Christians yet depart from the norms of the group as Ignatius understood them are the true enemies of the group. The latter are merely "plausible" or "specious" (Tr 6.2; Ph 2.2), and wholly untrustworthy (Pol 3.1). One is not to listen to them (Eph 9.1; Tr 9.1), one is not to receive them or meet them (Sm 4.1), one is not even to speak about them either in public or in private (Sm 7.2).

Before outlining what we know about the groups involved, it is important to stress the fact that aberrant theology and practice was not the only thing to distress Ignatius. Thus in a short exposition of the duties of the bishop written to Polycarp we find not only false teachers dealt with but also those whom Ignatius refers to as "the more troublesome" in contradistinction to "good disciples" (Pol 2.1). The bishop must learn to "bear with" such people (Pol 1.2). He must be like the pilot who guides his ship through the storm (Pol 2.3). He must expect to endure "as God's athlete" (Pol 2.3). In short, even in the ordinary course of affairs the bishop can expect to face difficulties from those who acknowledge his authority. Plutarch uses the same image of the ship of state to illustrate the difficulties of governing a Greek city under Roman rule (*Praecepta gerendae reipublicae* 19, 815b; 815d). The parallel may well be of more than literary interest. For it may furnish another example of the influence of Hellenistic civic ideals on Ignatius's view of the church, and it certainly illustrates the point that even the leader of the unified community must expect to absorb the distress of those entrusted to his care. Although all this advice is addressed to Polycarp of Smyrna, there can be no doubt that Ignatius would have described his own role in the church of Antioch in similar terms. At the same time, other bishops may have found themselves somewhat uncomfortable with the kind of advice that Ignatius gives Polycarp. Thus the "silence" of the bishop of Ephesus (Eph 6.1) and of the bishop of Philadelphia (Ph 1.1) suggests a less dominating stance. And the persistence of opponents to Ignatius in Philadelphia (cf. Ph 11.1) implies an unwillingness or inability of the local bishop to follow up his support of Ignatius effectively. Ignatius even shows some impatience with Polycarp when he advises him to "become more diligent

27. Ibid., 263–64.

than you are" (Pol 3.2). In this connection, Ignatius would surely have regarded as somewhat tepid Polycarp's promise to the Philippians to carry their congratulatory letter on to Antioch "if I have a convenient opportunity" (Pol. *Phil.* 13.1). On occasion Ignatius shows some awareness of the unfortunate consequences that stem from his own intensity and impatience (Mg 12; Tr 4),[28] and this may have contributed to the special difficulties that we think he had in maintaining his authority in the church of Antioch. In any event, as Ignatius saw it, a bishop must be prepared to accept a certain sense of isolation in the exercise of his office.

Much more commented on in the literature has been the problem of the theological fronts to which Ignatius addresses himself. In two letters he takes up the problems of docetism (Trallians and Smyrnaeans) and in another two letters he takes up the problem of Judaizers (Magnesians and Philadelphians). The question has been whether these represent one group or two and what exactly were the points at issue.[29] My own view, developed in my commentary on Ignatius, is that they were probably two groups but that Ignatius tended to treat the Judaizers in terms that he had developed in his thinking about the problem of docetists. Indeed, he dealt similarly with the visitors who came into the Ephesian community but who may have been no more than charismatic enthusiasts.[30] I believe that the docetists attacked by Ignatius had moved somewhat beyond the errorists alluded to in 1 John, but I do not think that their docetism presupposed a Gnostic cosmology. At most they claimed esoteric knowledge about angels and heavenly powers (Tr 5.2; cf. Sm 6.1).

The Judaizers attacked by Ignatius in his letter to the Magnesians may have actually been interested in the observance of the Sabbath (as Mg 9.1 suggests), but I do not think that this was necessarily the case. In any event, they seem to have been Christians (probably Gentiles) attracted by certain features of Judaism rather than adherents to some form of Jewish Christianity. Note Ignatius's closing argument that "Christianity did not believe in Judaism, but Judaism in Christianity" (Mg 10.3). The line apparently pits Christians who foolishly move toward Judaism against the Jewish apostles who rightly moved away from Judaism. Much the same seems to be true of the situation described in Ignatius's letter to the Philadelphians. For "it is better to hear Christianity from a man who is circumcised than Judaism from a man who

28. Ibid., 130, 144.

29. For a review of the discussion, see C. K. Barrett, "Jews and Judaizers in the Epistles of Ignatius," *Jews, Greeks and Christians: Essays in Honor of W. D. Davies* (ed. R. Hammerton-Kelly and R. Scroggs; SJLA 21; Leiden: E. J. Brill, 1976) 220–44.

30. For possible references to charismatics in the letters of Ignatius, see Christine Trevett, "Prophecy and Anti-Episcopal Activity: A Third Error Combatted by Ignatius?" *JEH* 34 (1983) 1–18.

is uncircumcised" (Ph 6.1). It is a matter, then, of uncircumcised Gentiles who have developed an interest in things Jewish. It seems even clearer in this instance that it was not Jewish practice—that is, the actual practice of circumcision—that appealed to this group. And if that is so, we are simply left guessing as to what it was that did appeal to them. My own tentative view is that they were interested in complex biblical exegesis akin to the sort of thing that is found in Hebrews and Barnabas and that in Ignatius's estimation it distracted the community from matters of more central importance (including solidarity under the bishop). In any event, their reference to the Old Testament as "archives" (Ph 8.2) finds its best parallels in Josephus (and Philo), and this probably indicates that the Judaizers of Philadelphia had fallen under the influence of a more Hellenized form of Judaism.[31]

Such Judaizers, then, were not Jewish Christians. That would seem to be true even if we choose to link the Judaizers more closely with the docetists attacked by Ignatius. In any event, they lived in Magnesia and Philadelphia, and it is not clear that Ignatius would necessarily have met people like them in Antioch. The only passage that could pass for a reference to Jewish Christianity in Ignatius is that in which he speaks of the Lord's cross set up as an ensign "for his saints and believers whether *among the Jews* or among the Gentiles in one body of his church" (Sm 1.2). But the sentiment is as general and idealized here as it is in the New Testament (Eph 2:16) and suggests no awareness of Jewish Christianity as a distinctive alternative to the type of Christianity taken for granted by Ignatius.

We may be inclined to think today that the Jewish Christianity of the Gospel of Matthew would qualify as just such an alternative. But we cannot be sure that it would appear so to Ignatius. Yet the difference is surely sufficient for us to wonder how it is that Ignatius can be so deeply indebted to gospel material of a Matthean type and yet so apparently unaffected by the general thrust of the Christianity reflected in Matthew. We shall return to this problem later.

In this connection, it should also be noted that Ignatius's discussion of the Judaizers presupposes a decisive distinction between Christianity and Judaism. For Ignatius deals with the prophets as Christians before their time and seems to deprive Jewish observance of roots in scriptural revelation (Mg 8–10). This suggests that the history of salvation for Ignatius consists of a thin line of saintly figures who stand apart from the life of Israel as a whole. The question that arises in Matthean scholarship as to whether the Christian community reflected in the Gospel had or had not broken with the synagogue is not one

---

31. William R. Schoedel, "Ignatius and the Archives," *HTR* 71 (1978) 97–106.

that would naturally occur to the reader of Ignatius's letters. There is no longer ambiguity on this point.

In Ignatius, as we have seen, the problem has to do with divergent tendencies within the Christian community. In this connection, it is worth returning for a moment to his description of the docetists in Smyrna where special light is thrown on how the communities known to Ignatius organized themselves and how such difficulties arose. We have already seen that the docetists apparently expressed their admiration for Ignatius even when he heatedly denied the validity of their Christianity (Sm 5.2). They were not, then, as radically distinct from the rest of the Christians in Smyrna as Ignatius would like to believe. It may have been precisely this that led Ignatius to say to Polycarp with reference to false teachers, "Become more diligent than you are" (Pol 3.2). At the head of their group was someone who had "office" (Sm 6.1). The reference is probably to an elder who led one of the house churches in the community. Ignatius declares that this group did not attend eucharist and prayer (Sm 7.1), but it is reasonably clear from his statements elsewhere that they held their own meetings (Sm 8.1). And it is because of this that he says that a eucharist is valid only under the bishop or under one whom the bishop appoints (Sm 8.1). In the mind of Ignatius a refusal to recognize the reality of the flesh of the Lord is connected not only with a refusal to recognize the real presence of the flesh of the Lord in the sacred meal but also with a refusal to meet the needs of brethren in physical distress (Sm 6.2–7.1). The celebration of the eucharist within the context of an ἀγάπη (love feast) where the well-to-do fed the less well-to-do probably helps explain the way in which these things are connected in Ignatius's mind.[32] Here again it is likely that Ignatius pushes theological logic beyond the facts. But it is also quite possible that the docetists in Smyrna represented something of an elite and as such tended to look down upon others in the Christian community, for docetism reflects a form of theological sophistication and suggests a certain independence of mind. It is perhaps such independence more than anything else that seemed to Ignatius to threaten the unity and concord of the community. To judge from such material in the letter to the Smyrnaeans it seems possible that before people like Ignatius came on the scene, churches in the places known to him (including Antioch) were characterized by a greater openness to the exploration of theological issues and less reliance on the leaders of the community for guidance in such matters.

The mention of house churches brings us finally to a consideration of the social units that made up the Christian congregation as far as can be made out from Ignatius. The existence of house churches is itself a guess based on

32. Schoedel, *Ignatius,* 241–42.

what seems to make sense of the sort of situation in Smyrna that we have just explored.[33] Ignatius's two letters to this same church also give us some insight into the regular components of the Christian community. The reason for this is that Ignatius spent more time in Smyrna than elsewhere and thus refers to more people in his greetings to that church. In his letter to the Smyrnaeans he first salutes "the households (οἴκους) of my brothers with their wives and children, and the virgins called widows" (Sm 13.1). If households broken by diverse religious loyalties (cf. Matt 10:34–36; Luke 12:49–53) or split between a Christian and a pagan spouse (cf. 1 Cor 7:12–16) ever formed a significant feature of the early church, there is no very obvious trace of that here in Ignatius. And if the complete household in antiquity included slaves and freedmen along with husband, wife, and children (Aris. *Pol.* 1253b), that is not noted here. There were, however, slaves in the Christian community of Smyrna, and there is a good chance that their presence there had something to do with the more extended sense of family that existed in classical antiquity. It may be noted that (if I understand the passage correctly) Ignatius once uses the image of household assistants and servants rising, working, and retiring together to illustrate the unified activity of the Christian community (Pol 6.1).[34] That may be a picture that fits the Christian (and non-Christian) households known to Ignatius.

Ignatius then names some of the people with whom he had become acquainted in Smyrna: Tavia, Alce, Daphnus, and Eutecnus (Sm 13.2). In his letter to Polycarp, the "wife of Epitropus" is singled out along with a certain Attalus and the as yet unappointed messenger to Antioch (Pol 8.2). In an afterthought, Alce is again mentioned (Pol 8.3). It is not actually Tavia but "the household (οἶκον) of Tavia" that is first saluted in the letter to the Smyrnaeans, but it is her firmness in the faith of which Ignatius boasts.[35] She may also be the one whom Ignatius greets in his letter to Polycarp as "the wife of Epitropus with the whole household of her and her children" (Pol 8.2). The name Epitropus is most unusual, and the word can also be taken as a common noun.[36] Thus the woman may actually be addressed as "the wife of the procurator." The term "procurator" covers a wide range of administrative positions of that day, but it would in any case suggest a household of somewhat higher status than usual. The woman was probably a widow now in charge of "the whole

33. For house churches in this period, see Harry Otto Maier, *The Social Setting of the Ministry as Reflected in the Writings of Hermas, Clement and Ignatius* (Ph.D. diss., Keble College, Trinity, 1987).
34. Schoedel, *Ignatius*, 274–75.
35. The verb is εὔχομαι which usually means "to pray." But it is the less familiar meaning of the verb (to express satisfaction with something of which one has a right to be proud) that seems to make sense here (Schoedel, *Ignatius*, 253 n. 29).
36. Ibid., 280 n. 14.

household." And that inevitably reminds us of Ignatius's greeting of the "household of Tavia." In any event, this woman, or each of these women, seems to have been a person of some substance and would very likely have opened her home to other Christians for eucharist and prayer.

Another woman of whom this may have been true is Alce. She is mentioned again in the *Martyrdom of Polycarp* (17.2) where she is identified as the sister of Nicetas who in turn was the father of a certain Herod, the police official (εἰρήναρχος) who arrested the aged Polycarp. If the passage can be trusted, Alce probably also belonged to a family of higher status. For the police officials of Asia in this period seem to have consisted of people of some standing.[37] Here, however, would be a woman whose family did not share her faith.

The three men referred to by Ignatius—Daphnus, Eutecnus,[38] and Attalus—were evidently somewhat more colorless than the women mentioned. Against this must be weighed the fact that all who are mentioned as officials in the communities known to Ignatius are men and that at least Polycarp probably provided as much by way of hospitality as anyone else in the Christian community of Smyrna.

A special group in the church of Smyrna was formed by "the virgins called widows" (Sm 13.1). It is not quite clear what the expression means. The likely reference, in my estimation, is to virgins (perhaps especially older women) who had been enrolled among the widows because they had no other means of support.[39] In any event, the topic of widows and children is given exceptional attention by Ignatius (Sm 6.2), and he counsels Polycarp to be the special guardian of widows (Pol 4.1). Support of this kind no doubt was one reason for the attractiveness of the Christian movement, and the fact that it was forthcoming shows that there were people (perhaps like Polycarp himself) with resources to meet such needs.

Virginity, however, played another role in the church of Smyrna. For Ignatius believed that some involved in that church ran the risk of boasting of their continence. Ignatius seems to be concerned about a threat to the authority of the bishop, for he says that if a person's virginity (it is not clear whether he is speaking of men or women or both) is known "beyond the bishop," such a person "is destroyed" (Pol 5.2). The reference is evidently to those who consciously adopted a life of special sanctity rather than to those who simply found themselves economically and socially isolated for lack of a mate. It is unlikely

37. Theodor Mommsen, *Römisches Strafrecht* (Leipzig: Duncker & Humblot, 1899) 308 n. 2.

38. Since Eutecnus does not occur elsewhere as a proper name, it may be taken as an adjective to describe Daphnus as one "blessed with children." That seems out of place here, however, and names similar to Eutecnus are found. Cf. Schoedel, *Ignatius*, 253.

39. Ibid., 252.

that these people had much to do with "the virgins called widows" since the latter would presumably have been well known to all for what they were.

Thus Ignatius takes marriage for granted as the normal and most trustworthy basis for the social interaction of Christians. And he moves a step beyond Paul, who called for marriage (or remarriage) "in the Lord" (1 Cor 7:39), when he urges Christian men and women who marry "to establish their union with the approval of the bishop" (Pol 5.2). There is to be what Bryan Wilson has called "group endogomy" as a contribution to the tightly knit texture of the Christian community.[40] It is important, then, that Ignatius's "sisters" in the faith "love the Lord and be satisfied with their mates in flesh and spirit" and that his "brothers" likewise "love their mates as the Lord loves the church" (Pol 5.1).

We turn finally to the slaves of this community. Widows, slaves, the married, and the celibate constitute the list of people to whom Polycarp is to give special attention (Pol 4–5). Slaves are singled out in a general admonition that individual attention be given by the bishop to all who belong to his congregation (Pol 4.3). Ignatius first advises Polycarp not to despise slaves. But he immediately turns the admonition around by urging the bishop not to allow slaves to be "puffed up." Slaves can hardly have formed the largest or most influential group in the church of Smyrna. At the same time, they were welcome and sometimes rose to high position at least in other Christian communities. In all likelihood the bishop of Ephesus, Onesimus, was a slave or former slave since his name was used almost exclusively (though not without exception) for slaves.

The most interesting point that Ignatius makes about Christian slaves is that they sometimes asked "to be set free out of the common fund." Ignatius rejects such requests "that they may not be found slaves of lust." The request to be set free out of the common fund was apparently met in other early Christian communities (cf. *1 Clem.* 55.2; *Herm. Man.* 8.10; *Herm. Sim.* 1.8), and some Hellenistic clubs (perhaps largely made up of servants and slaves) seem to have lent money from the common fund to members seeking manumission.[41] Since there are some similarities in organization between the Hellenistic clubs and the early Christian churches,[42] Christian conceptions of brotherly love may have received impulses from such practices.

Ignatius preferred to see the slaves remain slaves. He suggests that slaves will gain greater freedom before God the more faithfully they serve their

40. Bryan R. Wilson, *Patterns of Sectarianism* (London: Heinemann, 1967) 37.
41. Herbert Rädle, "Selbsthilfeorganisationen der Sklaven und Freigelassenen in Delphi," *Gymnasium* 77 (1970) 1–5.
42. Erich Ziebarth, *Das griechische Vereinswesen* (Leipzig: Hirzel, 1896) 130–32; Franz Poland, *Geschichte des griechischen Vereinswesens* (Leipzig: Teubner, 1909) 534.

masters. The view is that of Paul according to one reading of 1 Cor 7:21–22. A possible reason for such an attitude was that slaves were not always fully trusted even by churchmen. The author of the *Apostolic Constitutions* will speak of slaves who desire baptism as follows: "And if he is the slave of one of the faithful, let his master be asked [for a character reference]. . . . But if he is a slave of a gentile, let him learn to please his master 'so that' the Word 'be not blasphemed'" (8.32). The echo of Isa 52:5, which we have met before (Tr 8.2), is unmistakable. And it is interesting to note that it is also referred to already in 1 Tim 6:1–2 where slaves are advised to honor pagan masters so that "the name of God . . . be not blasphemed." In the same passage, slaves are told not to "despise" their Christian masters by taking advantage of their common faith. There seems to be a significant continuity of attitude in this connection.

When Ignatius says that the manumission of slaves leads them to become "slaves of lust," he possibly refers to the fact that manumitted slaves frequently had little choice but to take up low professions, especially those associated with prostitution.[43] I suspect that is why Ignatius goes on immediately to say in an obscure passage, "Avoid evil arts; better yet, preach sermons about them" (Pol 5.1). The expression "evil arts" may well refer to trades that minister to pleasure.[44] If so, there were enough people of low social standing in the Christian community of Smyrna to make sermons on the topic relevant. In any event, such people were welcome in the Christian community. Some preparation for such openness was to be found in the Hellenistic clubs and religious associations of the day. Many of the clubs drew their membership from only one class, "but it is possible to find all classes blended together" in them.[45] Especially interesting is an inscription that presents "rules of a private religious association in Philadelphia" from the first century B.C.E.[46] Here too we learn that "both men and women, both bond and free," are received into fellowship. Also reminiscent of the churches known to Ignatius is the (relatively) strict sexual ethic of this group: "A man [is not to take] another woman in addition to his own wife, either a free woman or a slave who has a husband. . . . Woman and man [alike], whoever does any of the things above written, let them not enter this house." It seems likely that the coherence of any marginal religious association is enhanced by such regulations. Finally, it is worth noting that the

43. Isaeus *De Philoctem. hered.* 12–20; Ps.-Demosthenes *In Neaeram* 18; Epictetus *Diss.* 4.1.35–40; cf. Aristide Calderini, *La manomissione e la condizione dei liberti in Grecia* (Milan: Hoepli, 1908) 350–71; Arnold M. Duff, *Freedmen in the Early Roman Empire* (Oxford: Clarendon, 1928) 103–15.

44. Schoedel, *Ignatius,* 271.

45. Reginald Haynes Barrow, *Slavery in the Roman Empire* (New York: Barnes & Noble, 1928) 165.

46. Frederick C. Grant, *Hellenistic Religions* (New York: Liberal Arts, 1953) 28–30. For an edition of the Greek text, see Karl F. W. Dittenberger, *Sylloge Inscriptionum Graecarum* (3d ed.; 4 vols.; Leipzig: Hirzel, 1915–24) 3.985,14–16.

Philadelphian cult was apparently established by the owner of the house in which the cult was practiced.[47] This arrangement, as we have seen, is likely to have obtained in Christian communities as well.

Ideally, an effort would be made at this point to compare our picture of the social and religious conditions of Christian Antioch in the days of Ignatius with what can be gleaned from Matthew about the community within which he worked. But the Gospel of Matthew does not lend itself to such comparison, and it is doubtful that much would be gained by such an exercise. It is surely obvious, however, from what has been said that the Antioch of Ignatius was not the context of the writing of Matthew's Gospel. The distance between Ignatius and Judaism or Jewish Christianity is enough in itself to preclude such a possibility. At the same time, the concentration of gospel materials of a Matthean type in Ignatius is sufficiently strong to compel us to take seriously the suggestion that the Gospel of Matthew was written in Antioch or near Antioch. And this possibility is probably strengthened (rather than weakened) if it is Matthean tradition rather than the Gospel itself that was known to Ignatius. For in that event Ignatius and Matthew still somehow shared the same theological culture in spite of the distance between them. A number of reasons or combinations of reasons can be suggested for this unusual state of affairs: an origin for the Gospel within a zone of Christian communities somehow connected with Antioch rather than in Antioch itself; a chronological gap between the time of Matthew and that of Ignatius; an imperfect assimilation of the Gospel on the part of Ignatius; or his acquaintance with a limited range of tradition of a Matthean type rather than the Gospel itself. Whatever the reason or reasons may be, much that is characteristic of Matthew and his theological world leaves no trace in Ignatius, even though the Gospel or tradition akin to it apparently loomed large in his world. The transition from the religious and social world of the Gospel to the religious and social world of Ignatius was apparently made without noticeable stress. This may mean that we should pay more attention to the linguistic and theological elements in Matthew that show him to be Hellenistic in a broad sense as well as Jewish.

IGNATIUS AND THE GOSPEL

The broad social and religious context reflected in Ignatius is not all that sets Ignatius apart from the Gospel of Matthew. The theological climate in which Ignatius worked also had undergone a sea change. And to this we now turn. As we do, however, it is important to keep in mind not only that Matthew or tradition of a Matthean type remains important for Ignatius, but also (as we

---

47. Grant, *Hellenistic Religions*, 28.

shall see) that the treatment of this material sometimes still reflects impulses that seem more at home in the world of Matthew than in the world of Ignatius.

The Religious Perspectives of Ignatius

Ignatius occasionally quotes Old Testament Scripture as authoritative (Eph 5.3; Mg 12; Tr 8.2) and from time to time reflects biblical phraseology (Eph 15.1; Mg 10.3; 13.1). He also attributes a high value to the prophets because they point forward to the fulfillment of their expectations in the figure of Jesus Christ (Ph 5.2; 9.2). In this connection, however, he insists that if people become preoccupied with Scripture as a source for what he considers idle theological speculation (cf. Ph 9.1), he is prepared to proclaim the sufficiency of Jesus Christ as opposed to the "archives" (Ph 8.2).

The "gospel," then, is decisive for Ignatius. Most commentators now agree that he uses this term of the Christian proclamation rather than of a written document (cf. Ph 5.1, 2; 8.2; 9.2; Sm 5.1; 7.2). Whether Ignatius at the same time used a written gospel is a question to which we shall return below. Suffice it to say at this point that his gospel material has a good deal in common with the Gospel of Matthew. No trace of a dependence on Mark can be found, and only a few possible echoes of distinctively Lukan materials can be identified (notably the resurrection tradition in Sm 3.2–3). Ignatius may quote the Gospel of John in one or two passages (Ph 7.1; cf. Rom 7.2; 7.3; Ph 9.1),[48] but that is regarded as unlikely by the majority of commentators today.[49] At the same time, Ignatius's theological outlook as a whole may be said to be closer to John than to Matthew or any other of our Gospels.

Ignatius looks to Paul as a prototype (cf. Eph 12.2), and his language of self-depreciation is modeled partly on Paul's designation of himself as the "last" of the Christians and a "miscarriage" (Rom 9.2; cf. 1 Cor 15:8–9). Yet certain usage of Pauline letters by Ignatius can be established only for 1 Corinthians. At the same time, Ignatius refers to Paul as the author of more than one letter (Eph 12.2), and it is likely that he had some familiarity with a number of them. Barnett states, "It is clear that Ignatius knew 1 Corinthians, Romans and Ephesians and that he probably knew Galatians, Philippians, and Colossians. He may also have known 2 Corinthians, 1 and 2 Thessalonians, and Philemon."[50] Yet the view that Ignatius used Ephesians depends primarily on the impression left by the salutation in Ignatius's own letter to the Ephesians,

---

48. Chr. Maurer, *Ignatius von Antiochen und des Johannesevangelium* (ATANT 18; Zürich: Zwingli, 1949).

49. Cf. Henning Paulsen, *Studien zur Theologie das Ignatius von Antiochien* (Forschungen zur Kirchen- und Dogmengeschichte 29; Göttingen: Vandenhoeck & Ruprecht, 1978) 36–37.

50. Albert E. Barnett, *Paul Becomes a Literary Influence* (Chicago: University of Chicago Press, 1941) 170.

and I doubt that real certainty is possible in this regard. Moreover, the most frequent and impressive echoes of Romans in Ignatius have to do with Rom 1:3–4, which we are more inclined to see today as dependent on a pre-Pauline formulation. Perhaps the safest thing to say would be that it is really only 1 Corinthians that Ignatius had read with any care.

Ignatius shares a theme with 1 John (Eph 14.2; cf. 1 John 3:9), but it is too isolated and indeterminate to establish clear literary interdependence. The same must be said about possible allusions in Ignatius to the Pastorals, *1 Clement, Hermas,* and *Preaching of Peter,* and the *Odes of Solomon.*

There is, then, in Ignatius a stock of traditional Christian themes in which the Pauline component plays an especially important role. But this stock of traditional themes "has been shaped by two somewhat antithetical yet ultimately reconcilable developments: (1) the emergence of more 'mystical' strains of Christianity (to which Ephesians and the Gospel of John are also indebted in different ways), and (2) the modification of Christian life and thought occasioned by a growing emphasis on discipline and ministerial authority (to which the Pastorals and the Gospel of Matthew also bear witness in different ways)."[51]

It is perhaps even more difficult to say anything with confidence about the influence of the broader religious movements of the day on Ignatius. Schlier convinced many with his interpretation of Eph 19 and other elements in Ignatius that Ignatius was swept up in a stream of well-developed Gnostic thought.[52] But the document to which Schlier pointed in particular for parallels, the *Ascension of Isaiah,* may better be viewed as emerging from an apocalyptic Jewish or Jewish-Christian background that had at most a family resemblance to Gnosticism.

Bartsch, in an almost equally influential study of Ignatius, saw the connection between Ignatius and Gnosticism primarily in the area of his teaching about God as the sphere of "unity" within which Christians were enclosed.[53] But I have been able to show in my commentary especially on Eph 4.2 and Mg 7.1 that the language of unity in Ignatius owes more to Hellenistic and Hellenistic Jewish culture than to Gnosticism.

Ignatius's relation with Judaism, then, is complex. He shows relatively little interest in Old Testament Scripture. Judaism of a distinctly Palestinian or rabbinic stamp has left no real mark on him. Nothing significant has come out of the Dead Sea Scrolls for the study of Ignatius.[54] Something close to the Jew-

---

51. Schoedel, *Ignatius,* 10.
52. Heinrich Schlier, *Religionsgeschichtliche Untersuchungen zu den Ignatiusbriefen* (BZNW 8; Giessen: Töpelmann, 1929).
53. Hans-Werner Bartsch, *Gnostisches Gut und Gemeindetradition bei Ignatius von Antiochien* (Gütersloh: Bertelsmann, 1940).
54. Herbert Musurillo, "Ignatius of Antioch: Gnostic or Essene?" *TS* 22 (1961) 103–10.

ish and Jewish-Christian world of the *Ascension of Isaiah* was important for Ignatius, but otherwise the vital connections are with themes of a Hellenistic or Hellenistic Jewish provenance. And as we have seen, Judaism as a social reality has no positive significance for Ignatius.

What enables Ignatius to pull all this diverse material together and to give it significant theological shape is his emphasis on the incarnation and crucifixion of Jesus Christ. The corollary here is a weakening of the emphasis on creation, the unfolding of the divine plan in history, and the coming of the end. Yet Ignatius does not have a Gnostic mentality. We may say instead that he works with vocabulary and themes rooted in primitive Christian conceptions, that the latter have fallen under the influence of a variety of widely diffused otherworldly impulses, and that the idea of the incarnation gives Ignatius the key to the underlying unity of the diverse theological tendencies at work in his thought. The emphasis on the incarnation deepens the sense of divine involvement in the sphere of the flesh but at the same time narrows the historical arena of divine activity and focuses it more sharply.

The Gospel according to Ignatius

What role, then, did the Gospel of Matthew or materials close to Matthew play in the religious world of Ignatius of Antioch? It is clear from what we have said that the theological traditions alive in Antioch in the time of Ignatius were diverse indeed and transcend the horizons of the Gospel of Matthew significantly. Yet Matthew or materials close to Matthew form the backbone of the gospel materials in Ignatius. The nature of the relation, in particular the question whether Ignatius knew Matthew in written form or not, has received extensive and careful treatment. In my view the discussion has focused somewhat too narrowly on parallels or possible parallels between Ignatius and Matthew and has failed to convey a sense of the religious impulses that lie in the background. Perhaps some progress may be made along these lines by asking ourselves what a gospel written by Ignatius himself would have looked like if he had chosen to write one. Such an approach should be viewed, of course, as a purely heuristic device and should not be unduly pressed. There is some justification for adopting it in the light of the quasi-credal materials found in various passages of Ignatius's letters. These have been shaped by the special tradition in which Ignatius stands or perhaps by Ignatius himself (either in whole or in part) with a view to opposing the docetic Christologies that were flourishing in many of the communities known to him. These materials, then, are marked by a tendency to list the major events in the life of Jesus in an effort to underscore the reality of the fleshly nature of the incarnate Lord.

The best example of such a list for our purposes is that found in Tr 9. There we are told that Jesus Christ was of the family of David, that he was of

Mary, that he was born, that he ate and drank, that he was persecuted under Pontius Pilate, that he was crucified and died, and that he was raised again.

More complete in some respects and less complete in others is the list in Sm 1 where we learn that Christ was of the family of David according to the flesh, that he was also God's son, that he was born of a virgin, that he was baptized by John, and that he was nailed to the cross under Pontius Pilate and Herod the tetrarch. And here after a brief theological comment by Ignatius there appears the account of the resurrection of Jesus that has such striking affinities to Luke 24:39.

Also worth mentioning here is the somewhat truncated list in Eph 18.2 where it is said that "our God, Jesus the Christ" was carried in the womb by Mary, that he was of the seed of David and of the Holy Spirit, that he was born, and that he was baptized. Immediately after comes the striking statement of Ignatius about "the three mysteries of a cry wrought in the stillness of God," namely, the virginity of Mary, her giving birth, and the Lord's death (Eph 19.1). Immediately after that appears the famous description of the star that heralded the Lord's coming and caused so much astonishment and perplexity (Eph 19.2–3). This description has been treated as a hymn by some; and whether that is true or not, it seems unlikely that Ignatius was the inventor of the remarkable materials contained in the passage.

Clearly some of the same impulses are at work here that lie behind the emergence of the Gospels in the early church. The antidocetic purpose of these lists provides a distinctive framework for the implied account of the events of the life of the Lord and may have something to do with the concentration on the events at the beginning and end of Jesus' career. And that suggests the wisdom of letting the beginning and end of the story stand out in the discussion of our imagined gospel according to Ignatius. The list in Tr 9 does, however, mention the eating and drinking of Jesus between references to his birth and crucifixion. That is a somewhat slender thread on which to hang a good deal of what we shall have to say below, but it does indicate that the ministry of Jesus as a whole was kept in view.

The beginning of the gospel: It is apparent from the material discussed above that if Ignatius had written a gospel, it would have contained a birth narrative. He was fascinated, as we have seen, with "the three mysteries of a cry" (Eph 19.1). These were events in the life of the Lord whose meaning was not immediately obvious, but which spoke volumes to the discerning. They were "wrought in the stillness of God," but like the silent deeds of the reticent bishops of Ephesus and Philadelphia were of greater significance than the idle clamor of the world. Two of the three mysteries, the virginity of Mary and her giving birth, are bracketed together by Ignatius in this connection.

In Ignatius's view, however, the indication that something of cosmic significance was taking place in the birth of Jesus was provided by a great star that outshone all other stars, caused astonishment and perplexity in the heavenly realms, and banished "all magic and every bond of wickedness" from the world (Eph 19.2–3). It is not entirely impossible (as Schlier argued) that the text is speaking about a star that appeared at the ascent of Jesus through the heavens after his resurrection.[55] But I think that the evidence is against such a solution and that we have to do with a star whose best parallel is the star that appears in the story of the Magi in the Gospel of Matthew (Matt 2:1–12).[56]

From this point of view, it is natural to think that what we have here in Ignatius is a kind of midrash on the text of the Gospel of Matthew and that perhaps even the story of the Magi lies concealed in the reference to the destruction of all magic and the banishment of the power of the stars over earthly destinies. Such an interpretation of the story of the Magi in fact appears later in the church fathers. We may say that in this way a mythological dimension was read into the story. And it is hard not to be intrigued by the possibility that the disturbance of Herod and "all Jerusalem" in Matthew (2:3) has something to do with the disturbance of the heavenly powers in Ignatius (Eph 19.2). The kind of approach imagined is neatly illustrated by the *(First) Apocalypse of James*, which has Jesus identify the earthly city of Jerusalem as "the dwelling place of a great number of archons" (Nag Hammadi Codex V, 3:25,15–19). For here too historical reality is invested with mythological significance. In fact, of course, such a reading of the birth narrative in Matthew does violence to its meaning. For Matthew's Magi are truly wise, and no polemic against magic or astrology is readily discernible.[57] Does this mean, then, that what we have in Ignatius is an early distortion of the Matthean account? Probably not, since no real trace of Matthew's narrative appears in Ignatius, and the description of events found in the passage is cosmological through and through. It may be better, then, to say (1) that the later patristic interpretations mentioned above link positive and negative approaches to the world of the Magi and astrology somewhat artificially and (2) that although Ignatius and Matthew are both responding to a story about the appearance of a star at the birth of Jesus, their treatment of it is sufficiently different to suggest that they are responding to it independently.

However we assess the problem of interrelation for this passage, it is clear that a birth narrative written in the spirit of Eph 19 would have shown more graphically than any New Testament Gospel what was going on behind

---

55. Schlier, *Untersuchungen,* 5–81.
56. Schoedel, *Ignatius,* 87–94.
57. Raymond E. Brown, *The Birth of the Messiah* (Garden City, N.Y.: Doubleday & Company, 1977) 168.

the scenes at the cosmological level. The mythology would be more vivid and explicit. Quite possibly we would have something more like the description of the birth of Jesus in the *Ascension of Isaiah* which Schlier found so useful in working out the background to Eph 19. The same tendency to mythologize the events of the gospel will be noted also elsewhere.

Ignatius, of course, would have avoided the naive docetism associated with this sort of thing in the *Ascension of Isaiah*. In this connection he would have emphasized Jesus' rootage in the lineage of David (Eph 7.2; 20.2; Tr 9.1; Rom 7.3; Sm 1.1). This very theme, however, undergoes revision here when measured by the birth narratives of the New Testament since Ignatius evidently ascribes Davidic lineage to Mary herself (Eph 18.2).[58] This point is also made by the *Ascension of Isaiah* (11.2) and other early Christian writings, and it no doubt originally aimed at a more persuasive application of proof from prophecy by placing the virgin Mary, the biological mother, rather than Joseph, the putative father, in the line of David. Whether this suggests ignorance of the Gospel of Matthew or an effort to supplement it is hard to say, for other writers of the church make the point long after the recognition of the canonical Gospels.[59] In any event, it represents a theme that is independent of what is now found in the New Testament; and it is perhaps unlikely that a gospel written by Ignatius would have included a genealogy that ended with the name of Joseph.

A gospel written by Ignatius would certainly have contained an account of the baptism of Jesus. As we have seen, it figures significantly in the quasi-credal materials that he develops. From one point of view Ignatius was perfectly comfortable with the story and saw it as some kind of anticipation of the crucifixion (Eph 18.2; cf. Luke 12:50; Mark 10:38–39). At the same time, he or his tradition sensed a difficulty in the implied subordination of Jesus to John the Baptist and was ready with an explanation. In fact Ignatius knew of two possible explanations. One was that Jesus was "baptized by John that all righteousness might be fulfilled by him" (Sm 1.1). The other was that he was "baptized so that he might purify the water by his passion" (Eph 18.2). The latter sounds like the sort of thing that would have been of greater interest to Ignatius. For again it deepens the mythological significance of the event, and there are rich developments in both heterodox and orthodox writers that illustrate just such an approach to the story.[60] Had Ignatius written a gospel, he might well have preferred to exploit such possibilities.

The former explanation, of course, is the Matthean formulation ("to fulfill all righteousness," Matt 3:15). Moreover, it is one of the most clearly

58. Ibid., 287, 511 n. 20.
59. Walter Bauer, *Das Leben Jesu im Zeitalter der neutestamentlichen Apokryphen* (Tübingen: J.C.B. Mohr [Paul Siebeck], 1909) 13–15; Grant, *Ignatius,* 48.
60. Schoedel, *Ignatius,* 85–86.

redactional lines in Matthew and reflects his characteristic vocabulary. In short, this is the passage above all others that convinces the commentators that Ignatius must have used the Gospel of Matthew in a written form.[61] It is a very strong argument indeed, and it is natural to suggest that this passage should be allowed to tip the balance when there is doubt about indebtedness to Matthew elsewhere in Ignatius. But if there are other passages in Ignatius that are close to Matthew and yet clearly or probably not derived from the Gospel of Matthew, the argument can be turned around: perhaps even the passage under discussion came to Ignatius by some other route. Thus it is possible either that Ignatius and Matthew are dependent on the same special tradition or that Matthew's formulation had been picked up by others and put to new use. It is perhaps significant that it is embedded in materials that are generally recognized as quasi-credal in character so that we may have before our eyes the evidence of the source that stands between Matthew and Ignatius. The fact that Ignatius would probably have preferred the alternative explanation of the baptism of Jesus in Eph 18.2 not only indicates that the explanation given in Sm 1.1 is not Ignatius's own but also suggests that he is not likely to have used it unless it had come to him already connected with other materials such as those with which it is associated here. Moreover, I have tried to show in my commentary on Sm 1 and on the possibly related tradition about Jesus' resurrection in Sm 3.2 (the Lukan parallel) that this material had been shaped at an early stage by apologetic concerns.[62] I do not know whether readers will be convinced by my arguments on that point. But if I am right, the possibility is increased that the Matthean theme in Sm 1.1 was picked up and used by someone other than Ignatius. For it too has some kind of apologetic purpose. It is interesting that examples can be found of a comparable use of a purpose clause in formulaic materials (1 Pet 3:18) and of a comparable and probably independent formulation of the reason for Jesus' baptism: "For this reason the Savior was baptized . . . that he might purify all water for those being reborn" (Clem. Al. *Eclog. proph.* 7.1). Matthew's formulation of the theme is distinctive, but the concern that it reflects apparently is not. It may well have been received and handed on by others as one suggestion among others.

It must be granted, to be sure, that the possibility of the use of the Gospel of Matthew is especially strong in this passage. But as we shall see, there are other passages in which we find materials close to Matthew yet not obviously derived directly from Matthew. I see no reason, then, not to allow for the possibility that Ignatius was familiar both with the written Gospel of Matthew and with the special tradition out of which the written Gospel emerged.

61. Wolf-Dietrich Köhler, *Die Rezeption des Matthäusevangeliums in der Zeit vor Irenäus* (WUNT 2.24; Tübingen: J.C.B. Mohr [Paul Siebeck], 1987) 77–79.
    62. Schoedel, *Ignatius*, 220–29.

Before leaving our discussion of the beginning of a gospel as Ignatius might have conceived it, it must be noted that he seems to have known one story in this connection that is not alluded to in the semicredal materials with which he was working—namely, that of the temptation of Jesus. For in declaring his readiness for martyrdom, Ignatius remarks that "the ends of the world and the kingdoms of this age shall profit me nothing; it is better for me to die in Christ Jesus than to rule the ends of the earth" (Rom 6.1). Here Ignatius seems to model his attitude on Jesus' resistance to Satan at his temptation. If this is correct, Ignatius knew the story in its Q form; and there are minute indications that he knew it in a form closer to Matthew than to Luke. For Ignatius refers to τὰ πέρατα τοῦ κόσμου and αἱ βασιλεῖαι τοῦ αἰῶνος τούτου; similarly, Matthew has the devil show Jesus πάσας τὰς βασιλείας τοῦ κόσμου (4:8), whereas Luke reads πάσας τὰς βασιλείας τῆς οἰκουμένης (4:5). The variation between Matthew and Ignatius and the unusual Semitic flavor of the formulation in Ignatius ("of this age") may indicate that Ignatius harks back to an earlier form.[63] Yet the wording may just as well be Ignatius's own since he speaks elsewhere of the "ends of the world" (Eph 3.2) and regularly refers to Satan as the "ruler of this age" (Eph 17.1; 19.1; Mg 1.2; Tr 4.2; Rom 7.1; Ph 6.2). Again it is striking that Ignatius's conception of the opening events of the life of Jesus points in the direction of the Gospel of Matthew rather than to any other source.

The end of the gospel : The same cannot be said of Ignatius's conception of the closing events of the life of Jesus, where there is a greater variety of materials. It is likely, however, that Ignatius did know the story of the anointing of Jesus by a woman before the crucifixion and that he knew it in a form close to that found in Matthew. For Ignatius speaks of the Lord receiving the ointment "upon his head" (Eph 17.1); and Matthew also has the woman pour the ointment "on his head" (Matt 26:7), whereas Luke and John in their partially parallel accounts of what happened in the house of Simon the Pharisee (Luke 7:36–50) or in the house of Lazarus (John 12:1–8) speak of her as pouring the ointment on Jesus' feet. Mark, of course, agrees with Matthew in placing the event at the beginning of the passion narrative and in having the woman pour the ointment on the head of Jesus (Mark 14:3–9); but in the absence of any other significant indication of a use of Mark by Ignatius, the parallel with Matthew is the one that must be taken most seriously.

Ignatius, however, gives the story of the anointing a special twist when he says that the Lord received ointment on his head "to breathe immortality on the church" and to oppose "the evil odor of the teaching of the ruler of this age"

63. J. Smit Sibinga, "Ignatius and Matthew," *NovT* 8 (1966) 267–68.

(Eph 17.1). The commentators are quite naturally reminded of the fact that in John's version of the story "the house was filled with the aroma of the oil" (John 12:3) and that when Jesus leaves his disciples at the end of the Gospel he "breathed" his spirit upon them (John 20:22). Direct influence from John on this point is not very likely. But the parallels do suggest the kind of theological context or religious atmosphere within which Ignatius instinctively interpreted the story. Deeper dimensions are read into the narrative and the symbolic possibilities of the scene are exploited. Something similar seems also to have happened in Ignatius's treatment of the silence of Jesus before his judges. First, a word about Ignatius and the last supper.

The eucharist was a central element, if not the central element, in the worship of the church in Antioch (cf. Eph 5.2; 13.1; Ph 4; Sm 7.1; 8.1). Thus although it seems likely that Ignatius would have known some account of the last supper, no clear echo of any of the relevant New Testament accounts of the event can be heard in his letters. He knows the sacred meal as the breaking of bread (Eph 20.2) as did Luke (Acts 2:46; 20:7) and Paul (1 Cor 10:16). And he refers to the "cup" of the eucharist (Ph 4) as do the Synoptic Gospels (Matt 26:27; Mark 14:23; Luke 22:17), Paul (1 Cor 10:16, 21; 11:25–28), and the Didache (9.2). But when he links the "cup" with the "flesh" of Christ, Ignatius sounds a Johannine note (John 6:52–59). Also more or less Johannine are the connections drawn elsewhere between the "bread of God" and Christ's flesh and between the drink and Christ's blood (Rom 7.3; cf. John 6:26–59). And in harmony with at least one level of redaction in the Johannine tradition, Ignatius puts all of this in the service of a strong sacramental realism (cf. Sm 7.1).[64] At the same time, the celebration still seems to have taken place within the context of a meal called the ἀγάπη (Sm 6.2–8.2). Thus there is contact here with early tradition, but again the tendency is to deepen it with themes from a theologically more reflective milieu.

Something similar, as we have suggested, also seems to have happened in Ignatius's treatment of the silence of Jesus before his judges—a motif that occurs in all of the canonical Gospels (when Jesus appears before Pilate in Mark 15:4–5; Matt 27:12–14; cf. John 19:9; before Herod in Luke 23:9; and before the high priest in Matt 26:63). This motif probably (though not certainly) lurks in the background when Ignatius says that "he who truly has the word of Jesus is able also to hear his stillness, that he may be perfect, that he may act through his speech and be known through his silence" (Eph 15.2). In this passage Ignatius seems not only to rework the popular theme about the

---

64. For the link between Ignatius and the presumed later stages of redaction of the Gospel of John, see Lothar Wehr, *Arznei der Unsterblichkeit: Die Eucharistie bei Ignatius von Antiochien und im Johannesevangelium* (Neutestamentliche Abhandlungen, n.f. 18; Münster: Aschendorff, 1987).

superiority of the silent deed over empty words, but also to exploit the silence of Jesus in order to characterize Jesus' ministry as a whole, drawing attention to the unobtrusive way in which his power was exercised from birth to crucifixion. If this is correct, Ignatius here universalized the significance of a single event in the life of Jesus much as he exploited the symbolic possibilities of the story of the anointing of Jesus.

A gospel written by Ignatius, unlike the Gospel of Matthew, would have had Jesus appear before both "Pontius Pilate and Herod the tetrarch" (as we learn from the semicredal material in Sm 1.2). Here the parallels are in Luke. For Jesus appears before Pilate and Herod in Luke (23:6–12), and in Luke Herod is identified as the tetrarch (3:1). Yet dependence directly on the Gospel of Luke is not necessary. For Pilate and Herod are mentioned again in Acts 4:25–28 in connection with Ps 2:2 with its reference to "kings" and "rulers" (in the plural) rising up against the Lord and the Lord's anointed. Thus on this point an exegetical tradition intent on squaring prophecy with the events of the passion may lie behind both Luke and Ignatius. Justin shows in an apparently independent line of argument how lively that concern continued to be (*Apol.* 1.40.5–18; *Dial.* 103.4).[65] And the fact that this point is embedded in semicredal material strengthens the impression that it was probably not derived by Ignatius from the New Testament.

The passion itself is at the heart of Ignatius's theology, and his emphasis on it suggests that any detailed nondocetic account of the crucifixion and death of Christ would have been welcome to him. At the same time, Ignatius may well have given some indication also here of what transpired behind the cosmic scenes "as heavenly, earthly, and subearthly things looked on" (Tr 9.1). The language is reminiscent of the Christ hymn in Paul's letter to the Philippians (2:10). In this connection, Ignatius may have gone on to picture the cosmic powers as baffled by what it was that was taking place just as they had been thrown into confusion by the appearance of the star. For "the death of the Lord" is also identified by Ignatius as one of the "three mysteries of a cry which were done in the stillness of God" (Eph 19.1). Ignatius may also have suggested that the powers soon got some inkling as to what it was that was overtaking them. For according to one plausible interpretation of Mg 9.2, Christ harrowed hell and raised the prophets from the dead.[66] Such scenarios place Ignatius's conception of the events of the ministry of Jesus outside of the range of any of the Gospels of the New Testament and suggest a mental horizon more in line with some of the later apocryphal gospels.

65. Helmut Koester, *Synoptische Überlieferung bei den Apostolischen Vätern* (TU 65; Berlin: Akademie-Verlag, 1957) 26–27.

66. Jean Daniélou, *The Theology of Jewish Christianity* (London: Darton, Longman & Todd; Philadelphia: Westminster, 1964) 236–37.

When Ignatius came to tell the story of the resurrection of Jesus, he fell back on something with close affinities to Luke 24:39. Here is what Ignatius says: "For I know and believe that he was in the flesh even after the resurrection. And when he came to those about Peter, he said to them: 'Take, handle me, and see that I am not a bodiless demon.' And immediately they touched him and believed. . . . And after the resurrection he ate and drank with them as a being of flesh, although spiritually united with the Father" (Sm 3.1–3). Luke has Jesus say: "Look at my hands and my feet; see that it is I myself. Touch me and see; for a ghost does not have flesh and bones as you see that I have" (24:39). Immediately before his account of the resurrection, Ignatius had already referred to docetists as condemning themselves to "being bodiless and demonic" by their beliefs about Christ (Sm 2). It has generally been argued that the terms "bodiless" and "demonic" are used by Ignatius in this unusual way because he is anticipating the mention of Jesus not being "a bodiless demon" in the story of the resurrection that he is about to recall. If that is so, Ignatius is working with a tradition independent of the Gospel of Luke. The argument, however, can also be turned around. The positive assessment of all that is bodiless in Hermetic and Gnostic texts suggests that Ignatius may have been taking a view of his opponents and throwing it back at them in distorted form when he identifies them as condemned to being bodiless—that is, demonic! If that is so, then he may have gone on to reformulate the Lukan passage under the influence of his own play on words.[67] Although it seems possible that Ignatius was playing on his opponents' views when he pictured them as condemned to being bodiless and demonic, would he have slipped so easily into altering the text of Luke in accordance with his own play on words? Would he not have accomplished more by letting the known form of the saying stand in his reference to the story of the resurrection so that the point of the play on words would be more obvious and that he might gain the advantage of quoting the saying in a familiar form? Certainty is impossible on such a point, but it seems to me more likely that here Ignatius is dealing with tradition parallel to Luke and not with the Gospel of Luke itself.[68]

It is interesting to note in this connection that the texts of Ignatius and Luke may be compared fruitfully with another in Philostratus's *Life of Apollonius* (8.12). Here we are told that after Apollonius mysteriously disappeared from the courtroom in which he was being tried by the emperor Domitian, he reappeared to two disciples, one of whom asks whether the sage is alive or

---

67. For details, see P. Vielhauer, "Jewish-Christian Gospels," *New Testament Apocrypha* (ed. Edgar Hennecke; rev. ed., ed. Wilhelm Schneemelcher, trans. and ed. Robert McL. Wilson; 2 vols.; London: Lutterworth; Philadelphia: Westminster, 1963–65) 1.129–30; Paulsen, *Studien zur Theologie des Ignatius von Antiochien*, 39–41, 141–42.

68. Schoedel, *Ignatius*, 225–29.

dead. Then "Apollonius stretched out his hand and said, 'Take me (λαβοῦ μου); if I slip from your grasp, I am a phantom (εἴδωλόν) come to you from Persephone . . .; if I remain firm under your touch (ἁπτόμενον), persuade also Damis that I am alive and that I have not thrown off my body.' They were no longer able to disbelieve (ἀπιστεῖν)." The points of contact are interesting: In Sm 3.2 Jesus also says λάβετε ("take"), whereas Luke does not have the expression. Philostratus's "phantom come to you from Persephone" and Ignatius's "bodiless demon" both refer to spiritual beings that lack corporeal substance. Ignatius has Jesus say ψηλαφήσατέ με ("handle me"), which has an exact parallel in Luke. Yet Ignatius also goes right on to say (more or less in harmony with Philostratus) that "they touched him" (αὐτοῦ ἥψαντο) and "believed" (ἐπίστευσαν). It is hard to know whether Philostratus writes with or without Christian religious propaganda in view and how old or reliable his sources may be. In any event, the variations in the three texts suggest that we have before us evidence for a debate that took place in apologetic contexts at the boundaries of the confrontation between Christians and pagans. Ignatius makes antidocetic use of the material. But this would not be the only instance of a reapplication of themes by Ignatius for such a purpose. The variations in the three texts also seem to suggest that Ignatius was in touch with developments that either went beyond what is found in the Gospel of Luke or that ran parallel to it and that he is less likely to have been using the written Gospel itself. The fact that Origen knew a saying from the *Teaching of Peter* (probably the apologetically oriented *Preaching of Peter*)[69] in which Jesus says, "I am not a bodiless demon" (*De principiis* 8) shows how alive the interest in this distinctive form of the story remained, however difficult it may be to decide whether literary dependence is involved and in which direction such dependence might point.

A word is in order here about the reference to Peter in the tradition about the resurrection known to Ignatius. The Gospel of Luke has the Emmaus disciples say that "truly the Lord is raised and has appeared to Simon" (24:34; cf. 1 Cor 15:5). But Peter is then ignored, and "the eleven and those with them" (Luke 24:33) are the ones involved in the Lukan scene under discussion (24:36–43). Ignatius, on the other hand, has the Lord speak the decisive words to "those about Peter." It is hard to know whether Ignatius possibly preserves a more primitive form of the tradition here (cf. the role of Peter as first witness to the resurrection in 1 Cor 15:5) or whether he might be running together things remembered from Luke. But since no very special interest in Peter is evident in Ignatius, it is perhaps more likely that he is simply reflecting his tradition on this point. Ignatius elsewhere mentions Peter along

69. Ernst von Dobschütz, *Das Kerygma Petri* (TU 11.1; Leipzig: Hinrichs, 1893) 82–84, 134.

with Paul as joint authorities that the Romans in particular would be likely to recognize (Rom 4.3). Remarkable for its absence from Ignatius is any reference to a connection between Peter and Antioch in spite of the evidence from Paul's letter to the Galatians that Peter had been there (and had perhaps won the day in the struggle with Paul over his attitude toward observance), and in spite of the (questionable) view of later authorities that Peter had established the line of bishops in Antioch either by appointing Ignatius himself (Origen) or Ignatius's immediate predecessor (Eusebius). Instead, Ignatius consciously models himself on Paul as we have already seen (Rom 9.2; cf. 1 Cor 15:8–9). Yet he does not do so because of any special association between Paul and Antioch. Instead, Ignatius speaks of Paul as having preceded him from Ephesus to suffer in Rome (Eph 12.2). An interest in living historical connections with the first generation of apostles is not a feature of Ignatius's Christianity. He works with sanctified tradition instead.

The middle of the gospel: There is not a great deal to go on when it comes to saying how Ignatius might have imagined the ministry of Jesus between the time of his birth and baptism on the one hand and his death and resurrection on the other hand. The semicredal materials, as we have seen, bridge the gap between these two periods only by mentioning the presumed fact that Jesus "both ate and drank" during his ministry (Tr 9.1). A reference here to Matt 11:19 where Jesus says that "the Son of Man came eating and drinking" seems to be beside the point. The remark sounds more like an echo of the resurrected Lord's eating in Luke 24:42–43 or John 21:5, 10 or to his eating and drinking in Acts 10:41. Justin in a rephrasing of the passion predictions of Jesus has him say that he will "eat and drink again with his disciples" after the resurrection (*Dial.* 51.2). Here the word "again" suggests how natural it would have been to read the apologetic emphasis on the resurrected Lord's eating and drinking back into the record of his life particularly when that was being looked at in antidocetic terms.

That Ignatius thought of the ministry of Jesus primarily in terms of a teaching ministry and with turns of expression that remind us particularly of Matthew will soon be clear. At the same time, a religious atmosphere akin to that found in the Gospel of John also lurks in the background. For Ignatius knows that "the Lord did nothing without the Father—being united with him—neither by himself nor through the apostles" during Jesus' ministry (Mg 7.1); or in other words (Mg 7.2), Ignatius knows (as John knows) that Christ "proceeded from the one Father" (cf. John 8:42; 13:3; 16:28; 17:8), "was with the one" during his ministry (cf. John 8:16, 29; 14:10), and "returned" to him (cf. John 13:3; 14:28; 16:10, 28).

Would Ignatius's Jesus also have taught with words that had a Johannine flavor? References in Ignatius to "living water" (Rom 7.2; cf. John 4:10; 7:38), to the "bread of God" and the eucharistic "flesh" of Christ (Rom 7.3; cf. John 6:51, 55), or to Christ as the "door" (Ph 9.1; cf. John 10:7, 9) do not seem distinctive enough to suggest literary dependence on the written Gospel. Moreover, some of these themes and images have parallels elsewhere that are at least as likely sources for Ignatius's usage. More significant is the line in Ph 7.1 in which Ignatius declares that the spirit "knows whence it comes and whither it goes and exposes hidden things." The famous line in John 3:8 ("the πνεῦμα blows where it wills . . . , but you do not know whence it comes and whither it goes," RSV) is the obvious parallel for the first part of the sentence, and the second part possibly also owes something to the Gospel (John 16:8), though here the terminology reminds us of other New Testament passages as well (Rom 2:16; 1 Cor 4:5; 14:24–25). But talk about the whence and whither of the spirit has a formulaic ring, and accordingly it is connected with figures other than the spirit in the Johannine writings (John 8:14; cf. John 7:27–28; 9:29; 12:35; 13:36; 14:5; 16:5; 1 John 2:11; Rev 7:13).[70] It is unlikely, then, that a literary relation between John and Ignatius is required to explain this line or that Ignatius would have had Jesus speak the language of the Gospel of John.

Jesus the teacher implies disciples; but to be a disciple for Ignatius implies above all else the willingness to suffer, especially in the case of Ignatius himself (e.g., Eph 1.2). This characteristic emphasis in our author could hark back to any of the Gospels. But it may be noted that the connection between the word "disciple" and suffering comes out most clearly in Luke 14:27 ("whoever does not carry the cross and follow me cannot be my disciple"). The parallel to this passage in Matthew lacks the term "disciple" (10:38). And the comparable materials in Mark do not have it (10:29–30 + 8:34). John gets somewhat closer to this usage in his emphasis on the incompleteness of discipleship among those with whom Jesus deals (John 8:31; 15:8). We learn very little about Ignatius's sources in this way, but we do gain some sense of how he may have read the record of Jesus' interactions with his disciples before the crucifixion.

Yet when Ignatius reflects materials from the teaching ministry of Jesus, there is little emphasis on words or actions of Jesus that might highlight the theme of suffering. Apparently nothing stood out in his mind as giving any special shape or direction to Jesus' activity between the time of his baptism and his crucifixion. There is no suggestion that he had in view any turning point comparable in importance to the scene at Caesarea Philippi in Mark, or to Jesus turning his face to go to Jerusalem as in Luke, or to Jesus' dramatic final

70. Cf. Gillis P:son Wetter, "Eine gnostische Formel im vierten Evangelium," ZNW 18 (1918) 49–63.

appearance in Jerusalem as in John. It may be fair to say that Ignatius carried to even greater lengths Matthew's tendency to subordinate action to teaching in this period of Jesus's ministry.

This may be illustrated by a passage in Ignatius that preserves a trace of the picture of Jesus as healer and, at the same time, of the concern about the fulfillment of prophecy. For Ignatius evidently models the role of a bishop of the church on the figure of Jesus when he says to Polycarp that he must "bear (βάσταζε) the illnesses of all" in coming to grips with "the more troublesome" in his congregation (Pol 1.3). The line reflects a form of Isa 53:4 found in Matt 8:17 (where it is taken as a prediction of the healing activity of Jesus). The Septuagint has something quite different. An effort has been made to argue for a source other than Matthew for the allusion in Ignatius by suggesting that Ignatius derived his version of the verse from some translation of the Bible other than the Septuagint. It has been observed that Aquila and Symmachus say of the servant of the Lord that "he took up our illnesses" and that the missing verb βαστάζειν ("bear") appears a few verses after in Aquila's version of Isa 53:11. The difference between Ignatius and Aquila or Symmachus on the verb ("bear" vs. "take up") is significant in view of the fact that the similarity between Matthew and Aquila or Symmachus on the noun ("illnesses") depends on the fact that both are closer to the Hebrew than to the Septuagint. We are probably dealing, then, with two different renderings of the Hebrew verb, and in all likelihood the appearance of one rather than the other represents more than a stylistic variation. To think that Matthew and Ignatius drew from the same version would involve the improbable assumption either that both independently took the verb "bear" from Isa 53:11 (Aquila) and combined it with Isa 53:4 or that there was some now unknown version that had the required reading.[71]

Unexpectedly, then, this little line presents one of the stronger pieces of evidence for a direct connection between Ignatius and the Gospel of Matthew. There has always been hesitation on the point, however, and no doubt that has something to do with the fact that a scriptural passage is involved so that Matthew and Ignatius may be dependent on the same exegetical tradition. There is some evidence that this is so here. For Irenaeus, who seems to have used collections of biblical texts for some purposes, quotes the relevant text of Isaiah in two forms. Thus at the end of one collection of passages from Isaiah he quotes Isa 53:4 in its Matthean form and like Matthew takes it to refer to Jesus as healer. He then goes on immediately to allude to the Septuagint form of Isa 53:3 which (along with other biblical material) he takes to refer to the passion (Adv. Haer. 4.33.11–12). Similarly in another passage he presents a full quotation of Isa 52:13—53:5 in its Septuagint form just after having introduced

71. Krister Stendahl, *The School of St. Matthew* (Philadelphia: Fortress, 1968) 106–7.

the Matthean form of the text (*Dem.* 67–68). This suggests the possibility that a list of biblical prophecies was known that made use of two forms of Isa 53:4. And although one of these may have been derived directly from the Gospel of Matthew, it also seems possible that it came from the school tradition that lies behind Matthew.

Whatever the solution to the problem of literary interdependence may be on this point, the passage retains a faint echo of the picture of Jesus as healer and a faint echo of the proof from prophecy that we find in Matthew. Characteristically, however, Ignatius makes use of the material for the purpose of defining episcopal authority and encouraging its wise and tolerant exercise. An image of Christ the healer has been replaced here by an image of the bishop who heals by patiently enduring all the distress to which one with such obligations is heir. There is a sense in which Ignatius here combines the two applications of Isa 53:4 that were known in the early period, and we are left wondering whether such a double application of the prophetic text may not be implicit in Matthew as well. Clearly, however, Ignatius does not work out proof from prophecy in the spirit of Matthew. Certainly he is concerned, as we have seen, to emphasize the fact that the prophets look forward to the coming of Christ. But he himself does not do the exegesis relevant to the point and is evidently not particularly interested in it. To judge from his discussion with the Philadelphians about the biblical "archives," Ignatius appreciated a more advanced form of interpretation involving in this instance a christological treatment of Christ as High Priest and only mediator of the mysteries enclosed in the Holy of Holies (Ph 7–9). Thus he was apparently more at home in the exegetical world of Hebrews and Barnabas. At the same time, he seems to warn against becoming too preoccupied even with this form of investigation into Scripture.

Two other passages in Ignatius's letter to Polycarp reflect the use of materials of a synoptic type to spell out the duties of the Christian bishop. Ignatius says to Polycarp, "If you love good disciples, you have no credit (χάρις)" (Pol 2.1). Luke has Jesus say, "If you love those who love you, what credit (χάρις) is that to you?" (6:32). Matthew has instead, "What reward do you have?" (5:46). But the sentiment in a form closer to Luke seems to be reflected elsewhere in sources prior to Ignatius. Thus 1 Peter calls for obedience to masters, both the good and the bad, and declares that it will be to one's "credit" if one suffers unjustly (2:18–19; cf. Did. 1.3; 2 *Clem.* 13.4). Direct dependence on Luke by Ignatius is not necessary or even very likely.

Closer to Matthew, on the other hand, is the line in Pol 2.2: "Be prudent as the serpent in everything and always pure as the dove." Matthew has Jesus send his disciples out "like sheep into the midst of wolves" with the advice to "be wise as serpents and innocent as doves" (10:16). The two passages are very close. But the sentiment is proverbial and something very similar to it appears in a late Jewish midrash (*Song of Songs* 2.14).[72] Paul also seems to reflect some such sentiment already in his letter to the Romans ("I want you to be wise in what is good and guileless in what is evil," Rom 16:19). Note, moreover, that the remark is immediately preceded in Ignatius by two medical proverbs. Ignatius, then, is not likely to have derived the passage directly from the Gospel of Matthew. Wolf-Dietrich Köhler, a recent defender of direct Matthean influence on Ignatius, recognizes the force of such arguments and concedes that the use of the Gospel in this instance is "only very possible."[73] Material of this kind suggests the possibility that Ignatius lived in an environment influenced not only by the Gospel of Matthew but also (or perhaps even exclusively) by some of the special materials that were taken up into the Gospel.

There is also a possibility that a noncanonical saying of Jesus was used by Ignatius in connection with his own role as bishop and martyr. His remark, "near the sword, near God; with the beasts, with God" (Sm 4.2), has affinities with a saying of Jesus preserved in the *Gospel of Thomas* (82), Origen (*Homiliae in Jeremiam* 20.3) and Didymus (*In Psalmos* 88.8). According to the latter, Jesus said: "He who is near me is near the fire; he who is far from me is far from the kingdom." The situation is complicated by the fact that we have a pagan proverb that also has affinities with the saying: "He who is near Zeus is near the lightning" (*Aesopi proverbia* 7).[74] Significant rewriting and reapplication is involved whether we think that Ignatius derived his remark from the saying or from the proverb. And the changes involved seem to be just about as great in either instance. Ignatius was not one to stick to any one type of material in his application of sentiments associated with the Gospels.

Still more of the allusions (or possible allusions) to Gospel material in Ignatius are used by him to reinforce calls to obedience and unity in the churches. Some of these concern themselves in a general way with the obedience due the Christian bishop: (1) If the "prayer of one or two have such power," how much more the prayer of the bishop and the whole church (Eph 5.2; cf. Matt 18:19–20). (2) One must "receive the bishop as him who sent him" (Eph 6.1; cf. Matt 10:40; Luke 10:16; John 13:20). (3) The difference between those who attend to the bishop and those who obey him is compared to "two coinages" (Mg 5.2; cf. Matt 22:19–22). (4) And in Sm 8.2: "*Wherever* Jesus Christ is, *there* is the whole church" (cf. Matt 18:20, "*where* two or three are gathered in my name, I am *there* among them"), and "what he [the bishop]

72. Koester, *Synoptische Überlieferung*, 43.
73. Köhler, *Die Rezeption des Matthäusevangeliums*, 86.
74. Johannes B. Bauer, "Echte Jesusworte?" W. C. van Unnik, *Evangelien aus dem Nilssand* (Frankfurt: Scheffler, 1960) 123–24.

approves is also pleasing to God" (cf. Matt 18:18, whatever the apostles bind on earth will be bound in heaven).

Most would agree that the last three of these passages point to no particular source though there are more or less minute indicators in each case of possible connections with the world of Matthew's Gospel. The New Testament passages about receiving the one sent are more complex than that which appears in Ignatius: in the New Testament, to receive the disciple = to receive the one sent (Christ) = to receive God (the sender). Ignatius's term "receive" (δέχεσθαι) is found in Matthew's version of the saying (10:40), but his term "the one who sent" (τὸν πέμψαντα) is found in John (13:20). Note that in the New Testament there is also a connection between this set of parallels and another set of parallels about "receiving" children (Mark 9:37; Matt 18:5; Luke 9:48). Here again three terms are usually involved: God, Christ, and the child. Only Matthew reduces the three terms to two: Christ and the child. There is a comparable reduction in Ignatius.

The links between Sm 8.2 and Matthew suggested above are not normally commented on in the literature. I think that the similarities formally and thematically are sufficiently close to suggest a common theological climate (and no more than a common theological climate). The same is less likely to be true of the passage about the two coinages (Mg 5.2). I have tried to show elsewhere that the image of the two coinages was widespread in the popular culture of Ignatius's day and that if it was connected in the Christian tradition with gospel material, it is just as likely to have been connected with the noncanonical saying, "Be approved money-changers," as with the discussion about taxation in Matthew.[75]

The allusion to the saying on prayer is more important for our purposes. For clearly it is closely related to distinctive Matthean materials and yet is sufficiently different to suggest the possibility of reliance on some other source. Ignatius may have blended the discussion in Matthew about the assembling of "two or three" (18:20) and his previous discussion of the need for "one or two" witnesses when quarreling brethren deal with one another (18:16). And that could account for Ignatius's reference to the prayer of "one or two." But it is recognized that this possibility is somewhat tenuous. The theme seems to have a background in Judaism. Thus Matthew's reference to two or three gathered together is illustrated by passages in *Avoth* that speak of the divine presence found between two who study the law together (3.2) or between three who do so (3.3). And the possibility of a variation on the theme like that found in Ignatius is also suggested by the Jewish source. For *Avoth* shortly after goes on to discuss the divine presence found among ten, or five, or three, or two, or even

75. Schoedel, *Ignatius,* 110–11.

one who attends to the study of the law (3.6). The theme also shows up in a variety of forms in what may be independent lines of tradition in later Christian sources.[76] Note especially the *Gospel of Thomas* in which we are told that Jesus is present where there are "two or one" (saying 30) or, in the Greek form of the saying, "one alone" (Oxyrhynchus Papyrus 1.1, 5). A veritable law of rhetorical variation on a stock theme seems to be at work here so that a reliance by Ignatius on tradition independent of Matthew yet closely related to Matthew seems a strong possibility indeed.

The passage is also important for another reason. The implication is clear that Ignatius is harking back to some well-known theme: if (as is well known) prayers of one or two are so effective, how much more the prayers of the whole community under the bishop. It has not been a mistake on the part of scholars to look for the possible sources of such materials. What is not clear is whether he would necessarily have associated them with Jesus as Matthew does. The more proverbial the passage, the greater the possibility that Ignatius still knew it in a form independent of any association with Jesus.

Other passages that possibly hark back to material of a synoptic type focus on the need not only to obey the bishop but also to follow him in opposition to false teaching: (1) False teachers are like "wild animals" (Eph 7.1) or more precisely like "wolves" (Ph 2.2; cf. Matt 7:15 where false prophets are likened to "ravenous wolves"). (2) The silent bishop of Ephesus is to be preferred to talkative false teachers since "the tree is manifest from its fruit" (Eph 14.2). (3) The silent bishop rather than false teachers should be followed since "one, then, is the teacher," Christ (Eph 15.1; cf. Matt 23:8, "for one is your teacher ... one is your leader, the Christ"). (4) False teachers will go "into unquenchable fire" (Eph 16.2).

Two of these remarks depend on imagery sufficiently indeterminate that they contribute little to our understanding of the sources of Ignatius's Christianity. This is especially true of the image of unquenchable fire. It occurs in connection with the Q account of John the Baptist's preaching (Matt 3:12; Luke 3:17) and in a phrase in Mark 9:43 that is verbally exactly what we find in Ignatius. The image of false teachers as "wolves" is especially striking in Matthew as we have indicated above, but it is also found elsewhere in the early church (John 10:12; Acts 20:29) and in pagan authors as well (Epictetus *Diss.* 3.22.35; Maximus of Tyre *Or.* 6, 7d; Libanius *Ep.* 194.1).

It is worth noting, however, that the imagery of false teachers as "wild animals" in Ignatius's letter to the Ephesians is followed a few sections later by a reference to knowing the tree from its fruit (Eph 14.2), and we may recall that

76. Jacques-E. Menard, *L'évangile selon Thomas* (Nag Hammadi Studies 5; Leiden: E. J. Brill, 1975) 124–26.

in a famous passage of Matthew's Sermon on the Mount there is a connection between the two themes (Matt 7:15–20). A common approach to the problem of the outside agitator is apparent in this instance. The exact form of the statement in Ignatius, however, is closer to another passage in Matthew where the Pharisees are attacked as "offspring of vipers": "for the tree is known by its fruit" (12:33b). At the same time, Ignatius's statement is also reasonably close to the form that it has in the Sermon on the Mount (especially in Matt 7:16, 20, "you will know them by their fruits"); and it is even closer to the form that it has in the Lukan parallel to the Sermon on the Mount (Luke 6:44, "for each tree is known by its own fruit"). Yet whereas the sentiment in Matthew has in view the problem of false teachers (the "ravenous wolves"), it serves in Luke only as a general exhortation. Thus the strongest connections are with Matthew, and yet the variations in the form of the statement and its appearance in more than one stratum of the tradition suggest reliance on something that has not yet achieved the fixed form that it has in the Gospels. It has been noted in particular that Ignatius uses the term φανερόν ("manifest") here instead of the synoptic term γινώσκεται ("is known") and that such a usage is "not otherwise typical for Ignatius."[77] Thus Ignatius is likely to have derived the statement from a source independent of the Gospel of Matthew. This conclusion is reinforced by the proverbial character of the sentiment; and in this connection Koester draws attention to the Jewish saying in b.Berakot 48a: "Every pumpkin can be told from its stalk."[78] It is worth noting that Köhler, in spite of his general emphasis on Ignatius's use of the written Gospel of Matthew, regards this passage as very "unlikely" to reflect direct dependence on the written Gospel.[79]

A more difficult problem is presented by the acclamation, "one, then, is the teacher" (Eph 15.1). The language and the use to which it is put is strikingly like that found in Matthew (23:8). And it may well be significant that the theme of the superiority of deeds to words is also found in this connection in both Matthew (23:3–7) and Ignatius (Eph 14.2). At the same time, Matthew develops the argument in a more complex form and is particularly concerned to warn against the appropriation of titles of honor such as "rabbi," "father," and "leader." This is part of an attack on the scribes and Pharisees; but the passage also seems to have in view problems of leadership in the Jewish-Christian community itself and, in any event, was apparently intended to rule out the development of overly specialized roles in the community. Ignatius, on the

---

77. Köhler, *Die Rezeption des Matthäusevangeliums*, 92 (citing C. S. Morgan).
78. Koester, *Synoptische Überlieferung*, 42–43.
79. Köhler, *Die Rezeption des Matthäusevangeliums*, 92 ("unwahrscheinlich" for Köhler has to do with allusions in Ignatius least likely to be derived from the Gospel of Matthew; it ranks after the already weak prospects of a connection "allenfalls theoretisch möglich"; four classes of allusions are recognized in all).

other hand, appeals to the uniqueness of Christ's authority to support the bishop; and the bishop, especially as Ignatius defines the office, is a figure who plays a significantly specialized role in the community. This argument must not be pressed too hard. We have already seen that Ignatius can take language from the letters of Paul and reapply it without much concern for its original context. And further examples of that could be provided. But it is perhaps less likely that we have such a reapplication before us here. For Matthew and Ignatius carry the argument to almost opposite conclusions. Thus an appropriation of a theme older than both Matthew and Ignatius seems more likely. That it was rooted in a broader rhetorical context is suggested by the fact that we find other comparable acclamations in the early period that serve to focus hearts and minds on a common object of veneration. Thus Paul announces that though there are many gods and lords, "for us there is one God, the Father" and "one Lord, Jesus Christ" (1 Cor 8:6). And Ignatius himself elsewhere in his letter to the Ephesians sets forth a string of christological paradoxes that begins with the words, "one is the Physician" (7.2). Here again the point of the discussion is that one should avoid listening to those who behave like "wild beasts" and "ravening dogs" as they challenge the authority of the taciturn bishop of Ephesus (6.1–7.2).

The emphasis on Christ as the one authority in the church is used elsewhere by Ignatius to resist not just false teachers in general but Judaizers in particular (Ph 9.1). Two possible allusions to gospel materials play a role here: (1) In Mg 10.2 Judaism is compared to old leaven (cf. 1 Cor 5:7–8; Gal 5:9) and set in opposition to Jesus Christ in whom we may be "salted" (cf. Matt 5:13; Luke 14:34–35; Mark 9:49–50). (2) In Ph 6.1 Judaizers are compared to "tombstones and graves of the dead" (cf. Matt 23:27, the scribes and Pharisees are compared to "graves" that are filled with bones "of the dead").

The use of the imagery of "salt" is too indeterminate to help us much. Perhaps the curious line found in Mark 9:49, "for everyone will be salted with fire," would lend itself most readily to a christological application of the image such as we have in Ignatius. But Mark is the least likely of the Gospels to have left a trace on Ignatius here or elsewhere. The imagery of "tombstones" and "graves" is almost equally indeterminate. For the commentators have recognized that there are parallels in pagan literature that are at least as striking as that found in Matthew.[80]

Two possible allusions to gospel materials of a more interesting kind are found in connection with Ignatius's attack on docetists: (1) It is said of the docetists of Tralles that "they are not the *planting* of the *Father*" (Tr 11.1; cf. Matt 15:13, where Jesus says of the scribes and Pharisees, "Every *plant* that my

80. Schoedel, *Ignatius*, 203.

heavenly *Father* has not planted will be uprooted"). (2) The docetists of Smyrna are told that even the heavenly powers will be judged if they do not believe in the blood of Christ; and to this is added the remark, ὁ χωρῶν χωρείτω (Sm 6.1, "he who can receive this, let him receive it"; cf. Matt 19:12 where almost exactly the same formula closes off the hard saying about becoming eunuchs for the sake of the Kingdom of Heaven: ὁ δυνάμενος χωρεῖν χωρείτω).

There is a broad background in biblical and postbiblical literature both in Judaism and Christianity for the image of God as the divine planting.[81] But the formulation of the thought in Ignatius is strikingly close to that found in Matthew where it is also put to polemical use. This must be judged one of the strongest pieces of evidence for the direct dependence between Matthew and Ignatius.[82] At the same time, it is the kind of vivid image that may well have migrated freely from one context to another. It occurs again in Ignatius's letter to the Philadelphians where it is directly linked with the image of "evil plants" or "weeds" (3.1). And that, as we shall see presently, means that it intersects a range of images reminiscent of certain New Testament parables that appear to have been treated in the environment of Ignatius in a very independent way.

The line "he who can receive this, let him receive it" finds no other parallel more precise than that provided by Matthew. But it looks so much like a formula that it would be unwise to claim too much for it. When the letters of Ignatius were expanded in the fourth century, the present passage was rendered as follows: "He who can receive this, let him receive it; he who can hear, let him hear." That author rightly sensed an affinity between the formula in Ignatius and the expression in the Gospels, "Let anyone with ears to hear listen!" (Mark 4:9). A noncanonical saying of Jesus quoted by Epiphanius has, "He who can hear, let him hear; and he who disobeys, let him disobey" (*Pan.* 78.24). Along similar lines is a passage near the end of the New Testament apocalypse: "Let the evildoer still do evil; and the filthy still be filthy, and the righteous still do right, and the holy still be holy" (Rev 22:11). It appears that we have before us a rhetorical pattern from the exhortation of the early church, and at least some forms of it seem to have been used particularly for the sake of commending hard sayings. It is likely, then, that Ignatius and Matthew were drawing on the same local variation of the formula.

We turn finally in this connection to language in Ignatius apparently associated with parables in the Gospel of Matthew and used here to support the authority of bishops against false teachers: (1) Ignatius speaks of the Ephesian bishop as God's representative "whom the householder (οἰκοδεσπότης) sends

81. Jean Daniélou, "The Vine and the Tree of Life," *Primitive Christian Symbols* (Baltimore: Helicon, 1964) 25–41.
82. Köhler, *Die Rezeption des Matthäusevangeliums,* 80.

into his stewardship (οἰκονομίαν)" [(Eph 6.1; cf. the parable of the wicked husbandmen in Matt 21:33–41). This is part of the line (studied above) about receiving the one sent as the one who sent him. Apparently the motif of "sending" linked the two themes in Ignatius's mind.] (2) Ignatius speaks of false teaching as "sown" (σπειρόμενα) among the Ephesians (Eph 9.1; cf. the parable of the tares in Matt 13:24–30). (3) Elsewhere in the same letter Ignatius speaks of the need for patience in the face of outside pressure as a matter of avoiding any "plant (βοτάνη) of the devil" (Eph 10.3), and in other letters he employs the same term "plant" again to refer to false teaching (Tr 6.1; Ph 3.1). Here too we may have an echo of the parable of the tares.

Matthew's version of the parable of the wicked husbandmen is the one generally referred to by the commentators rather than that of Mark or Luke because only Matthew mentions the "householder." A reliance by Ignatius on a source of some kind is suspected since he uses the term "householder" only here, and uses the term "stewardship" only here in this sense.[83] Since the latter term does not occur in Matthew, however, language from other parables with comparable themes may have influenced the formulation. Thus Matthew's version of the parable of the good and wicked servants (24:45) has the lord set his good servant over his "household" (οἰκετείας), and Luke's version (12:42) has the lord address his good servant as a faithful "steward" (οἰκονόμος). Naturally, the use of the term "stewardship" in Ignatius may also have been derived from the simple logic of the situation in the story. In any event, a continuing interest in the parable of the wicked husbandmen is made evident by the relatively independent versions of it found in the *Gospel of Thomas* (sayings 65–66) and Hermas (*Herm. Sim.* 5.2). The latter is particularly important for our purposes. For it refers to God as the "master" (δεσπότης), and on this point approaches the language of Ignatius (and Matthew). It also demonstrates the variety of applications that could be made of the parable since it develops the role of Jesus as God's servant and pictures him as one who for his merits was destined to become coheir with the divine Son of God.

Hermas's formulation of the parable is also interesting for another reason. It makes much of the servant's concern to root out the weeds from the master's vineyard. Here the term βοτάνη is used for the noxious plants (*Herm. Sim.* 5.2.3–5). This is also the term used by Ignatius in some of the passages already noted as possibly containing echoes of the parable of the tares. In fact, however, Matthew's version of the parable of the tares uses the unusual word ζιζάνια for the weeds. Ignatius, then, may be relying on something else. And since the term βοτάνη is used of the uprooting of noxious "plants" in Hermas's version of the parable of the wicked husbandmen, there is a possibility that

---

83. Koester, *Synoptische Überlieferung*, 39–42.

themes and images from related parables flowed together to account for what we find in Ignatius. Similarly, the identification in Ph 3.1 of those who are not the "planting of the Father" as "evil plants" may represent another element in a complex system of associations of related themes and images.

This is all very tenuous and can hardly be more than suggestive. But if such a complex system of associations existed, it would show once again that the world of Matthew is closest to Ignatius as far as the use of gospel material is concerned and that either the Gospel itself or the special form of the tradition that lies behind the Gospel was drawn on with the greatest freedom by Ignatius and others. If a recognized text lies in the background, it has been exploited in such a way that there has emerged from it a secondary tradition as loosely formulated as anything that may have existed before the emergence of such a text.

We turn finally to a passage where we find a possible allusion to gospel material used to encourage patience in the face of pagan hostility: "Before their anger be gentle, before their boastfulness be humble, before their slanderings (offer) prayers, before their deceit be fixed in faith, before their fierceness be mild, not being eager to imitate them in return" (Eph 10.2). It is hard not to be reminded of the comparable sentiments in the Sermon on the Mount (Matt 5:39–42, 44) and the Lukan parallel to it (Luke 6:27–28). The formulation is rhetorically so free, however, that not much can be learned from it. There is one tiny indication that Ignatius may be closer to Luke than to Matthew, for he speaks to the Ephesians of offering prayers in face of the "slanderings" (βλασφημία) of their neighbors. In the parallel passages, Matthew talks of praying for those who "persecute" you (5:44), and Luke of praying for those who "abuse" or "revile" (ἐπηρεαζόντων) you (6:28). The slightly softer Lukan word is perhaps more in harmony with the language of Ignatius. In this connection, it may be worth recalling that something close to the related sentiment in Luke 6:32 is echoed in Ignatius's letter to Polycarp (2.1). At the same time, the Lukan elements in Ignatius are so few that such contacts are more likely to suggest reliance on free tradition than on written sources.

IGNATIUS AND MATTHEW

One conclusion that emerges from this account is that a use of the Gospel of Matthew is almost certain in one or two passages of Ignatius and that a use of gospel material of a Matthean type not derived from the Gospel is almost certain in one or two passages. Under the circumstances it would seem wise to admit the possibility that Ignatius knew both the Gospel and elements of the special tradition that lay behind it. But since certainty is impossible, it is understandable that strong evidence for the use of the Gospel convinces some that materials of the same type are also likely to come from the Gospel (Massaux,

Köhler) and that strong evidence for the use of material not derived from the Gospel convinces others that materials of the same type are likely to derive from free tradition (Koester).[84] Forced to choose between these views, I would opt for the latter.

Another distinction may be relevant here. It is conceivable that we are dealing in some or all instances with materials derived from the Gospel that have been cut loose from their original context and freely reused in a variety of ways. Ignatius's use of Paul makes the suggestion plausible. For, as we have seen, he knows Paul as the writer of numerous letters, yet seems fairly well acquainted with only one of them and in general makes a very free use of Pauline motifs that appealed to him. Such a free use (by Ignatius himself or by those about him) of gospel material from a written but as yet uncanonical Matthew must, of course, be distinguished from the use of materials that lie behind the Gospel. At the same time, some of the passages studied above (for example, the line about the power of the prayer of one or two in Eph 5.2 and its Matthean parallel) suggest that if such material was dependent on Matthew, it went on developing as it was reused in ways that must have characterized developments in a pre-Matthean context as well. Even in these circumstances, then, certain mental habits evidently carried over from one stage to the next in the transmission and use of gospel material.

It is difficult to know what to conclude when so many different possibilities must be allowed. Perhaps enough has been said, however, to show that when the Gospel of Matthew was received in Antioch, it was in all likelihood received along with aspects of the theological culture that spawned it, or at least that it was used within a context in which mental habits were still operative comparable to those operative in the development of the tradition behind the Gospel. If the Gospel was actually written in Antioch, then we are speaking of a theological culture and certain mental habits that were once more apparent in

84. Edouard Massaux, *Influence de l'évangile de Saint Matthieu sur la littérature chrétienne avant Saint Irénée* (Universitas catholica Lovanensis 2,42; Louvain: Publications universitaires, 1950; reprint with supplements, Louvain: University Press, 1986) 94–135; Köhler, *Die Rezeption des Matthäusevangeliums*, 73–96; Koester, *Synoptische Überlieferung*, 24–61. Massaux wrote without having absorbed the lessons of form criticism for the study of the New Testament. Koester for his part gave no real attention to Massaux. Köhler may be said to have attempted a direct confrontation between the claims of the two earlier works. He favors the conclusions of Massaux over those of Koester. But although he concludes that in no case was an appeal to oral tradition necessary to explain what was found, the text of the Gospel is by no means the only possible source that he takes into account, and in this connection the use of oral tradition is sometimes recognized as one possibility among others. I have attempted to refrain as much as possible above from speculating about the way in which material presumably not derived from the text of the Gospel may have reached Ignatius. I suspect that it was a school tradition that worked with written material and certainly produced written material (the Gospel) but that also worked in the context of an oral culture that both contributed to what was written and derived inspiration from it.

Antioch than they appear to be in the letters of Ignatius. In any event, clues to the state of the tradition that lay behind the Gospel of Matthew may well be found in the letters of Ignatius, however minute and tenuous they may be.

8

Matthew and Ignatius:
A Response to
William R. Schoedel

_____ JOHN P. MEIER

I would be remiss not to begin my remarks with a sincere word of thanks to Professor Schoedel for an insightful and stimulating essay. His ability to read between the lines of Ignatius's letters and to ferret out information most of us would miss testify to his mastery of the material. From so rich an article one could easily compile a long list of questions for discussion. But, since the space allotted is necessarily limited and since one of our major concerns is the history of the Matthean community and Ignatius's possible relation to it, I shall focus on two key questions, each of which involves problems of both method and content.

I

The first question touches on the legitimacy of using Ignatius's letters to sketch the state of the church at Antioch in his own time. Theoretically, there is a whole range of possible responses to this question, from declaring that Ignatius's remarks are totally directed to the local churches of Asia and so tell us nothing about the Antiochian church, to declaring that Ignatius was obsessed by the problems in his home church and thus sees the local Asian churches only through the filter of Antioch. As usual, neither extreme is correct. Simply as a matter of fact, Ignatius speaks pointedly at various times both of Syrian Antioch (e.g., Rom 9.1–2; Ph 10.1–2; Sm 11.1–3) and of events in the various Asian churches (e.g., Eph 1–2; Mg 2–3).[1] The task of the exegete,

1. The following abbreviations will be used in this chapter for the letters of Ignatius:

then, is to try to distinguish the reference or locus of any given remark—easier said than done!

At the very least, though, Ignatius clearly did not suddenly create his theological views about Christ, church, triple hierarchy, unity, eucharist, and docetism while on the road to Smyrna or Troas. The very fact that all commentators sketch some sort of coherent picture of Ignatius's mind on these questions argues for a basic synthesis formed by Ignatius before his arrest. Presumably, then, the fundamental theological positions in his letters reflect his preaching and teaching at Antioch over some time. At times, in fact, we *are* tempted to suggest that Ignatius sees the Asian churches through the filter of his home church. For instance, one wonders whether all the Asian churches understood their leaders to be "monarchical" bishops in the same sense that Ignatius understood his own office at Antioch. The chairman of the board of presbyters in a local Asian church may have been surprised to hear his office spoken of in such exalted terms by the holder of the bishop's chair at Antioch. In such cases, we may be learning more about Antioch than about Asia Minor.

All this is important when we raise the question of possible allusions to Matthew's Gospel in Ignatius. For, if such allusions exist, the natural presupposition is that they reveal not Ignatius's sudden discovery of Matthew on the road to Troas, but rather a knowledge and use of Matthew in the Antiochian church.

II

We come, then, to our second and larger question, a question occasioned by the "strong" influence exercised on Ignatius by "gospel tradition like that found in Matthew," to use Prof. Schoedel's careful formulation of the problem. The heart of the problem is whether Ignatius knew the Gospel of Matthew itself or whether he simply knew something of the special M tradition which was also incorporated into Matthew's Gospel. Schoedel candidly admits his preference for the view of Helmut Koester, which emphasizes the predominance of oral tradition in the Apostolic Fathers.[2] While I have great respect for Koester's work, I have always thought that his book on the Apostolic Fathers achieved its unified thesis by playing down some fairly clear examples of dependence on the books of the New Testament. I feel this is especially true in the case of Ignatius, and so, willy-nilly, I find myself—to that degree—in the camp of Edouard Massaux and, especially, Wolf-Dietrich Köhler.[3] In my opinion,

---

Rom (Romans), Ph (Philadelphians), Sm (Smyrnaeans), Eph (Ephesians), Mg (Magnesians), Pol (Polycarp), Tr (Trallians).

2. Helmut Koester, *Synoptische Überlieferung bei den apostolischen Vätern* (TU 65; Berlin: Akademie-Verlag, 1957); see esp. 24–61.

3. Edouard Massaux, *Influence de l'évangile de Saint Matthieu sur la littérature*

four texts from the Ignatian letters supply clear proof of the dependence of Ignatius on the Gospel of Matthew.[4]

1. I think the most striking argument for Ignatius's dependence on Matthew is found in Sm 1.1. The larger context of 1.1–2 is a concise summary of the story of Jesus, stretching from virginal birth to resurrection and consequent proclamation of universal salvation to both Jews and Gentiles. The story begins with Jesus being declared both of the stock of David according to the flesh and Son of God according to the will and power of God, truly born of a virgin, baptized by John "that all justice might be fulfilled by him," truly nailed [to the cross] under Pontius Pilate and Herod the tetrarch, truly raised from the dead for all who believe in him, both Jews and Gentiles, in one body, his church.[5]

A number of things should strike us immediately about this summary of the story of Jesus.

(a) It is not the summary that would flow naturally from a précis of

---

chrétienne avant Saint Irénée (Universitas catholica Lovanensis 2,42; Louvain: Publications universitaires, 1950; reprint with supplements, Louvain: University Press, 1986); see esp. 94–135. This great work was a trailblazer in its time. Today many would feel that it is not sufficiently critical and needs various corrections. Yet its basic thesis is sustained—though with a more rigorous method and more nuanced conclusions—by Wolf-Dietrich Köhler, *Die Rezeption des Matthäusevangeliums in der Zeit vor Irenäus* (WUNT 2/24; Tübingen: J.C.B. Mohr [Paul Siebeck], 1987); see esp. 73–96. Nevertheless, Köhler does mark a real advance beyond Massaux, and I shall be using his work rather than Massaux's in this essay.

4. The most careful sifting of the evidence in recent literature is that of Köhler, *Die Rezeption des Matthäusevangeliums*, 73–96. Köhler tries to distinguish between references that are "probable," "quite possible," "theoretically possible but not likely," and "improbable." In the first category he puts Sm 1.1 (= Matt 3:15) and Ph 3.1 (= Matt 15:13). In the "quite possible" category he puts Eph 5.2 (= Matt 18:19–20); Eph 15.1 (= Matt 23:8); Eph 17.1 (= Matt 26:6–13); Eph 19 (= Matt 2:2, 9); Ph 2.2 (= Matt 7:15); Ph 6.1 (= Matt 23:27); Pol 1.2–3 (= Matt 8:17); Pol 2.2 (= Matt 10:16); Sm 6.1 (= Matt 19:12); and the use of μαθητής vocabulary. In the category of only "theoretically possible," he puts Eph 6.1 (= Matt 10:40; 21:33–41); Eph 10.3 (= Matt 13:25); Eph 11.1 (= Matt 3:7b); Eph 16.2 (= Matt 3:12); Mg 5.2 (= Matt 22:19); Ph 7.2 (= Matt 16:17); Rom 9.3 (= Matt 10:41–42; 18:5); Sm inscription (= Matt 12:18); Sm 6.2 (= Matt 6:28); Tr 9.1 (= Matt 11:19); use of the word ἄξιος with genitive of the person. In the category of "improbable" he puts Eph 4.4 (= Matt 5:16; 25:31–46); Eph 14.2 (= Matt 12:33); Mg 3.2 (= Matt 6:4); Mg 8.2 (= Matt 5:11–12); Mg 9.2 (= Matt 27:52); Pol 1.1 (= Matt 7:25); Pol 3.2 (= Matt 16:3); Rom 6.1 (= Matt 16:26); Sm 10.1 (= Matt 10:42); Tr 8.2 (= Matt 5:23).

Naturally, judgments about where a particular passage belongs on this sliding scale will vary among scholars. As is clear from what follows, I would put Pol 2.2 and Eph 19.2–3 in the "probable" category. Köhler's own conclusion is that his two "probable" cases show, with a probability bordering on certainty, that Ignatius did know and "received" the Gospel of Matthew (p. 95).

5. The full text of the relevant passage reads: ... τὸν κύριον ἡμῶν, ἀληθῶς ὄντα ἐκ γένους Δαυεὶδ κατὰ σάρκα, υἱὸν θεοῦ κατὰ θέλημα καὶ δύναμιν θεοῦ, γεγεννημένον ἀληθῶς ἐκ παρθένου, βεβαπτισμένον ὑπὸ Ἰωάννου, ἵνα πληρωθῇ πᾶσα δικαιοσύνη ὑπ' αὐτοῦ. ἀληθῶς ἐπὶ Ποντίου Πιλάτου καὶ Ἡρώδου τετράρχου καθηλωμένον ὑπὲρ ἡμῶν ἐν σαρκί, ἀφ' οὗ καρποῦ ἡμεῖς ἀπὸ τοῦ θεομακαρίστου αὐτοῦ πάθους, ἵνα ἄρῃ σύσσημον εἰς τοὺς αἰῶνας διὰ τῆς ἀναστάσεως εἰς τοὺς ἁγίους καὶ πιστοὺς αὐτοῦ εἴτε ἐν Ἰουδαίοις εἴτε ἐν ἔθνεσιν ἐν ἑνὶ σώματι τῆς ἐκκλησίας αὐτοῦ.

either Mark or John. Neither has an infancy narrative, neither mentions a virginal birth, and neither ends his Gospel, at least in its original form, with the risen Jesus proclaiming a universal mission to both Jews and Gentiles. While Ignatius is often close to John in his theology, John, unlike Ignatius, places no emphasis on Jesus being of the family of David.

(b) Moreover, while Ignatius, like John, has a strong sense of pre-existence and incarnation, those motifs are not explicitly mentioned in Sm 1.1. Rather, both "stock of David" and "Son of God" (notice the order!) naturally refer in the context to the beginning of Jesus' life on earth, followed as they are by "truly born of a virgin" as a further explication of Jesus' stock and sonship. We are naturally reminded of the Christology found in the infancy narratives of Matthew and Luke (e.g., Matt 1:18–25; 2:15; Luke 1:26–35). True, there may also be an echo of the pre-Pauline formula in Rom 1:3–4. But what has happened to that formula in the Gospel infancy narratives has also happened in Ignatius: A two-stage, somewhat antithetical Christology of Davidic descent during Jesus' earthly life and his exaltation to divine sonship after his resurrection (the pattern in Rom 1:3–4) has been collapsed into the beginning of the story of Jesus, in connection with birth from a virgin. By the way, we should remember a point that Joseph A. Fitzmyer has stressed in recent years: It is Matthew, not Luke, who emphasizes that Jesus' conception and birth were precisely from a virgin.[6]

(c) If I may jump ahead just for a moment to the end of the story in Sm 1.1, I would like to underscore the fact that the story ends with cross, resurrection, and universal mission to Jews and Gentiles as a consequence of cross and resurrection—a motif that fits the end of Matthew's Gospel perfectly.[7]

(d) Granted, then, this framework at the beginning and end of the Jesus story in Sm 1.1, let us look at the reference to Jesus being baptized by John "that all righteousness might be fulfilled by him" (ἵνα πληρωθῇ πᾶσα δικαιο-σύνη ὑπ' αὐτοῦ). This description of Jesus' baptism by John is most naturally seen as a direct reference to Matt 3:15, πρέπον ἐστὶν ἡμῖν πληρῶσαι πᾶσαν δικαιοσύνην. We can argue, at the very least, that the phrase occurs only in Matthew's version of the baptism of Jesus by John. The conjunction of two of Matthew's favorite theological words, πληρόω and δικαιοσύνη, is the telltale signature of Matthew himself, as I have tried to show elsewhere.[8] Each of the two words is typically Matthean. Indeed, a case could be made that every

---

6. See the stronger form of his position in his article, "The Virginal Conception of Jesus in the New Testament," *TS* 34 (1973) 541–75; and then his moderated stance in *The Gospel according to Luke (I–IX)* (AB 28; Garden City, N.Y.: Doubleday, 1981) 338.

7. See, e.g., John P. Meier, *The Vision of Matthew* (New York: Crossroad, 1991) 26–39.

8. John P. Meier, *Law and History in Matthew's Gospel* (AnBib 71; Rome: Biblical Institute, 1976) 76–81.

occurrence of δικαιοσύνη in Matthew is redactional,[9] and the same could be said for most of the occurrences of πληρόω.[10] Certainly, no other text in the New Testament draws these two words together in this way. Moreover, if one holds, as I do—and as I think the majority of exegetes do—that Matthew is directly dependent on Mark and Mark alone for this narrative of the baptism, the case for πληρῶσαι πᾶσαν δικαιοσύνην being a redactional insertion into the Marcan narrative becomes all the stronger. Apart from the Matthean vocabulary, this concern about why the sinless Jesus should be baptized by John, his inferior, ties in with other redactional changes Matthew makes in Mark's text, from the removal of εἰς ἄφεσιν ἁμαρτιῶν in the description of the baptism conferred by John (Matt 3:1–2; cf. Mark 1:4) to the insertion of the same phrase into the words of institution over the cup at the last supper (Matt 26:28; cf. Mark 14:24).

All in all, then, the understanding of Matt 3:15 as Matthean redaction is the simplest explanation. Likewise, I would maintain that Ignatius's direct dependence on Matthew is the simplest explanation of "baptized by John that all righteousness might be fulfilled by him" in Sm 1.1. Koester's attempt to get around this conclusion seems to me curious and contorted. He admits that Sm 1.1 does show that Matthew's Gospel had already been written. To uphold his own thesis about the predominance of oral tradition, Koester is reduced to making Ignatius's connection with Matthew an indirect one. Smyrnaeans 1.1 is declared to contain a kerygmatic formula that had already incorporated Matt 3:15, but no proof for this assertion is given. At this point, one should remember Occam's razor: *entia non multiplicanda sine necessitate* (to use a modern paraphrase: amid competing explanations, one should prefer the explanation that can explain all the data in the simplest way). We have Matthew's redactional composition in 3:15; we have Ignatius's clear echo of it in Sm 1.1. Why invent an otherwise unverifiable "kerygmatic formula" except to rescue Koester's endangered thesis?[11]

2. However, Sm 1.1 does not stand alone as a probable reference to Matthew's Gospel. Among some twelve or so other fairly probable candidates, the constraints of space allow me to mention only three.

9. This seems clear in cases where we have Marcan or Q parallels (Matt 3:15; 5:6; 6:33) and quite likely when we are dealing with Q material with a strong redactional flavor (5:10, 20; 6:1; 21:32). It is noteworthy that the only other occurrence of δικαιοσύνη in the Synoptics is Luke 1:75, in a phrase of the *Benedictus*.

10. The great exception being Matt 26:56 (= Mark 14:49).

11. Köhler (*Die Rezeption des Matthäusevangeliums*, 78–79) takes something of a middle position. He grants to Koester the existence of a credal formula used in Sm 1.1, but claims that ἵνα πληρωθῇ πᾶσα δικαιοσύνη is so loosely connected with its context that it does not seem to belong to the credal formula. While Köhler thus winds up maintaining dependence on Matthew, he does not provide sufficient reasons why one should accept Koester's hypothesis of a credal formula to begin with.

A text to which Köhler gives his highest ("probable") rating is Ph 3.1: "Keep yourselves from the evil plants, which Jesus Christ does not cultivate, because they are not a planting of [i.e., they are not plants planted by] the Father (Ἀπέχεσθε τῶν κακῶν βοτανῶν, ἅστινας οὐ γεωργεῖ Ἰησοῦς Χριστός, διὰ τὸ μὴ εἶναι αὐτοὺς φυτείαν πατρός). The probable source is Matt 15:13–14: "Every plant that my heavenly Father has not planted will be uprooted. Let them alone" (πᾶσα φυτεία ἣν οὐκ ἐφύτευσεν ὁ πατήρ μου ὁ πατήρ μου ὁ οὐράνιος ἐκριζωθήσεται. ἄφετε αὐτούς). A careful comparison of the two texts brings to light three significant points. First, the context of the two admonitions is basically the same: a warning against those (αὐτούς in each case) who spread false teaching (in Ignatius naturally yoked with a warning against schism); hence the imperatives ἀπέχεσθε and ἄφετε. Second, the noun φυτεία occurs in the New Testament only in Matt 15:13 and in other early Christian literature only in Ignatius.[12] Third, the phrase paralleled in Ignatius occurs in a Matthean insertion into the Marcan text which recounts the dispute over clean and unclean; most likely the phrase in question is a redactional creation of Matthew rather than M tradition. Hence the fact that Ignatius echoes this phrase cannot be explained by his knowing similar M tradition, but only by his knowing Matthew's Gospel.

3. There is a significant parallel between a logion in Matthew's missionary discourse and an exhortation in Ignatius's letter to Polycarp. Matthew's missionary discourse in chapter 10 is a pastiche of the Marcan and Q missionary discourses plus passages from the Marcan eschatological discourse and various Q sayings. Right in the midst of all these sayings paralleled elsewhere in the synoptic tradition stands a saying unique to Matthew, v. 16b: "So be wise as serpents and innocent as doves" (γίνεσθε οὖν φρόνιμοι ὡς οἱ ὄφεις καὶ ἀκέραιοι ὡς αἱ περιστεραί). Commentators often point to similar sayings in the Greco-Roman world, yet as far as I can tell no saying in any pagan, Jewish, or early Christian document *prior* to Matthew[13] contains this precise

12. Interestingly, Walter Bauer, in his *Greek-English Lexicon of the New Testament and Other Early Christian Literature* (Chicago: University of Chicago Press, 1957), lists as occurrences of φυτεία in early Christian literature only Matt 15:13 and two passages in Ignatius (Tr 11.1 [οὗτοι γὰρ οὔκ εἰσιν φυτεία πατρός] and Ph 3.1).

13. It is telling that, e.g., Alan Hugh McNeile, when supplying parallels to this verse in his *The Gospel according to St. Matthew* (Grand Rapids: Baker Book Hosue, 1915; repr. 1980) 139, can find a close parallel only in a saying of Rabbi Juda (ca. 200 C.E.) contained in the rabbinic midrash on the Canticle of Canticles: "God says of the Israelites, toward me they are sincere as doves, but toward the Gentiles they are prudent as serpents." The parallel McNeile adduces from the *Testament of Naphtali* 8.9 [10] is not close, and the problematic dating of the *Testaments of the Twelve Patriarchs* makes any argument drawn from them shaky. Interestingly, while Schoedel claims that the sentiment in this maxim "was more widely spread" (*Ignatius of Antioch* [Hermeneia; Philadelphia: Fortress, 1985] 263), he too supplies no pre-Matthean example, though he concludes: "Thus Ignatius is probably in touch with a traditional saying." The lack of any precise

combination of verb, adjectives, and nouns: γίνεσθε, φρόνιμοι, ὡς ὄφεις, ἀκέραιοι, ὡς περιστεραί.[14] Hence, I think this precise formulation is a Matthean composition. At any rate, we find precisely this concatenation of verb, adjectives, and nouns in Ignatius's letter to Pol 2.2, where, of course, everything has to be put into the singular because of the direct address to Polycarp: "Be thou clever as a serpent in all things and innocent forever as the dove" (φρόνιμος γίνου ὡς ὄφις ἐν ἅπασιν καὶ ἀκέραιος εἰς ἀεὶ ὡς ἡ περιστερά). The "in all things" (ἐν ἅπασιν) and the "forever" (εἰς ἀεί) seem to be Ignatius's neat, two-part addition to the neat, two-part exhortation from Matthew.

4. A fourth intriguing Matthean parallel in Ignatius is not a single saying but a whole homiletic midrash on Matthew's "star of the Magi." The Ignatian midrash is found in Eph 19.2–3:[15]

> How then was he [Christ] manifested to the world [or: to the aeons]? A star [ἀστήρ] in heaven shone more brightly than all the [other] stars, and its light was beyond all telling, and its newness caused amazement. All the other stars together with sun and moon gathered like a chorus around the star; but with its light it outshone them all. There arose a disturbance [ταραχή] as all asked the origin of this new star, so unlike them [literally: whence the newness unlike them].
>
> By this all magic [μαγεία] began to be destroyed[16] and every bond began to vanish. The ignorance that evil causes was being dispelled, and the old kingdom was being dissolved, as God appeared in human form to [confer] the newness of eternal life. What had been prepared in God's presence [from all

---

parallel before Matthew would seem to argue in the opposite direction, i.e., for direct dependence of Ignatius on Matthew.

14. Köhler (*Die Rezeption des Matthäusevangeliums*, 86) ranks Pol 2.2 only as "quite possible" because of Koester's emphasis on the proverblike nature of the logion. Yet neither Koester nor Köhler produces an exact parallel from the Greco-Roman or Jewish milieu prior to Matthew; see n. 13 above.

15. Some authors have claimed that Eph 19.2–3 refers to the gnostic motif of the secret descent and the public ascent of the redeemer figure; see Heinrich Schlier, *Religionsgeschichtliche Untersuchungen zu den Ignatiusbriefen* (BZNW 8; Giessen: Töpelmann, 1929) 29; also Koester, *Synoptische Überlieferung*, 31–32. Against this opinion is Hans-Werner Bartsch, *Gnostisches Gut und Gemeindetradition bei Ignatius von Antiochien* (Gütersloh: Bertelsmann, 1940) 140–54. For a more recent critique of Schlier's interpretation, see Schoedel, *Ignatius*, 88–89; Schoedel leans in the direction of Bartsch. On p. 90, Schoedel argues well that the primary reference in this text is to the incarnation/birth of Christ, though that event is of course connected in Ignatius's mind with the passion/death.

16. My translation emphasizes that all the main verbs in this final part of chap. 19 are in the imperfect tense in the Greek, indicating a process or the beginning of a process. The sense is, "By this all magic was being destroyed" or "began to be destroyed," etc. In Schoedel's view (*Ignatius*, 94), "all . . . the preceding verbs . . . should be understood as inceptives. . . ." Schoedel suggests that Ignatius would probably have seen the passion as the culmination of this plan.

eternity] was receiving its beginning [in time]. Hence all things began to shake because the abolition of death was being carried out.

The star motif, connected with Jesus' manifestation to the world, is of course present in the New Testament only in Matt 2:2, 9–10.[17] In both texts, the word ἀστήρ is used for the star announcing the coming of Christ, the disturbance of the powers (the political power of Herod in Matthew, the astral powers in Ignatius) is described by ταράσσω/ταραχή, and Ignatius pointedly states that this star destroys all μαγεία, a nice echo of the μάγοι.[18]

Indeed, Ignatius does more than merely echo words from the Matthean text. The basic thrust of Matthew's story is seized upon by Ignatius's midrash and projected onto a cosmic screen. In Matthew, the coming of the gentile Magi to the Christ child at the beginning of the Gospel foreshadows the coming of all the Gentiles to faith in the risen Christ at the end of the Gospel (Matt 28:16–20). The universal scope of salvation, proclaimed openly at the climax of the Gospel, is proclaimed symbolically in the heavens as the Gospel begins. Ignatius simply extends the universal thrust of the symbolism from "all the nations" to all the cosmos. By making the Gentiles in chapter 2 astrologers who bear the title μάγοι, Matthew may indeed be hinting at the overcoming of pagan magical belief by the light of Christian faith. In this case, the Ignatian midrash ("by this all magic [μαγεία] was destroyed") would again be explicating what lies implicit in the Matthean midrash.

5. I think a final cumulative argument, an argument from converging lines of probability, can be drawn from these four cases taken from the dozen or so texts that could be adduced if space allowed. To restrict myself to the four Matthean texts I have cited: Notice that they occur each within a different strand of early Christian tradition. The "fulfill all justice" text is found in a Marcan narrative, the baptism of Jesus by John. The "plant planted by the Father" text is located in a Marcan dispute story on clean and unclean. The "wise as

17. The approach of Schoedel (ibid., 92) at this point is curious. He affirms quite correctly: "The star of Matt 2:1–12, then, still presents the parallel most relevant to *Eph.* 19.2." But then he proceeds: "But Ignatius reaches back to a more mythological version of the account." This is a strange conclusion, since Schoedel has to reconstruct this more mythological account to which "Ignatius reaches back" from chronologically later Christian writings (e.g., the *Ascension of Isaiah,* the *Odes of Solomon,* Justin Martyr, Cyril of Jerusalem, and some of the Nag Hammadi codices). The more natural approach, in my view, is to see Ignatius's text as a conscious homiletic development of the one text we can be sure preexisted the Ignatian epistles, the one text that "presents the parallel most relevant," namely, Matt 2:1–12. Hence I think Schoedel is reading the history of the tradition backward when he suggests (92 n. 30): "It may be that the 'disturbance' of Herod and 'all Jerusalem with him' (Matt 2:1–12) represents an application on the historical plane of the disturbance of the stars."

18. Köhler, however, thinks that the style of Eph 19.2 could indicate that Ignatius had taken over or recycled a poetic composition known to him (*Die Rezeption des Matthäusevangeliums,* 83–84); hence Köhler gives this passage only a "quite possible" rating.

serpents" saying appears in a discourse immediately after some Q sayings. The star motif occurs in a section of the infancy narrative tradition unique to Matthew. Now, how are we to explain these data? Are we to posit one written M document containing all these heterogeneous traditions, a document that Matthew drew upon and that Ignatius then drew upon as well? Despite the position of G. Kilpatrick, almost all Matthean scholars have rejected the idea of one written M document, a source more rudimentary than Q.[19] But without such a single M document, we are hard-pressed to explain how Ignatius just happened to cite—in some cases practically word for word—these various so-called M traditions, traditions presumably emanating from very different matrices, traditions that all just happened to wind up in Matthew's Gospel too. I feel that such a scenario is too much of a coincidence. To invoke Occam's razor: The simplest and most obvious solution is that Ignatius knew and used Matthew, which he may actually refer to at times as εὐαγγέλιον.[20] I think that this position, once accepted, has tremendous implications for drawing up a history of the church in Antioch that reaches from Barnabas and Paul, through Matthew, to Ignatius. Such a genealogy gives the Matthean church a "before" and "after," forebears and progeny, and thus supplies a framework for writing the social history of the Matthean community in Roman Syria.

19. For the position of G. Kilpatrick, see his *The Origins of the Gospel according to St. Matthew* (Oxford: Oxford University Press, 1946) 36.

20. See my remarks in "Locating Matthew's Church in Time and Space," in Raymond E. Brown and John P. Meier, *Antioch and Rome* (Ramsey, N.J.: Paulist, 1983) 25. Of course, Koester (*Synoptische Überlieferung*, 8–9, 25) does not agree. Yet in Ph 8.2 the εὐαγγέλιον is opposed to the ἀρχείοις ("archives") of the Jews (probably the written Old Testament); hence in this context it may well mean "written gospel." If it does, the written gospel would be Matthew's. While rejecting Koester's position that εὐαγγέλιον in Ignatius always means the oral kerygma, Köhler (*Die Rezeption des Matthäusevangeliums*, 74–77) argues that for Ignatius εὐαγγέλιον always means the content of the Christian message, Jesus Christ himself. Therefore, the question whether εὐαγγέλιον means oral or written gospel is wrongly put. In my view, it may be a mistake to claim that εὐαγγέλιον must *always* mean one thing. Certainly, there are passages in Ignatius that could argue for "oral kerygma" or "Christ, the content of the kerygma." But I think that the context of Ph 8.2 does argue for the meaning of "written gospel" *in this one passage*. For a study of this obscure passage in Ph, see William R. Schoedel, "Ignatius and the Archives," *HTR* 71 (1978) 97–106.

IV

MATTHEW:
SOCIAL SITUATION
AND LOCATION

9

Antioch as the Social Situation for Matthew's Gospel

RODNEY STARK

For sociologists, the most important single fact about early Christianity is that it was, at least subsequent to the crucifixion, an *urban movement*—as Wayne Meeks (1983) chose to emphasize in the title of his marvelous book. Hence, despite the fact that the sayings attributed to Jesus often reflect the village culture of Judea or Galilee, the New Testament was set down by urbanites. Indeed, many scholars believe that the Gospel of Matthew was composed in Antioch, the fourth largest city of the Roman Empire at the time.

If we want to understand how the New Testament may have been shaped by the sociocultural environment of those who first put it into written words, we must comprehend the physical and social structures of the Greco-Roman city. Moreover, if we want to understand the immense popular appeal of the early church we must understand how the message of the New Testament and the social relations it sustained solved acute problems afflicting Greco-Roman cities. Here too Antioch is of special interest because it was unusually receptive to the Christian movement, sustaining a relatively large and affluent Christian community quite early on (Longenecker, 1985).

For these reasons, I have been trying to discover some basic facts about Greco-Roman cities in order to understand the physical realities of everyday life. What was it like to live there? Frankly, I was amazed to discover how difficult it is to find any answers. Despite libraries filled with books on many Greco-Roman cities, the truth is, as Lewis Mumford (1974) has pointed out, that the "city itself remains a shadow." Even when books have titles indicating that they are about cities of the Greco-Roman era, there usually is next to nothing in them about the physical environment of the city. Let me hasten to acknowledge that John E. Stambaugh's (1988) book, *The Ancient Roman City,* is a fine exception to this rule. Indeed, it guided me to many valuable sources from which I could document points I had initially been forced to infer on the basis of what is known to be true of premodern cities in general.

Nonetheless, the widespread lack of interest in the city per se means that it usually is easier to find out the approximate seating capacity of a city's theater than it is to discover the size of a city's population. Indeed, were it not for the many decades of work by Tertius Chandler, assisted finally by Gerald Fox, we would have very little knowledge of the population of the major Greco-Roman cities (Chandler and Fox, 1974). As for other aspects of the city, whatever facts exist are fugitive to say the least. Since I am neither a historian nor a biblical scholar, but a sociologist of religion who sometimes works with historical and biblical materials, I am greatly hindered whenever good secondary sources are lacking. Nevertheless, I have managed to glimpse some aspects of the cities within which Christianity arose. What I see are extraordinary levels of urban disorder, social dislocation, misery, and cultural chaos. I shall attempt to share with you my vision of these cities, and especially of Antioch.

My interest in Greco-Roman cities is rooted in my more general effort to construct a theoretically informed account of the rise of Christianity (Stark, 1986a, b)—how did this obscure movement, born on the eastern fringe of the empire, ultimately triumph over the whole of the Greco-Roman world?

Keep in mind that new religions almost never amount to much and that it is very rare for a new faith to sweep through a large-scale social system in the way that Christianity, Buddhism, and Islam did. Moreover, we would do well to heed Peter Brown's (1964:109) warning not "to take the end of paganism for granted." Since paganism had served the religious needs of the Greco-Roman world for centuries, its demise must have involved extraordinary factors.

And, indeed, a consensus has been developing among social scientists that a cultural shift so extreme as the rise of Christianity is possible only during periods of acute social disruption. Let me outline the basic notions involved here, and then I will show how they apply to specific facts about the Greco-Roman city, giving special attention to Antioch. Then I will sketch some of the ways in which these urban environments not only shaped Christian consciousness, but gave Christianity immense competitive advantages vis-à-vis paganism and other religious movements of the day.

In a now famous essay, Anthony F. C. Wallace (1956) argued that successful new religions always arise as *revitalization movements* responding to acute social crises. He used the term "revitalization movement" to capture how new religions revitalize the cultural and social capacity of a society to overcome its problems. The cultural aspect of revitalization involves the discovery and adoption of new religious beliefs and practices. The social aspect involves the ways in which the movement effectively mobilizes and unites people to attempt collective actions. Let me briefly sketch each aspect.

Crises produced by natural or social disasters often are translated into crises of faith. This is because the disaster places demands upon the prevailing religious culture that it appears unable to meet. For example, classical paganism appeared to offer no protection against the two deadly epidemics that swept the empire in the second and third centuries, nor could it offer an explanation of these terrible events. In contrast, as we shall see, Christianity seemed both to protect against these epidemics and to explain their occurrence. A much-studied example is how the inability of Native Americans in North America to withstand encroachments by European settlers caused them frequently to abandon their traditional religion and magic and to embrace new messianic movements. These movements revitalized Indian societies, at least initially, by providing an effective cultural justification for uniting fragmented bands into a political unit capable of concerted action (Mooney, 1896).

Social and natural disasters often do more than overload a society's religious culture; they also disrupt social relations. Human groups rely on networks of interpersonal relationships to bind members together and particularly to sustain commitment to the moral order. That is, our attachments to others serve as our primary stake in conforming to the norms—to deviate from the moral order is to risk the loss of our relationships. When the average member of a group suffers a substantial loss of attachments, social disorganization occurs and conformity to the conventional moral order declines. In this sense, disasters free many members of a group to adopt new culture. That is, if most of your friends and relatives have perished or fled, you have much less at risk should you deviate from the conventional religious culture. Moreover, by joining a new religious movement a person lacking attachments gains new ones—indeed, people typically affiliate with new religion because they have formed attachments to members (Stark and Bainbridge, 1985, 1987).

Against this explanatory background, let me now focus on the Greco-Roman city. I shall suggest that in the days during which Christianity arose, the Greco-Roman city imposed severe physical and social stress on most residents most of the time, and that this everyday misery was punctuated frequently by appalling natural and social disasters. In this regard, Antioch offers an excellent case study.

PHYSICAL SOURCES OF
CHRONIC URBAN MISERY

The first important fact about Greco-Roman cities is that they were small, both in terms of area and population. When founded, about 301 B.C.E., the walls of Antioch enclosed slightly less than one square mile, laid out along a southwest to northeast axis. Eventually Antioch grew to be about two miles long and about one mile wide, for a total area of about two square miles (Finley, 1977). Like many Greco-Roman cities, Antioch was small in area because it was founded initially as a fortress (Levick, 1967). Once the walls were up, it was very expensive to expand.

Given the small area of the city, it is astonishing that its population was as large as it was—at the end of the first century Antioch had a total population of about 150,000 (Chandler and Fox, 1974). This population total applies to inhabitants of the city proper—those living within, or perhaps immediately against, the walls of Antioch. It does not apply to those living on the nearby rural estates or in the various satellite communities such as Daphne (Levick, 1967). Given this population and the area of the city, it is easily calculated that the population density of Antioch was roughly 75,000 inhabitants per square mile or 117 per acre. As a comparison, in Chicago today there are 21 inhabitants per acre, San Francisco has 23, and New York City overall has 37. Even Manhattan Island has only 100 inhabitants per acre, and keep in mind that Manhattanites are very spread out vertically, while ancient cities crammed their populations into structures that seldom rose above five stories—and, as MacMullen (1974) pointed out, these low-rise tenements of classical times had a terrible tendency to collapse. Therefore, given the constant earthquakes in Antioch, it is unlikely that any of their tenements were more than several stories tall. Keep in mind too that New Yorkers do not share their space with livestock nor are their streets fouled by horse and oxen traffic.

Even so, these density comparisons are quite misleading because large areas of Greco-Roman cities were occupied by public buildings, monuments, and temples. In Pompeii this area amounted to 35 percent of the area of the city (Jashemski, 1979), in Ostia 43 percent was taken up in this way (Meiggs, 1974), and in Rome the public-monumental sector occupied half of the city (Stambaugh, 1988). If we assume that Antioch was average in this regard we must subtract 43 percent of its area in order to calculate density. The new figure is 205 persons per acre. This contrasts with Stambaugh's (1988) estimate of 302 per acre in Rome (MacMullen [1974] estimated Rome's density as 200 inhabitants per acre). As a comparison, the density in modern Bombay is 183 per acre and it is 122 in Calcutta.

But even these figures fail to convey fully the crowded conditions of everyday life in these cities. Despite the fact, as Michael White (1987) has noted, that many writers seem to assume that everyone lived in huge atrium houses like the ones built by MGM for *Ben-Hur* (cf. Koester, 1987:73), most people lived in tiny cubicles in multistoried tenements, in conditions wherein privacy was, as Stambaugh (1988:178) tells us, "a hard thing to find." Not only were people terribly crowded within these buildings, the streets were so narrow that if people leaned out their window they could chat with someone living across the street without having to raise their voices.[1] Indeed, Packer (1967) doubted that people actually could spend much time in quarters so cramped and squalid. Thus he concluded that the typical residents of Greco-Roman cities spent their lives mainly in public places and that the average "domicile must have served only as a place to sleep and store possessions" (Packer, 1967:87).

One thing is certain when human density is high: urgent problems of sanitation arise. However, I have found very few activities more frustrating than attempting to discover details about such matters as sewers, plumbing, garbage disposal, or even water supply in Greco-Roman cities. One can spend an afternoon checking the indexes of scores of histories of Greece and Rome without finding any of these words listed. The aqueducts are, of course, often mentioned as are the public baths and the public latrines often constructed next to the baths. It is all well and good to admire the Romans for their aqueducts and their public baths, but we must not fail to see the obvious fact that the human and animal density of ancient cities would place an incredible burden even on modern sewerage, garbage disposal, and water systems. Hence, it is self-evident that, given the technological capacities of the time, the Greco-Roman city must have been extremely filthy.

Consider the water supply. Aqueducts brought water to many Greco-Roman cities, but once there it was poorly kept and quite maldistributed. In most cities the water was piped to fountains and public buildings such as the baths. Some also was piped to the homes of the very rich. But, for the rest of the residents, water had to be carried home in jugs. This necessarily greatly limited the use of water. There could have been very little for scrubbing floors or washing clothes. Nor could there have been much for bathing, and I very much doubt that the public baths truly served the public in the inclusive sense. Worse yet, the water often was very contaminated. In his exceptional study of Greek and Roman technology, K. D. White (1984) pointed out that whether their water came via aqueducts or from springs or wells, all of the larger Greco-Roman cities had to store water in cisterns. He also noted that "untreated water . . . when left stagnant, encourages the growth of algae and other organisms, rendering the water malodorous, unpalatable, and after a time, undrinkable" (1984:168). No wonder Pliny advised that "all water is the better for being boiled" (in White, 1984:168).

Upon closer examination, the notion that Greco-Roman cities enjoyed

1. The main thoroughfare of Antioch, admired throughout the Greco-Roman world, was only 30 feet wide (Finley, 1977).

efficient sewers and sanitation also turns out to be largely an illusion. Granted that an underground sewer carried water from the baths of Rome through the public latrines next door and on out of the city, we can ask, What about the rest of the city? Indeed, just as it is obviously silly to suppose that the wretched masses of Rome soaked nightly in the Roman baths, hobnobbing with senators and equestrians (the capacity of the baths reveals this to be a physical as well as social absurdity), it is equally silly to think everyone jogged off to the public latrines each time that nature called. Rome, like all cities until modern times, was dependent on chamber pots and pit latrines. Indeed, Stambaugh (1988) suggests that most tenements depended entirely on pots. As for sewers, they were, for the most part, open ditches into which slops and chamber pots were dumped—frequently out the window at night from several stories up (de Camp, 1966).

Given limited water and means of sanitation, and the incredible density of humans and animals, most people in Greco-Roman cities must have lived in filth beyond our imagining. Tenement cubicles were smoky, dark, often damp, and always dirty. The smell of sweat, urine, feces, and decay permeated everything. Outside, on the street, it was little better—mud, open sewers, manure, and crowds. In fact, human corpses—adult as well as infant—were sometimes just pushed into the street and abandoned (Stambaugh, 1988). And even if the wealthiest households could provide ample space and cleanliness, they could not prevent many aspects of the filth and decay surrounding them from penetrating their homes. Given that the stench of these cities must have been overpowering for many miles—especially in warm weather—even the richest Romans must have suffered. No wonder they were so fond of incense. Moreover, Greco-Roman cities must have been smothered in flies, mosquitoes, and other insects that flourish where there is much stagnant water and exposed filth. And, like bad odors, insects are very democratic.

The constant companion of filth, insects, and crowding is disease. This is especially so when societies lack antibiotics or, indeed, have no knowledge of germs. Here too one pages uselessly through nearly all of the books on Roman and Greek society and on the rise of Christianity, for words such as epidemic, plague, and even disease almost never appear. This seems incredible, for not only was the Greco-Roman world periodically struck by deadly epidemics that raged for years and killed 20 to 30 percent of the population each time, but illness and physical affliction were probably the dominant features of daily life in this era.

The Greco-Roman city was a pesthole of infectious disease—because it was always thus in cities. Indeed, it was not until the twentieth century that urban mortality was sufficiently reduced so that the cities of Western Europe and North America could sustain their populations without additional in-migration from rural areas. If this was true of modern cities, think what must have been the case in places like Rome and Antioch. In fact, historical demographers agree that "the average lifetime of the ancients was short" (Durand, 1960:365). Although there have been some disagreements among those who have attempted to estimate life expectancies from Roman tomb inscriptions (Burn, 1953; Russell, 1958; Durand, 1960; Hopkins, 1966), none challenges that life expectancy at birth was less than thirty years—and probably substantially less. Where these levels of mortality are found, very high levels of fertility are required to prevent the population from shrinking— levels far higher than anyone would attribute to residents of Greco-Roman cities (Hopkins, 1966; Wrigley, 1969).

It is important to realize that where mortality rates are very high, the health of those still living is very poor. The majority of those living in Greco-Roman cities must have suffered from chronic health conditions that caused them pain and some degree of disability, and of which many would soon die.[2] Stambaugh (1988:137) pointed out that, compared with modern cities, sickness was highly visible on the streets of Greco-Roman cities: "Swollen eyes, skin rashes, and lost limbs are mentioned over and over again in the sources as part of the urban scene." Little wonder that healing was such a central aspect of both paganism and early Christianity (MacMullen, 1981; Kee, 1983, 1986).

Moreover, women in Greco-Roman times were especially afflicted because of chronic infections resulting from childbirth and abortion. This, combined with female infanticide, which was widely practiced in many Greco-Roman cities (Grant, 1970), resulted in highly imbalanced sex ratios—a relative shortage of adult females. J. C. Russell (1958) estimated the sex ratio of Rome at 131 males per 100 females and set the ratio at 140 for Italy and North Africa.

Sociologists have recently come to recognize that sex ratios greatly influence sex roles (Guttentag and Secord, 1983). To the extent that males outnumber females, women will be enclosed in more restrictive sex roles, as in the case of ancient Athens. Conversely, to the extent that women outnumber men, they will enjoy substantially greater freedom and equality, as in the case of ancient Sparta (Guttentag and Secord, 1983; Pomeroy, 1975). That males probably far outnumbered females in Antioch, at least into the second century (Stambaugh, 1988), ought to have influenced the gender roles that Wire detects within the Matthean texts (see chap. 5).

However, since the early Christians rejected both abortion and female

2. In the first data on urban mortality ever published, John Graunt found that more than five percent of those who died in London during 1632 had been killed by infected teeth. Moreover, that year—in which there were no epidemics and mortality was relatively low—the number buried equaled the number christened. In most other years for which he reported data, burials substantially exceeded christenings and London could not sustain its population without substantial in-migration.

infanticide[3] while pagans continued to practice both, contrasting sex ratios would soon have developed within these two relatively endogamous sub-cultures. That is, the ratio of males to females ought to have been substantially less among Christians than among pagans. Over time this factor ought to have enhanced the relative status of Christian women. Evidence that the average Christian female married at a later age than did the average pagan female, and that Christian girls were far less likely than pagan girls to be wed at prepubic ages (Hopkins, 1965) is fully consistent with predictions from the theory linking sex ratios to the status of women.

SOCIAL CHAOS AND CHRONIC URBAN MISERY

Historians have tended to present a portrait of the Greco-Roman city as one in which most people—rich and poor alike—were descended from many generations of residents. But nothing could be further from the truth, espe-cially during the first several centuries of the Christian era. As noted, Greco-Roman cities required a constant and substantial stream of newcomers simply to maintain their populations. Moreover, given the immense cultural diversity of the empire, newcomers were of very diverse origins and therefore fractured the local culture into numerous ethnic fragments. Again, Antioch offers an instructive example.

When founded by Seleucus I, the city was laid out in two primary sections—one for Syrians and one for Greeks—and, taking a realistic view of ethnic relations, the king had the two sections walled off from one another (Stambaugh and Balch, 1986). According to Downey (1963), the ethnic origins of the original settlement consisted of retired soldiers from Seleucus's Macedonian army, Cretans, Cypriotes, Argives, and Herakleidae (who had pre-viously been settled on Mt. Silipius), Athenians from Atigonia, Jews from nearby Palestine (some of whom had served as mercenaries in Seleucus's army), native Syrians, and a number of slaves of diverse origins. As the city grew, its Jewish population seems to have increased markedly (Meeks and Wilken, 1978). And, of course, a substantial number of Romans were added to this mixture when the city was seized by the empire in 64 B.C.E. During the days of Roman rule, the city drew an influx of Gauls, Germans, and other "bar-barians," some brought as slaves, others as legionnaires. Smith (1857:143) esti-mates that the "citizens were divided into 18 tribes, distributed locally." I take him to mean that there were eighteen identifiable ethnic quarters within Antioch.

3. The Didache (2.2) warned: "Thou shalt not murder a child by abortion nor kill them when born."

Ramsay MacMullen (1981:xi) describes the Roman world in this period as "a proper melting pot." But it is not clear how much melting actually went on. What does seem clear is that the social integration of Greco-Roman cities was severely disrupted by the durability of internal ethnic divisions which typically took the form of distinctive ethnic precincts. Ethnic diversity and a constant influx of newcomers tends to undercut social integration thus exposing residents to a variety of harmful consequences, including high rates of deviance[4] and disorder. Indeed, this is a major reason why Greco-Roman cities were so prone to riots.

NATURAL AND SOCIAL DISASTERS

When we examine the magnificent ruins of classical cities we have a tendency to see them as extraordinarily durable and permanent—after all, they were built of stone and have endured the centuries. But this is mostly an illusion. We usually are looking at simply the *last* ruins of a city that was turned to ruins repeatedly. And if the physical structures of Greco-Roman cities were transitory, so too were their populations—cities often were almost entirely depopulated and then repopulated and their ethnic composition often was radically changed in the process. The following summary of natural and social disasters which struck Antioch is instructive and rather typical (a complete listing is provided in Appendix A). The list probably is not complete. In fact, I have skipped the many serious floods because they did not cause substantial loss of life. Still, the summary shows how extremely vulnerable Greco-Roman cities were to attacks, fires, earthquakes, famines, epidemics, and devastating riots. Indeed, this litany of disasters is so staggering that it is difficult to grasp its human meaning.

During the course of about 600 years of intermittent Roman rule, Antioch was taken by unfriendly forces eleven times, was plundered and sacked on five of these occasions, and was under seige, but did not fall, two other times. In addition, Antioch burned in whole or in major part four times,[5] three times by accident and once when the Persians carefully burned the city to the ground after picking it clean of valuables and taking the surviving population into captivity. This does not include the substantial fires set during several of the six major periods of rioting that racked the city. By a major riot I mean one

---

4. Stambaugh (1988) reports that the sources are unanimous that the streets of Greco-Roman cities were dangerous at night because of many sorts of roaming human predators.

5. Because the temples and many public buildings were built of stone, it is easy to forget that Greco-Roman cities were built primarily of wood-frame buildings, plastered over, that were highly flammable and tightly packed together. Severe fires were frequent and there was no pumping equipment with which to fight them.

resulting in substantial damage and death, as distinct from the city's frequent riots in which only a few were killed.

Antioch probably suffered from literally hundreds of significant earthquakes during these six centuries, but eight were so severe that nearly everything was destroyed and huge numbers died. Two other quakes may have been nearly this serious. At least three killer epidemics struck the city—with mortality rates probably running above 25 percent in each. Finally, there were at least five really serious famines. That comes to forty-one natural and social catastrophes, or an average of one every fifteen years.

Why in the world did people keep going back and rebuilding? One would suppose that the earthquakes alone might have caused Antioch to be abandoned. The answer is simple. Antioch was of immense strategic importance as the key stronghold for defending the border with Persia. As Barbara Levick (1967:46) explained, "The Romans thought it dangerous to leave such a site unsupervised and settled veterans there as soon as they could." And wherever Rome planted such colonies there always was a rush of civilian settlers in pursuit of economic opportunity. Thus Antioch continued to change hands and to be rebuilt and resettled again and again. Indeed, it lived on to be retaken from Islam several times by Byzantine forces and then by Crusaders.

Any accurate portrait of Antioch in New Testament times must depict a city filled with misery, danger, fear, despair, and hatred. Antioch was a city where the average family lived a squalid life in filthy and cramped quarters, where at least half of the children died at birth or during infancy, and where most of the children who lived lost at least one parent before reaching maturity. This city was filled with hatred and fear rooted in intense ethnic antagonisms and exacerbated by a constant stream of strangers. This city was so lacking in stable networks of attachments that petty incidents could prompt mob violence. Crime flourished and the streets were dangerous at night. And, perhaps above all, Antioch was repeatedly smashed by cataclysmic catastrophes. A resident could expect literally to be homeless from time to time, providing that he or she was among the survivors.

People living in such circumstances must often have despaired. Surely it would not be strange for them to have concluded that the end of days drew near. Surely too they must often have longed for relief, for hope, indeed, for salvation.

CHRISTIAN REVITALIZATION

In the remainder of this essay I shall attempt to show how Christianity served as an effective revitalization movement that greatly mitigated the chronic misery, disorder, and periodic disasters that afflicted Greco-Roman cities.

The simple phrase "For God so loved the world" would have puzzled an educated pagan. The notion that the gods care how we treat one another would have been dismissed as patently absurd.

From the pagan viewpoint, there was nothing new in the Jewish or Christian teachings that God makes behavioral demands upon humans—the gods have always demanded sacrifice and worship. Nor was there anything new in the idea that God will respond to human desires—that the gods can be induced to exchange services for sacrifices. But the idea that God *loves* those who love God was entirely new. MacMullen (1981:53) has noted that from the pagan perspective what mattered was "the service the deity could provide, since a god (as Aristotle had long taught) could feel no love in response to that offered."

Moreover, the corollary that *because* God loves humanity, Christians may not please God unless they *love one another* was something entirely new. Perhaps even more revolutionary was the principle that Christian love and charity must extend beyond the boundaries of family and tribe, that it must extend to "all those who in every place call on the name of our Lord Jesus Christ" (1 Cor 1:2). Indeed, love and charity must even extend beyond the Christian community. As Cyprian instructed his Carthaginian flock (as reported by his biographer Pontianus):

> There is nothing remarkable in cherishing merely our own people with the due attentions of love, but that one might become perfect who should do something more than heathen men or publicans, one who, overcoming evil with good, and practicing a merciful kindness like that of God, should love his enemies as well.... Thus the good was done to all men, not merely to the household of faith. (Harnack, [1908] 1962:172–73)

This was revolutionary. Indeed, it was the cultural basis for the revitalization of a Roman world groaning under a host of miseries. Chief among these was the cultural chaos produced by the crazy quilt of ethnic diversity and the blazing hatreds entailed thereby.

In uniting its empire, Rome created economic and political unity at the cost of cultural chaos. Ramsay MacMullen (1981:xi) has put it well:

> If we imagined the British Empire of a hundred years ago all in one piece, all of its parts touching each other, so one could travel ... from Rangoon to Belfast without the interposition of any ocean, and if we could thus sense as one whole an almost limitless diversity of tongues, cults, traditions, and levels of education, the true nature of the Mediterranean world ... would strike our minds.

Greco-Roman cities were microcosms of this cultural diversity. In my judgment, a major way in which Christianity served as a revitalization movement within the empire was in offering a coherent culture that was *entirely stripped of ethnicity*. All were welcome without need to dispense with ethnic ties. Yet, for this very reason, among Christians ethnicity tended to be submerged as new, more universalistic, and indeed cosmopolitan, norms and customs emerged. In this way Christianity first evaded and then overwhelmed the ethnic barrier that had prevented Judaism from serving as the basis for revitalization. Unlike the pagan gods, the God of Israel did indeed impose moral codes and responsibilities upon God's people. But, to embrace the Jewish God one had also to don Jewish ethnicity, albeit that, as Segal suggests, the Judaism of the first century may have been more inclusive than has been recognized (see chap. 1). I agree with him that the existence of the God-fearers demonstrates this inclusiveness, but it also seems clear that the God-fearers were limited to the social fringes of the diaspora Jewish communities precisely because of their failure to fully embrace the law, and hence the law remained the primary ethnic barrier to conversion. In fact, elsewhere I (1986a) have argued that many Hellenized Jews of the Diaspora found Christianity so appealing precisely because it freed them from an ethnic identity with which they had become uncomfortable.

Not only did Christianity seek to reach across all nations, it also greatly mitigated relations among social classes—at the very time when the gap between rich and poor was growing (Meeks and Wilken, 1978). It did not preach that everyone could or should become equal in terms of wealth and power in *this* life. But it did preach that all were equal in the eyes of God and that the more fortunate had a God-given responsibility to help those in need. Consider the duties of deacons, as outlined in the *Apostolic Constitutions*:

> They are to be doers of good works, exercising a general supervision day and night, neither scorning the poor nor respecting the person of the rich; they must ascertain who are in distress and not exclude them from a share in church funds, compelling also the well-to-do to put money aside for good works. (Harnack, [1908] 1962:161)

Similarly, as Schoedel has noted, Ignatius stressed the responsibility of the church to care for widows and children. Indeed, Ignatius made it clear that he was not simply discussing doctrines about good works, but was affirming the reality of a massive structure of Christian voluntarism and charity. Tertullian (*Apology* 39) noted that members willingly gave to the church, which unlike the pagan temples, did not spend it on gluttony,

> but for feeding and burying the poor, for boys and girls without money and

without parents, and for old men now house-ridden, for the shipwrecked also, and for any in the mines, or in the islands, or in the prisons.

Indeed, Paul Johnson (1976:75) noted that the Christians soon "ran a miniature welfare state in an empire which for the most part lacked social services."

The apostate emperor Julian, who made his capital in Antioch, bitterly agreed. In a letter to the high priest of Galatia in 362, Julian stressed that if Christianity was to be withstood, paganism must match its charitable activities:

> We must pay special attention to this point and by this means effect a cure. For when it came about that the poor were neglected and overlooked by the priests, then I think the impious Galilaeans observed this fact and devoted themselves to philanthropy.... For when ... the impious Galilaeans relieve both their own poor and ours, it is shameful that ours should be destitute of our assistance. (Ayerst and Fisher, 1971:179–81)

But Julian soon discovered that the means for reform were lacking. Paganism had not only failed to develop the kind of voluntary system of good works that Christians had been constructing for more than three centuries, but it lacked the religious ideas that would have made such organized efforts plausible. Indeed, as E. A. Judge has noted in detail, classical philosophers regarded mercy as a pathological emotion and defect of character to be avoided by all rational men. Indeed, Plato eliminated "the problem of beggars from his ideal state by dumping them over its borders" (Judge, 1986). In this moral climate Christianity taught that mercy is one of the primary virtues—that a merciful God requires humans to be merciful. Nowhere were these new and revolutionary moral teachings of Christianity so fully and eloquently expressed as in Matthew.

I suggest it would be fitting at a conference on the Gospel of Matthew to try to listen to one of its most famous passages as if hearing the words for the very first time, in order to grasp the power of this new morality when it was *new*, not centuries later in more cynical and worldly times:

> For I was hungry and you gave me food,
> I was thirsty and you gave me something to drink,
> I was a stranger and you welcomed me,
> I was naked and you gave me clothing,
> I was sick and you took care of me,
> I was in prison and you visited me, ...
> Truly I tell you, just as you did to one of the least of these who are members of my family, you did it to me. (25:35–40)

Did it matter? Did Christian good works really change the quality of life in Greco-Roman times?

I think they did, in many ways. On a day-to-day level there were very tangible fruits of Christian commitment. Substantial resources were available to those in dire need, and the lot of Christian widows and orphans was far better. But to conclude my essay, I would like to sketch the really critical difference that Christian social services made when disasters struck. Here I shall draw upon work I have done linking differential pagan and Christian responses to the great epidemics of the second and third centuries to the rapid growth of Christianity.

As noted previously a devastating epidemic swept the Greco-Roman world beginning in 165 C.E. It lasted for about 15 years, frequently doubling back on itself. Eventually, from 25 to 30 percent of the population died, including the emperor Marcus Aurelius (McNeill, 1976; Gilliam, 1961; Russell, 1958; Boak, 1947). Hans Zinsser ([1934] 1960:101) noted that the epidemic was so severe that "it completely demoralized social, political, and military life and created such terror there were none who dared nurse the sick." Indeed this was the pattern reported in exquisite detail by Thucydides[6] about the great epidemic that struck Athens in 431 B.C.E.:

> [The victims] died with no one to look after them; indeed there were many houses in which all the inhabitants perished through lack of any attention. . . . The bodies of the dying were heaped one on top of the other, and half dead creatures could be seen staggering about in the streets or flocking around the fountains in their desire for water. . . . As for the gods, it seemed to be the same thing whether one worshipped them or not, when one saw the good and the bad dying indiscriminately.

In 251 a new and equally devastating epidemic struck the empire (McNeill, 1976; Gilliam, 1961; Russell, 1958; Zinsser [1934] 1960). Again, there are widespread reports of flight from the afflicted and of their utter neglect.

But I have thus far withheld a vital element. Contrary to Zinsser's assertion that none dared to nurse the sick, the Christian communities seem to have had no shortage of such persons. Dionysius, bishop of Alexandria during the second great epidemic, wrote in an Easter letter about 260 that a substantial number of his presbyters, deacons, and laymen had given their lives:

> Heedless of danger, they took charge of the sick, attending to their every need and ministering to them in Christ, and with them departed this life serenely happy. . . . Many, in nursing and curing others, transferred their death to

6. He contracted the disease early in the outbreak.

> themselves and died in their stead. . . . The best of our brothers lost their lives in this manner.
>
> The heathen behaved in the very opposite way. At the first onset of the disease, they pushed the sufferers away and fled their dearest, throwing them into the roads before they were dead, and treated the unburied corpses as dirt.

There is no reason not to believe the bishop. His parishioners would have had direct knowledge of whether many leading members had died nursing the sick. As for his claims about how non-Christians responded, the pagan sources agree. Indeed, they regarded it as the sensible thing to do—unless, of course, one believed that death was a beginning, not an end.

William H. McNeill (1976), in his pioneering study of plagues and history, pointed out that "even quite elementary nursing will greatly reduce mortality" during epidemics such as these. Large numbers die not directly from the disease, but from dehydration and lack of calories because they become too weak to obtain food and liquids. In fact, modern medical experts estimate that conscientious nursing *without any medications* could cut the mortality rate by two-thirds or even more. So, if the Christians nursed their sick, they would have had a far lower mortality rate than pagans—a difference that would have been obvious to all. Moreover, this would tend to compound as the epidemic recurred, since the far greater proportion of Christians who had survived the first time would now be immune. To the extent that Christians had sufficient resources to nurse their pagan friends and neighbors, they too would have been very likely to survive. And who was to say whether it was the prayers or the soup that produced the cure?

Elsewhere I have shown how the differential mortality of pagans and Christians during these two great epidemics would have caused a substantial shift in the relative size of the two populations. I also have suggested how Christian responses to the epidemics would likely have prompted a substantial amount of conversion (Stark, 1991).

It also is worth noting that Christian doctrine did more than undergird effective responses to catastrophes. Christianity made human history *purposeful* even in the face of what to pagans seemed mere caprice. During the massive epidemic in the third century, pagan priests admitted they did not know if the gods were involved or even cared (Harnack, [1908] 1962), while sophist philosophers "prattled vaguely about the exhaustion of virtue in a world growing old" (Cochrane, 1957:155). But to Cyprian, bishop of Carthage, the epidemic was an opportunity for Christians to grow in faith and virtue:

> How suitable, how necessary it is that this plague and pestilence, which seems horrible and deadly, searches out the justice of each and every one and examines the mind of the human race; whether the well care for the sick,

whether relatives dutifully love their kinsmen as they should, whether masters show compassion to their ailing slaves, whether physicians do not desert the afflicted begging their help.... Although this mortality has contributed nothing else, it has especially accomplished this for Christians and servants of God, that we have begun gladly to seek martyrdom while we are learning not to fear death. These are trying exercises for us, not deaths; they give to the mind the glory of fortitude; by contempt of death they prepare for the crown ... our brethren who have been freed from the world by the summons of the Lord should not be mourned, since we know that they are not lost but sent before; that in departing they lead the way; that as travellers, as voyagers are wont to be, they should be longed for, not lamented ... and that no occasion should be given to pagans to censure us deservedly and justly, on the ground that we grieve for those who we say are living with God. (*Mortality,* 16; 20)

It is revealing to compare Cyprian's views about the duties of physicians with pagan norms as reflected in the behavior of Galen, the most renowned physician of the age, during the epidemic in the time of Marcus Aurelius. As soon as the epidemic appeared, Galen fled Rome and retired to his country estate in Asia Minor until the danger receded. Indicative of his haste to leave is the fact, oft-noted by modern medical historians, that his description of the disease is so "uncharacteristically incomplete" that it offers no clues as to what disease it was (Hopkins, 1983). Although Galen's flight may have been rational for an individual, collectively the pagan response was irrational in that it caused huge numbers of needless deaths and undermined all semblance of social solidarity.

This brief account of how pagans and Christians responded to epidemics sets the stage for the major point I wish to draw about the basis for Christian success in the urban Greco-Roman world. If too many historians of the early church seem to take its success as a foregone conclusion, far too many social scientists recoil in utter amazement that any normal person would have become a Christian. How could people sacrifice so much? What could possibly have compelled them to risk so much and give up so much on behalf of purely subjective benefits?

Of course, it did cost a lot to be a Christian in those days. Not only was there a certain amount of risk and social stigma involved in being a Christian, but the tangible demands on those who wished to remain in good standing were high. You were expected to be your brother's keeper. You were expected to dig deep to help feed, clothe, and shelter the less fortunate. You were asked to devote time and energy to good works. You were asked to observe a far more restrictive moral code than that observed by pagans. And when epidemics struck, you were expected to risk your life gladly to nurse the sick, bury the dead, and console the living.

Viewed in this light, Christian behavior strikes many social scientists as utterly irrational, even to those willing to grant that the "otherworldly" promises made by the faith were highly valued by adherents. But this is the wrong light for seeing the full picture. It was not simply the promise of salvation that motivated Christians, but the fact that they were greatly rewarded here and now for belonging. Thus, while membership was expensive it was, in fact, a bargain. That is, because the church asked much of its members, it was thereby possessed of the resources to *give* much (Iannaccone, 1990). For example, because Christians were expected to aid the less fortunate, many of them received such aid, and all could feel greater security against bad times. Because they were asked to nurse the sick and dying, many of them received such nursing. Because they were asked to love others, they in turn were loved. Because of the tangible fruits of their faith, the average Christian could lead a far more comfortable and rewarding life than could the average pagan. Demographers regard life expectancy as the best summary measure of the quality of life. It is thus significant that Burn (1953) found, based on inscriptions, that Christians had longer life expectancies than pagans.

And herein lies the very utilitarian link between Christianity and its social situation. Christianity revitalized life in Greco-Roman cities by providing new norms and new kinds of social relationships able to cope with many urgent, urban problems. To cities filled with the homeless and impoverished, Christianity offered charity as well as hope. To cities filled with newcomers and strangers, Christianity offered an immediate basis for attachments. To cities filled with orphans and widows, Christianity provided a new and expanded sense of family. To cities torn by violent ethnic strife, Christianity offered a new basis for social solidarity. And to cities faced with epidemics, fires, and earthquakes, Christianity offered effective nursing services.

In closing, let me note that earthquakes, fire, plagues, and invasions did not appear for the first time at the start of the Christian era. People had been enduring catastrophes for centuries without the aid of Christian theology or Christian social structures. I am by no means suggesting that the misery of the ancient world caused the advent of Christianity. I am arguing that once Christianity did appear, its superior capacity for meeting these chronic problems soon became evident and played a major role in its ultimate triumph.

Since Antioch suffered acutely from all of these urban problems, it was in acute need of solutions. No wonder the early Christian missionaries were so warmly received in this city. For what they brought was not simply an urban *movement,* but a new culture capable of making life in Greco-Roman cities more tolerable. I leave it to those far more learned than I to detect how these urban facts of life are refracted through the lens of Matthew's Gospel.

APPENDIX A

Disasters at Antioch

The list is based primarily on Downey (1963).

B.C.E.

64   Pompey occupied the city and Romans replaced Persians as the administrative and social elite.

51   Parthians laid siege to Antioch. The Romans successfully held the city, but the suburbs were plundered.

C.E.

24   A major fire destroyed many public buildings.

37   A severe earthquake smashed the city causing immense damage and substantial loss of life.

40   A series of bloody and very destructive anti-Jewish riots broke out.

42   Another severe earthquake flattened three major temples and many homes.

46–47   All Asia Minor was gripped by famine, and in Antioch there was widespread hunger and some rioting.

66–70   A new wave of even more destructive anti-Jewish riots took place.

70   That winter a fire destroyed a major section of the city.

115   A huge earthquake leveled Antioch with great loss of life.

165–80   The empire was ravaged by an epidemic. Antioch was among the first cities to be hit, mortality there probably exceeded 30 percent, and substantial numbers fled.

193–94   Pescennius Niger was proclaimed emperor by his legions, which led to civil war with Emperor Severus. After defeat in the field, Pescennius fell back to Antioch. Shortly thereafter the city was taken by imperial troops, and Pescennius was executed along with some of his officers.

251   A new epidemic swept the empire and Antioch again lost a large segment of its population.

253   The city was sacked by King Sapor of Persia, and many inhabitants were carried off as captives.

260   The Persians captured the city and once again sacked it and sent residents into captivity.

272   The city was retaken by Emperor Aurelian.

333   Famine caused a substantial number of deaths.

354   Severe famine was accompanied by destructive riots.

361–62   Drought caused crop failures and brought on another serious famine.

C.E.

382–84 Famine hit again. Fearing mob violence, all of the bakers fled Antioch. Thereupon substantial rioting took place.

387 An imperial edict raising taxes touched off riots that turned into a full-scale insurrection. Initially the mobs destroyed portraits and statues of the imperial family. Then they began to burn public buildings and the homes of the rich. Troops led by the Count of the East arrived, rounded up the mobs, and executed everyone they caught, including children.

458 Once again a devastating earthquake knocked down the city, this time even shattering the city walls, and the death toll was immense.

484 A rebellion was led by Leontius who made Antioch his headquarters. Troops sent by Emperor Zeno defeated the rebels and forced them to flee Antioch.

490 A series of bloody and recurrent riots began, often accompanied by anti-Jewish attacks. During one of the worst of these riots, mobs burned the governor's headquarters and the Forum.

507 Once again mobs burned synagogues, homes, and government buildings with substantial loss of life. When the Count of the East arrived with imperial troops, the loss of life was even higher as the troops executed everyone suspected of having been involved.

525 A massive fire broke out and burned down major portions of the city; smaller fires recurred for six months.

526 An earthquake struck at mealtime during the festival of Ascension Day when Antioch was crammed with visitors. The city literally fell down. As is often the case, the quake started fires and so many of those trapped beneath the rubble burned to death or were suffocated by smoke. Downey (1963) says the "the figure of 250,000 dead, which is given in the sources, is by no means impossible."

528 Just as the city began to recover, a major quake struck once again. It is claimed that the walls of the city and all buildings not destroyed last time, or which had been subsequently rebuilt, were leveled.

540 Hardly had the emperor Justinian managed to have Antioch rebuilt than the Persians came, laid siege to the city, captured it, sacked it, and then very carefully burned everything including the suburbs and rural estates. Procopius reported that the destruction was so complete that as residents returned they often could not even locate the sites where their houses had stood. Justinian immediately sent large numbers of laborers and craftsmen to rebuild the city.

C.E.

542   Bubonic plague arrived from Egypt. The death toll in Constanti-
           nople was estimated to have been from 30 to 50 percent. The toll in
           Antioch was high, but unknown.

551   Another devastating earthquake damaged the city.

557   The walls of the city fell again to a huge earthquake.

573   Most residents fled when they heard Persian raiders were coming.
           The Persians did arrive, but did not try to take the city, being
           satisfied to burn all of the suburbs.

577   An earthquake totally destroyed the luxury resort suburb of Daphne,
           five miles beyond the walls, but the city itself was not badly damaged.

588   An estimated 60,000 persons were killed by an earthquake.

606–7   Again the city was sacked by Persians.

610   Bloody riots took many lives, and more were lost when the Count of
           the East arrived with his troops to restore order.

611   Antioch was captured by Persians with great loss of life. The Per-
           sians garrisoned the city.

628   The Persians evacuated Antioch, and the Romans returned.

638   Islamic troops captured Antioch causing a substantial exodus of
           refugees to the West.

REFERENCES

Ayerst, David, and A.S.T. Fisher. 1971. *Records of Christianity.* Vol. 1. Oxford: Basil
     Blackwell.
Boak, Arthur E. R. 1947. *A History of Rome to 565 A.D.* 3d ed. New York: Macmillan.
Brown, Peter R. L. 1964. St. Augustine's Attitude to Religious Coercion. *Journal of
     Roman Studies* 54:107–16.
Burn, A. R. 1953. Hic breve vivitur. *Past and Present* 4:2–31.
Chandler, Tertius, and Gerald Fox. 1974. *Three Thousand Years of Urban Growth.*
     New York: Academic.
Cochrane, Charles Norris. 1957. *Christianity and Classical Culture.* London: Oxford
     University Press.
Cyprian, 1958. *Treatises.* Translated by Mary Hannan Mahoney and edited by Roy J.
     Deferrari. New York: Fathers of the Church.
de Camp, L. Sprague. 1966. *The Ancient Engineers.* Norwalk, Conn.: Burndy Library.
Downey, Glanville. 1962. *Antioch in the Age of Theodosius the Great.* Norman:
     University of Oklahoma Press.
———. 1963. *Ancient Antioch.* Princeton: Princeton University Press.
Durand, John D. 1960. Mortality Estimates from Roman Tombstone Inscriptions. *The
     American Journal of Sociology* 75:365–73.

Finley, M. I. 1977. *Atlas of Classical Archaeology*. New York: McGraw-Hill.

Gilliam, J. F. 1961. The Plague under Marcus Aurelius. *American Journal of Philology* 64:243–55.

Grant, Robert M. 1970. *Augustus to Constantine: The Thrust of the Christian Movement into the Roman World*. New York: Harper & Row.

———. 1977. *Early Christianity and Society: Seven Studies*. San Francisco: Harper & Row.

Guttentag, Marica, and Paul E. Secord. 1983. *Too Many Women? The Sex Ratio Question*. Beverly Hills, Calif.: Sage.

Harnack, Adolph. [1908] 1962. *The Mission and Expansion of Christianity in the First Three Centuries*. New York: Harper & Row.

Hopkins, Donald R. 1983. *Princes and Peasants: Smallpox in History*. Chicago: University of Chicago Press.

Hopkins, Keith. 1965. The Age of Roman Girls at Marriage. *Population Studies* 18:309–27.

———. 1966. On the Probable Age Structure of the Roman Population. *Population Studies* 20:245–64.

Iannaccone, Laurence R. 1990. Religious Practice: A Human Capital Approach. *Journal for the Scientific Study of Religion* 29, no. 3:297–314.

Jashemski, Wilhemina F. 1979. *The Gardens of Pompeii*. New Rochelle, N.Y.: Caratzas.

Johnson, Paul. 1976. *A History of Christianity*. New York: Atheneum.

Judge, E. A. 1986. The Quest for Mercy in Late Antiquity. In P. T. O'Brien and D. G. Peterson, eds. *God Who Is Rich in Mercy: Essays Presented to D. B. Knox*. Sydney, Australia: Macquarie University Press.

Kee, Howard Clark. 1983. *Miracle in the Early Christian World*. New Haven: Yale University Press.

———. 1986. *Medicine, Miracle and Magic in New Testament Times*. Cambridge: Cambridge University Press.

Koester, Helmut. 1987. *History, Culture and Religion of the Hellenistic Age*. New York: de Gruyter.

Levick, Barbara. 1967. *Roman Colonies in Southern Asia Minor*. Oxford: Clarendon.

Longenecker, R. N. 1985. Antioch of Syria. In R. K. Harrison, ed. *Major Cities of the Biblical World*. Nashville: Thomas Nelson.

MacMullen, Ramsay. 1974. *Roman Social Relations: 50 B.C. to A.D. 284*. New Haven: Yale University Press.

———. 1981. *Paganism in the Roman Empire*. New Haven: Yale University Press.

———. 1984. *Christianizing the Roman Empire*. New Haven: Yale University Press.

———. 1988. *Corruption and the Decline of Rome*. New Haven: Yale University Press.

McNeill, William H. 1976. *Plagues and Peoples*. Garden City, N.Y.: Doubleday.

Meeks, Wayne A. 1983. *The First Urban Christians*. New Haven: Yale University Press.

Meeks, Wayne A., and Robert L. Wilken. 1978. *Jews and Christians in Antioch in the First Four Centuries of the Common Era*. Missoula, Mont.: Scholars.

Meiggs, R. 1974. *Roman Ostia*. 2d ed. Oxford: Oxford University Press.

Mooney, James. 1896. *The Ghost Dance Religion and the Sioux Outbreak of 1890*. Fourth Annual Report of the Bureau of Ethnology to the Secretary of the Smithsonian Institution. Washington, D.C.: United States Government Printing Office.

Mumford, Lewis. 1974. Foreword in Chandler and Fox.

Packer, James E. 1967. Housing and Population in Imperial Ostia and Rome. *Journal of Roman Studies* 57:80–95.

Pomeroy, Sarah B. 1975. *Goddesses, Whores, Wives, Slaves: Women in Classical Antiquity*. New York: Schocken Books.

Russell, J. C. 1958. *Late Ancient and Medieval Population*. Philadelphia: Transactions of the American Philosophical Society.

Smith, William, ed. 1857. *Dictionary of Greek and Roman Geography*. London: Walton & Maberly.

Stambaugh, John E. 1988. *The Ancient Roman City*. Baltimore: Johns Hopkins University Press.

Stambaugh, John E., and David L. Balch. 1986. *The New Testament in Its Social Environment*. Philadelphia: Westminster.

Stark, Rodney. 1986a. Jewish Conversion and the Rise of Christianity: Rethinking the Received Wisdom. In Kent Harold Richards, ed. *Society of Biblical Literature Seminar Papers*. Atlanta: Scholars.

———. 1986b. The Class Basis of Early Christianity: Inferences from a Sociological Model. *Sociological Analysis* 47:216–25.

———. 1987. How New Religions Succeed: A Theoretical Model. In David G. Bromley and Phillip E. Hammond, eds. *The Future of New Religious Movements*. Macon, Ga.: Mercer University Press.

———. 1991. Epidemics and the Rise of Christianity. *Semeia* 53, edited by L. Michael White.

Stark, Rodney, and William Sims Bainbridge. 1985. *The Future of Religion: Secularization, Revival, and Cult Formation*. Berkeley: University of California Press.

———. 1987. *A Theory of Religion*. Bern and New York: Peter Lang.

Thucydides. 1953. *The Peloponnesian War*. Translated by F. Smith. Cambridge: Harvard University Press.

Wallace, Anthony F. C. 1956. Revitalization Movements. *American Anthropologist* 58:264–81.

White, K. D. 1984. *Greek and Roman Technology*. London: Thames & Hudson.

White, L. Michael. 1987. Scaling the Strongman's 'Court' (Luke 11:21). *Foundations and Facets Forum* 3:3–28.

Wrigley, E. A. 1969. *Population and History*. New York: McGraw-Hill.

Zinsser, Hans. [1934] 1960. *Rats, Lice and History*. New York: Bantam.

10

Crisis Management and Boundary Maintenance: The Social Location of the Matthean Community

_____ L. MICHAEL WHITE

THE QUEST FOR THE COMMUNITY

Where, when, and for whom was the Gospel of Matthew written? In one way or another all the studies in this volume are attempts to sight the Matthean community in its social and historical setting. Discussions of social history necessarily imply attempts to describe the social setting in which a given population or group operated within a given span of time. In such discussion it is assumed that the role and status of individuals are directly affected by the social order in which they operated. Attitudes, behavior, and beliefs are part and parcel of the social fabric of the larger cultural context. Thus, social historians typically analyze the primary historical data (including literary, documentary, and archaeological sources) from a given context in order to reconstruct its social order and its cultural framework.[1]

In the case of the Christian Gospels, as with much of the Jewish and Christian literature of the first centuries C.E., one faces a slightly different and more complex problem, precisely because they are literary compositions (rather than documentary sources) detached by subsequent usage from their original context. The task at hand goes something like this: Using the Gospels as

1. The task at hand is well defined by John H. D'Arms, _Commerce and Social Standing in Ancient Rome_ (Cambridge: Harvard University Press, 1981) 1–18. The work of Ramsay MacMullen, _Roman Social Relations, 50 B.C. to A.D. 284_ (New Haven: Yale University Press, 1974), is exemplary; cf. Géza Alföldy, _The Social History of Rome_ (rev. ed.; trans. D. Braund and F. Pollock; Baltimore: Johns Hopkins University Press, 1985) ix–xi; Naphtali Lewis, _Life in Egypt under Roman Rule_ (Oxford: Clarendon, 1983) 18–35.

primary sources for the earliest periods of the Christian movement, one should
be able to deduce from them data to reconstruct the religious and social history
of the movement. However, the ability to reconstruct concrete information
from a given document is correlative with and dependent upon locating the
particular document in its own historical context, that is, chronologically, geographically, and socially. The task is further complicated when issues of historiographical or theological perspective have to be factored into the analysis of
a given text. Traditional questions of authorship, place, and date, while certainly central, are only part of a larger picture of the social setting.

While such issues have been discussed in other areas of early Christian
studies, the turn toward social history analysis of the Gospels, and of Matthew
in particular, has been prompted further by two concurrent and intersecting
lines of inquiry in contemporary scholarship. The first, it may be argued, has
been the outgrowth of redaction criticism on the Gospels, as it began to focus
attention on the editorial process of literary composition. With it (and its offspring, the various modes of literary criticism) came a greater recognition of
the audience for whom the documents were intended. Audience setting constitutes a social context behind the compositional strategy.[2] To put it another way,
following Leander Keck, scholarly attention shifted from the original *Sitz im
Leben Jesu* of gospel materials to their *Sitz in der Kirche* and beyond—to the
social ethos of those early churches in which the gospel traditions were
preserved, used, and modified.[3] It has become a quest for the historical community in earliest Christianity.

The second area is in part a result of the first, as it comes from the
current state of scholarship (including implications of redactional and literary
analysis) on Luke-Acts. From the time that W. C. van Unnik forecast "a storm
center in contemporary scholarship"[4] it has proven increasingly difficult to use
the theologically and historiographically conditioned picture presented in
Luke-Acts as the normative outline of Christian origins.[5] In particular, the

---

2. Cf. Marinus de Jonge, *Christology in Context: The Earliest Christian Response to
Jesus* (Philadelphia: Westminster, 1988) 21–29; John Gager, *Kingdom and Community: The Social
World of the Early Christians* (Englewood Cliffs, N.J.: Prentice-Hall, 1975) 1–18; Howard Clark
Kee, *Christian Origins in Sociological Perspective: Methods and Resources* (Philadelphia: West-
minster, 1980) 11–29; Wayne A. Meeks, *The Moral World of the First Christians* (Philadelphia:
Westminster, 1986) 11–39; Robert Morgan (with John Barton), *Biblical Interpretation* (Oxford
Bible Series; New York: Oxford University Press, 1988) 139–45.

3. Leander E. Keck, "On the Ethos of the Early Christians," *JAAR* 42 (1974) 446.

4. "Luke-Acts, A Storm Center in Contemporary Scholarship," *Studies in Luke-Acts* (ed.
L. E. Keck and J. L. Martin; Philadelphia: Fortress, 1966) 15–32. The current literature on
Luke-Acts is too extensive to cite here. The forecast has more recently shifted to Matthew; cf.
Graham N. Stanton, "Matthew's Gospel: A New Storm Centre," *The Interpretation of Matthew*
(ed. G. Stanton; Philadelphia: Fortress, 1983) 1.

5. Cf. Ernst Haenchen, "The Book of Acts as Source Material for the History of Earliest
Christianity," *Studies in Luke-Acts,* ed. Keck and Martin, 258–78; cf. Martin Hengel, *Acts and the
History of Earliest Christianity* (Philadelphia: Fortress, 1980) 35–50; J. Jervell, *The Unknown
Paul: Essays on Luke-Acts and Early Christian History* (Minneapolis: Augsburg, 1984) 13–25.

idealized (or harmonized)[6] portrayal of Luke-Acts tends to telescope back onto the early days of the Christian movement practices, beliefs, and perspectives that did not and could not have existed. As a result the development of distinct groups or strands of early Christianity tend to get lost in the mix. This effect has been most noticeable in its treatment of Jewish groups and in the degree of a distinctive group identity among Christian communities.[7] Instead, there has been a greater awareness of the diversity of Jewish and Christian groups operating in their own social context throughout the early period.[8] One can no longer simply plug Matthew into the historiographical landscape or the geographical spread motif of Luke-Acts as the starting point for analysis. The question of social location of any given group or document is central to the process and must look both to social historical analysis and to literary analysis as means to this end.[9] To these modes of analysis one should bring more awareness of both archaeological and sociographic data in reconstructing the social location of the Matthean community.

LOCATING THE MATTHEAN COMMUNITY

To date most attempts to locate Matthew have looked primarily toward its geographical setting in conjunction with an analysis of its polemic against the Pharisees. Despite Papias's attributions of a "Hebraic" (conceivably meaning Aramaic) original, the present form clearly presupposes a Greek idiom and composition, even in the wording of the most central prophecy-fulfillment passages.[10] Thus the discussions have concentrated on sighting the Matthean authorship (and by derivation, the audience as well) along a spectrum between Palestinian and Greek culture or between Jewish and gentile Christianity. The suggestions range from Palestine (understood broadly) to Alexandria,[11] based

---

6. See the comment in this volume by Anthony Saldarini.

7. Jack T. Sanders, *The Jews in Luke-Acts* (Philadelphia: Fortress, 1987) passim.

8. L. M. White, "Adolf Harnack and the Expansion of Early Christianity," *SecCent* 5 (1985/86) 108–10; Helmut Koester, "*GNOMAI DIAPHOROI*: The Origins and Nature of Diversification in the History of Early Christianity," *Trajectories through Early Christianity* (ed. J. M. Robinson and H. Koester; Philadelphia: Fortress, 1971) 114–57.

9. Thus, in current New Testament work it is important to balance between a traditional exegetical, or text-centered approach (as some would term it), and culturally cued analysis of language and customs. One might call this an attempt at social and historical *triangulation,* which would involve both synchronic and diachronic placement of the document and the community it represents.

10. Eus. *Hist. Eccl.* 3.39.16; cf. W. G. Kümmel, *Introduction to the New Testament* (rev. ed.; trans. H. C. Kee; Nashville: Abingdon, 1975) 119–20 (though this point is far too widely discussed and accepted to require further discussion here).

11. Among others, see Julius Schniewind, *Das Evangelium des Matthäus* (12th ed.; Göttingen: Vandenhoeck & Ruprecht, 1968) 3; and Martin Hengel, *Judaism and Hellenism* (Philadelphia: Fortress, 1974) 1. 105 (for Palestine); S.G.F. Brandon, *The Fall of Jerusalem and the Christian Church* (2d ed.; London: SPCK, 1957) 221; and S. van Tilborg, *The Jewish Leaders*

upon suppositions about the use of Hebrew, Aramaic, and Greek in the Jewish homeland. The predominant view places Matthew among the mixed Jewish and Christian groups of the nearer Syrian Diaspora in the decades after the First Revolt. Antioch in particular has been favored as a likely location because of (1) its well-established and predominantly Greek-speaking Jewish community and (2) the traditions of early Christian activities (and tensions) there.[12] Yet others have suggested the Greek cities of the Phoenician coast, Caesarea Maritima, or the Transjordan.[13]

What must be recognized is that such suggestions regarding the geographical setting are implicitly determined by suppositions about the social setting as well. More often than not, the argument proceeds from a description of the social situation (usually predicated on exegetical considerations in pointing to the character of the audience or community) to posit a likely place for it to have occurred.[14] The social factors most often discussed in this regard are language (Greek versus Aramaic), socioeconomic status, ongoing Jewish-Christian relations and tensions, gentile contacts (and converts), and a Jewish scribal heritage (for use of the Scriptures). Also at work are assumptions regarding the development of both Judaism and Christianity in the period after 70 C.E. In particular the separation of the Christian movement away from Judaism to a distinct religious and institutional identity within the Roman world is of great significance. Conclusions regarding the geographical location

in Matthew (Leiden: E. J. Brill, 1972) 172 (for Alexandria). Neither position has received wide acceptance.

12. First suggested by B. H. Streeter, The Four Gospels (London: Macmillan [1924] 1957) 500–507, but widely followed; cf. Schweizer, "Matthew's Church," Interpretation of Matthew, ed. Stanton, 129; Farmer, "Jesus and the Gospels," Perkins (School of Theology) Journal 28 (1975) 31; "The Post-Sectarian Character of Matthew and Its Post-War Setting in Antioch of Syria," Perspectives in Religious Studies 3 (1976) 235–47; Wayne Meeks and Robert Wilken, Jews and Christians in Antioch in the First Four Centuries of the Common Era (SBLSBS 13; Missoula, Mont.: Scholars, 1978) 18; Meeks, Moral World of the First Christians, 137; Helmut Koester, Introduction to the New Testament (2 vols.; Philadelphia: Fortress, 1982) 2.171–77; R. E. Brown and J. P. Meier, Antioch and Rome: New Testament Cradles of Catholic Christianity (New York: Paulist, 1983) 22–27; J. D. Kingsbury, Matthew (Proclamation Commentary; Philadelphia: Fortress, 1977) 93, 97–98. By way of caution, it must be noted that many of the older discussions of the early Christian community at Antioch have been heavily dependent upon Acts as a source. But as noted above (n. 5), some of these assumptions need to be tested, as in the more recent studies (cf. Meeks and Wilken, Jews and Christians in Antioch, 14–17). More specifically in regard to traditional treatments of Matthew, the tendency to assume a close tie between Christian groups in Antioch and Jerusalem (following Acts) should now be tested, not only for Antioch itself but also for other areas, especially Galilee and the nearer Syrian regions.

13. G. D. Kilpatrick, The Origins of the Gospel according to St. Matthew (Oxford: Oxford University Press, 1946) 133–34 (for the Tyrian coastal cities); B. T. Viviano, "Where Was the Gospel according to Matthew Written?" CBQ 41 (1979) 182–84 (for Caesarea); D. L. Slingerland, "The Transjordanian Origin of Matthew's Gospel," JSNT 3 (1979) 18–28 (for the Transjordan, leaning particularly toward Pella on the basis of the Pella-flight legend).

14. Brown and Meier, Antioch and Rome, 18–23.

of Matthew often imply conclusions regarding its degree of Jewishness or Greekness.

Both the process and the progress of the separation of Christian groups away from their Jewish roots are social factors that must be assessed more carefully to understand the social location of Matthew. Whereas traditional Christian historiography (usually following Luke-Acts) assumed that a complete separation had been achieved within the early years, such does not seem likely. The process of separation must have taken different courses or progressed at different rates in different communities and geographical regions, and one cannot use later traditions, such as the Pella legend, to claim that Christianity had made an official break with Jerusalem by 70 C.E. The first official Roman recognition of Christians as a distinct group did not come until the early decades of the second century, and then only in diaspora contexts.[15] In some recent studies of Matthew a geographical location in southern Syria (nearer to Galilee and an indigenous Jewish population) has been suggested, while other studies have reassessed the degree of separateness or similarity between the Matthean "school" and its Jewish neighbors (or opponents).[16]

Such studies have brought reconsideration of Matthean Christianity in the context of emergent Pharisaism in the post-70 period. In this light, one begins to ask new questions or question old assumptions. For example, given Matthew's polemical tone regarding *"their* synagogues" (Matt 4:23; 9:35; 10:17; 12:9; 13:54; cf. 23:34 *"your"*),[17] one must ask what kinds of boundaries

15. Gerd Lüdemann, "The Successors of Pre-70 Jerusalem Christianity: A Critical Evaluation of the Pella-Tradition," *Jewish and Christian Self-Definition,* vol. 1: *The Shaping of Christianity in the Second and Third Centuries* (ed. E. P. Sanders; Philadelphia: Fortress, 1980) 161–73; Helmut Koester, "The Origin and Significance of the Flight to Pella Tradition," *CBQ* 51 (1989) 90–106; Steven T. Katz, "Issues in the Separation of Judaism and Christianity after 70 C.E.: A Reconsideration," *JBL* 103 (1984) 43–76; Reuven Kimelman, *"Birkat Ha-Minim* and the Lack of Evidence for Anti-Christian Jewish Prayer in Late Antiquity," *Jewish and Christian Self-Definition,* vol. 2: *Aspects of Judaism in the Graeco-Roman Period* (ed. E. P. Sanders et al.; Philadelphia: Fortress, 1981) 226–44; L. M. White, "Adolf Harnack and the Expansion of Early Christianity," 108–9.

16. W. Grundmann, *Das Evangelium nach Matthäus* (3d ed.; Berlin: Evangelischer Verlagsanstalt, 1972) 43; W. D. Davies, *The Setting of the Sermon on the Mount* (Cambridge: Cambridge University Press, 1964) 27–32; Krister Stendahl, *The School of St. Matthew* (Philadelphia: Fortress, 1968) 30–35. Most recently, see J. Andrew Overman, *Matthew's Gospel and Formative Judaism: The Social World of the Matthean Community* (Minneapolis: Fortress, 1990) passim.

17. In each case where the passage is found in double or triple tradition material, the use of the possessive pronoun is a uniquely Matthean editorial insertion. The only exception is the first (Matt 4:23), a triple tradition unit (= Mark 1:39; Luke 4:44) which is probably the literary prototype for the Matthean redactional shaping of the rest. (So cf. the repetition of Matt 4:23 at 9:35.) While the possessive (αὐτῶν) is used in the Mark 1:39 par., it should be noticed that (unlike Matthew) this passage is not the first reference to Jesus' teaching in *the* synagogue (cf. Mark 1:21, 29), and in both cases the simple definite article is used. In the Matthean ordering of material, these two units have been shifted to a later position in the narrative (Matt 7:28 and 8:14 respectively), their direct literary interdependence severed, and the synagogue references removed. As a result the Matthean unit at 4:23–25 comes to have a more pivotal place in establishing Jesus' relationship to "their" synagogal authority. The Lukan emendation of τῆς Ἰουδαίας

(between "us" and "them") are being drawn. What stage of development or separation between Christians and Jews (or just Pharisees) is envisioned? What was a synagogue in Matthew's day? Where does Matthew's group stand in relation to both Jewish and Greek culture?

Recent archaeological work has led to the conclusion that the synagogue was not a religious institution in the later rabbinic sense prior to 70 C.E.[18] There is no evidence for synagogue architecture in the homeland dating from the first century, and all the known Palestinian synagogues come from the third to sixth centuries C.E.[19] The earliest archaeological evidence for synagogues comes from the Diaspora, though it reflects considerable diversity and lack of rabbinic influences on institutional or liturgical order.[20] Instead, it appears that only in the period after the destruction of the temple did the new institutional organization begin to develop in the homeland and come under the influence of the emergent Pharisaic leadership. In the villages of the Galilee and Golan,

---

serves a similar function but must be seen as dependent upon the rejection of Jesus in the synagogue in Nazareth a few verses earlier (Luke 4:16). In contrast, the Markan usage of the possessive (which occurs only twice in reference to the synagogue) has a different function, as may be seen from its usage in Mark 1:23. In this case it seems that the possessive is meant to connote locality (the synagogue of the Caperneans), rather than the Matthean sense of distinctiveness (of "us" vs. "them"), and here Luke 4:33 follows this tone in Mark (while Matthew drops the passage entirely). Thus, the usage of αὐτῶν in Mark 1:39 may also be taken to refer to geographical locality (referring back to the mission in other towns of Galilee in Mark 1:35, another unit omitted in Matthew). Its distinctive syntactic position relative to the prepositional phrase εἰς ὅλην τὴν Γαλιλαίαν would support this reading, and once again both Matthew and Luke have modified the construction to fit their own emphasis. Thus, in Mark 1:39 "their synagogues" serves as a geographic reference (the synagogue of each town) in conjunction with the so-called Sammelberichten (3:7–12; cf. 6:53–56) and in service to the geographical progression of Jesus' ministry (cf. Mark 6:1, 6b). The Matthean redaction, however, has transformed the usage of the possessive to serve an oppositional function and has repeated the usage for emphasis. For Matthew, "their *synagogues*" stand in direct opposition to "our *church*" in a unique way.

18. Joseph Gutmann, "The Origin of the Synagogue: The Current State of Research," *The Synagogue: Studies in Origins, Archaeology, and Architecture* (ed. J. Gutmann; New York: Ktav, 1975) 72–76; idem, "Synagogue Origins: Facts and Theories," *Ancient Synagogues: The State of Research* (BJS 22; Atlanta: Scholars, 1981) 1–4; L. M. White, "The Delos Synagogue Revisited: Recent Fieldwork in the Graeco-Roman Diaspora," *HTR* 80 (1987) 133–35.

19. M. Avi-Yonah, "Ancient Synagogues," *Synagogue: Studies in Origins, Archaeology, and Architecture,* ed. Gutmann, 95–109; E. M. Meyers, "Ancient Gush Halav (Giscala), Palestinian Synagogues and the Eastern Diaspora," *Ancient Synagogues,* 71–74; M. J. Chiat, "First-Century Synagogue Architecture: An Overview," *Ancient Synagogues,* 49–60; A. J. Seager, "Ancient Synagogue Architecture: An Overview," *Ancient Synagogues,* 39–47; E. M. Meyers and A. T. Kraabel, "Archaeology, Iconography, and Nonliterary Written Remains," *Early Judaism and Its Modern Interpreters* (ed. R. A. Kraft and G.W.E. Nickelsburg; SBL Centennial; Atlanta: Scholars, 1986) 175–95.

20. A. T. Kraabel, "The Diaspora Synagogue: Archaeological and Epigraphic Evidence since Sukenik," *ANRW* 2.19.1: 489–510; idem, "The Social Systems of Six Diaspora Synagogues," *Ancient Synagogues,* 79–89; idem, "Unity and Diversity among Diaspora Synagogues," *The Synagogue in Late Antiquity* (ed. L. I. Levine; Philadelphia: ASOR, 1987) 49–60; White, "Delos Synagogue Revisited," 135–60; idem, *Building God's House in the Roman World: Architectural Adaptation among Pagans, Jews, and Christians* (Baltimore: Johns Hopkins University Press, 1990) 60–77.

"prayerhalls" (προσευχαί) may have originated as places of public assembly (cf. ✓ Joseph. *Vit.* 277–80).[21] But until the later second century, when architectural renovation becomes more prominent after the Second Revolt, it seems that Jewish groups met for worship in household assemblies or other less formal "prayerhall" (προσευχαί) settings.[22] In the Diaspora there were often several synagogue congregations in any given locale, much like the picture of the early house churches. As a result social and theological diversity and group tensions were common. It may be argued that the development of the synagogue as the central religious institution of post-70 Judaism was a product over a considerable time (ca. 70–200 C.E.) of converging streams of development: (1) the collegial experience of diaspora communities, (2) the leadership of the rabbinic schools, and (3) the profound transformations effected in Jewish social life after the failure of the two revolts against Rome. Coming in the last decades of the first century, Matthew's polemic against "*their* synagogues" cannot be understood as having broken away from the established order of Judaism in Jesus' day. Rather it was generated within the context and convulsions of an emerging new order, with both theological and social implications. In this context, hearing Matthew's "Jewish voice"[23] has greater significance.

PROGRESS IN THE HELLENISTIC
URBAN ENVIRONMENT

If one sightline for Matthew places it in relation to its Jewish cultural heritage, then another sightline must consider it in the light of the social placement of Jewish and Christian groups within the Hellenistic environment of the Roman East. Usually cited in this context is Matthew's legitimation of the gentile mission (28:18) in contrast to the earlier, exclusively Jewish mission (10:5–6, 17–18, 23). It has also been speculated, based on 21:43, that a majority

---

21. Cf. Gutmann, "Origin of the Synagogue," 75–76; and idem, "Synagogue Origins," 4. Gutmann follows Solomon Zeitlin, "The Origin of the Synagogue: A Study in the Development of Jewish Institutions," *Synagogue: Studies in Origins, Archaeology, and Architecture,* ed. Gutmann, 20–21. His conclusions may be taken in concert with the work of Jacob Neusner regarding the development of the Pharisaic movement after 70 C.E. The best discussion on lines of development from the civic assembly is that of S. Hoenig, "The Ancient City-Square: The Forerunner to the Synagogue," *ANRW* 2.19.1:448–76.

22. White, *Building God's House in the Roman World,* 79, 85–101; E. M. Meyers, J. F. Strange, and C. L. Meyers, "The Ark of Nabratein," *BA* 44 (1981) 237–43. Neither sacred orientation nor the architectural definition of the sacred ark (Torah Shrine) is demonstrable prior to the last decades of the second century. Thus, it would appear that the canonization of the synagogue liturgy and the architectural adaptation for worship were products of the later phases of development after 70 and leading up to the codification of the Mishnah. It may well be that many of these developments did not begin, or at least did not have their full significance, until after the failure of the Second Revolt in 135 C.E. Cf. Franz Landsberger, "The Sacred Direction in Synagogue and Church," *Synagogue: Studies in Origins, Archaeology and Architecture,* ed. Gutmann, 239–60.

23. As suggested above in the chapter by Alan Segal.

of Christians in Matthew's community were non-Jews. Thus for many a
"melting pot" for Jews in Antioch or Syria has seemed a logical location.[24]
Jewish groups ranged from Galilee to Antioch throughout the first century,
while the Matthean emphasis on "Galilee of the Gentiles" (4:15) must also be
noted. As a result it becomes increasingly difficult to maintain old distinctions between Jewish and Hellenistic culture or between Palestinian and
Hellenistic Judaism.[25] Instead, the difference often lay in the experience
of Jewish groups either as a "homeland" culture or as a minority culture in an
alien environment. Given the cultural diversity of northern Palestine and
southern Syria in the first century C.E., local Jewish groups could have faced
both kinds of experience in rather close proximity. When one takes into
account sectarian group consciousness, then further tensions or divisions might
arise within the larger Jewish population. The development of Jewish and
Christian groups must be analyzed by looking first at the social diffusion within
the local environment.

Rodney Stark's discussion of the urban environment of Antioch is an
instructive case study of how social factors can come into play once one begins
to assess the local environment.[26] It brings home graphically the role of an
urban setting and the sense of crisis that could be produced there. Most
notably it posits a correlation between religious adherence and social networks,
especially in times of social crisis. Stark's observations regarding the importance of social bonds especially in times of crisis have been borne out in Peter
Garnsey's work, *Famine and Food Supply in the Graeco-Roman World*. Two
points in particular deserve attention. First, Garnsey's study shows the crucial
relationships between the cities themselves and their immediate surroundings,
including smaller towns and villages and rural farming districts.[27] While large-
scale agricultural estates were not uncommon, especially in Italy, the bulk of
food production for most cities of the Roman world still fell on small local farmers (both smallholders and tenants). One must think, therefore, in terms of
city-territories and market exchange districts within which each local urban
environment tended to work. What are the natural lines of trade and commerce for any given group and locality? What are the administrative and tax
structures that might be involved, and does their operation shed light on the
relationships of ethnic and religious groups?

24. Schweizer, "Matthew's Church," 129; cf. Brown and Meier, *Antioch and Rome,* 23.
Regarding Matt 21:43, see n. 48, below.
25. Shaye J. D. Cohen, *From the Maccabees to the Mishnah* (Philadelphia: Westminster,
1987) 35–46.
26. Clearly not everyone would agree with the untested premise of an Antiochian location
for Matthew, as we shall discuss below. But for the purposes of Stark's discussion, that is really
beside the point.
27. Peter Garnsey, *Famine and Food Supply in the Graeco-Roman World: Responses to
Risk and Crisis* (Cambridge: Cambridge University Press, 1988) 43–55.

Second, networks of patronage established and reinforced the reciprocal obligations and expectations between groups and individuals of different status in Roman society. They thereby bound the social structure together both in functional terms and in terms of an operative cultural ideology.[28] Religious and ethnic subgroups, such as Jews living in urban contexts, were dependent upon such socioeconomic ties. The diffusion of Jewish-Christian groups into the urban matrix was also affected by these channels, most notably in the organization of trade contacts and household associations.[29] The most immediate Matthean point of reference comes in the redacted instructions regarding households in the so-called missionary discourse material (Matt 10:5–42) and its implicit suggestion of group bonds and boundaries (Matt 18:15–20; 22:1–14; 25:31–46). Both of these points indicate the need to be aware of the social and cultural boundaries within which both Jewish and Christian groups operated.

The impact of urban crisis may be assessed more clearly when one can locate the actions of a particular group in the situation of a documented crisis. Unfortunately, there is no such clear linkage for Matthew in Antioch. Instead, it would seem more profitable to do the kind of close analysis in relation to the chronology of disasters suggested by Stark for Antioch for the cases of Libanius[30] or John Chrysostom[31] in the fourth century. Perhaps even more interesting is the case of Paul of Samosata during the third century.[32] The latter is particularly important since Paul's "schismatic" episcopate in Antioch fell (ca. 260–270 C.E.) during the period of Persian takeover, in which the city was twice sacked and there was a continuing epidemic.[33] The accounts clearly

28. Ibid., 55–68; cf. Richard P. Saller, *Personal Patronage under the Early Empire* (Cambridge: Cambridge University Press, 1982) 7–40.

29. Wayne A. Meeks, *The First Urban Christians: The Social World of the Apostle Paul* (New Haven: Yale University Press, 1983) 26–32, 74–85; White, "Adolf Harnack and Expansion of Early Christianity," 115–26.

30. With reference to Stark's list of Antiochian disasters, note the years 354, 361–384, and 387 C.E. Libanius wrote letters to the Patriarch of Tiberias dated 364 and 388–393 that mention sufferings of the Jewish people. Also he delivered an oration (*Or.* 47) entitled "On Patronage" (Περὶ τῶν προστασιῶν), in which he mentions the situation of Jews and Christians (chap. 13) as well as the concern for patronage in times of natural disaster (chap. 19). For text and further discussion, see Meeks and Wilken, *Jews and Christians in Antioch*, 59–81.

31. While John Chrysostom was a presbyter in Antioch, he preached eight *Homilies against the Jews* in fourteen months during 386–387. In addition to showing a much higher degree of separation between Jewish and Christian institutions, the text also refers to a number of points of social interaction in situations of distress. For text and further discussion, see Meeks and Wilken, *Jews and Christians in Antioch*, 83–127; R. L. Wilken, *John Chrysostom and the Jews: Rhetoric and Reality in the Late Fourth Century* (Berkeley: University of California Press, 1983) passim.

32. The crucial sources for Paul of Samosata come from Eus. *Hist. Eccl.* 7.30; and for Aurelian's dealings in the East during the Persian crisis from the *Historia Augusta*, Fl. Vopiscus, *Divus Aurelianus* 22.1–28.9. Cf. Fergus Millar, "Paul of Samosata, Zenobia, and Aurelian: The Church, Local Culture and Political Allegiance in the Third Century," *JRS* 61 (1971) 126–34; Ramsay MacMullen, *The Roman Government's Response to Crisis, A.D. 235–337* (New Haven: Yale University Press, 1976) 93.

33. The Persian armies of Queen Zenobia captured Antioch and other cities in 260 C.E.

indicate that Paul was allied with a number of powerful figures and the local village churches. While Eusebius's account makes the case primarily on theological grounds (Paul's "heretical" Christology was too Jewish!), it is apparent that factionalism and social ties played an important role as well. The controversy was resolved in favor of the opposition ("orthodox") clergy only after the emperor Aurelian had recaptured the city. The case would seem to be susceptible to Stark's analysis, since it suggests that the religious allegiances and group boundaries were dependent upon the social ties of local groups and the social disruption of the crisis situation.

By the same token, one can document the impact of similar natural disasters in other areas suggested for locating the Matthean community, such as in the Galilee and Golan.[34] Such possibilities suggest that one needs to con-

---

Antioch was sacked yet again, after the earlier Sassanid incursions of 253–256 (which wrenched much of the eastern frontier from Roman control). One should guess that for an imperial city like Antioch, being sacked by hostile forces must have had a profound impact, easily the equivalent of a natural disaster in terms of social disruption and psychological despair. In this case the situation was compounded by an epidemic and more, since it must be remembered that the emperor Valerian was captured by the Persians near Edessa in 260. There was a profound sense of crisis, reflected in religious terms as in the account of Trebellius Pollio (in the *Historia Augusta*), *The Two Gallieni* 3–5. The tone of the response can be seen in the following passage (which corresponds to events in either 262 or 267): "In the consulship of Gallienus and Fausianus, amid so many calamities of war, there was also a terrible earthquake and a darkness for many days. There was heard, besides, the sound of thunder, not like Jupiter thundering, but as though the earth were roaring. And by the earthquake many structures were swallowed up together with their inhabitants, and many died of fright. . . . Therefore the favor of the gods was sought by consulting the Sibylline Books, and according to their commands, sacrifices were made to Jupiter Salutaris. For so great a pestilence, too, had arisen [from the east] that both in Rome and the cities of Achaia in a single day 5000 men died of the same disease. While Fortune thus raged, and while here [there were] earthquakes and there clefts in the ground, in diverse places pestilence devastated the Roman world, while Valerian was held in captivity" (*Gallieni duo* 5.2–6 [LCL, trans. D. Magie] adapted). It may be added that Pollio's account is retrospective from a period of Diocletianic reform, not unlike what one finds in Eusebian historiography a few years later.

It is interesting that Eusebius also mentions this period of crisis and its impact on the diffusion of the church, though he does so more in reference to Alexandria and the exemplary episcopate of Dionysius (247–65 C.E.), after which he contrasts the situation at Antioch under Paul. Much of Eusebius's description of the Alexandrian church under Dionysius is devoted to the medical care of Christians during the great plague (*Hist. Eccl.* 7.22). In this light it may be worth noting that one of the great theological issues that Dionysius faced was a literalist interpretation of the Apocalypse by the chiliast followers of Nepos, the bishop of Arsinoe (cf. *Hist. Eccl.* 7.24.1). Dionysius responded with a discussion of the Johannine authorship to prove unsubstantiated their basis for a literal sense of "prophecy" (ibid., 7.25). It seems that no one has considered the possibility that these two issues, the one a theological debate and the other a social concern, were related within the crisis circumstances of the period. One begins to suspect, however, that the literalists were equating the crises (wars, plague, and famine) of their day with the eschatological horrors found in the Apocalypse (chaps. 6–9) and so concluding that they were witnessing the final days. This sentiment touched Dionysius, too (cf. *Hist. Eccl.* 7.21.10). If true, their religious response to the crisis was not so unlike that of their pagan neighbors. Also on the larger issues of the sense of crisis see MacMullen, *Roman Government's Response to Crisis*, 6–23, 38–40.

34. Cf. K. W. Russell, "The Earthquake Chronology of Palestine and Northwest Arabia from the Second through the Mid-Eighth Century A.D.," *BASOR* 260 (1985) 37–59.

sider other factors in the social transformation of the region that might have prompted a "crisis" context. For example, the growth of Pharisees and their social impact in the later first through the mid-second century needs to be explored in these terms as well.[35] They too were affected by shifting social alignments in the periods of crisis following the two revolts against Rome. In such situations the competition or cooperation of social groups to maintain their identity and boundaries is very important.[36] It is also the case that shifting social alignments, resulting in the dislocation of groups or individuals, might be perceived by the disenfranchised as part of the crisis. In such cases reconfiguring of the boundaries by which a group defines its identity occurs, as with the Pharisees themselves after 70 C.E. Boundary maintenance becomes a mechanism of crisis management.

MARKING THE BOUNDARIES OF
THE MATTHEAN COMMUNITY

Further clues to the social location of the Matthean community may be found by examining its boundary definition language relative to its surrounding environment. Several studies have suggested that tensions both with Jewish neighbors and within the Christian community were prevalent.[37] The usual set of boundary-defining terms is assumed from the polemic against the Pharisees and "their" synagogues (cf. Matt 23:2–7), but there are other boundary markers as well. A good test case comes in Matt 18:15–20, in the uniquely Matthean discourse material on church order.[38] There, as part of the disciplinary

35. Anthony J. Saldarini, *Pharisees, Scribes, and Sadducees in Palestinian Society: A Sociological Approach* (Wilmington, Del.: Michael Glazier, 1988) passim. By way of response, however, I wonder if the connection between the scribes and the Pharisees (suggested by Saldarini as derived from their role as retainers of Rome) was rather a product of a later, post-70 shift of alliance, at least insofar as the two groups are equated in Matthew. It seems to me that the civil or public scribes, especially in local contexts, were more likely the "retainers" of the Roman bureaucracy.

36. Garnsey, *Famine and Food Supply*, 15, also mentions some of the rabbinic evidence in relation to the nature of food shortages and drought in the period, citing esp. *b.Ta'anit* 25a and related passages for breaking droughts through prayer and fasting. It should be noted that the mishnaic tractate was ordered around prescriptions for what to do if the rains had not begun according to their proper time to insure the annual crops (cf. *m.Ta'anit* 1.4; 3.1; 3.9).

37. W. G. Thompson, *Matthew's Advice to a Divided Community: Matthew 17:22–18:35* (Rome: Pontifical Biblical Institute, 1973) passim; Davies, *Setting of the Sermon on the Mount*; Goran Forkman, *The Limits of the Religious Community: Expulsion from the Religious Community within the Qumran Sect, within Rabbinic Judaism, and within Primitive Christianity* (Lund: Gleerup, 1972) passim, esp. 90–105.

38. The import of this material for Matthean redactional activity is inestimable for two main reasons (cf. G. Bornkamm, G. Barth, and H. J. Held, *Tradition and Interpretation in Matthew* [Philadelphia: Westminster, 1963] 84, 205): (1) It has strong similarities to disciplinary procedures found in the Qumran *Rule* (1QS 5.8–6.4) but also to mishnaic ideas of community (cf. *Pirqe Aboth* 3.2); (2) It is directly related to other Matthean redactional materials, most notably Matt 16:17–19, the only other place where the term ἐκκλησία is used. Cf. also Matt 9:2–8 (cf. Bornkamm, Barth, and Held, *Tradition and Interpretation*, 270, 273) and Matt 5:46–47.

procedures, the ultimate sanction under the church's authority to "bind and loose" is emphatic: "If the member [the offender] refuses to listen even to the church, let such a one be to you as a Gentile and a tax collector (ὁ ἐθνικὸς καὶ ὁ τελώνης)" (18:17). What is significant about this sanction is the way it establishes the boundaries of the religious community. Disciplinary exclusion from the church of an unworthy person (whether a Jew or Gentile by birth) is conceived of as putting one in the same category as "Gentiles and tax collectors." The sentiment is also echoed in Matt 5:46–47 (a note of superiority to the ethics of tax collectors and Gentiles) in the injunction on loving one's enemies. Thus, despite the apparent antipathy toward the synagogue (cf. 6:2 in relation to 5:46–47) Matthew consistently presents the nature of the community in Jewish, not Greek, terms.[39] Its worldview is dominated by categories from Jewish apocalyptic thought. In this light the Matthean community must be viewed still as a *sect* within the larger fabric of Judaism in its day, rather than having obtained the status or self-definition of a separate religion.[40]

Sectarian self-definition in early Judaism and Christianity has received considerable attention in recent scholarship.[41] Hence some definitions are in order. From a cross-cultural perspective a *sect* may be defined as "a divergent (i.e., deviant or separatist) revitalization movement which arises out of an

39. Cf. the prescriptive nature of boundaries along similar lines in the mishnaic code; cf. *Nedarim* 3.4 and *Baba Kama* 10.1–2 (tax collectors lumped together with murderers and robbers, or their trade is considered polluted by robbery). Esp. noteworthy are the contact boundaries (guarded by rules of uncleanness) in *Hagigah* 3.6 and *Tohoroth* 7.6. The latter is especially noteworthy as it lumps tax collectors together with other classes of "outsiders" that include Gentiles, *Amme ha-aretz*, and Samaritans (cf. also the commentary on *Tohoroth* in *Eliyahu Rabbah* 20, 22).

40. Here I would want to push even beyond Stendahl (*School of St. Matthew*, ix–xiii, 30–35) against the view of Bornkamm (Bornkamm, Barth, and Held, *Tradition and Interpretation*, 50) regarding the Jewish versus Greek self-definition of Matthean Christianity. I would agree with Bornkamm that one should not think of Matthew in terms of "retrograde process of re-Judaizing" (cf. his "The Authority to 'Bind' and 'Loose' in the Church in Matthew's Gospel," *Interpretation of Matthew*, 92). However, I think he goes too far in saying that "Matthew and his congregation presuppose hellenistic Christianity which had already outgrown its Jewish origin" (ibid., 95). The power "to bind and loose" is found in later rabbinic tradition for defining community boundaries, even if those boundaries are in dispute (against Bornkamm, "Power," 88; cf. also Meeks, *Moral World of the First Christians*, 136–39). The terminology is also found in magical usage; cf. Richard H. Hiers, "'Binding' and 'Loosing': The Matthean Authorizations," *JBL* 104 (1985) 233–50; Dennis C. Duling, "Binding and Loosing," *Forum* 3 (1987) 3–31. Josephus (*BJ* 1.111) uses the terms of administrative or bureaucratic powers in conjunction with the early Pharisees. The latter case may suggest further that the real context behind Matthew derived from the competition for influence and authority by religious leaders in interpreting theological norms for use in civil legislation in local *synedria* (a suggestion offered by David Balch; see chap. 4 above).

41. Robin Scroggs, "The Earliest Christian Communities as Sectarian Movements," *Christianity, Judaism, and Other Graeco-Roman Cults* (ed. J. Neusner et al.; part 2: *Early Christianity*; Leiden: E. J. Brill, 1975) 1–23; John Gager, *Kingdom and Community: The Social World of the Early Christians* (Englewood Cliffs, N.J.: Prentice-Hall, 1975) 19–49; Meeks, *Moral World of the First Christians*, 98–104; Joseph Blenkinsopp, "Interpretation and the Tendency to Sectarianism: An Aspect of Second Temple History," *Jewish and Christian Self-Definition*, ed. Sanders, 2:1–26.

established, religiously defined cultural system, with which it shares a symbolic worldview."[42] A central feature of this definition is its location of the sect's origins and development within its parent culture, but where there is tension with the dominant cultural idiom, usually referred to as "the world." As with the Dead Sea Covenanters, the sectaries thought of themselves as Jews even though there was a high degree of tension with the "worldly" Jewish culture exemplified by Jerusalem. Yet the dominantly Jewish worldview, deeply etched by apocalyptic expectations, remains in place. The points of tension or divergence are expressed in terms of disagreements over commonly accepted practices or beliefs. The piety and purity of a "righteous remnant" is a way of demarcating the boundaries of the sect from the masses of Jews who are not, from its perspective, keeping the faith rightly.[43]

Sects operate as "deviant" groups within their parent culture; therefore, a further distinction may then be made in the case of a new religious movement that develops in the context of an alien or foreign cultural environment. This type of group is more properly called a *cult* and may be defined as "an integrative, often syncretistic, revitalization movement which is effectively imported (by mutation or mobilization) into another religiously defined cultural system, to which it seeks to synthesize a basically foreign (or novel) symbolic worldview."[44] Both types of groups are "deviant" (or divergent) in that they stand in tension with their environment. From the moment of origin both types of groups will be in a process of flux, balancing tensions against "the world" with

42. The following discussion is based on the more detailed treatment in L. M. White, "Shifting Sectarian Boundaries in Early Christianity," *BJRL* 70.3 (1988) 7–24; the definitions both here and below may be found on p. 17.

43. Cf. Meeks, *Moral World of the First Christians,* 75–80. While the Qumran group is truly a sect, not all Jewish groups in first-century Judaea were. The term "sect" has been overused in referring to the various groups within first-century Judaism, and more technical specificity is needed. See also the recent discussions by Cohen, *From the Maccabees to the Mishnah,* 124–37; Alan Segal, *Rebecca's Children: Judaism and Christianity in the Roman World* (Cambridge: Harvard University Press, 1986) 58–59. The Sadducees, e.g., should generally not be considered a sect in the early first century C.E.; nor should the Samaritans in the fourth and third centuries B.C.E. Indeed, the Samaritans represented the indigenous Israelite ethno-cultural group, and the "exiles" who had returned to restore Jerusalem represent the minority faction who broke away from other forms of Israelite culture. Yet, in the long run the Jerusalem group would become the dominant cultural idiom (hence no longer a sect), and over time their historiography served as a legitimation of that position. See the discussion by White in "Shifting Sectarian Boundaries," p. 11 (with further bibliography). See also the excellent discussion of these matters of boundary definition in Judaism in Meeks, *Moral World of the First Christians,* 66–91. The question still remains, however, how to define the social organization of Pharisaic groups in the various periods prior to the codification of the Mishnah. One must suspect that not all subgroups or "schools" of Pharisees were truly sectarian in character, though some likely were *at certain times.* One must consider the shifts of sectarian order among the pre- and post-70 Pharisees a very real possibility, as suggested by the work of Jacob Neusner. See esp. Neusner's work on the pre-70 traditions, summarized nicely in his *From Politics to Piety: The Emergence of Pharisaic Judaism* (New York: Ktav, 1979) 82–96; cf. Cohen, *From the Maccabees to the Mishnah,* 143–64.

44. White, "Shifting Sectarian Boundaries," 17.

accommodation and assimilation. Yet the impulses of this tension will cause *sects* and *cults* to respond to their respective cultural settings in different ways. Nor are the two terms altogether exclusive. It would be possible either for a sect, having been transported from its native environment, to become effectively a cult in its new environment, or for a cult, having become established within a dominant culture, to have internal, hence effectively sectarian, splits. Thus, some Jewish and Christian groups may properly be called sects, while others were effectively cults, once they were transplanted from their native soil into the larger Roman environment.[45] Still, sects and cults (even from the same basic religious background) tend to behave differently. Whereas sects tend to stress (at least at the level of symbols and rhetoric) rigid boundaries of separation as a way of keeping the founding tensions alive, cults tend to stress similarities with their host culture as a means to synthesis between the conflicting symbol systems. Boundary definition and maintenance are crucial to this process.[46] Ultimately the tendency is for each type to be assimilated into its resident culture. The key point is that the group's message or theology embodies its basic self-defining tensions, and it takes its boundary markers from its own setting and experience. Also, in times of crisis, when the group feels that its identity or existence is threatened, it will tend to cause key defining boundaries to be hardened and symbolic markers to receive more stress.

As seen in Matt 18:15, the boundary markers for the Matthean community are still essentially of a Jewish character. No matter how hellenized their language or their intellectual climate, they define a Jewish worldview, including a basic division of humanity into Jews and non-Jews.[47] Yet, the dominant tension of the Matthean community is with its Jewish cultural heritage, or with at least some groups within the larger fabric of post-70 Judaism. The Greek-speaking Matthean church should still be thought of as a sectarian Jewish community. To become a member of the community is to become a member of the congregation of the *true* nation of Israel, the kingdom (Matt 5:9; 13:38, 52; 21:43).[48] The ethical obligations of membership are defined in

45. Hence Pauline communities in the Aegean should be thought of as cultic forms of Judaism in the larger Hellenistic-Roman environment, even though some of Paul's tensions with other Jewish (or Jewish-Christian) groups may be considered sectarian; cf. White, "Shifting Sectarian Boundaries," 20.

46. Cf. the "cult" boundary-defining language found in 1 Cor 5:9–10 (also from a case concerning disciplinary exclusion of an offender) with that in Matt 18:15–20.

47. In particular, notice the tone of the Hellenistic Jewish wisdom tradition, which had already entered into Christian usage (in the Q tradition) and into proto-rabbinic usage (*Wisdom of Solomon*), but which receives further redactional modifications in Matthean usage. Cf. M. J. Suggs, *Wisdom, Christology, and Law in Matthew's Gospel* (Cambridge: Harvard University Press, 1970) 7–10, 26–48, 56–59; James M. Robinson, "*LOGOI SOPHON*: On the Gattung of Q," *Trajectories through Early Christianity*, ed. Robinson and Koester, 103–12.

48. We may take issue with those who see the Matthean adaptation of the allegory of the wicked tenants to indicate a rejection of Israel in favor of another "nation" (ἔθνει, Matt 21:43), understood to mean the separated gentile church. See the discussion in Kingsbury, *Matthew*,

remarkably Jewish (explicitly Pharisaic) terms of Torah observance (Matt 5:17–21; cf. 28:19–20), where the distinction is in terms of superiority to other Jewish modes of observance. To be cast out of the church (Matt 18:17) is a binding consignment to the outer darkness reserved for non-Jews at the eschatological judgment (Matt 13:41–43, 47–49; 22:11–14). In contrast the boundary markers and self-definition of Antiochian Christianity as found in Ignatius have lost this sense of sectarian identity within a Jewish matrix. In Ignatius the separation from Judaism is more complete, and his perspectives on the "church" are more in line with a cultic identity being presented in the Roman cultural environment.[49]

It seems, then, that a fuller sociographic analysis is needed of the internal and external boundary markers for the Matthean community in order to understand its social location. Some indications of boundaries may be seen in the redaction of key passages. For example, the uniquely Matthean insertion of the temple tax pericope (Matt 17:24–27) as the introduction to the discourse unit on church order (Matthew 18) carries an important notice. It recommends paying the tax, "so that we do not give offense" (σκανδαλίσωμεν) to the collectors of the δίδραχμα (17:24, 27). One has to wonder about the function

---

72–77; and idem, "The Parable of the Wicked Husbandmen and the Secret of Jesus' Divine Sonship in Matthew," *JBL* 105 (1986) 645, for further references. Instead it should be noted that the very conception of the kingdom as an elect *nation* still comes from the self-consciousness of Israel's heritage filtered, to be sure, through a sectarian hermeneutic based on the prophetic tradition of the righteous remnant. In this sense, *the nation* (or "people," τὸ ἔθνος, Matt 21:43) is still distinct from *the nations* (i.e., "Gentiles," τὰ ἔθνη, Matt 6:32); cf. a "Gentile" (ὁ ἐθνικός, Matt 18:15; cf. 5:47: οἱ ἐθνικοί). Thus, even the final legitimation of the gentile mission in Matthew is framed in Jewish terms of "making disciples of all nations" (μαθητεύσατε πάντα τὰ ἔθνη) and "teaching them to observe" (διδάσκοντες αὐτοὺς τηρεῖν). It is not as yet a self-definition of the church as a "third race." At the very least, then, Matt 21:43 and 28:18–20 seem to reflect a sense of the church as grounded in the identity of *the nation* of Israel, though made up of a mixed population that also included disciples drawn from among the gentile *nations*. (Cf. Brown and Meier, *Antioch and Rome*, 69, n. 157.) The question that remains is whether this redactional posture reflects the accepted self-definition in its context; or is it an apologetic offered in the face of some implicit criticism of the Matthean community? The Matthean shaping of the wicked tenants pericope (Matt 21:33–46) suggests the latter (so also Kingsbury, "The Parable of the Wicked Husbandmen," 643–55), and this reading is reinforced by its intertextual redactional links with the following pericope, the marriage feast (Matt 22:1–14), with its allusions to the eschatological judgment of the "bad and good" within the kingdom.

49. William Schoedel's work on Ignatius demonstrates this basic difference most clearly; see above, p. 129; see also idem, "Theological Norms and Social Perspectives in Ignatius of Antioch," *Jewish and Christian Self-Definition,* ed. Sanders, 1.30–56; and idem, *Ignatius of Antioch* (Hermeneia; Philadelphia: Fortress, 1985) 16–17. The distinctive quality of what might be called the "vectors" of acculturation that Schoedel illustrates in Ignatius may give further indication of the ways in which earlier Christian materials from even a proximate region could result in a different theological presentation. Hence one may also reconsider the debated issue of whether or not Ignatius knew Matthew directly. Cf. esp. the seminal work of Helmut Koester, *Synoptische Überlieferung bei den Apostolischen Vätern* (TU 65; Berlin: Akademie Verlag, 1957) 24–61. Others would see more direct connections; cf. Brown and Meier, *Antioch and Rome,* 24–25 (as an argument for locating Matthew in Antioch); cf. Jean Daniélou, *The Theology of Jewish Christianity* (London: Darton, Longman & Todd, 1964) 39–43.

of this insertion in the context of a discourse unit having such important literary links to other major elements in the composition. It is all the more peculiar given the fact that the temple was no longer standing at the time of Matthew's composition. Does this reflect Vespasian's appropriation of the temple tax after 72 C.E. as a kind of dues for Jewishness? Or is this merely a literary device aimed at other issues? There are further connections between this notion of offense and a sense of crisis through the indications that the Matthean community had faced (or was facing) persecution at the hands of other Jewish groups.[50] What is the real concern over offending others? It is interesting that this notion of offending (σκανδαλίζειν) shows up often in Matthew in reference to: (1) clearly opposing factions (such as the Pharisees; cf. Matt 15:21), (2) others within the Christian matrix (such as the "little ones," Matt 18:6), (3) sympathizers (i.e., potential "disciples") who fall away under duress (Matt 13:21, 57; 24:10), and (4) the disciples themselves (Matt 5:29; cf. 18:8; 11:6; 13:41; 26:31–33).

The range of materials suggests that "giving offense" represents tensions at the boundaries of the community, both internal and external, in the midst of some sort of crisis. Rhetorically, for Matthew's community, it seems that offense has been given and received. The Matthean community was facing conflicts, probably on several fronts, and these conflicts have produced the sense of crisis. It may be possible, then, to use such boundary markers to provide a sociographic analysis of the Matthean community's environment. One may look to the social relationships reflected in order to visualize the social ecosystem in which the community was operating. The biographical narrative of Jesus' interactions with and teachings to others is shaped in such a way as to symbolize key relationships in the formation of the Matthean community.[51] From the boundaries and relationships reflected one can gain a sense of the symbolic prosopography, a "who's who," not so much by name but by their relative position in the social framework.

To be outside the community is to be considered as a "Gentile and tax collector" (18:15), yet Jesus as Messiah is identified prophetically as the "hope of the Gentiles" (12:15–21). He is criticized for consorting with "tax collectors and sinners" (9:10–13; 11:19; cf. 21:32), and he calls a tax collector (redacted as "Matthew," the namesake of the Gospel) to become a disciple (9:9). The status

50. On the temple tax after 70, cf. E. Mary Smallwood, *The Jews under Roman Rule from Pompey to Diocletian* (SJLA 20; Leiden: E. J. Brill, 1976) 344–45; S. Applebaum, "The Legal Status of Jewish Communities in the Diaspora," *The Jewish People in the First Century* (CRINT 1.1; Philadelphia: Fortress, 1974–76) 460–63. For further discussion of the implications for Matthew, see below, n. 86. On persecution, see Douglas R. A. Hare, *The Theme of Jewish Persecution of Christians in the Gospel according to Matthew* (Cambridge: Cambridge University Press, 1967) passim.

51. Cf. Meeks, *Moral World of the First Christians*, 136–43. Note Schweizer's discussion of the various groups reflected in Matthew ("Matthew's Church," 130–39).

of disciple is very important throughout Matthew and is defined in terms of Torah observance by the conditions of "righteousness" (δικαιοσύνη; cf. 5:21; 10:41) and being "perfect" (τέλειος; cf. 5:48).[52] At the same time, the "lawless" (ἀνομία; cf. 7:23; 13:41; 23:28; 24:12), equated with "offenders" (13:41), will be relegated to the outer darkness. Certain boundaries and polarities become apparent and yet at times are clouded. The scribes and Pharisees do not represent unrighteousness, but rather a lower level of righteousness since they are mired in hypocrisy (5:21; 6:1; 15:7; 23:23). Yet they are part of the antagonism toward the Matthean community that has been linked to the persecution in "their" synagogues (9:35; 10:17; 12:9; 23:6, 34) and has historically resisted the prophets (23:37). There are some ambiguous relationships here, too. While the scribes are often lumped together with the negative judgment on the Pharisees (23:29), the disciples are encouraged to act in the manner of "good scribes" (13:51–52). Even the term "prophet" in Matthew carries a note of ambiguity, since there are both true prophets, messengers of divine Wisdom (11:9–10), and false prophets still within the Christian community (7:15–16). Similarly, the "little ones," who are apparently itinerant Christian charismatics, are treated with some ambivalence, even though they are not to be offended (7:41–42; 18:10–14).[53] Finally, there are recurrent warnings of a coming apocalyptic judgment to be visited not only on outsiders but also on insiders who have not lived up to the righteousness of the church (13:41; 18:15; 22:11–14; 25:41–45).

⚹ Three further observations may be made regarding these polarities and relationships. First, the terminology used of key relationships is often ambivalent, in that the same term (e.g., scribes or prophets) may have both positive and negative referents. These key terms, therefore, reflect certain arenas of tension between the Matthean community and others who use similar terminology but place different valuations. Thus, it is precisely the similarity and proximity of the opposition that is the source of much of the tension and sense of crisis. Second, there are both internal and external tensions reflected, and on several different fronts. There is a balance between the judgment against external opponents, the Pharisees (chap. 23), and judgment within the church (chap. 25). Thus, the seeming radicalization of Jew versus Christian, of synagogue versus church, is only symptomatic of, or perhaps the catalyst for, a

52. Cf. Bornkamm, Barth, and Held, *Tradition and Interpretation,* 105–20; D.R.A. Hare and D. Harrington, "Make Disciples of All the Gentiles (Matt 28:19)," *CBQ* 37 (1975) 359–69; Kingsbury, *Matthew,* 78–90.

53. Bornkamm, Barth, and Held, *Tradition and Interpretation,* 121–24; Gerd Theissen, "Wanderradikalismus: Literatursoziologische Aspekte der Überlieferung von Worten Jesu im Urchristentum," *ZTK* 70 (1973) 245–71; and idem, *Sociology of Early Palestinian Christianity* (trans. J. Bowden; Philadelphia: Fortress, 1978) 8–14; but see also the recent criticism of Theissen by R. Horsley, *Sociology and the Jesus Movement* (New York: Crossroad, 1990) 3–18.

more complex set of relationships between the Matthean community and its Jewish-Gentile matrix.[54] Third, there are both vestigial (i.e., derived from earlier phases of the Jesus movement) and new relational forces within these boundary tensions (cf. 13:52).[55] Here, the scribes and "little ones" probably represent accepted forms of Jewish and/or Jewish-Christian activity going back to an earlier day, while the Pharisees and the synagogue seem to be recent developments that are in some way a threat to Matthew's community over issues of religious authority. As a community-founding document, the Matthean Gospel presents a picture of Jesus that will allow for the maintenance and balancing of these boundary tensions by showing the divine sources, in Jesus as the embodiment of Wisdom, of its own authority and ethical structure.[56]

CONFLICT AND CRISIS:
SOME GEOGRAPHICAL CONSIDERATIONS

Given these circumstances, then, how may one locate the crisis situation at work in Matthew? For a variety of reasons, both Antioch and Galilee proper would seem to be ruled out. At least from Ignatius's perspective of urban Christianity at Antioch, there is a substantial difference from the sectarian elements in Matthew.[57] The portrayal of Galilee in Matthew largely serves the literary intentions of the Gospel. The ministry of Jesus is confined for the most part to Lower Galilee, though the geographic progression is much less clear than that in Mark. The Matthean use of "Galilee" is designed to authenticate the messianic visitation on Israel, and thereby serves as a narrative (rather than

54. It should also be noted that there is a remarkable consistency in this emphasis on balancing between external and internal judgments that runs throughout the Matthean redaction, most notably in the composition of the discourse units. E.g., cf. those in chaps. 23 and 25 with 5:21 (cf. 6:33) and 7:21 (from the Sermon on the Mount discourse unit), with 13:12, 24–43, and 47–50 (from the parables discourse), and with the juxtaposed allegories of 21:33–46 and 22:1–14 (from the first portion of the Jerusalem discourse). It is also significant that these paired judgment teachings are set in contexts of debates over Jesus' authority (cf. 13:34–35; 21:23–27).

55. Here it is clear that a number of the standard categories of authority in Matthew are drawn from Q material, the vestigial source par excellence, but that through redactional shaping new situations are being addressed (cf. Suggs, *Wisdom, Christology, and Law*, 31–62). There may also be other sources of vestigial material reflected in Matthew, such as the so-called M material or a Matthean school of prophetic interpretation. Cf. Stendahl, *School of St. Matthew*; L. Cope, *Matthew: A Scribe Trained for the Kingdom of Heaven* (CBQMS 5; Washington: Catholic Biblical Association of America, 1976) 32–52. In either case, they are also likely to have been in some disagreement with the vestigial claims to tradition by the Pharisees themselves looking to pre-70 sources of authority.

56. Meeks, *Moral World of the First Christians*, 139–41; Suggs, *Wisdom, Christology, and Law*, 99–116; Kingsbury, "The Parable of the Wicked Husbandmen," 652–54 (cf. his *Matthew*, 95–99); de Jonge, *Christology in Context*, 91–96.

57. See above, n. 49.

real) geography from the perspective of the audience.[58] Yet with these qualifications, Matthew might have come from anywhere in between these two geographic limits. As a way of focusing in on some of the historical problems of social location, it may be best to think in terms of regionalization throughout this area, a Syro-Phoenician arc from Upper Galilee northward to Coela-Syria.

Extensive archaeological work has recently begun to shed new light on the history, geography, and culture of the Galilee and the Golan in the first centuries.[59] Most notably, an awareness of Galilean "regionalism" makes clearer some of the social conditions of that time. Galilee was not isolated from surrounding regions, nor was it one homogeneous territory. It was broken up into subregions along ethnic, topographical, and social lines. The languages of the region likewise reflect this mix; Greek was the common language for all. Classical Hebrew and official Latin had only limited usage. Both Greek and Aramaic were common among Jews, even though Aramaic may have been the colloquial language of rural areas. For many Jews, however, Greek seems to have been the first language. Many people were comfortably bilingual; numerous legal documents have been found in duplicates of Greek and Aramaic.[60] As in Egypt, such conditions would make professional scribes central to civic life. It was also a religious mix, as Galilee itself had been largely a gentile area until settled by Jews during the later Hasmonean period. Still, the population was religiously and culturally diverse, from village to village or especially within larger towns and cities. Under Herod the Great immigrant Jews from Babylonia had been induced to settle villages in the northern, largely non-Jewish regions of the Transjordan (Trachonitis and Batanea; cf. Joseph. *AJ* 17.23–31). They were considered ethnically distinct even by other Jews, and they remained loyal to Agrippa II and Rome throughout the revolt. In the process they were harassed by others from the region of Ituraea (apparently a coalition of pagans and renegade Jews; cf. Joseph. *Vit.* 54–61).

58. So Sean Freyne, *Galilee, Jesus, and the Gospels: Literary Approaches and Historical Investigations* (Philadelphia: Fortress, 1988) 90.

59. In addition to the literary study of Freyne (ibid.), see his *Galilee from Alexander the Great to Hadrian: A Study of Second Temple Judaism* (Wilmington, Del.: Michael Glazier, 1980). Cf. Martin Goodman, *State and Society in Roman Galilee*, A.D. *132–212* (Totowa: Rowman & Allenheld, 1983); idem, *The Ruling Class of Judaea: The Origins of the Jewish Revolt against Rome*, A.D. *66–70* (Cambridge: Cambridge University Press, 1987); and M. Avi-Yonah, "Historical Geography of Palestine," and M. Stern, "The Reign of Herod and the Herodian Dynasty," both in *The Jewish People in the First Century* (CRINT 1.1); 78–115 and 216–307, respectively; D. Sperber, *Roman Palestine 200–400: The Land, Crisis and Change in Agrarian Society as Reflected in Rabbinic Sources* (Ramat-Gan, Israel: Bar Ilan University, 1978).

60. Gerhard Mussies, "Greek in Palestine and the Diaspora," *Jewish People in the First Century* (CRINT 1.2), 1040–64; E. M. Meyers and James F. Strange, *Archaeology, the Rabbis, and Early Christianity: The Social and Historical Setting of Palestinian Judaism and Christianity* (Nashville: Abingdon, 1981) 62–91, esp. 84–86, discussing Greek inscriptions among Jewish burials at Beth Shearim.

The main geographic division fell between Upper and Lower Galilee demarcated (following Josephus) along the sharp Beth Ha-Kerem valley and the Meiron mountains (see map 1). On its eastern side, the boundary was marked by the upper ravines of the Nahal 'Ammud (which runs off toward the Sea of Galilee near Genesaret), but the line continues eastward along the gentle runoff of the Galilean highlands toward the upper Jordan valley and the Golan. Roughly speaking, the village of Chorazin would have been near this border, while Capernaum and the other cities along the sea would have been considered part of Lower Galilee. Bethsaida-Julias represented the gateway to the Golan, though still closely associated with the cities of Lower Galilee.[61] Lower Galilee became more hellenized and urbanized throughout the first century. A testimony to this mixed character has been found in recent excavations of Sepphoris. A free city, it served as the capital of the region, remained loyal to Rome in the First Revolt, and yet served as the seat for Rabbi Judah ha-Nasi at the time that the Mishnah was being codified. Towns and villages (such as Nazareth, only three and one-half miles to the southeast) tended to be grouped into market networks connected to one of the free cities, a kind of city-territory or toparachy organization.[62] In contrast, Upper Galilee did not have any free

61. Joseph. *BJ* 3.35–43, 58; cf. E. M. Meyers, "Galilean Regionalism as a Factor in Historical Reconstruction," *BASOR* 221 (1976) 93–101; idem, "The Cultural Setting of Galilee: The Case of Regionalism and Early Judaism," *ANRW* 2.19.1:686–702; cf. Meyers and Strange, *Archaeology, the Rabbis, and Early Christianity*, 38–45. See n. 98, below, with implications for the woe-saying on Chorazin and Bethsaida (Matt 11:20–24).

62. Urbanization in Lower Galilee began under Herod the Great, but his great building programs were concentrated elsewhere. The boom came under Antipas (4 B.C.E.–37 C.E.), who built up Sepphoris, the first *synedria* of the Roman period and then capital of the tetrarchy. Antipas later founded Tiberias (ca. 17–19 C.E.) as the new capital of Galilee, also to serve as a trade center with the Decapolis and Transjordan trade routes. Sepphoris, Tiberias, and Gabara were the largest urban centers and held free-city status. Sepphoris commanded the highways and trade routes to the Mediterranean coast and south toward Samaria and Caesarea Maritima; Tiberias anchored the Sea of Galilee and access to the Transjordan. In addition, there were several other large towns such as Arav, Tarichaea, or Capernaum. They were not free-cities as such, but were local hubs nonetheless. Finally, there were further programs of "urbanization" under Vespasian and Titus (i.e., in the period after the First Revolt) and later under Hadrian (in the time of the Second Revolt). Both Sepphoris and Tiberias played important roles in the First Revolt as depicted in Josephus. In particular Sepphoris quickly capitulated to Vespasian and was subsequently rewarded by imperial favors for remaining loyal to Rome. (There are too many references in Josephus's works to list, but note, e.g., *Vit.* 30–39.) Vespasian then embarked on a new campaign of urbanization throughout the region. Further attention needs to be given to the role of local city councils or *synedria* as used in Josephus and inscriptions. On urbanization see A.H.M. Jones, "The Urbanisation of Palestine," *JRS* 21 (1933) 265–75; S. Applebaum, "Jewish Urban Communities and Greek Influences," *Scripta Classica Israelitica* 5 (1979) 158–77; and J. Andrew Overman, "Who Were the First Urban Christians? Urbanization in Galilee in the First Century," SBLSP 1988 (ed. D. Lull; Atlanta: Scholars, 1988) 160–69. On Sepphoris, see E. Meyers, "Sepphoris, Ornament of All Galilee," *BA* 49 (1986) 4–19; E. Meyers, E. Netzer, and C. L. Meyers, "Artistry in Stone: The Mosaics of Ancient Sepphoris," *BA* 50 (1987) 223–31; Y. Meshorer, "Sepphoris and Rome," *Greek Numismatics and Archaeology: Essays in Honor of Margaret Thompson* (ed. O. Morkholm and N. Waggoner; Brussels: Cultural Press, 1979) 159–71; S. Miller, *Studies in the History and Traditions of Sepphoris* (Leiden: E. J. Brill, 1984). On Tiberias, see M. Avi-Yonah, "The Foundation of Tiberias," *IEJ* 1 (1950) 160–69; Smallwood, *Jews under Roman Rule*, 183–84.

cities and remained a nonurbanized village culture. These villages tended to be clustered more tightly in their own social organization in contrast to village patterns found in Lower Galilee. It was called *Tetracomia* ("Four Villages") through the early Byzantine period.[63]

These regional differences also created distinct political, social, economic, and cultural contacts as well. Lower Galilee tended to trade east and west between the Sea of Galilee (including the Transjordanian cities and the lower region of the Decapolis) and the Mediterranean ports of Caesarea Maritima and Acco-Ptolemais (which was politically part of Phoenicia-Syria). Upper Galilee, however, tended to trade with the very Romanized cities of Tyre and Sidon (on the Mediterranean coast) and, to the northeast, with the Hellenistic cities of the upper Golan and Ituraea (including Paneas-Caesarea Philippi) and up toward Damascus. There is, therefore, a Syro-Phoenician axis especially for the Upper Galilean cultural and economic contacts. There was also a substantial Jewish population in the Golan and in Greek cities, especially Ptolemais, Tyre, Caesarea Philippi, and Damascus.[64] The entire region of Phoenicia, almost down to Caesarea Maritima, and the region around the free city of Damascus (as with most of the cities of the Decapolis) were administered under the Legate of the Province of Syria until the time of Septimius Severus (193–211 C.E.). At times, however, certain regions or city-territories were placed under local procuratorial control of client-kings, as in the cases of the Nabataean king Aretas IV at Damascus,[65] Herod of Chalcis (d. 48 C.E.), and later Herod Agrippa II (ca. 50–93 C.E.) in Chalcis and Abilene.

63. Dennis E. Groh, "Jews and Christians in Late Roman Palestine: Towards a New Chronology," *BA* 51 (1988) 80–96 (with a good overview of chronology and bibliography). For archaeological reports see, among others, E. M. Meyers and A. T. Kraabel, "Archaeology, Iconography, and Nonliterary Written Remains," *Early Judaism and Its Modern Interpreters*, ed. Kraft and Nickelsburg, 177–80; E. M. Meyers, C. L. Meyers, and J. F. Strange, *Excavations at Ancient Meiron, Upper Galilee, Israel 1971–77* (Meiron Excavations 3; Cambridge: ASOR, 1981).

64. Cf. R. Hanson, *Tyrian Influences in Upper Galilee* (ASOR Monographs; Cambridge: ASOR, 1980) passim. There are also similarities between the village culture of Upper Galilee and that found in the Golan. Josephus's accounts of John of Gischala, his chief rival among the Jewish revolutionary leadership in Galilee, are indicative of these cultural contacts. Gischala was one of the main villages of the Upper Galilee. It appears that John had held some role in the local Roman administration since Josephus refers to "his [John's] region" (ἐν τῇ αὐτοῦ ἐπαρχίᾳ, *Vit.* 73). John had also amassed a sizeable fortune (which he was using to finance his forces) through trade between Upper Galilee and the cities of the Tyrian coast, a fact supported by recent archaeological discoveries at Gischala (Gush Halav). Cf. E. M. Meyers, "Excavations at Ancient Gush Halav (Giscala) in Upper Galilee," *Ancient Synagogues Revealed*, ed. L. I. Levine (Jerusalem: IES, 1981) 75–77. Among other things, John traded in oil (for anointing) that was deemed "pure" for Jewish usage (ἔλαιον ᾧ χρίσονται καθαρόν, *Vit.* 74), but Josephus accuses him of profiteering and price gouging during the war by charging the Jewish residents of Caesarea Philippi a rate ten times higher than in Gischala. Cf. D. Urman, *The Golan: A Profile of a Region during the Roman and Byzantine Periods* (British Archaeological Reports International Series 269; Oxford: BAR, 1985).

65. Aretas IV (9 B.C.–40 C.E.) was the Nabataean king, but served as procurator of Damascus, apparently during the time that Paul was there (cf. 2 Cor 11:32). His daughter had been married to Herod Antipas, tetrarch of Galilee, until ca. 27/28, when Antipas divorced her to

One does not have to go as far as Antioch to find a cosmopolitan Jewish presence in the midst of a thriving and diverse Greek culture. This was the "near Diaspora," and it was viewed by Galilean Jews quite differently from the faraway Greek Diaspora. The Greek cities of Ptolemais, Tyre, Berytus, Caesarea Philippi, and Damascus were part of the Jewish matrix, despite their highly syncretistic religious environment.[66] Yet there were cultural and religious tensions, especially in the years surrounding the First Revolt.[67] The escalation of social banditry prior to the revolt and the political and social reconstruction afterward are important conditions that need to be considered for their impact both within the two Galilees (or specific toparchies) and in their respective relations with surrounding territories.[68] What needs to be

---

marry Herodias (the sister of Agrippa I and former wife of Herod Boethus). The divorce not only evoked the fabled condemnation of John the Baptist, but also provoked a war between the Nabataeans and Antipas that forced the Romans to intercede in 37 C.E. with the intent of removing Antipas from office (cf. Joseph. *AJ* 18.109–12). Eventually he was replaced by Agrippa I. The Nabataeans remained hostile and assisted the Romans and Agrippa II against the Jewish forces during the First Revolt. See Smallwood, *Jews under Roman Rule*, 185–87. See also below, n. 70.

66. One may note the story of Rabban Gamaliel's (II) encounter with the pagan philosopher Proclus in the Baths of Aphrodite at Ptolemais (*m.Abodah Zara* 3.4). It seems to me that the argument advanced by this story (to justify the Rabbi's presence in a pagan edifice, dedicated to a foreign god) is akin to that used by Paul to justify eating diverse foods (1 Cor 8:1–7). There are other indications of free travel between Upper Galilee or the domain of Agrippa II with the Tyrian coastal cities (cf. Joseph. *Vit.* 49), and Agrippa II apparently had royal residences in Berytus (*Vit.* 181–82) and as far north as Arca, a hundred miles away (*BJ* 7.97). These cities were also known for their syncretistic culture, in many respects like that of Herod's port at Caesarea Maritima. Cults of merchants from the Tyrian coastal cities were also found throughout the eastern Mediterranean all the way to Italy. Usually they are identified by collegial associations dedicated to a hellenized form of their ancestral god, a local patronymic version of Ba'al. Thus, one finds the Poseidoniasts of Berytus and the Heracleiasts of Tyre (at Delos), the cult of Helios Sareptenos from Sarepta and Tyre (at Puteoli and Rome). Diaspora Jewish enclaves moved in these same networks, and it may be surmised that it was produced by alliances in their native regions. For discussion and bibliography see my *Building God's House in the Roman World*, 31–39. It is also the case that the Herodian client-kings had contacts throughout the eastern Mediterranean through similar mechanisms. Note then the statue dedications in honor of Herod Antipas (dating ca. 6 C.E.) from Delos, Athens, and Cos in *Orientis Graeci Inscriptiones Selectae* 417 and 416; cf. Smallwood, *Jews under Roman Rule*, 184–85.

67. See, e.g., Joseph. *Vit.* 25–27 (a pogrom against Jewish residents in the "Syrian" regions of Scythopolis and Damascus; cf. *BJ* 2.466, 559); *Vit.* 43–45 (an attack on Gischala by Tyrians and their allies who were loyal to Rome). Also, in one incident (*Vit.* 112), Josephus resisted the attempts of Jewish insurgents at Tarichaea to force the circumcision of two wealthy supporters of the Revolt, who had fled there from Trachonitis (an area still loyal to Agrippa II and Rome). Although they were uncircumcised, Josephus implies that they were worshipers of the Jewish God, and it is not inconceivable that they came from one of the predominantly Jewish settlements or from the Babylonian Jewish enclave of Batanea (cf. *Vit.* 55–57).

68. For incidents of banditry or terrorism in neighboring districts under Syrian control, see Joseph. *Vit.* 42 (cf. 410), 126–31, 341–42, 371–72 (John of Gischala had troops from his own city and allies from the metropolitan region of Tyre). These cases underscore a further point regarding the use of the term "Galileans" in Josephus. It seems to have gone unnoticed in much of the scholarship that Josephus clearly identifies the population based on not only religious background or revolutionary sympathies but also political boundaries. Thus, on the relationship between Sepphoris and the "Galileans," cf. Freyne, *Galilee from Alexander the Great to Hadrian*, 122–28. Josephus, e.g., never refers to the Jewish insurgents of the free cities Tiberias or Tari-

observed is the way political and social boundaries were operating in this period down to the time of Domitian and Trajan.

At this point the relations of Christian and Pharisaic groups in the period of reconstruction become a significant issue. Sean Freyne has suggested that the emergence of the Pharisees needs to be reconsidered in light of the Hellenistic urban social setting of the Lower Galilee.[69] What has often been missing in the discussion of the setting of the Gospels is a careful assessment of the shifting social and political boundaries after the Revolt. Too often, studies of the Gospels assume simplistically that the political boundaries and social alignments reflected therein were the same as those during the life of Jesus. But one cannot simply take the threefold division of Herod's kingdom among his sons and apply it to the geographic setting of the Gospels. Thus, on the basis of these two issues—the emergence of the Pharisees and the geopolitical boundary shifts—in the period from ca. 75–125 C.E. the setting of Matthew's Gospel may be given further consideration.

The political or administrative boundaries of the Galilee changed in some significant ways during the period under consideration. The traditional area called Galilee (with subdivisions of Upper and Lower) came from the tetrarchy of Herod Antipas that he inherited from his father (see map 2). After the deposition of Antipas in 39 C.E. the region might have been reorganized under provincial authority.[70] Instead, it was ceded to Herod Agrippa I along with the regions that had previously belonged to the tetrarchy of Philip. Then in 41 the remaining areas of Herod's kingdom (Samaria and Judaea) were added, along with some territories to the north of Ituraea, both of which had been under direct Roman procuratorial rule. Thus, Agrippa I managed to reunite the entire kingdom of Herod under a hereditary rule. Agrippa I could

---

chaea as "Galileans"; rather, he calls them "Tiberians" or "Tarichaeans." Likewise, the people of Sepphoris, who had capitulated to Rome early on, are always called "Sepphorites." In non-urbanized areas, regional designations are used, such as the non-Jewish (probably Bedouin or Nabataean) peoples of Trachonitis' border, called "Trachonites" (cf. *AJ* 17.23). Josephus seems to reserve the term "Galileans" for the residents of the primarily Jewish villages (or toparchies) not associated with one of the major free cities (cf. *Vit.* 311–13, 349–51, 373–80, 381–85). More generally on the problem of banditry and the beginnings of the Revolt, see R. Horsley and J. Hanson, *Bandits, Prophets, and Messiahs: Popular Movements at the Time of Jesus* (New York: Winston-Seabury, 1985) passim; and the response by S. Freyne, "Bandits in Galilee: A Contribution to the Study of Social Conditions in First-Century Palestine," *Social World of Formative Judaism and Christianity*, 50–68 (stressing the distinctive experience of the Galilee in the period of the revolt). Freyne's criticisms are well taken, and I would add a further note. Horsley has used the term "peasantry" indiscriminately to describe the Galilean insurgents when, in fact, Josephus's account (regarding John of Gischala and Justus of Tiberias) clearly shows that the leading revolutionaries were often people of substance with important political contacts. Yet there is a subtle distinction to be made between the sympathies of those from the free cities and those (like John) who were residents of the rural toparchies. Cf. M. Goodman, "The First Jewish Revolt: Social Conflict and the Problem of Debt," *JJS* 33 (1982) 417–26.

69. Freyne, *Galilee, Jesus, and the Gospels*, 213–18.
70. Joseph. *AJ* 18.143–60; cf. Smallwood, *Jews under Roman Rule*, 187–92.

claim both Herodian and Hasmonean lineage, and, according to Josephus, he was widely supported by the Jewish population despite his taste for Roman culture.[71] In particular, his reign enlarged the political-administrative borders of the Galilee to the north and expanded the trade networks with adjacent regions through civic benefactions (most notably to the Tyrian coastal cities) and alignments with other client-kings in the Syro-Phoenician region (see map 3).[72] This new kingdom was short-lived, however, as Agrippa I died suddenly at Caesarea Maritima in 44 C.E. Since his son, Agrippa II, was too young to assume the throne, the emperor Claudius placed the entire Herodian kingdom under direct procuratorial control.

It should be noted, then, that whereas Judaea had experienced procuratorial rule from 6 to 41 C.E. (after Archelaus was deposed), Galilee had never been under direct Roman rule until after the death of Agrippa I. There is further significance to this perceived change in the status of Galilee. Whereas political resistance and unrest had occurred sporadically from the early Herodian period, the real escalation began only after the death of Agrippa I and the arrival of the new series of Roman procurators. In contrast to the situation in Judaea, the known cases of insurrection prior to 66 from the Galilee involved situations of changing the administrative borders and the implications for taxation.[73]

Another change in the administrative situation arose in 48 C.E. after the death of a brother of Agrippa I, Herod the client-king of Chalcis. In the following year, the ethnarch of Ituraea Soemus (or Sohaemus) also died.[74] It was then that Claudius granted to Agrippa II the city-territory of Chalcis along with additional territories in Ituraea. The local nobility became his vice-regents.[75]

---

71. *AJ* 19.292–96, 331; cf. Smallwood, *Jews under Roman Rule*, 193–95.

72. *AJ* 19.338–42. Significantly, Agrippa was able to bully Tyre, Sidon, Damascus, and Philadelphia in trade negotiations by exercising economic restrictions and blockades. Cf. Smallwood, *Jews under Roman Rule*, 198.

73. Given the Hasmonean sympathies that had haunted Herod the Great in his early years of Galilean rule (*AJ* 14.158–60, 416–30), it may be that Agrippa was able to consolidate nationalistic hopes around his own Hasmonean lineage. Thus, his unexpected death, combined with the arrival of non-Jewish administration in Galilee, may well have been perceived with increased trepidation. Taxation as a cause for political unrest was already signaled at the time of the census of Quirinius in 6 C.E. when Judas of Gamala ("the Galilean") rose up as a bandit chieftain (*AJ* 18.3–10). Shortly after the death of Agrippa I, two sons of Judas, James and Simon, were executed for insurrection (ca. 46–48) by the procurator Tiberius Julius Alexander (Philo's nephew, whose brother was married to the sister of Agrippa II; cf. *AJ* 20.102). Another son of Judas was Menahem, who led the group that captured Masada at the outbreak of the war (cf. *BJ* 2.433–45). The background of John of Gischala in this regard has already been mentioned (above, n. 64).

74. Cf. Joseph. *BJ* 2.481; Tac. *Ann.* 12.23. Sohaemus seems to have been a local noble of the Antilebanon region, whose kin ruled as clients in the city-territory of Emesa, near Antioch. It appears that Sohaemus was made tetrarch of Ituraea in 39 C.E., after the death of Agrippa I, when portions of Agrippa's kingdom were taken under direct administration of Syria, cf. Cass. Dio *Hist.* 59.12.2.

75. Cf. *Vit.* 55. Varus, Viceroy to Agrippa II, is said to be a hereditary claimant to Sohaemus's "kingdom," and hence resentful of Agrippa. In part Agrippa's takeover in Ituraea may

By ca. 50–52 Agrippa II was granted the Transjordan regions (Gaulanitis, Batanea, Trachonitis, and Hauranitis) along with portions of the district of Lisanius around the city-territory of Abilene.[76] Finally, it seems to have been the intention of Claudius and his successor, Nero, eventually to cede all of the kingdom of Agrippa I to Agrippa II by annexing additional territories in piece-meal fashion. One such provision occurred ca. 54–56, when the Galilee was split down the middle from north to south. The eastern half (including the Sea of Galilee and its major cities) was annexed to his Transjordan kingdom (see map 4). Tiberias then became one of the chief free cities of the kingdom of Agrippa II, while Sepphoris once again became the capital of the Roman pro-vincial district of Galilee.[77]

This was the political situation when the Revolt broke out in 66 C.E. It is perhaps indicative that the Jewish insurgents in Galilee immediately took over a good portion of Agrippa's kingdom both in the Galilee and in the Transjordan (see map 4).[78] It may be suggested, then, that the change of administrative boundaries had some impact on the situation, since territorial borders usually marked tax districts for trade and market goods. A.H.M. Jones suggests that the duty on goods crossing such territorial boundaries in the provinces could range from 2 percent (at interprovincial boundaries) to as high as 20 percent (on the frontier).[79] The administrative changes just prior to the revolt had perhaps disrupted the market exchange system of Galilee in unique ways by establishing new duty zones that crossed traditional market lines. Agrippa II had important links with Ituraea, Chalcis, and Abilene and with the Tyrian coastal cities. He held territories as far away as Coela-Syria and Armenia Major.[80] He also made frequent trips to Antioch to confer with the Legate of

have been facilitated through contracted marriages; his sister Drusilla, before marrying Antonius Felix, was married to Azizus of Emesa, where Soemus (Sohaemus) also had relations. Cf. *AJ* 20.158. Herod of Chalcis and, later, Agrippa II exercised the hereditary authority of confirming the high priest in Jerusalem following the death of Agrippa I.

76. Cf. Joseph. *AJ* 20.189–96; Smallwood, *Jews under Roman Rule*, 278–79. Because of the nature of these client-kingships, Agrippa II dealt directly with the Legate of Syria from his capital at Caesarea Philippi, though he also maintained the Herodian palace at Jerusalem and kept close contact with the procurator of Judaea.

77. This provision seems to have been a reward by the emperor for Agrippa's assistance in sending troops to face the Parthians, cf. Tac. *Ann.* 13.7.1. At this time Tiberias began striking coins of Agrippa, while Sepphoris began striking imperial coinage. Agrippa II was also given two toparchies in the region of Peraea, Abila and Livias-Julias. Cf. Smallwood, *Jews under Roman Rule*, 273. Note that when Jesus is reported as leaving Capernaum and going to his own country (Mark 6:1 = Matt 13:53, though it is a more distinct departure in Mark), it may reflect this sense of the division between eastern and western Galilee in the time of Agrippa II.

78. Cf. Joseph. *BJ* 2.569–79; 3.55–58; *Vit.* 28–29, 46–61, 77–79. In numerous references Josephus details Agrippa's role in cautioning the insurgents and supporting Rome, cf. *BJ* 2.345–407. Eventually, Vespasian went to consult with Agrippa II at Caesarea Philippi, *BJ* 3.443.

79. A.H.M. Jones, *The Decline of the Ancient World* (London: Longmans, Green, 1966) 21.

80. The last by virtue of another grandson of Herod the Great, Tigranes IV of Armenia, a

Syria while his sister, Drusilla, was married to Antonius Felix, the procurator from ca. 52–60.[81] Jewish communities lived far and wide in Agrippa's domain.

During the Revolt, much of Galilee, especially the larger cities, capitulated very quickly, and the entire region was pacified by the end of 67. After the war ended in 74, the provincial status of Judaea was upgraded and placed under its own Roman *legatus*. In the north, much of the territory of Agrippa II was returned to him with additional territories in Syria as a reward for his loyalty.[82] It seems, however, that some of the hotly disputed lands of the eastern Galilee were retained under Roman control of the Legate of Judaea.[83] On the death of Agrippa II (ca. 92–93) his domain reverted to the Province of Syria, thus producing the peculiar boundaries that existed down to the time of the Second Revolt (see map 5).[84] It also appears that a portion of the northern expansion of Galilee achieved under Agrippa I was ceded once again to Phoenicia (Syria).[85] With this new provincial status, the political boundaries for the Jewish population of Galilee, the Transjordan, and the Syro-Phoenician cities were once again subject to administrative changes, while culturally there was a lively exchange.

It is to this era of administrative reorganization that one should look for keys to the crisis behind Matthew's Gospel, since the issues of taxation and political boundaries were changed sharply. It is also the case that the situation of Jewish communities in the "near Diaspora" was directly affected by these same changes, especially in the requirement that all Jews pay the *didrachma* tax to Rome.[86] Jewish communities formerly in the Galilee or in the domain of

portion of whose land was entrusted as a hereditary bequest to Agrippa II in 60 C.E. while his cousin Aristobulus, son of the late Herod of Chalcis, was given charge of Armenia Minor; cf. Joseph. *AJ* 20.158; Tac. *Ann.* 13.7.2; 14.26.

81. Joseph. *AJ* 20.139.

82. One such prize was the city-territory of Arca, near Emesa in Coela-Syria (cf. *BJ* 7.97). At about the same time (ca. 72–73, when Vespasian set about reorganizing the eastern provinces after becoming emperor), his cousin Aristobulus (having lost Armenia Minor when it was once again annexed to Syria for strategic purposes) was given the city of Chalcis (Chalcidice) near Antioch (cf. *BJ* 7.219–43). Agrippa was honored with the *ornamenta praeatoria* on a state visit to Rome in 75, cf. Cass. Dio *Hist.* 66.15.3–4. He received other honors as well, such as dedications at a temple of Atargatis (cf. Smallwood, *Jews under Roman Rule*, 339 n. 35).

83. It is possible, however, that Tiberias (and thus the access around the southern end of the Sea of Galilee) remained in Agrippa's domain, while the Upper Galilee and part of the Golan seem to have become part of the province of Judaea. Cf. Smallwood, *Jews under Roman Rule*, 339–40.

84. On the date of Agrippa's death, see the discussion by Smallwood, *Jews under Roman Rule*, 572–74.

85. The two regions of Phoenicia (Prima, with capital at Tyre, and Libanensis, with capital at Damascus) were not organized in this fashion and made independent of the Province of Syria until the reign of Septimius Severus (ca. 193–211 C.E.). Meanwhile, the areas of the Hauran and the Decapolis were reorganized as a separate province of Arabia under Trajan in 106 C.E.

86. On taxation in Judaea after 70, see Smallwood, *Jews under Roman Rule*, 343–45, with special notice regarding Vespasian's appropriation of the temple tax in 71–72; also Applebaum, in *The Jewish People in the First Century*, CRINT 1.1:460–63; and idem, I.2:698–99.

Agrippa II (hence with direct ties to the homeland) were now part of the province of Syria.[87] Here, too, there evolved a complex and checkered history for the diffusion of Christian groups in this mixed Jewish and gentile environment, as evidenced by the later appearance of a "Marcionite synagogue" in the region of Damascus.[88] Would that the Matthean community had left a lintel stone to signal its precise geographic location.

The breakup of the kingdom of Agrippa II was a time of massive administrative changes, not only for the Galilee and Golan but for the regions formerly in his domain from Ituraea to Coela-Syria. The loss of a "Jewish" monarch in these regions meant there was now a greater vacuum for those Jewish (and Christian) communities living outside the borders of the homeland. It is also possible to see it as the occasion for the expansion of new lines of religious authority associated with the consolidation of the rabbinic academy in the Yavnean period (from ca. 90–120 C.E.).[89] Over time it would give rise to the development of both the patriarchate and the uniquely Galilean synagogue organization.[90] It may be argued that the patriarchate developed as much from

87. Note the epitaph of Alexandra daughter of Alexander (CIJ I.501) for epigraphic evidence (albeit somewhat confused in previous interpretations) of Jews from Arca (Agrippa's territory in Lebanon) later in Rome. Against Frey's reading of this as evidence for a "Synagogue of the Jews of Arca," however, see H. J. Leon, *The Jews of Ancient Rome* (Philadelphia: Jewish Publication Society, 1960) 163–65; cf. Smallwood, *Jews under Roman Rule*, 505. Similarly, compare CIJ I.500 (= IGRR I.180), an epitaph of a Jew named Agrippas from Phaena in Trachonitis.

88. A lintel inscription from the Synagogue of the Marcionites, dating perhaps to the beginning of the fourth century C.E. from the village of Lebaba (Deir-Ali, about three m. south of Damascus), was published in P. Le Bas and J. Waddington, *Inscriptions Grecques et Latines de Syrie* (Paris: F. Didot, 1898) 3.2558. See also the discussion of the regional spread of Christian groups in Adolf von Harnack, *The Mission and Expansion of Early Christianity* (trans. J. Moffatt; London: Williams & Norgate, 1908) 2. 108–35.

89. The traditional date of the so-called council of Yavneh is ca. 90 and would correspond to some of these same developments. However, as many recent studies have shown, the developments of the Yavnean period were in no way enacted at one time, but were a more gradual process. So see Shaye J. D. Cohen, "The Significance of Yavneh: Pharisees, Rabbis, and the End of Jewish Sectarianism," *HUCA* 55 (1984) 27–53; Neusner, *From Politics to Piety*, 97–122. As with the traditions attributed to Hillel and Shammai in an earlier generation, so too with Yavneh there tends to be a telescoping of later developments onto the earlier period. One must be very careful in using the chronology of a "final separation" suggested by James Parke (*The Conflict of Church and Synagogue: A Study in the Origins of Antisemitism* [New York: Meridian; Philadelphia: Jewish Publication Society, 1961] 71–91) by claiming that letters to Palestinian synagogues denouncing Christians were already being used between 80 and 90. On the developments relative to Christian groups in the synagogues see R. Kimelman, "*Birkat Ha-Minim* and the Lack of Evidence for an Anti-Christian Jewish Prayer in Late Antiquity," *Jewish and Christian Self-Definition*, ed. Sanders, 2. 226–44; Asher Finkel, "Yavneh's Liturgy and Early Christianity," *Journal of Ecumenical Studies* 18 (1981) 231–50; W. Horbury, "The Benediction of the *Minim* and Early Jewish-Christian Controversy," *JTS* 33 (1982) 19–61.

90. On the patriarchate, see Goodman, *State and Society in Roman Galilee*; Lee I. Levine, "The Jewish Patriarch (Nasi) in Third Century Palestine," *ANRW* 2.19.2:649–88; and A. I. Baumgarten, "The Politics of Reconciliation: The Education of R. Judah the Prince," *Jewish and Christian Self-Definition*, ed. Sanders, 2. 213–25. For recent archaeological evidence on the beginnings of Galilean synagogue architecture, see Meyers and Kraabel, "Archaeology, Iconography, and Nonliterary Written Remains," *Early Judaism and Its Modern Interpreters*, ed. Kraft and Nickelsburg, 177–81 (with further bibliography); E. M. Meyers, "Ancient Synagogues in the

the role of local Jewish nobility in the toparchy and city-territory organization as from rabbinic organizational norms. Jewish communities in the Upper Galilee and Golan through the Amoraic period would develop their own peculiar style once rabbinic norms had come into force at the end of the second century. Following the breakup of the last Herodian kingdom, existing communities of Jews or Jewish-Christians might well have found the new authority to be intrusive, especially if it began to impose strictures on observance and liturgy or on their traditional exercise of social boundaries between Jews and Gentiles.[91] There are further indications that Jews and Christians in and around the homeland faced crises during the reign of Domitian.[92]

MATTHEW'S SOCIAL LOCATION:
A SUGGESTION

It is possible to suggest the following scenario under which the Matthean Gospel was produced. The Gospel of Matthew was composed not only to reinforce longstanding beliefs of an existing Christian community, but also to respond to a crisis that had recently arisen. The identity of the Christian group was being threatened. Matthew's christological image is part of a response to contemporary issues of authority by recasting the traditional source materials of the life of Jesus. The conflict between Jesus and the Pharisees, heightened and polemicized through Matthean literary redaction, represents the core of this crisis (albeit not from Jesus' day but) from the immediate experience of the Matthean community itself. The disciples of Jesus have been persecuted from one village to the next, hated and betrayed by kinsfolk, flogged in "their" synagogues, and brought to trial before councils (συνέδρια), governors (ἡγεμόνας), and kings (10:17–25; cf. 23:34).[93] The redactional position and

Galilee: Their Religious and Cultural Setting," *BA* 43 (1980) 97–108; idem, "Ancient Gush Halav (Giscala), Palestinian Synagogues, and the Eastern Diaspora," *Ancient Synagogues,* 61–78; idem, "Early Judaism and Christianity in the Light of Archaeology," *BA* 51 (1988) 69–79. On relations with synagogues from the Golan, see also Zvi Ma'oz and A. Killebrew, "Ancient Qasrin: Synagogue and Village," *BA* 51 (1988) 5–19; and Zvi Ma'oz, "Ancient Synagogues in the Golan," *BA* 51 (1988) 116–28. See also the study of the city square as a possible line of development as suggested in the article of S. Hoenig, "The Ancient City-Square" (n. 21, above).

91. See the suggestive article by L. A. Hoffman, "Censoring In and Censoring Out: A Function of Liturgical Language," *Ancient Synagogues,* 19–38.

92. It strikes me now as more than coincidence that Domitian's economic reorganization was perceived as part of a persecution against several Jewish (including Christian) groups or individuals in the mid-90s, cf. Cass. Dio *Hist.* 67; Eus. *Hist. Eccl.* 3.13–20; E. M. Smallwood, "Domitian's Attitudes toward the Jews and Judaism," *Classical Philology* 51 (1961) 1–13.

93. These terms, including συνεδρία, come from the technical vocabulary of local authority of city-districts, local ἐπάρχοι and procurators, and client-kings. The conflict is one in which the Matthean Christians, having previously been accepted or tolerated, have recently been undercut before local secular authorities by the emerging Pharisaic authority. Thus, see also the suggestion made above, n. 40.

shape of this unit of material in Matthew is at the heart of the conflict and the crisis. For it is also the discourse unit that sets up the understanding of the mission of the sectarian community, the ἐκκλησία, relative to both its Jewish heritage and its gentile environment.

Initially, the Matthean Jesus had sent out "disciples" to proclaim the coming apocalyptic kingdom "only to the lost sheep of the house of Israel" (10:5; cf. 15:24) and only in the towns and villages of Israel (10:23). Gentiles and Samaritans were initially excluded (10:5). But in the end, after the rejection of Jesus by his own townsfolk (13:53–58) and ultimately by Jerusalem (23:37–39), the door was opened for them to "make disciples of all nations" (28:18–20; cf. 15:21–28; 21:43).[94] Those who now persecute the disciples (23:34) are seen as direct descendants of those who rejected both Jesus and the prophets before him (21:33–46). Their rejection legitimates the formation of a new "people" (ἔθνος, 21:43).[95] Significantly, it is not the message or identity of Jesus alone (a vestigial element from a previous generation) that is the new element of debate within Matthew's context. Rather, it seems to be a question of using the tradition and authority of Jesus (God's Wisdom, the source of Torah) to define and legitimate the nature of the Matthean community as a Jewish sect. Central are the themes of discipleship and faith and the place of Jews and Gentiles in the better righteousness. Thus, the character of the religious community has been called into question by others, who likewise have strong boundaries of piety and observance. The Matthean apologetic here reflects charges of moral laxity that had been leveled at the community. They had abrogated proper Jewish observance and were consorting with outsiders. At the same time, it was difficult to escape the fact that their own vestigial claims of Jewishness seemed to validate these criticisms, while there were other traditions in Matthew's background that legitimated contact with Gentiles.[96]

94. The Matthean redactional placement of the rejection at Nazareth relative to the geographical progression of Jesus' ministry (and death) is significantly different from that in Mark. (Luke-Acts, of course, has its own redactional shift on this same material, cf. Luke 4:16–30.) Cf. Freyne, *Galilee, Jesus, and the Gospels*, 70–90.

95. On the redaction of 10:5–42, see A.-J. Levine, *The Social and Ethnic Dimensions of Matthaean Salvation History: "Go nowhere among the Gentiles" (Matt 10:5b)* (Lewiston, N.Y.: Edwin Mellen, 1988) passim. It seems that despite the generally negative portrayal of the Pharisees throughout Matthew, the real emphasis is less on their role in killing Jesus and more on their present rejection of the Christians' proclamation about him. Cf. Jack D. Kingsbury, "The Developing Conflict between Jesus and the Jewish Leaders in Matthew," *CBQ* 49 (1987) 57–63.

96. Here I agree with Schweizer ("Matthew's Church," 141–43) that the document clearly reflects an awareness of earlier stages in the life of the community. He suggests that what we have here called the internal tensions (reflected in the Matthean reshaping of Q material) are a result of differing lines of development within the Christian matrix over the ideal of "discipleship." This is consistent also with the vestigial element described above. Schweizer suggests further (pp. 143–45) that one may track some of these alternative lines from the diverse elements in Matthew to later Syrian Christian forms. While such analysis is beyond the scope of this discussion, it seems to me that such analysis is most desirable in the light of recent work on the social history of the region, as suggested in nn. 30–33, 47, and 88 above.

The emergence of a *new* Pharisaic alliance in the aftermath of the First Revolt and the ensuing provincial reorganizations precipitated a conflict with an already existing Christian community. The parameters of this new alliance involve an alignment of Pharisaic groups with both a professional scribal class and local civic and "synagogal" organizations.[97] While none of the major free cities of the Lower Galilee are ever mentioned, an urban location for the Matthean community in the outlying regions is not precluded. What is more at issue in Matthew is the growing tension felt by the community over the intrusion of Pharisaic authority into their region so that they were being marginalized. A significant narrative unit to read in this light is the Q woe-saying against Chorazin, Bethsaida, and Capernaum (Matt 11:20–24 = Luke 10:13–15). These three towns mark the boundaries of Lower Galilee (narratively the arena of Jesus' confrontation with the Pharisees) with the surrounding village cultures of the Upper Galilee and Golan (the arena of gentile contact). In the same unit Jesus says that it will be better for the Greek cities of Tyre and Sidon in the final apocalyptic judgment.[98] This geographic tension symbolizes the

97. Cf. Morton Smith, *Jesus the Magician* (New York: Harper, 1978) 157. I am not persuaded by the criticism of Smith by James D. G. Dunn, "Pharisees, Sinners, and Jesus," *The Social World of Formative Christianity and Judaism*, 280, though his discussion of factionalism is helpful. On the role of "scribes," it should be noted that the term could designate both secular and religious officials. Thus, it may be worth considering the notion that they represented a local class of professional "retainers" associated with the administration, who after the reorganization were forced to new social, political, and religious alliances. Cf. Freyne, *Galilee, Jesus, and the Gospels*, 206 and n. 62. See also the discussion of role and status for scribal groups by Antoinette Wire (above, p. 87).

98. The redactional position of this unit (Matt 11:21–24) should be noted; cf. Celia Deutsch, *Hidden Wisdom and Easy Yoke: Wisdom, Torah, and Discipleship in Matthew 11:25–30* (JSNTSup 18; Sheffield: JSOT, 1987) chap. 3. In Matthew the unit is placed well after the mission discourse (10:5–42) but before the rejection at Nazareth (13:53), after which Jesus actually goes to the regions of Tyre and Sidon (15:21). This is a reversal of the geographic progression in Mark: rejection (Mark 6:1–6a), expanded mission (6:6b–13), and then the journey to regions of Tyre and Sidon (7:24–30). Matthew has also used the Q mission material in a different way to supplement this shaping. For in Luke the woe against Chorazin and Bethsaida (Luke 10:13–15) appears directly in the mission discourse material (Luke 10:2–12, 16 = Matt 10:7–16, 40), where the blessing on Tyre and Sidon is balanced nicely by a parallel blessing on Sodom and Gomorrah (Luke 10:12). By this parallelism, also, the woeful response of Chorazin and Bethsaida is equated with the implied judgment upon those households that do not properly receive the traveling Christian teachers (Luke 10:10–11). The original form of the Q unit as followed by Luke, therefore, was already used to legitimate an existing gentile mission. In Matthew, however, the Chorazin-Bethsaida/Tyre-Sidon unit is used to demonstrate that those to whom the mission was first intended (i.e., "the lost sheep of the house of Israel," 10:5), had in fact failed to respond. It thereby foreshadows the turn toward a broader audience, though not an immediate abandonment of the mission to its primary Jewish audience. Even after the Matthean rejection at Nazareth, Jesus is still resisting a mission to Gentiles, until the "faith" demonstrated by the Syro-Phoenician woman begins to show that non-Jews also could demonstrate appropriate signs of true discipleship. It becomes an important way of legitimating the transformation of the exclusively Jewish mission material for a wider audience of mixed Jews and Gentiles. Nonetheless, for Matthew it does not mean an abrogation of a basically Jewish self-understanding of the mission, since it retains its traditionally Jewish sectarian markers. When combined with the final commissioning (Matt 28:18–20) it authorizes the current self-understanding of the Matthean church, so that even Gentiles can become disciples.

conflict situation of Matthew's community, although it does not necessarily betray an explicit location.

The Matthean community clearly looks to the Galilean ministry of Jesus for its roots, but Lower Galilee represents a distant place. It would appear, then, that the Matthean community looked to the mixed environment—mixed both as Jew-Gentile population and village-urban society—of the Syro-Phoenician region as a symbol of its own situation. Previously, the Matthean community had felt less tension and more openness to both Jewish and Gentile sympathizers in its local environment. With the relaxation of tensions had come a softening of boundaries, a greater sense of acculturation to the Hellenistic environment.[99] The emergence of a new religious leadership has brought a new sense of conflict over authority for both groups and was serving to produce new boundary-defining tensions. The level of polemic against the Pharisees and "their" synagogues also suggests that they had, in fact, managed to disenfranchise some local Christian groups. The new Pharisaic leadership was gaining the upper hand, and the Christian group was losing ground. It was forcing the Christian community to redefine its own identity accordingly through heightened sectarianism and communal boundaries. The pressures from external opposition were also producing internal tensions. Thus, there was not just one Christian group or response at work, just as the Christians were viewed as part of a diverse spectrum of Jewish activity.

The conflict in Matthew, therefore, represents one of the earliest stages of the rift between emerging institutions of Judaism and Christianity in the period between 70 and 132 C.E. Yet it is a localized case. It likely comes from the waning years of Agrippa II or just after his death, when there was reorganization of his territories under direct Roman provincial administration. In this context, local groups of civic and religious leaders began vying for power. Matthew's community could have come from any of the regions of the "nearer diaspora" where the reign of Agrippa had been influential. The rise of Pharisaic groups may have come from the Lower Galilean cities but was now given opportunity to expand into these other areas as well. On many fronts the definition of piety by Christians was virtually identical to that of their Jewish neighbors. Yet there is a competition for "disciples," though one hears nothing of "converts." The tension of the Matthean community with other Jewish groups (or to be more precise, the Pharisees and "their" synagogues) was born of proximity rather than distance, of similarity rather than difference.[100] It is a

99. In this way we may begin to account for some of the decidedly Hellenistic elements of Matthew as well. The Syro-Phoenician region and even the region from the Golan to Ituraea were thoroughly infused with Greek cultural elements, including a famous school of Greek philosophy at Gadara. Thus, see the discussion of Hellenistic elements by Hans Dieter Betz, "The Sermon on the Mount (Matt 5:3—7:27): Its Literary Genre and Function," *Essays on the Sermon on the Mount* (ed. L. L. Welborn; Philadelphia: Fortress, 1985) 1–16.

100. Cf. Segal, *Rebecca's Children*, 146–58. Notice (in sharp contrast to Paul) that

case of "marginal differentiation," where minutiae—or marginal features of faith and practice—are used to preserve a sense of difference between organisms that are otherwise substantially similar.[101] Moreover, because they are dealing in local contexts, where social makeup of the groups is a significant issue, networks of relationships and influence become increasingly important. An alliance of other "discipling" Jews who have won the favor of local leaders (city councils, governors, even kings) was a serious threat. For the Matthean community righteousness and faithfulness are the watchwords of true discipleship for an embattled sect seeking to establish its self-definition on the margins of a Hellenistic Jewish society.

---

circumcision plays no part in the dispute. Matthew assumes circumcision as a given for all who are part of the community. In such contexts the notion of "conversion" has a different force, since all members of the sect are in effect Jews (by birth or adoption). Therefore, the stress on "discipleship" is the distinctive feature of sectarian identity, just as it would be for Pharisees seeking to attract followers from among the broader spectrum of Jews. Cf. Overman, *Matthew's Gospel*, for a convincing discussion of this sense of proximity.

101. The terminology comes from advertising, as a means of distinguishing between two products that are essentially the same in content or substance. It is also closely related to discussions of purity regulations for delimiting the arena of the "sacred" in cultural anthropology; cf. Bruce Malina, *The New Testament World: Insights from Cultural Anthropology* (Atlanta: John Knox, 1981) 137–50. Here, however, we are most concerned with the symbolization of marginal boundaries by which a group (especially one that might be feeling marginalized) seeks to mark off its identity from another group that is largely similar in terms of other boundary maintenance devices. In traditional Jewish categories, purity regulations might serve such purposes as well. In other words, the more the two groups might be alike in social makeup, organization, and basic values, the more likely they will stress marginal features, often based on issues open to debate and interpretation, in order to maintain a distinct identity. Cf. S. Freyne, "Vilifying the Other and Defining the Self: Matthew and John's Anti-Judaism in Focus," *'To See Ourselves as Others See Us': Jews, Christians, and Others in Antiquity* (ed. E. Frerichs and J. Neusner; Atlanta: Scholars, 1985) 117–44.

MAP 1

Regional divisions in the Galilee and environs
from the time of Herod the Great

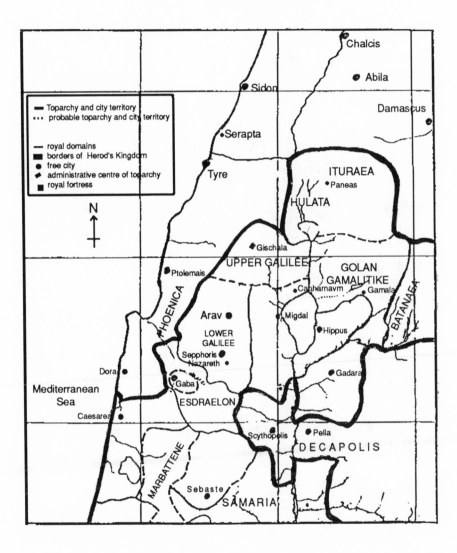

MAP 2

The divisions of Herod's kingdom down to the time of Agrippa I
(4 B.C.E.–41 C.E.)

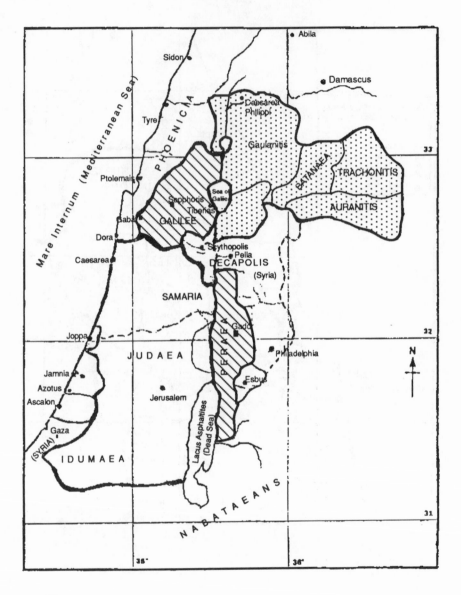

⊠ Tetrarchy of Herod Antipas

▫ Tetrarchy of Philip

MAP 3

The kingdom of Herod Agrippa I
(41–44 C.E.)

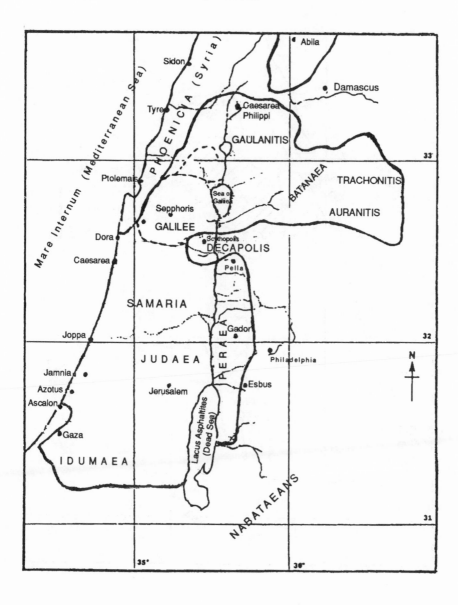

MAP 4

Judaea and the kingdom of Agrippa II
(44–93 C.E.)

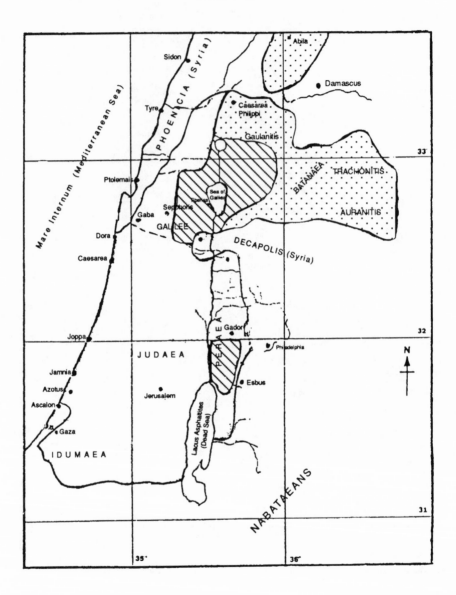

☐ Territories under Agrippa II (52–93 C.E.)

☒ Agrippa's territories taken by insurgents in
the First Revolt (66–67 C.E.)

MAP 5

Provincial boundaries after the death of Agrippa II
(93–211 C.E.)

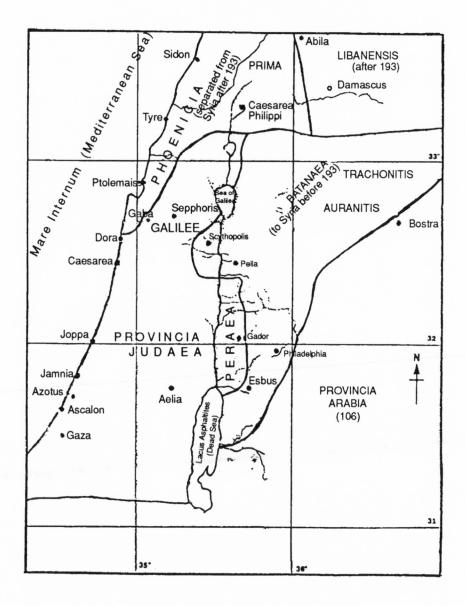

11

Artifacts from Antioch

 FREDERICK W. NORRIS

Near the end of the first century and the beginning of the second century C.E., Antioch on the Orontes was no less than the fourth largest city of the Mediterranean world behind Rome, Alexandria, and Seleucia on the Tigris. Yet information about its entire history is sorely lacking. Theodor Mommsen indicated that inscriptions from greater Antioch were worthy of a small North African town; the excavations of 1932 to 1939 only strengthened that judgment.[1] The great Hellenistic histories of the city are lost.[2] Most of our written sources deal only obliquely with Antioch as they tell of other things. With the

This essay is an edited version of a slide lecture given at the conference. That lecture pictured the topography of Antioch proper, the artifacts for Isis and Sarapis worship in greater Antioch, and the argument against Festugière's comment on the mosaics of greater Antioch. Only the latter portion appears here and that in a revised form, particularly in response to criticism by William Babcock of Southern Methodist University.

1. Theodor Mommsen, *Römische Geschichte*, Bd. 5 (Berlin: Weidemann, 1885) 460. Only 245 Greek or Latin inscriptions, mostly fragmentary, were published in the reports of the excavations. They provide little information about the city. See G. W. Elderkin, "Greek and Latin Inscriptions," *Antioch-on-the-Orontes I: The Excavations of 1932* (Princeton: Princeton University Press, 1934) 52–53; Glanville Downey, "Greek and Latin Inscriptions," *Antioch-on-the-Orontes II: The Excavations of 1933–1936* (Princeton: Princeton University Press, 1938) 148–65; and idem, "Greek and Latin Inscriptions," *Antioch-on-the-Orontes III: The Excavations 1937–1939* (Princeton: Princeton University Press, 1941) 83–115. The journal *Syria* has published a few Antiochian inscriptions discovered since the publication of the last excavation report that includes inscriptions, but none of them adds anything to our knowledge of the period upon which this conference focused. All subsequent references to the archaeological reports will use the abbreviation *AO* with the volume and page numbers.

2. Glanville Downey, *A History of Antioch in Syria from Seleucus to the Arab Conquest* (Princeton: Princeton University Press, 1961) 35–38, discusses those histories.

exception of John Malalas's sixth-century C.E. world chronicle, which includes parts of the city's archives from throughout its history, and Libanius's fourth-century C.E. *Oration* 11, which praises the metropolis and thus gives us a look at one rhetorician's view of its life over the course of its existence, we have little written record of its days. Some texts, particularly John Chrysostom's sermons and the corpus of Libanius from the fourth century C.E., tell us many things about its social history but they are too late for first-century interests.

For those concerned with the social history of the Matthean community in Roman Syria, the evidence from or about Antioch is meager or totally lacking. I see no particular reason to doubt the information that the book of Acts supplies concerning Christianity in the city. As Acts 11 indicates, earliest Antiochian Christianity grew out of at least two preaching traditions, one limited to the Jewish community, the other open to direct contact with Gentiles. That context clarifies the agreements and disagreements among Paul, Peter, Barnabas, and James's people from Jerusalem—referred to in some way within Acts 15 and Galatians 1–2. The Latin and Jewish names of leaders within the Antiochian Christian community, mentioned in Acts 13, appear appropriate given the two preaching traditions, the large Jewish community, and the Roman influence in the city after the conquest of the region in 63 B.C.E. Indeed the strange figure of Menaen (Menahem?), the σύντροφος of Herod Antipas, well fits Antioch's fragmentary history. Herod the Great, in order to show his appreciation of Roman hegemony, poured part of his wealth into the metropolis by paving its main street with marble sometime between 30 and 20 B.C.E. It seems likely that he had Jewish agents in the city to oversee the project. Perhaps his son, Herod Antipas, continued that kind of embassy, and one of them, a friend from his earliest days, was a leader in Antiochian Christianity.[3]

Disappointingly, however, there is no specific archaeological information known to me that would link the Gospel of Matthew with Syrian Antioch. The coin evidence used by B. H. Streeter proved to be of little value since that type of issue was not restricted to the city. Streeter's main argument rests upon the assumption that a Gospel as important as Matthew must come from a large urban center with great influence.[4] Such an assumption is unprovable on the basis of the information we have. Even on the level of proposed models for interpretation, church history will not sustain the presupposition that influential writings must come from large urban centers. It may be the case

3. Ibid., 173–74; Malalas, *Chronographia*, ed. L. Dindorfii (1831) 223; Joseph. *BJ* 1.425; idem, *AJ* 16.148.

4. B. H. Streeter, *The Four Gospels: A Study of Origins* (New York: Macmillan, 1929) 500–528, esp. 504. The stater mentioned in Matt 17:24–27 had been interpreted as one that equalled two drachma, but the text can be understood as referring to a stater that was equal to four drachma.

that they must be accepted in such important places to reach a wide audience, but many oft-copied writers from the patristic period did not live or work in major centers. Leisure and learning were necessary for the writing of Matthew, but they are not restricted to urban centers in any century. Even the apparent knowledge of the written Matthew or of oral tradition similar to Matthew that one sees in Ignatius does not secure an Antiochene origin for that Gospel. That knowledge only means that a Matthean tradition or the written Gospel circulated in the Antiochene Christian community of Ignatius's time.[5]

The discoveries of the 1932–1939 excavations sponsored by Princeton, the Sorbonne, and others have been most helpful for describing the city of Antioch, but they have provided no important artifacts for early Christianity or first- and second-century C.E. Judaism.[6] The Jewish community in Antioch was large, perhaps occupying not only a specific quarter in the southeastern part of the city proper but also a section outside the city in the plain to the northeast. But because the modern city of Antakya covered the Jewish quarter, only a few trial trenches were sunk in the southeastern region, where the largest part of the Jewish community probably lived, and none in the northeastern area outside the walls of the ancient city.[7]

What may be of interest and can be provided, however, by an armchair archaeologist—one who has visited Antakya twice and has studied the artifacts on display in the Louvre, the McCormick Museum at Princeton, and the city museum at Antakya—are some suggestions about what constitutes appropriate canons for interpreting artifacts as evidence for religious attitudes. Not many New Testament scholars feel confident in interpreting nontextual sources. Perhaps this essay can offer some introduction to what a person can learn from one portion of that kind of data. Antioch is an interesting test case because its epigraphic materials are so sparse and the materials from its previous excavation in such disarray. Few of the artifacts, which the Sorbonne, Princeton, and the other colleges and universities took away with them after the 1932–39 excavations, are actually on display. The bulk of the materials outside Turkey are in Paris and Princeton. Most of those at Princeton are housed in the Armory.

5. In his section of *Antioch and Rome: New Testament Cradles of Catholic Christianity* (New York: Paulist, 1983) 18–27 [written with Raymond E. Brown], John P. Meier handily collects the various arguments concerning the place of Matthew's composition. He cautiously claims only that Antioch is "the most viable hypothesis." It was clear, however, at the conference, that other regions, particularly Upper Galilee, still have their supporters.

6. A crude menorah was scratched on one monument along with the word *GOLB*, but it was difficult to date and provided no real information of value. See *AO* II.150–51; and Edwin R. Goodenough, *Jewish Symbols in the Greco-Roman Period* (New York: Pantheon, 1954) 4.71–98.

7. In terms of the broader history of Antioch, neither the campus martius nor the Syrian quarter were excavated. The latter was covered by the modern city, and the former contained no landmarks that suggested places the archaeologists should dig. Thus lack of information for the social and religious aspects of Roman legions or Syrian citizens cannot be used as negative answers. We simply do not have specific data about those sections of the population.

The greatest single collection of materials at Antakya, modern Antioch, poses a large problem because the pieces are not numbered in any way that corresponds to the numbers that appear in the published reports or the field notes from the dig. Furthermore, other sites in greater Antioch have been excavated since 1939 and a number of materials have been purchased by the Antakya museum since that date. Another complication arises from the knowledge that Antakya has a small but potent industry devoted to the creation of forged artifacts. Thus pieces within its museum that have no well-documented history must be tested not only for provenance but also for genuineness. Yet Andrew Overman's suggestion in his portion of the closing summary of the conference is correct. If Antioch remains a possible site for the place of Matthew's community, both on the basis of allusions to material similar to that in Matthew which appears in Ignatius and on the basis of suggestions in early church fathers, it stands as a place that might be redug and certainly a site whose museum holdings should be carefully examined. The local officials at Antakya have tried to be careful about preserving their ancient heritage by supervising any excavations for private or public projects. There is also much to be gleaned from the artifacts that are already out of the ground.

For the purposes of this essay, however, focus on the mosaics of Antioch makes the most sense. Dated primarily from the second through the fifth centuries, they are the acknowledged treasures discovered during the excavations. Festugière, however, warned thirty years ago that the figures depicted in these decorations could not be trusted as indicative of the religious values or beliefs held by the home's occupants. For him they are reminiscent of the seventeenth-century wealthy French residences which held a conglomeration of pagan artifacts all chosen on the basis of their owners' sense of art and decoration, not their Catholic faith.[8] I wish to challenge that view, but with certain cautions. Many of the mosaics from greater Antioch contain only varied designs and nonreligious representations.[9] Had the quality of the art been the

---

8. A. J. Festugière, *Antioche painne et chrétienne: Libanius, Chrysostome et les moines de Syrie* (Paris: E. de Boccard, 1959) 12, specifically argues that many Christian families had apparently pagan artifacts in their homes just as seventeenth-century French families did. Their faith was not to be read from the decorations of their homes.

9. The excavation reports list the number of mosaics as 180, but some of those mosaics have multiple panels. See G. W. Elderkin, "The Figure Mosaics," *AO* I.42–48. References to mosaics made up entirely of geometric patterns occur in relation to the buildings on pp. 4, 12, and 23. See also "Catalogue of Mosaics," *AO* II.180–204; and W. A. Campbell and Richard Stillwell, "Catalogue of Mosaics," *AO* III.171–219. Sheila Campbell, *The Mosaics of Antioch* (Subsidia Mediaevalis 15. Corpus of Mosaic Pavements in Turkey; Toronto: Pontifical Institute of Mediaeval Studies, 1988), is republishing the mosaics in two volumes. She numbers the mosaics at 178. Volume 2 includes an appendix on the various geometric designs (pp. 85–100).

A number of the mosaics have figured panels as their distinctive features, but enough are of geometric design or have the representation of nonreligious figures that intentional choice can be defended for some specific mosaics.

only concern, such geometric designs, representations of hunts, or depictions of various flora and fauna as well as birds and animals would have sufficed. The selection of particular themes within the emblemata of the mosaics may indicate choices based on specific ideals important to the family, ideals different from a general desire to make the home attractive. All figures in the mosaics found in greater Antioch are not related to such ambiguous concerns. Some are distinctive enough to be representations of significant values within the lives of the homeowners. One mosaic, now displayed at Princeton in the McCormick Museum, has been identified as a scene from a Hellenistic novel, one that concerned Ninus and Semiramis. It lead to the designation of the house in which it was found as the House of the Man of Letters.[10] What its presence reinforces is the sense that intentional representation of things important to the home owners could be a strong part of the choice of mosaics, rather than a general concern for decoration. The owner of this home evidently loved literature and wanted that aspect of the family's life depicted in mosaic.

It is of course true that mosaics were often constructed on the basis of pattern books depicting the various choices available to the home owners. Those decisions at times appear to have been made solely on the basis of quite eclectic or decorative criteria that are not clearly related to any particular religious preferences. One of the largest mosaics, now on display in the museum in Antakya, came from a house uncovered in the excavations at Daphne, a complex named the House of the Red Pavement. This mosaic measures 5.7 by 5.8 meters and can be dated no earlier than the mid-second century. It depicts the myths of Meleager and Atalanta, Phaedra and Hippolytos, Io and Argos, and Adonis's Farewell in the four oblong, outside panels; personifications of the four seasons on the outside corners; and, perhaps, Andromache and Astyanax in the badly damaged center panel.[11] The selection of Io and Argos as one of the panels might give some indication of a specific Antiochian religious interest since Zeus was a principal god of the Seleucid founders of Antioch and is well attested in texts and artifacts.[12] But it seems more likely that this entire depiction represents a joy in the beauty of the various ancient Greek myths than that some special religious intention is involved in the selections. Those who made the decision about mosaics for this home apparently treasured these myths and

10. Doro Levi, *Antioch Mosaic Pavements* (Princeton: Princeton University Press, 1947) 1.117; 2. pl. XXa. See fig. 1.

11. Ibid., 1.68–89, fig. 28; 2, pls. XI–XIII. *AO* III, pls. 66–68, no. 140. See fig. 6. One fragmentary inscription was found under a badly broken mosaic in the same room of this house. The inscription's letter form and broken words suggest that it was created in the early imperial period and probably refers to Tiberius. Thus the earliest date for this mosaic would be after his reign. See Downey, "Greek and Latin Inscriptions," *AO* III.96, inscription no. 160.

12. See the section on Zeus in my article, "Antioch on-the-Orontes as a Religious Center, Part I," *Aufstieg und Niedergang der römischen Welt* 2.18.4 (ed. Haase; Berlin: de Gruyter, 1990) 2322–79.

wanted them prominently displayed. Their choice may have been related to some religious concerns, but there is no way to establish such interests from the mosaic itself. Unfortunately no other information is available about the household.

Another mosaic from the large House of the Buffet Supper in Daphne is similar in size to that of the House of the Red Pavement—somewhat narrower—and depicts Ganymede watering the eagle. It includes many decorative design elements, but it is focused on the tale of Zeus's conquest. Although the central panel is damaged, there is enough of the eagle itself and the youth doing the watering to suggest that Doro Levi's identification of it is correct. In interpreting the panel, Levi also observed that Ganymede watering the eagle is not a common depiction in ancient art.[13] If that is true, the owner of this house evidently wanted this particular scene represented, perhaps because of some specific interest in tales of Zeus. Again, we are not in a position to say that this home belonged to faithful worshipers of the Olympian ruler, but we are dealing with a more clearly defined decision than can be gleaned from the mosaic in the House of the Red Pavement. Here one panel, infrequently depicted in Hellenistic and Roman mosaics, is featured in the most prominent mosaic of the building complex. Why? Religious motivation is one distinct possibility.

A similar situation is suggested by the depiction of Daphne and Apollo in one emblem of a mosaic from Daphne. Here the specific legend of the founding of Daphne is pictured; in it Daphne turns herself into a tree as Apollo approaches. The pursuit of Daphne by Apollo is a common scene represented in ancient art, but the figure here is of that variation on the common legend known from textual sources related to Antioch, one not involved in the tales of Apollo from other cities.[14] At the least this mosaic contains a recognition of the importance of Apollo for the beautiful suburb of Daphne. Given the religious sensitivity of the ancient world, it is perhaps a signal that the owner of the home took pride in the legend, the myth, that Apollo was involved in the city. A large temple dedicated to Apollo dominated Daphne. Thus the inclusion of the specific legend about his presence in the city fits the intertwined aspects of life in greater Antioch: civic pride and religious concern.[15]

---

13. Levi, *Antioch Mosaic Pavements*, 1.130–32; 2, pls. XXIIIa, XXIVa–b. See fig. 3. Although the theme is represented in "several mosaics," particularly the rape of the boy in the air, Levi claims that the depiction of Ganymede watering the eagle is "much rarer." That suggests that there is more likelihood of this theme representing a specific value of the home than the more commonly attested figure.

14. Ibid., 1.211–14; 2, pl. XLVIIb. See fig. 2.

15. The eleventh oration of Libanius insists that Antioch proper is a world-class city because the gods are clearly represented in its temples; in fact, some deities actually migrated to the metropolis because they desired to be there.

Another way that we can see how religious or philosophical symbols were appropriated in mosaics is by looking at the personifications. There are a number of these representations in the Antiochian mosaics. I mention only two. A mosaic, found about nine kilometers east of Antioch at Narlidja, contains the personification of *Soteria* (Σωτηρία, "salvation, deliverance") in what the excavators called the Bath of Apolausis because of another mosaic within the building. The *Soteria* mosaic probably points up at least an interest in healing and good pleasure as Levi indicates.[16] Three personifications of *ktisis* (κτίσις, "founding") were found, two in Daphne-Harbiye and one uncovered just west of the circus outside the walls of Antioch proper. They probably honor proper foundation or the pursuit of acquisition.[17] Dated in the fourth and fifth centuries, these mosaics do not reflect Christian concerns, but they do indicate religious ones. A bath dedicated to Apolausis that pictures *Soteria*, and homes whose floors feature a Bacchic Thiasos and personifications of *Ananeosis* (ἀνανέωσις, "renewal"), *Dunamis* (δύναμις, "power") and *Euandria* (εὐανδρία, "manliness"), *Ge* (γῆ, "earth") and the Seasons, and *Ktisis* (κτίσις) are best identified as emphasizing pagan themes. The religious influence behind the selection of these medallions is pagan even though the words themselves, put in a Christian context, have substantial, even structural importance in Christian doctrine. Libanius provides clear epigraphic evidence that paganism was influential in Antioch during the last half of the fourth century. The intertwining of philosophical and religious concerns in late antiquity is probably the best explanation of why any building would have such panels on its floors.

One of the strangest mosaics from greater Antioch is the Yakto Floor, which measures 7 by 7.2 meters. Discovered just outside of ancient Daphne in the village of Yakto, it has a border that depicts a journey through the city of Antioch as it would have looked in the middle of the fifth century.[18] In one

16. Levi, *Antioch Mosaic Pavements*, 1. 304–6; 2, pls. LXVIId, LXVIIIa–b. See fig. 5. On the basis of pottery sherds, coins, and mosaic style, Lassus dated the building to no earlier than the mid-fifth century, but Levi suggests that since most of the coins found under the mosaics were from the second half of the fourth century, the building and the mosaics may have come from that date and been rearranged in a fifth-century renovation.

17. Ibid., 1. 255, 347, 357–58; 2, pls. LXIc, LXXXIIb, and LXXXVa. See fig. 7–9. The villa in Daphne-Harbiye was dug hurriedly at the end of the 1935 season because the landowner wanted the land for his own agricultural purposes. One Constantinian coin was found under its mosaics; thus they are probably not earlier than the second quarter of the fourth century. The House of Ge and the Seasons in Daphne-Harbiye, in which the second personification appears, was dated in the fifth century. The House of Ktisis was found in 1934 outside the west wall of the circus. No sherds or coins were found that would help fix its date of origin, but its depiction of a beribboned parrot and thus its Persian influence may suggest a fifth-century date, as does a similar, dated mosaic in the House of the Beribboned Parrot, found in Daphne-Harbiye.

18. Ibid., 1. 323–45; 2, pl. LXXXc. See fig. 4. One building represented in the topographical border is designated as τὸ πριβάτον Ἀρδαβουρίου. Because there is an Ardaburius who was *magister militum per Orientum* from 450–457 it is quite likely that this mosaic represents Antioch during that period.

portion the great church of Constantine is pictured with a worshiper at its door. Although much of the border has been destroyed, indeed all of one side, the mosaic does give a sample of what a visitor to Antioch might have seen. It is interesting for the question of religious values because the Constantinian church is featured. That imposing building is not mentioned in Libanius's *Oration* 11 that follows a similar itinerary around the city, even though that church had stood for decades before Libanius wrote. Unfortunately the side of the mosaic that might have featured the various pagan temples that so interested Libanius is the one that had been broken off. We cannot tell how the home-owner reacted to those temples. Thus the evidence is difficult to assess because it cannot be persuasively argued that the owner of the mosaic had any particular Christian convictions and specific focus on paganism, only that he did not have the anti-Christian convictions of Libanius.

Two mosaics from greater Antioch, however, demand a specific religious interpretation. The first from Daphne-Yakto, although difficult to date since it was discovered by accident and had no pottery sherds or coins underneath it, is unmistakably a partial representation of an Isis-Sarapis festival. The figure on the far right carries a sistrum, and the figure on the far left wears the *palla contabulata*, the stole with the half moon, stars, and special fringe. Those features identify the figures as representations of Isis priestesses or perhaps the one on the left as Isis herself.[19] This mosaic was not laid with primarily artistic or decorative purposes in mind since those purposes could have been fulfilled by many other themes. It represents the religious views of the home's owner or family.

The second mosaic found in Antioch proper, and also difficult to date, was identified by Levi as related to Isis worship.[20] It may, however, be a depiction of an initiation into the mysteries of Demeter, as I have argued elsewhere.[21] The figure on the right is Hermes, identified by the caduceus, but in mythology Hermes is also a consort of Demeter. The headdress of the goddess is not the one of the horns around the disk so prominently a part of the crushed bronze figurine found in the Doric temple at Seleucia Pieria and is the type of headdress at times associated with Demeter. Texts from Libanius and Theodoret tell us about a Demeter temple that still existed at least in the fourth century C.E.[22] The family that lived in this complex had a strong

19. Ibid., 1.49–50; 2, pl. VIIIb. See fig. 10.
20. Ibid., 1. 163–66; 2, pl. XXXIIIa. See fig. 11.
21. Norris, "Isis, Sarapis and Demeter in Antioch of Syria," *HTR* 75 (1982) 189–207. In the article I sought to identify the data that deal with Isis-Sarapis in Antioch including texts, a temple ruin, coins, lamp fragments, sculpture, and mosaics.
22. Libanius *Or.* 11.21; 11.125; 15.79. Theodoret *H.E.* 4.21. Louis Jalabert and René Mouterde, *Inscriptions greques et latines de la Syrie* (2.2; Paris: Geuthner, 1929); no. 1672 speaks of a mission from Eleusis to Antioch and Laodicea of Syria in connection with the Demeter festival in Eleusis.

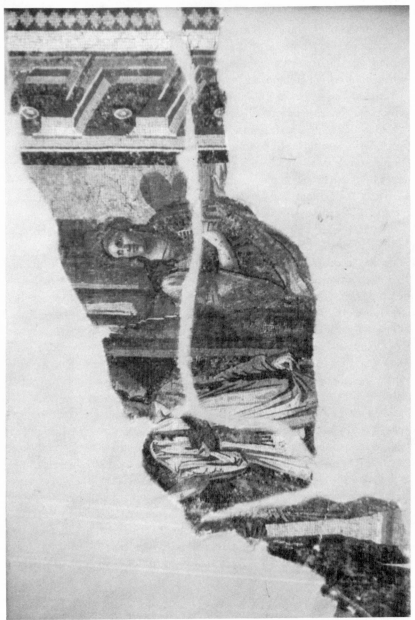

Mosaic of the Isiac Ceremony. Daphne-Yakto, Area 117

concern for mystery religion and had this initiation depicted on its floor. This mosaic is related to specific religious concerns, ones that cannot be explained on the basis of other values.

Finally three apotropaic mosaics from the villa at Jekmejeh village southwest of Antioch are definitely related to religious views. Because of them the building was designated as the House of the Evil Eye, even though the bulk of its mosaics are filled with geometric patterns rather than figures. None of the three figure mosaics represents common public Christian values nor the more public Hellenistic or Roman worship of the acknowledged pantheons. The first two were found under the third in a vestibule opening into the great room of a villa in a village just west of Daphne. The first mosaic is a less frequently attested image, that of the lucky hunchback with his large exposed phallus and his magical sticks. The second depicts Heracles strangling snakes, a picture of that god's power over diseases. The inscription καί σύ is intended to bring laughter and thus to break the spell of any evil spirits. The phrase is perhaps comparable in some sense to the proverbial "you too, buddy," or some other such gesture or word now focused on an enemy rather than a powerful spirit. Plutarch mentions the use of such sentences and pictures to ridicule the powers of magic and evil spirits.[23]

What is most interesting about this particular set of mosaics is that sometime after the earthquake of 115 C.E. the villa seems to have been abandoned only to be refurbished in the fourth or fifth century. There were signs that the structure had been abandoned for a considerable period of time. For some reason a new owner in the fourth or fifth century had the third mosaic laid over the other two. Rather than trying to rely on the lucky hunchback with its ridicule of threatening powers and the tales of Heracles, this new mosaic (in much less elegant detail) clearly depicts the evil eye and attacks it with all sorts of specific tearing animals or gouging implements: a leopard, a bird, a trident, a sword, a scorpion, a snake, a dog, and perhaps a millipede. The inscription καί σύ remains, but now a dwarf with his magic sticks aims his giant phallus at the eye. It is difficult not to think that some disaster had befallen the home, perhaps one well after the earthquake of 115 C.E. There was no evidence for a claim that the structure was always unoccupied between 115 and the fourth or fifth century. The sense of the fourth- or fifth-century homeowner, however, was that more stringent and explicit remedies were called for.[24] Here, more clearly than in any villa at Antioch, the religious intention of mosaics appears. The inability of the first set of apotropaic images to ward off the effects of the

23. Plutarch *Quaestiones convivales* 5.7.3–4 (681E–682B). See Joseph Engemann, "Zur Verbreitung magischer Übelwehr in der nichtchristlichen und christlichen Spätantike," JAC 18 (1975) 22–48, esp. 30–45.

24. Levi, *Antioch Mosaic Pavements*, 1. 28–34; 2, pl. IVa–c. See figs. 12–14.

evil eye moved the new owner to put in place a more specific attack on such evil powers. A clear magical or religious motivation explains the choice of this new mosaic.

It seems then that although many mosaics in Antioch do have only decorative purposes and some are ambiguous concerning the values behind their selection, others warrant the conclusion that religious commitment is the reason for their existence. Artifacts, specifically mosaics, continue to be important, though often ambiguous, evidence for religious values in antiquity.

12

Conclusion:
Analysis of a
Conversation

_____ JACK DEAN KINGSBURY

In the ongoing conversation among authors, respondents, and participants at the conference in Dallas, the steady focus was on the social history of
the Matthean community in Roman Syria. In attempting to draw an initial
balance on this conversation, I should like to discuss, both appreciatively and
critically, (1) matters having to do with methodology, (2) the tentative picture
that emerged of the character and makeup of the Matthean community, (3) the
use of source theories, and (4) directions future research might take.

CONSIDERATIONS REGARDING
METHODOLOGY

In a conference such as that in Dallas, one could well anticipate that the
invited authors would not all make use of the same method of inquiry. Even
granting this, one is still struck, in reading the major papers, by the differences
in methodology characterizing them. Briefly, I should like to sketch the three
methods used by four of the scholars and evaluate them.

The method used by Alan Segal is what I prefer to term "traditional historical inquiry." In his paper on "Matthew's Jewish Voice," Segal concentrates
on Christian attitudes toward the Jewish law as found in the New Testament.
He develops a historical trajectory that extends from the earliest Christian community in Jerusalem to Matthean Christianity. In establishing the historicity of
this trajectory, Segal moves from the literary world of texts and documents
to the social, or real, world to which he argues they refer. Seemingly, the

principle on the basis of which Segal makes this move is that commonly known as "transparency." According to the principle of transparency, select texts or documents may be construed as "windows" because they allegedly provide the interpreter with a direct view into any given historical situation, or context. Apparently, it is with this principle in mind that Segal affirms, "The Christian record ... gives us a unique window into Judaism ..."[1]; and again, "What Matthew offers us is a window on the developing trouble."[2] If there is a weakness to the method of traditional historical inquiry involving use of the principle of transparency, it is that the judgments the interpreter makes concerning which—or to what extent—texts are or are not transparent to the social, or real, world tend to be private in nature and therefore open to the charge of being unduly subjective. Potentially, this weakness could be overcome were we to have at our disposal a rich store of independent data (i.e., data not derived from Matthew's Gospel itself) that would enable us to corroborate results derived from the application of the principle of transparency. Unfortunately, however, the opposite is true: There is a great dearth of such independent data. Consequently, the major problem besetting the method of traditional historical inquiry as employed by Segal is the relative inability of the interpreter to demonstrate that he or she has, in fact, accurately defined the social, or real, world lying behind the text.

The method William Schoedel uses in his social and religious study of Ignatius is also that of "traditional historical inquiry." Like Segal, Schoedel, too, operates with the "principle of transparency." In line with this, he constructs from his reading of Ignatius's letters a historical portrait of Ignatius's own religious and social situation and, to the extent the letters permit, of Ignatius's church in Syria as well. In a summarizing remark, Schoedel explicitly attests to his use of the principle of transparency: "Such are the points that I have been able to glean from the letters of Ignatius that tell us *something directly* (emphasis added) about the Christians in Antioch sometime early in the second century."[3] As for the accuracy of the historical results Schoedel infers, it appears that, theoretically at any rate, he occupies a position that is stronger and not so vulnerable as that of Segal. The reason is that Schoedel, in his historical inquiry, is aided by the genre of the literature he investigates. This genre is that of the Greco-Roman letter. Typically in a Greco-Roman letter, the author and the audience are identified, and it belongs to the purpose of the author to address directly both his or her own situation and that of the audience. By contrast, in attempting to use the Gospel of Matthew to reconstruct the historical and social matrix within which this Gospel arose, the

1. Segal, "Matthew's Jewish Voice," 15.
2. Ibid., 34.
3. Schoedel, "Ignatius and the Reception of the Gospel of Matthew in Antioch," 133.

interpreter can count on neither of these factors: The mark of both author and audience is that they remain hidden from view, and what the author purports to do is to tell neither his own story nor that of his audience but the story of Jesus of Nazareth. From the standpoint of genre, therefore, the results of Schoedel's traditional historical inquiry are perhaps less fragile and more secure than those of Segal.

In Rodney Stark's chapter on "Antioch as the Social Situation for Matthew's Gospel," one has to do with what may be called a "social mode of historical inquiry." Stark first constructs a typology setting forth the features that would have been characteristic of any Greco-Roman city. Drawing on this typology, he next shows how early Christianity could be understood as a revitalization movement that enabled the pagan populations of urban centers to overcome problems they faced, which were associated with both their religious beliefs and social practices. Methodologically, the direction in which Stark moves in his paper is the opposite of that observed in the papers of Segal and Schoedel. In the latter two papers, the methodological movement is from the literary world of the texts and documents being investigated to the postulation and reconstruction of the social, or real, world to which this literary world is thought to refer. In Stark's chapter, the methodological movement is from an understanding of the social world in which particular texts or documents could conceivably have originated to an understanding of both the message these texts or documents conveyed within that social world and the impact this message had upon that world. If the weakness of the traditional mode of historical inquiry with its principle of transparency is that one may question how accurate a picture it can produce of the social situation lying behind the text, the weakness of Stark's social mode of historical inquiry, at least as he has applied it to the Gospel of Matthew, is that it does not seem that one must even have recourse to Matthew's Gospel to make sense of the social situation in which it arose. Although Stark makes prominent reference to Matt 25:35–40, he could just as easily have written his paper without referring to Matthew's Gospel at all. Indeed, Stark simply presupposes, without demonstrating on the basis of an analysis of the Matthean text, that Matthew's Gospel originated in an urban area in general and in Antioch in particular.

In her study of "Gender Roles in a Scribal Community," Antoinette Clark Wire also makes use of a "social mode of historical inquiry" but one that differs markedly from that of Stark. Specifically, Wire undertakes a "distant, trans-cultural comparison" of what she terms scribal communities: the Qing ("Ch'ing") Dynasty of China (1644–1911 C.E.) on the one hand and the Qumran Covenanters, the Pharisees, and especially the community of Matthew on the other. On the basis of her probe of what is known of the Qing Dynasty, Wire constructs a typology of a scribal community in an agricultural society that contains five characteristics. She then examines, in terms of these five characteristics, source materials attributed to the Qumran Covenanters, the Pharisees, and Matthew in order to cast light on the respective communities or groups that can be assumed to have existed behind these source materials. Methodologically, therefore, Wire moves (1) from the social world she constructs on the basis of her typology (2) to an examination of the literary world of the ancient documents in terms of her typology, and then posits (3) a social world analogous to that of the Qing Dynasty for the Qumran Covenanters, the Pharisees, and the community of Matthew. If there is a danger in this particular mode of social inquiry, it is that one mistakenly assumes that comparative materials taken from one culture, in this case the Qing Dynasty, can be treated as "social laws" and thus used to prove that what was the case in the social world of the Qing Dynasty must also (or necessarily) have been the case in, say, the social world of the Matthean community. By the same token, the value of comparing one culture with another in specific respects is that such a comparison can serve as the basis for forming new hypotheses and generating new questions. As one reads Wire's paper, one notes that she herself is aware of both the danger and the potential of the method she employs.[4]

Before we leave this topic of methodology, there is a final matter to treat. Should we now stand back and view these brief analyses synoptically, it becomes clear that these four authors have used two different kinds of inquiry to approach their materials in three different ways. This notwithstanding, there does appear to be a point at which the approaches of all four converge: In each case, the text itself is not regarded as the primary concern but as a vehicle for getting at something else, namely, the social situation of the community of Matthew (or of Ignatius). To call attention to this is not to suggest that it is illegitimate to use the text of Matthew's Gospel to gain insight into the social situation of his community. But having said this, I should in fact wish to suggest that social historians might want to give far more thought than they perhaps have done thus far to answering the question of how one may properly move from "text" to "social situation." To move from text to social situation by simply invoking the principle of transparency is, owing to the high degree of subjectivity involved and the paucity of independent evidence for corroborating one's findings, hazardous indeed. On this score, witness the shipwreck so many redaction-critical hypotheses regarding the community of Matthew have suffered. Similarly, to move from text to social situation by means of a model or typology brought to the text from the outside runs the risk of forcing the text into a procrustean bed. In what direction, then, lies progress in coming to grips with this problem of moving from text to social situation? Generally speaking,

4. See, e.g., Wire, "Gender Roles in a Scribal Community," 94, 110–13.

one must wonder whether biblical social historians, in trying to solve this problem, might not do well to throw in their lot with biblical literary critics. Presently, biblical literary critics are devoting no little attention to this problem because of their desire to learn as much as possible about the intended audience for whom Matthew wrote. Could it be, then, that the time is ripe for biblical social historians and biblical literary critics to engage one another in conversation about this problem? Such a conversation could enrich both groups: Whereas social historians could apprise literary critics of an entirely new set of questions to ask, literary critics could teach social historians how to be more adept at probing a text for information concerning social situation.

THE CHARACTER AND MAKEUP OF
MATTHEW'S COMMUNITY

As one could have surmised, the major papers presented at the conference convey no uniform picture of Matthew's community. Within limits, however, one can discern in them some shared notions about what this community was like. Since Matthew's community tends to be described in light of Matthew's Gospel, the date of the writing of the Gospel also becomes important.

In dating Matthew's Gospel, none of the authors of the major papers specifies a particular year or even decade. Indirectly, however, all disclose that they think of the Gospel as having been written in the years following the destruction of Jerusalem. The common assumption, therefore, is that Matthew's Gospel arose at some point in the years between 85 and 100 C.E. In keeping with this assumption, Wire[5] construes Matthew as having made use of Mark and Q, and Segal,[6] who apparently regards Matthew as having incorporated Q into his Gospel, speaks approvingly of the notion that Matthew represents a form of Christianity existing a generation or two after Paul. Though more cautious in what he will concede, Schoedel, too, seems to work with this assumption. In his view, Ignatius wrote his letters and died as a martyr in the years between 105 and 135 C.E. In the environment in which Ignatius lived, Schoedel posits the existence of "gospel material of a Matthean type."[7] More to the point, although Schoedel does not think that Ignatius had direct access to Matthew's Gospel in written form, he does believe that Ignatius had access to a passage such as Matt 3:15 as this passage was mediated to him through a "setting" other than the First Gospel itself.[8] In any event Schoedel, in

5. Ibid., 102 n. 56.
6. Segal, "Matthew's Jewish Voice," 4 n. 4.
7. Schoedel, "Ignatius and the Gospel of Matthew," 129.
8. Ibid., 157–58.

his historical scheme, likewise appears to trace the origin of Matthew's Gospel to the years 85 to 100 C.E.

In the last decades, Matthean scholars have almost unanimously identified the city of Antioch of Syria as the place where Matthew's Gospel was written and his community was at home. In part, the authors of the major papers break with this consensus. True, Stark is prepared to presuppose that Antioch was the place where Matthew penned his Gospel.[9] Still, as far as the thesis of his paper is concerned, the only thing he need insist upon is that Matthew's community be an urban community.[10] For his part, Schoedel, while not wishing to rule Antioch out as the home of Matthew's community, is less certain than Stark that Matthew's Gospel necessarily points to Antioch as its place of origin. Thus, while Schoedel affirms that "the influence of gospel tradition like that found in Matthew is . . . strong . . . in the religious world of Ignatius," he also affirms that "the theological traditions alive in Antioch in the time of Ignatius were diverse indeed and transcend the horizons of the Gospel of Matthew significantly."[11] In the boldest statement made by any of the authors, Segal contends that the evidence pinpoints no exact location as the home of Matthew's community and that one must reckon with the possibility that this community could have resided almost anywhere within that arc that extends from Galilee to Antioch.[12]

Although one cannot, as I have said, derive from the major papers of the conference a uniform picture of Matthew's community, one can find in them any number of points on which the authors either appear to agree or, at a minimum, to which they would not seem to object. These points are such as the following:

1. In Matthew's Gospel, one has to do with a Christian community living toward the end of the first century C.E.
2. This Matthean community was situated in an urban environment, perhaps in Galilee or perhaps more toward the north in Syria but, in any case, not necessarily in Antioch.
3. By the time of Ignatius of Antioch, the most one can say for certain is that Ignatius was living "in an environment in which gospel material of a Matthean type prevailed."[13]
4. The constituency of the Matthean community, though it encompassed gentile converts, was, ethnically, predominately Jewish Christian.

9. Stark, "Antioch as the Social Situation for Matthew's Gospel," 189.
10. On the "urban" nature of Matthew's community, see also Wire, "Gender Roles," 115–16.
11. Schoedel, "Ignatius and the Gospel of Matthew," 154.
12. Segal, "Matthew's Jewish Voice," 19, 26–27.
13. Schoedel, "Ignatius and the Gospel of Matthew," 129, 151, 175.

5. The Matthean community is best thought of as a sect within Judaism.

6. The Matthean community was, at the writing of Matthew's Gospel, encountering severe opposition from Pharisaic, or formative, Judaism.

7. At the center of the Matthean community's quarrel with Pharisaic Judaism was the interpretation and practice of the Jewish law (and, as Segal would add, the divinity of Jesus[14]).

8. The Matthean community's interpretation of the law and the sacred past was sophisticated and reflects the presence in it of those who may be termed "classically [or scribally] educated."[15]

9. In the Matthean community, the figure of Peter played a prominent role relative to the community's sense of self-identity and link with the past.

10. The Matthean community was patriarchal in nature so that men occupied the social roles involving responsibility and authority, and women were assigned social roles that made them passive and dependent.

11. Judging from Matthew's Gospel, the Matthean community exhibited in its communal life that peculiar Christian ethic that, in time, revitalized life in Greco-Roman cities "by providing new norms and new kinds of social relationships able to cope with many urgent, urban problems."[16]

As compiled from the major papers of this conference, this description of Matthew's community is as yet rough and unfinished. Also, one may question how accurate it is in this or that particular. Despite these deficiencies, it does possess sufficient substance so as to commend itself as the basis for further investigation and discussion.

THE USE OF SOURCE THEORIES

To the extent that the authors of the major papers made use of any source theory in their historical reconstructions of the community of Matthew, their theory of choice is quite obviously the two-source hypothesis.[17] As commonly understood, this theory presumes that the evangelists Matthew and Luke, in composing their respective Gospels, each drew upon Mark and the sayings-document Q.

14. Segal, "Matthew's Jewish Voice," 32.
15. Wire, "Gender Roles," 110, 108–13.
16. Stark, "Social Situation," 205.
17. See, e.g., Segal, "Matthew's Jewish Voice" (cf. 4 n. 4); Wire, "Gender Roles," 102, 119.

In recent years, the two-source hypothesis has, as is well known, increasingly come under attack. In fact, one of the persons who played a prominent role in planning the conference at Dallas is also the man who, perhaps more than any other, has led this attack; I refer, of course, to William Farmer.[18] Farmer, and others who participated in the conference as well, have found reason to break with the two-source hypothesis and to advocate some other source theory, to wit: the Augustinian model (according to which Matthew is the earliest Gospel, Mark is dependent on Matthew, and Luke is dependent on both Matthew and Mark); or Farmer's own preferred model, the two-gospel hypothesis (according to which Matthew is the first of the Synoptic Gospels, Luke used Matthew, and Mark made use of both Matthew and Luke). In addition to these two theories, other source theories have likewise been advanced, by Austin Farrer, Robert Lindsey, B. C. Butler, and Pierson Parker.[19] Be that as it may, what is clear from recent discussion of the various source theories meant to explain how the Synoptic Gospels are related to one another is that the two-source hypothesis is not unassailable, as might once have been thought. In light of this, the question one must raise vis-à-vis the conference is this: What difference would it have made in the major papers had the authors presupposed either no source theory or a theory other than the two-source hypothesis? My own preliminary judgment is that while any historical trajectories developed in them would necessarily have to be altered, the major conclusions the authors have drawn on the social profile of Matthew's community would stand.

SUGGESTIONS
FOR FUTURE RESEARCH

The final question is the obvious one: Where might one go from here? As I see it, the overriding importance of the conference at Dallas is that it constituted, certainly as far as Matthean studies are concerned, an undertaking of a new kind. For the first time, a concerted effort was made on several fronts and across disciplinary lines to come to grips with the vexing problem of the "self-definition" of the Matthean community. For this reason alone, this conference must be judged to have been highly significant. Still, one must also look to the future, and as one does, perhaps two or three suggestions are in order.

18. See, e.g., Farmer's classic volume, *The Synoptic Problem: A Critical Analysis* (Dillsboro, N.C.: Western North Carolina Press, 1976).
19. For a good review of the various source theories and the arguments that have been made "for" and "against" both Markan priority and the Q Hypothesis, see A. Bellinzoni, Jr., *The Two-Source Hypothesis: A Critical Reappraisal* (Macon, Ga.: Mercer University Press, 1985).

Judging from the major papers, one of the topics in which biblical social historians are most interested concerns the relationship between Matthew's community and formative Judaism. As a key part of understanding this relationship, social historians will be obliged, it seems to me, to focus careful attention on the way Matthew presents the religious authorities in his Gospel and relates the various groups they form to one another. Although Matthew's presentation of the authorities is not uncomplicated, a glance at Matthean studies will show that scholars have routinely dealt with it by means of one or two sweeping observations. First, the interpreter will often note that Matthew employs the term "Pharisees" far more frequently than does Mark (29 times to 12 times) and that he employs the term "Sadducees" only seven times. Then, invoking the principle of transparency, the interpreter will deduce from these statistics that, by the time of Matthew, the Sadducees had disappeared from the scene and that it was Pharisaic Judaism with which Matthew's community was both closely associated and embroiled in conflict.

A close look at Matthew's depiction of the religious authorities, however, suggests that this rush to judgment is not unproblematic. Consider, for example, the expression "the Pharisees and Sadducees." This expression is exclusive to Matthew's Gospel and occurs four times (3:7; 16:6, 11–12). Also, there is virtually unanimous agreement among scholars that it stems from the hand of Matthew and therefore constitutes Matthean redaction. Grammatically, the two nouns in this expression are bound together by one article. The upshot is that Matthew combines "Pharisees" and "Sadducees" so as to form a single, larger group. Indeed, he even ascribes to this group a common teaching (16:12).

The problem Matthew has ostensibly created in minting this expression is, of course, apparent: Historical record does not support the notion that Pharisees and Sadducees ever formed a single, larger group or espoused a common teaching. For the social historian, therefore, the expression "the Pharisees and Sadducees" poses a baffling question: How is he or she to deal with it in any reconstruction of the social history of Matthew's community? Closely related to this question is another, equally important, question: What does the presence of this expression in Matthew's Gospel augur for the continued use of the principle of transparency? If one applies this principle to this expression, one posits historicity for a peculiar grouping that scholars otherwise believe never existed as such. If one forgoes the use of this principle in the case of this expression but not elsewhere, one leaves oneself open to the charge that one engages in historical reconstruction on a convenient, selective basis. And if one forgoes the use of this principle altogether, does one have an alternative method for reconstructing the social history of Matthew's community? In eminently practical terms, the problem with which the expression "the

Pharisees and Sadducees" confronts the social historian is this: If the religious authorities within the text of Matthew's Gospel are an index to the opponents outside the text with whom Matthew's community had to contend, how does one go about defining accurately who those opponents outside the text were?

A second matter to which biblical social historians might want to give attention has to do with another aspect of the relationship between Matthew's community and formative Judaism: the extent to which Matthew's community had broken with formative Judaism and begun to think of itself as distinct. The firm impression one gets from the major papers that addressed this issue is that Matthew's community is to be viewed as still embedded within Judaism. To be sure, this may have been the case, but one must wonder. In tracing the flow of Matthew's story, one observes that although the mission to the Jews is to continue to the Parousia (10:23), there is a gradual, yet perceptible, movement away from the Jews and toward the nations. Apropos the flow of any story, it is a sound literary-critical principle that the last impressions the author conveys to the reader are of special consequence. Looking at Matthew's story with this in mind, one quickly discovers that the last direct reference Matthew makes to "Judaism" occurs at 28:15. In this passage, Matthew as narrator bursts the bounds of his story and addresses the reader directly. Specifically, Matthew reports that "this word" (i.e., the false rumor to the effect that the disciples came by night and stole the body of Jesus) is being spread "among the Jews" until this day. If this passage is any indication, it strongly suggests that the evangelist Matthew, in his own day, drew a sharp distinction between himself and his community on the one hand and the "Jews over there" on the other. To put it differently, as Matthew momentarily abandons his story to speak directly to the reader, he points to himself and his community as being something other than a part of Judaism. What this "something other" is appears to be identified by Jesus elsewhere in Matthew's Gospel: Matthew's community is Jesus' "church" (16:18) or the "nation that produces [the fruits of the kingdom]" (21:43).

A final matter to which biblical social historians will want to attend as they advance their reconstructions of Matthew's community has to do with reading the text of Matthew's Gospel itself. In the last analysis, for social historians to make a case for some particular view of Matthean communal "self-definition," or "self-understanding," they cannot avoid the task of guiding others through the story of Matthew to show how clues in the text progressively lead the reader to understand himself or herself in light of that view. Thus, if at the time Matthew wrote his Gospel his community were in fact embedded in Judaism, it should be possible to show, on the basis of a careful reading of his story, that the reader is so guided that the self-understanding with which he or she leaves the world of this story is that of a Christian Jew still living within the bounds of first-century Judaism. If there is any overriding weakness in the major papers of the conference, it is that they treat one to no sustained reading of any portion of Matthew's story. Instead, what they offer are reconstructions of the social situation of Matthew's community based on a random selection of passages that, one is assured, provide a reliable "window" or "typological aid" for catching sight of Matthew's social situation. Still, however impressive these reconstructions may be, the truth of the matter is that it is difficult, if not impossible, to build a convincing case regarding the social situation of Matthew's community if this case is supported by no more than a fragmentary, piecemeal reading of Matthew's story. What this ultimately implies, therefore, is that social historians will need to lead others through the sweep of Matthew's story simply as part of the case they would make concerning the social situation of Matthew's community. Or to put it another way, what this implies is that there comes a point where the social historian must become something of a literary critic, just as it is also incumbent upon the literary critic to pay close attention to social history. In any event, I myself find the prospect that social historians might see it as their task to take others on a tour of Matthew's story thoroughly appealing. From such a tour could only come new appreciation for the power and riches inherent in this ancient document.

In the latter paragraph, I have tipped my hand as to my own wish for the future. Thus far, the two subdisciplines of biblical literary criticism and biblical social history have been traveling in parallel lanes. While scholars in each sub-discipline know of the existence of the other, dialogue among scholars from each subdiscipline has been sparse. What I learned firsthand from the confer-ence in Dallas is how potentially rewarding such a dialogue could be. My hope for the future, then, is that this dialogue will now get underway.

Scripture and
Ancient Sources

HEBREW BIBLE

Genesis		Deuteronomy		52:13–53:5	166
15:6	13	6:5	8	53:3	166
		24:1–4	82 n.42	53:4	166, 167
Exodus				53:11	166
15:3	32	1 Samuel			
20:2	32	1:6	6	Hosea	
20:4	80			6:6	7, 52
20:8	80	Isaiah			
		7:14	64	Psalms	
Leviticus		9:1	28	2:2	161
15:31	80	42:7	68		
19:18	8	52:5	150	Daniel	
				7:9–13	32

NEW TESTAMENT

Matthew		1:21	64	2:5, 15, 17,	
1:1	99	1:22	98 n.49	23	89 n.49
1:1–2	101	1:23	xviii, 64	2:9	180 n.4
1:18–2:23	62 n.5	2	51, 185	2:9–10	185
14:28–33	62 n.5	2:1–12	156, 185	2:11	116 n.79,
1:18–19	48		n.17		117
1:18–25	38 n.1, 100,	2:1–23	117	2:13, 14, 20,	
	181	2:2	180 n.4, 185	21	103
		2:3	156		

OTHER ANCIENT JEWISH LITERATURE

OTHER EARLY CHRISTIAN LITERATURE

GREEK AND ROMAN SOURCES

Modern Authors

Alfoldy, C., 211 n.1
Alon, G., 33 n.46, 36 n.53
Anderson, J., 87 n.1, 102 n.56
Applebaum, S., 226 n.50, 230 n.62
Arnim, J., 70 n.6
Aune, D., 83 n.44
Avi-Yonah, M., 216 n.19, 229 n.59, 230 n.62
Ayerst, D., 201

Babcock, W., 248
Balch, D., 76 n.22, 222 n.40
Bammel, C., 130 n.2
Barnard, L. W., 30 n.37
Barnett, A., 152, 152 n.50
Barrett, C., 17 n.18, 144 n.29
Barrett, D., 58 n.61
Barrow, R., 150 n.45
Barth, G., 39 n.4
Bartsch, H., 153, 153 n.53, 184 n.15
Bauer, J., 168 n.74
Bauer, W., 82 n.43, 157 n.59, 183 n.12
Becker, H., 45 n.24
Bellinzoni, A., 266 n.19
Ben Yuda, N., 39 n.2, 44 n.21, 46 n.30
Betz, H., 78, 78 n.29, 80 n.35, 99 n.52, 241 n.99

Boak, A., 202
Bockmuehl, M., 49 n.37
Bonnard, P., 55 n.46
Bornkamm, G., 39 n.3, 55 n.46, 77 n.26, 221 n.38, 222 n.40, 227 nn.52–53
Brandon, G., 19 n.19, 213 n.11
Brawley, E., 23 n.23
Brown, P., 190
Brown, R., 9 n.9, 49 n.38, 77 n.24, 156 n.57, 214 n.12, 218 n.24
Brown, S., 39 n.5, 49 n.38
Burn, A., 195, 205
Butler, B., 266

Calderini, A., 150 n.43
Campbell, S., 251 n.9
Campbell, W., 251 n.9
Chandler, T., 190, 192
Chiat, M., 216 n.19
Cochrane, C., 303–4
Cohen, B., 82 n.42
Cohen, S., 36 n.53, 96 n.38, 97 n.46, 102 n.55, 218 n.25, 237 n.89
Cohen, Y., 46 n.26
Collins, J., 136 n.16
Cope, L., 228 n.55
Cullmann, O., 10 n.11

282